I0825488

Praise for *Incorruptible*

"*Incorruptible* is the only business book I've ever read that weaves 'fiduciary duty' and 'human flourishing' into a single, convincing argument. Eric Ries shows why so many idealistic founders collide headfirst into a system that turns noble intentions into nasty outcomes—and then he points a way forward. By treating ownership and governance as design problems and by drawing on vivid case studies of unfashionable but enduring enterprises, Ries offers a bracingly practical vision of how companies can stay true and still win."

—Daniel H. Pink, author of *The Power of Regret* and *Drive*

"*Incorruptible* destroys the myth that only sleazy founders and companies get rich. Eric Ries shows how to build a mission-driven company that will be humane and ethical and make piles of money for decades. A rare joy to read."

—Robert I. Sutton, Professor Emeritus at Stanford; author of eight books, including *The No Asshole Rule*

"After authoring the most important business book of the 2010s, Eric Ries has done it again. No business book became standard practice more quickly than Eric's first book. If you're a founder, a CEO planning an IPO, an investor seeking epic outcomes—stop now and read this book. It will change your life. Eric unveils the unspoken truths about how to build a legendary success . . . and how to keep it successful. When will it be seen as founder malpractice to not have read this book?"

—Scott Cook, cofounder of Intuit

"*Incorruptible* is a must-read for anyone who cares about protecting the productive power of capitalism from the dangers of short-term thinking—and for anyone who recognizes the importance of trustworthy and enduring institutions for a thriving democracy."

—Reid Hoffman, cofounder of LinkedIn; author of *Superagency*

"If you want to build a company that will be making the world a better place a hundred years from now, it's not enough to be a great person with good intentions—you need to consciously build incorruptible governance. Ries shows you how. Indispensable!"

—KIM SCOTT, author of *Radical Candor*

"*Incorruptible* is the rare business book that is both a moral compass and a practical playbook. Ries shows us, with rigor and optimism, how to build organizations that are worthy of our trust."

—FRANCES FREI, UPS Foundation Professor of Service Management at Harvard Business School

"*Incorruptible* demonstrates the importance of mission-driven leadership and defying the *status quo* to build organizations that withstand the test of time. Through Eric's decades of experience building and running businesses, he articulates how companies avoid the traps of corruption and lead with values to thrive as organizations and reshape industries."

—KEN CHENAULT, chairman and managing director of General Catalyst; former chairman and CEO of American Express

"This profound book will inform and infuriate, and then it will help you see a path forward. It should be required reading for anyone who manages (or has a manager). Gravity is real."

—SETH GODIN, author of twenty-one books, including *This Is Strategy*

"*Incorruptible* is Eric Ries at his most ambitious and original. He argues that corruption—extracting value from successful companies—results not from moral failure but from flaws in our institutions. Ries shows how organizations can be engineered to resist these flaws. This is a practical manifesto for building mission-driven companies that survive success without killing the golden goose."

—THOMAS R. EISENMANN, Howard H. Stevenson Professor of Business Administration and Peter O. Crisp Faculty Chair at Harvard Business School

"Every founder eventually faces the board meeting where the mission is on the table. I've been in that room. Eric has too—and this book will help you walk out with your soul intact. *Incorruptible* is as practical as it is inspiring."

—Matt Blumberg, author of *Startup CEO* and *Startup Boards*

"I've read countless business books, but this is the first that had me in tears not out of sadness, but because it gave me hope.

Incorruptible is not just a book. It's permission. It's a blueprint. And it's proof that you're not crazy for wanting to build something that's both wildly successful and deeply good, something that lasts. For any founder who truly wants to make a difference, this is a must-read."

—Vlada Bortnik, founder and CEO of Marco Polo

"As a mission-driven founder, this is the book I wish I'd had while building. Ries offers both a new vocabulary and concrete, hard-won examples for how to create real value without losing your soul at scale. He explains why mission and massive growth so often end up at odds—and more importantly, how founders can be intentional about choosing a different path."

—Leah Solivan, founder of TaskRabbit

"Every founder hopes their path is a straight line. It won't be. They hope they will have the right mentor to help them avoid problems. They won't. Eric Ries gives founders a playbook to help avoid the inevitable pitfalls and find their path to the business they set out to create."

—Mark Cuban

"As a first-time founder, the only thing I knew about corporate governance was what my lawyer told me. He didn't tell me much. If I'd had the knowledge in *Incorruptible* up front, it would have helped me structure my company better, and it would have helped me make better and more accountable leadership decisions as we grew."

—Kieran Snyder, founder of Textio;
VP of AI Transformation at Microsoft

"We've thought of the role of business—to make money for shareholders, full stop—as immutable because for most of our lifetimes, it has been that way. But a deeper view of history shows that this wasn't always the case, and Ries does a masterful job of outlining an even bolder view for our future."

—Seth Levine, partner at Foundry VC; author of *Capital Evolution* and *The New Builders*

"If you want the world to be a better place than it is, this book is a good place to start."

—Tim O'Reilly, founder and CEO of O'Reilly Media

"This is an important book for any mission-driven leader or investor. It describes what we all feel: company after company turning their backs on their users and their founding values. It also offers a framework for avoiding that fate, packed with advice, research, and case studies of organizations that have stayed true to their mission and have thrived. It's a timely reminder that enshittification is a choice, not an inevitability, that there is a better way, and that you're not alone in trying to find it."

—Eli Luberoff, founder of Desmos Studio PBC

"After decades as a venture capitalist and then founding Wealthfront, I've learned it's incredibly hard to keep a company truly mission-driven as it scales. *Incorruptible* is the most practical guide I've seen to doing exactly that. It shows how special leaders built breakthrough business models, cultures, incentives, and governance to ensure their mission endured. At a time when Silicon Valley feels increasingly mercenary, this book is a refreshing reminder that idealism and performance are not trade-offs. If you're a founder, investor, or engineer who wants to change the world or build a great enterprise, then this book is well worth your time."

—Andy Rachleff, cofounder of Wealthfront and Benchmark Capital; lecturer at Stanford Graduate School of Business

INCORRUPTIBLE

Also by Eric Ries

The Lean Startup

The Startup Way

The Leader's Guide

INCORRUPTIBLE

WHY GOOD COMPANIES
GO BAD . . .
and
HOW GREAT COMPANIES
STAY GREAT

Eric Ries

Authors Equity
1123 Broadway, Suite 1008
New York, New York 10010

Cover design and chapter opening illustrations by Marcus Gosling
Interior design by Anna B. Knighton
Interior diagrams by Janis Ozolins (ozo.art)

Library of Congress Control Number: 2026930769
Print ISBN 9798893311860
Ebook ISBN 9798893312065

Printed in the United States of America
Second printing

www.authorsequity.com

For Aurelia

Contents

PART III: TO BEND THE LIGHT

Introduction

It was happening again.

"I need your help," The Professor said. "I think I'm about to screw everything up."

My ears hurt from pressing the earbuds closer to hear over traffic as The Professor manically explained the complex wonders of cellular biology. His call had caught me at the end of a long week advising startups, and I was exhausted. Before I could get home to my family, I had just one more stop, a celebration for a friend. But The Professor's voice had an intensity—and fear—that was impossible to ignore.

He was on the verge of a discovery that could redefine medicine, like a ChatGPT for biology: an AI that could design new medicines to fight cancer, Alzheimer's, maybe even the next pandemic. The promise was staggering. So was the nightmare. In the wrong hands, the same technology could design a perfect poison, a targeted bioweapon, or a plague we have no defense against.

This wasn't science fiction. His lab had already created the breakthrough that could turn these possibilities into reality.

As he kept going, I pulled over and parked outside the gathering I was supposed to be attending. The music from the venue rattled my windshield, and I could see throngs of people arriving: employees, ex-employees, colleagues old and new. The board of directors, notably, had not been invited.

I was too engrossed in The Professor's story to go inside.

I could hear the fatigue and panic in his voice. His potential employees—the brilliant scientists he was trying to recruit from the best university labs in the world—were relentlessly asking him the same hard questions. "They see the danger," he told me, his voice strained. "They want to know how I can guarantee we won't sell out. What happens when investors demand we prioritize short-term profits over everything else? What happens if they fire me and put someone else in charge—someone who doesn't care how our technology is used?"

I wasn't surprised. Everyone involved had seen *Jurassic Park.*

"When I talk to investors, they say these worries prove we're not serious about business. I can already see how they'd be perfectly comfortable making money while I become a monster who can't sleep at night. It feels like I have to choose between saving lives and saving my soul."

The Professor continued, oblivious to my queasy sense of déjà vu, "But surely I'll be able to safeguard what we build as we grow. I'll be CEO. I know my own values. I'll have control . . ."

I'd heard this line of thought many times before. From so many others who thought their success would protect them. They were wrong. *We* were wrong. We hadn't seen far enough ahead.

My book *The Lean Startup* gave a generation of founders the tools to build quickly, to scale, and to create massive value. But I failed to anticipate what came next. I taught people how to build something worth protecting—but not how to protect it.

Like the founder whose gathering was just outside. I hadn't known how to help him, or many others who used Lean Startup ideas to build incredible companies, only to watch their evolution—and often their destruction—with mounting horror.

Over time, I started to feel like I was feeding one company after another into a meat grinder.

I told The Professor, "Look, I have to go to this event. There are nearly a thousand people here to commemorate a founder and the company they built with him. People have flown in from all over the country, even ex-employees he'd fired."

The Professor brightened. "That's so rare—what a sign of respect. That's exactly the kind of company I want to build. Enjoy the party."

I paused for a second before answering, "Yeah, except he doesn't work there anymore. This isn't a party; it's a wake."

Silence.

I had to explain. After years of pressure to abandon the very ethos that made the company great, after years of being pushed to focus on the stock price—more than product, more than customers—this founder had been ousted. The billions he had made for investors were not enough. They wanted more.

"Wait, are you saying that's going to be me someday?" His voice cracked. "How do I protect this company? Is that even possible?"

"The answer is yes," I told him. "I believe it *is* possible." I could hear him exhale. "But you're not on track to accomplish it. You're about to lock yourself into exactly the future you fear."

"Is it too late?" he asked.

"It's not too late, but you've taken some steps in the wrong direction. The time to change course is right now."

I promised we'd speak again soon.

That night, at a very unusual celebration, a thousand of us mourned together. Every person who helped build something extraordinary, only to watch it be slowly eroded by something we couldn't quite name. We all felt a shared sense that this was not how business is supposed to work. I left grimly determined that this reality—one affecting so many companies and creators—had to change. The next generation deserves better.

Over the weeks that followed, The Professor and I forged a different path for his fledgling company. A path that would allow them to shape their own future.

Discovering that path required me to unlearn everything I thought I knew about business, from the very definition of profit itself to the fundamental way we build and structure organizations.

Now let me share it with you.

LEADING FROM THE BATHROOM FLOOR

I've written books on entrepreneurship and innovation. I've built organizations myself and helped others do the same: AI research labs, law firms, non-profits, and companies pursuing every kind of advanced technology and scientific breakthrough you can imagine. And, sadly, after helping so many companies scale through initial public offering (IPO) and beyond, I've had a front-row seat to the process by which they get surgically deboned.

So I built a brand-new stock exchange to try to stop the meat grinder from turning. Crazy, I know. In Silicon Valley, everyone thought so too. No joke, I've had founders working on immortality ask me if I *really* think my project is realistic.

The Long-Term Stock Exchange (LTSE) was designed to be a sanctuary against short-term thinking. But the closer we got to pulling it off, the more hostile the world became (and I'm not talking about healthy competition). A top investment banker offered me a quiet deal to add loopholes to our rules so his bank could profit. A major customer launched a technical attack on our systems "by accident," then tried to use the resulting chaos to extract concessions.

The term *status quo* sounds so passive, so plain. But the *status quo* can throw quite a punch.

The pressure reached its breaking point when a coalition of hedge funds and governance experts made us "an offer you can't refuse," in the middle of the night, while I was thousands of miles from my team. The deal was simple: Abandon our principles and adopt the same "best practices" as our competitors, and all our problems would disappear. Otherwise, they would see to our failure.

My team had given up lucrative careers to follow me on this quest. If they wanted to compromise, who could blame them? On the conference call, we debated every angle. Say yes, and we'd at least have something to show for our years of work. Say no, and bankruptcy was a real possibility. I asked each person to choose yes or no. The silence on the line was agonizing. Then, one by one, every single voice came back with the same answer: no.

The fallout was severe. Our partners abandoned us. From the brink of victory, we had to start over.

I wish I could tell you it was my visionary leadership that helped us through that awful night. The truth is, I was the one curled up on the bathroom floor.

It was 3:15 a.m. I still remember the contrast of the cool tile and the heat of humiliation. I thought we had chosen to die to save a principle.

But I was wrong.

We had started LTSE to help *other companies* resist exactly this kind of pressure, but its guardrails ended up saving *us* first. We rebuilt the exchange from scratch. Today, it is the first new exchange to both list and trade multiple stocks since the creation of the NASDAQ fifty years ago.

TO BUILD IS A RADICAL ACT

The Professor's fear, the grief of every person at that party, and the futility I felt the night I thought we'd lost LTSE are all related. Each of us was a casualty in a much larger war being fought in every boardroom, every startup, and on every factory floor.

The truth is, we're all one acquisition, one IPO, one board meeting away from watching something we love turn into something we hate. But we lack the vocabulary to call it what it really is. "Mission drift" sounds like a navigation error. "Bureaucracy" sounds like paperwork. Neither captures the gut punch of betrayal when something precious is corroded beyond recognition.

So I call it by a simple, old-fashioned name: *corruption.*

I'm willing to bet you've felt it yourself in your own life and career. Maybe it was the day your favorite company killed the product you (and everyone else) loved. Or when your own company canceled its innovation projects to help "make the quarter." Or when you watched helplessly as the "professional CEO" brought in to replace the founder drove the company into the ground. Or when leadership changed and the mission became just words on a website.

Maybe you've wondered why everyone accepts this as inevitable. Maybe you, too, have wondered if there's a better way.

There is.

To find it, we have to accept something that almost everyone understands intuitively yet rarely says out loud: Not every form of making money is equally good.

The Professor did not see himself as a revolutionary or a social reformer (me neither!). He wanted to make a great product, to save lives, and—yes—to make money for himself, his team, and his investors. But, like many builders, he was not interested in making money by any means necessary. He wanted his company to prosper by creating a product that was useful, trustworthy, and healing to his customers. In today's hyper-financialized economy, these simple aspirations have become radical acts. Every one of them has become expendable, too often sacrificed on the altar of growth, share price, and short-term returns.

THE FORCE THAT NO ONE CONTROLS BUT EVERYONE OBEYS

I've spent years trying to understand who is responsible for this treacherous state of affairs. Managers blame executives, executives blame the board, the board blames investors. Then you talk to the investors—and I have!—and they act dismayed too. Many are horrified by all this short-termism. But they blame executive greed: the stock buybacks, the golden parachutes. Executives fire back that investors say they want sustainable, long-term returns, but they also want to be able to liquidate their position at any moment. It's like watching two people pointing at each other, each yelling "You did it!" while standing in a house they both set on fire.

Nobody seems to be in charge.

The force behind this—one that no one controls but everyone obeys—affects far more of your daily life than you probably realize. Everywhere at once, like gravity, it radiates far beyond the corporate boardroom, explaining phenomena as diverse as the spiraling cost of American transit construction, the gutting of local journalism, the malignancy of social media, the stubborn persistence of medical errors, the fact that the owners of your local sports team drive you crazy, the "social contagion" of corporate layoffs, and why customer service would rather put you on hold than solve your problem.

Yet look around. In almost every industry, there are outlier companies that remain purpose-driven despite massive scale: Vanguard in finance, Patagonia in apparel, Costco in retail. Once you know how to look, you'll discover them everywhere, quietly fulfilling their promise day after day, year after year, while making huge profits. We admire them as exceptions that prove the rule.

We've come to accept that the gradual corruption of successful companies is as natural and inevitable as gravity. Yet if there are so many exceptions that prove the rule, maybe the rule is broken?

In fact, once you understand how these exceptional organizations are structured, you will realize that they violate practically every conventional business "best practice" we've been taught. That I, in my own ignorance, used to teach.

Most people walk right past the secret of these outliers' success, focusing instead on their cultures or founders or missions. But culture dies, founders leave, and missions drift—unless something deeper protects them.

THE *INCORRUPTIBLE* BLUEPRINT

Here is what I have learned about how that deeper protection is forged. Organizations that seek to flourish over the long term can intentionally activate it by following the right blueprint:

> **First, create something worth protecting.** An incorruptible organization begins with an aspirational mission aligned with human flourishing, and a principled ethos that instills in everyone it touches the determination to see the mission through. Such *mission-driven organizations* generate a high level of trust and loyalty among customers, employees, and investors. They resist the temptation to take shortcuts, exploit customers, or trade long-term endurance for the temporary dopamine hit of short-term rewards.

> **Second, build with structural integrity.** The more successful an organization is at that first step, the more valuable it becomes as a target. Profits attract predators. This is where the gravity of our financial system buckles most standard structures. To resist requires powerful and carefully designed defenses, and a whole new theory of corporate governance to match. We must rethink corporate purpose, board composition, voting rights, and—eventually—embrace entirely new corporate forms.

Both parts are essential. In the long run, neither works without the other. Everything worth protecting will eventually need protection.

The companies that master this blueprint share unmistakable characteristics. They build cultures of extreme alignment, practice superlative care, and pursue missions that maximize human flourishing (as they each define it).

But they go further than internal alignment. They forge structures that defy "best practices." Costco has a *governance fortress* that has fended off decades of attacks on their distinctive approach. Patagonia has an ownership structure that transcends our typical binary distinction between for-profit and non-profit, embodying the best of both. We will see the stories of many others as we go. This book will show you how to build organizations that are neither investor-controlled nor founder-controlled. Instead, they are *mission-controlled* organizations.

This is not a niche affair. Companies with these "alternative" structures today account for a significant chunk of the world's gross domestic product (GDP), including millions of employees and trillions in value.

Years ago, Airbnb CEO Brian Chesky shared this insight with me: "The greatest product Steve Jobs designed was Apple. Your company is the most important product you'll ever design."[1] In *The Lean Startup*, I offered a new way to build products. This book does the same for designing, building, and protecting organizations.

Success, determination, and hard work are not enough. If an organization has a weak structure, it is vulnerable to being captured. No matter your aspirations, if what you build is not sufficiently strong, those aspirations are mere wishes. In the long run, what happens will not be up to you.

THE INVISIBLE EVIDENCE

The good news is that we have overwhelming evidence that mission-driven organizations systematically outperform their conventional competitors. They deliver superior returns to shareholders. They create more value than they capture. They are far more likely to endure over generations, not just quarters. And above all, they stay true to their intentions—while being more profitable too. In the chapters that follow, I will share the research and case studies that prove this.

However.

This does not mean that mission-driven companies always win. The reality of our contemporary financial system is that it supports many ways to make money without creating any value at all. There are plenty of bad actors out there who intentionally seek to exploit these "opportunities" to enrich themselves. These are people who insist that it's impossible for a company to actually be both truly mission driven and successful. They say exploitation is "just the way it is." Maybe because it's all they've ever known.

The reason their message has any power at all is simple. Although many of the techniques in this book have long-established precedents, some going back as far as 1885; are backed by extensive research; and are embodied in global-scale companies, they remain—to most leaders anyway—completely invisible.

The goal of this book is to offer a clear, concrete alternative to today's "best practices" so that you will have a choice when the time comes—whether you're starting a company, choosing where to work, or simply deciding which organizations deserve your trust and your money.

HOW TO USE THIS BOOK

The book unfolds in three parts:

> **Part I: The Shape of the Abyss** (Chapters 1–4) explores why even well-intentioned companies end up betraying their promises. Here lie the forces that can breach the hull and drag organizations down into corruption.
>
> **Part II: Escape Velocity** (Chapters 5–11) provides the specific tools and structures that make corruption not just difficult but impossible. Incorruptible organizations are those engineered to have the strength to break free.
>
> **Part III: To Bend the Light** (Chapters 12–15) shows how the strongest organizations reshape entire industries around their values, creating new paths for others to follow.

The chapters build on each other, but you can start where you need to.

To understand the core mistakes builders commit that make corruption inevitable, start with Part I. If you've already encountered the dangers and need solutions now, start with Parts II and III and then go back and read Part I. If you're focused on systemic change that can work on the scale of whole industries and even society at large, feel free to begin with Part III.

MEET THE MOMENT

We are at an inflection point.

The Professor's breakthrough, which could design both cures and bioweapons, isn't unique—or even, these days, unusual. As I write this, my daily practice is working with organizations large and small that are all grappling with the same thing: breakthrough technologies that could serve humanity or corrupt it, depending on how they're structured and who controls them. We know how this ends if we follow the old playbook: another wave of promise turned to betrayal.

The disruption is coming regardless. The years ahead will require rebuilding many of the core institutions that govern our shared civic life. If we build them to be incorruptible from the start, we can usher in an era of organizations that truly serve human flourishing. Miss this moment, and we'll be locked into another century of institutional betrayal.

This book is the manual I wish I'd had when The Professor—and countless other founders and leaders just like him—first came to me. It's the culmination of everything I've learned about why good companies go bad and how great companies stay great.

After reading this book, you'll know in your bones the difference between a real mission-controlled organization and those that are just whitewashing their corruption.

You'll be able to start building something incorruptible, even if you're not yet in a leadership role. Many of the most successful mission-driven organizations were shaped by the beliefs people held long before they had formal power.

Let's talk about those beliefs for a moment. Not every leader has or even needs a grandiose-sounding vision at the start. Many of the leaders we will study in this book began in a much humbler way. They simply wanted to make some corner of the world, and our experience in it, better. By staying true to their principles, they ended up doing more good than they ever imagined.

If you're building something right now, you'll learn the principles and practices that will allow you to protect what you're building for the long term.

It may feel like a matter of chance, or luck, or willpower whether the thing you are building will stay true or fall to corruption.

What if I tell you that it is, instead, a matter of design? And that this design is available to anyone with the courage to attempt it. And that it is available today, right now, without having to wait for the world to change. Does that sound impossible?

Wouldn't you like to know how to do this impossible thing?

Take heart. Every organization that chooses sovereignty over surrender makes it easier for the next one.

Turn the page. The exceptions are about to become the rule.

Part I

THE SHAPE OF THE ABYSS

Chapter One

THE MYSTERY OF THE GOLDEN GOOSE

> These principles will prove themselves unerringly true and will by their irresistible truth pervade society to the utmost bounds of the earth; for silence will not retard their progress, and opposition will give increased celerity to their movements.
>
> —**Robert Owen**
>
> *A New View of Society*
>
> 1813

I was born in San Diego in 1978. Little did I know at the time that I had just missed a pivotal moment of business history, which took place just down the street three years earlier.

In 1975, retail innovator Sol Price, founder of FedMart, headed into a meeting where he was about to be blindsided. Despite creating a revolutionary business that transformed American retail with its membership-based discount stores, low markup philosophy, and employee-centric policies, Price found himself facing a hostile board. The company he built from nothing was thriving financially, yet his investors were frustrated. Within hours, Price was ousted from his own company.[1]

Sol Price wasn't just another retailer. He was a man with a radical philosophy of business. Born to immigrant parents in 1916, he came of age during the Great Depression. He practiced law, where he learned to act as a "fiduciary"—legally bound to act in his clients' best interest.

In 1954, Price left his career as a lawyer behind to found a new kind of retail store. The first FedMart was a no-frills warehouse near Harbor Drive in San Diego, offering high-quality goods at rock-bottom prices to members only. "Fortunately, most of us had backgrounds that were alien to retailing," he later recalled. "We didn't know what wouldn't work or what we couldn't do."[2]

He ranked the new company's priorities in a clear hierarchy: "Our first duty is to our customers. Our second duty is to our employees. Our third duty is to our stockholders."[3] He believed that "if you recognize you're really a fiduciary for the customer, you shouldn't make too much money."[4] In an industry obsessed with maximizing profits, Price insisted on capping margins. While most retailers saw customers as targets for profit extraction, Price saw them as clients he was duty-bound to represent.

When other retailers paid workers fifty cents an hour, Price paid a full dollar. He doubled the prevailing wage because "people could not live on 50 cents an hour."[5] He believed staunchly in his employees' rights not just to fair wages but to every kind of flourishing he could encourage, as he made clear in an early employee memo:

> You must feel confident that you are working for a fine and honest company. Somehow, we must make this mean to each of you that you will be permitted, encouraged and sometimes even harassed into growing with the company to the limit of your ability. We believe that you should be paid the best wages in your community for the job you perform. We believe that you should be provided with an opportunity to invest in the company so that you can prosper when it prospers. We believe that you should be encouraged to express yourself freely and without fear of recrimination or retaliation. We believe that you should be happy with your work so that your occupation becomes a source of satisfaction as well as a means of livelihood.[6]

His stores operated with a pristine ethical code that prohibited employees from taking any form of gratuity from suppliers, even a free lunch. He treated suppliers with the utmost fairness. His protégé, Jim Sinegal, told the story this way:

> One time we were selling ladies' hosiery for $3.99 and Sol got the idea we should sell the package for $2.99, so he said we would give up 50 cents if the supplier would also give up 50 cents. And so we did. . . . After about six months it had not really moved the needle, so Sol asked Ira to go back to the supplier and give them back the 50 cents. The factory could not believe it; they had never had anyone buy from them who had that type of integrity in terms of the business—and that was Sol.[7]

THE CONFRONTATION

By 1975, Price's approach was working brilliantly, with forty stores boasting annual sales north of $350 million (billions in today's dollars), all without spending a dollar on advertising.[8] "The best advertising," Price would say, "is the unsolicited testimonial of the satisfied customer."[9]

He had created a thriving business, but growth required capital. He'd taken FedMart public in 1969 to fund expansion, only to discover that public market investors constantly pressured him to abandon the very principles that made the company successful. "I wished I'd never placed FedMart stock in the open market,"[10] Price later admitted. Frustrated by this fundamental misalignment, he arranged to take the company private again at a premium price, both to reward shareholders and to secure patient capital from new partners who, he believed, would support his long-term vision.

But to the investors on FedMart's board in 1975, these principles looked like missed opportunities to make more money. In their eyes, Price's ethos was an impediment to maximizing their returns: Why cap margins or pay workers double when you don't have to? Perversely, they understood that the very trust Price engendered with customers meant the company could get away with more shenanigans. They wanted faster expansion, higher margins, and a more conventional approach to retail.

The confrontation had been brewing for months. Price resisted pressure to compromise his principles. At that fateful board meeting in December 1975, the investors made their move. Despite FedMart's financial success and loyal customer base, Price was voted out of the company he had built from nothing. That night, the locks on his office doors were changed.[11]

THE AFTERMATH

Put yourself in Sol Price's shoes. At fifty-nine years old, what he thought of as his life's work was abruptly taken from him. It was a devastating and humiliating blow, but it was not the end of his story.

Unfortunately, it *was* the end of FedMart.

FedMart's investors got what they wanted but still lost everything—a self-inflicted devastation. Driven by its new ethos of greed, FedMart abandoned Price's philosophy. It spent $150 million trying to replace it with conventional retail practices.

This pursuit of faster profits turned profoundly unprofitable by 1978, when losses began to mount. Leadership churned; one president after another came and went. Customer loyalty eroded, employee morale crumbled, and the distinctive advantages Price had built disappeared.

By 1982, FedMart closed all forty-six stores. Eight thousand workers lost their jobs. FedMart was completely liquidated—a textbook case of investors killing their own golden goose.[12]

THE VINDICATION OF SOL PRICE

Sol Price understood something that his investors did not. FedMart's success was powered by a philosophy composed of three mutually reinforcing elements that defied conventional business wisdom:

First, Price believed in what he called "the intelligent loss of sales"—deliberately limiting selection to focus on high-volume, high-value items.[13] While competitors stocked more than fifty thousand items, FedMart carried just a fraction but sold them in high numbers, allowing for massive buying power on those products. This retail heresy demonstrated tremendous care for the customers' experience. Careful curation respected their time and reduced decision fatigue. Each item on FedMart's shelves had to earn its place, sending a clear message: We've done the hard work of selection for you so you can trust every choice.

Second, he embraced what might be called *harder-is-easier* thinking. Price consistently chose difficult short-term paths that built long-term advantages. Paying double the market wage in San Antonio and higher in other locations like Phoenix and San Diego was harder on immediate profits but created extraordinary employee loyalty and productivity.[14] Capping margins was harder on quarterly earnings, but it built unshakable customer trust.

Third, Price built his entire business around trust as the ultimate currency.[15] Every policy at FedMart was designed to convince customers that "we're on your side." His unconditional refund policy, transparent pricing, and strict ethical standards created a personal bond with customers. Members would drive miles to shop at FedMart, not just for savings but because they trusted Price's judgment.

So FedMart's decline was not due simply to the loss of its charismatic leader. Its success had been powered by something deeper, something transferable. As a result, Price knew he could do it again.

As his son Robert Price recalled, "About a week after being locked out of his office, he called John Alessio, owner of the Fifth Avenue Financial Center office building, to inquire about another office. Suite 729, directly above his former FedMart office, was empty and ready for Sol to occupy immediately. He signed a lease that day, purchased some furniture, and ordered a sign for the door."[16] By the time I was growing up in San Diego, Price Club was a local fixture. FedMart was a distant memory.

As a kid, I experienced the power of these commitments firsthand. My grandfather was one of those evangelists who would tell anyone who would listen about the greatness of Price Club. In my family, every school year began with a pilgrimage to Price Club for supplies. Somehow, despite its deliberately limited inventory, it always had exactly what we needed. When a friend or family member needed something—a new TV, a refrigerator, anything significant—the solution was always the same: Back to Price Club we would go.

We never met Sol Price. I didn't even know that his name was the

"Price" in Price Club. It would be many years before I would understand even the first thing about business strategy or work with my first retailer. But we nonetheless had a very intimate relationship with Sol Price because we experienced the expression of his deepest beliefs every time we shopped at his store. We did not need to read a manifesto to know exactly what he—and the company he founded—stood for.

You may never have heard of Price Club, but its influence still radiates out and touches nearly every American. Price's philosophy was eventually—and thoroughly—vindicated. Today, it powers a corporate behemoth worth $400 billion, a story with a happy ending we will pick up in Chapter 6.

THE MYSTERY

Who is to blame for what happened to FedMart? I bet you have one of two answers in mind. Greedy investors? Sure. A naive founder? Also. But there is a problem with both of these explanations: The investors were sophisticated retail experts. And Sol had spent two decades building one of the most successful retail operations in America.

When I share this story with leaders, they always ask the same questions: Why would investors destroy something so successful? Why didn't Sol protect what he had built?

Or, if they've been around this weary business long enough, they don't ask any questions at all. I once had an executive tell me, with complete confidence, "If the mission-driven model were broadly superior to quarterly profit-chasing companies in the long-term, we'd expect the economy to be mostly composed of mission-driven companies by now through Darwinian competition, yet that's not what we see."

This argument sounds compelling. It has the clean logic of natural selection. There's just one problem: It assumes the market selects for value creation. Entrepreneurs have been making this mistake for centuries.

THE TRAGEDY OF ROBERT OWEN

Scotland, January 1, 1800. Mill manager Robert Owen took over the unprofitable New Lanark Cotton Mills with two partners, acting on the belief that in a factory, care for the workers was just as important as care for the machines.[17]

After inheriting a workforce of about two thousand, including five hundred children from poorhouses working in harsh conditions, Owen implemented a comprehensive overhaul guided by his personal ethos. His contemporaries saw machines as worthy of investment, but their human workers as a cost to be minimized. His idea, radical for the time, was to treat these "vital machines" as deserving of investment too.[18] He provided free medical care, childcare, and education for workers and their families; reduced daily shifts to ten and a half hours (when twelve to fourteen were standard); refused to employ children under ten; and invested in housing for his employees. He set up a village store selling quality goods at near-cost prices.

Owen's insight remains bold today; consider how revolutionary it sounded in 1800: "If, then, due care as to the state of your inanimate machines can produce such beneficial results, what may not be expected if you devote equal attention to your vital machines, which are far more wonderfully constructed?"[19]

Within just a few years, productivity and profits increased dramatically and the mill achieved consistently exceptional quality standards.[20] In 1806, when other mills laid off employees during a four-month cotton embargo, New Lanark continued to pay workers. The firm became so successful that New Lanark became a "pilgrimage site" for social observers, with royalty and statesmen visiting to witness Owen's revolutionary approach. The firm's value more than doubled by 1813.[21]

The scope of Owen's philosophy was immense and forward thinking. Even his performance management system, called the "silent monitor," was centuries ahead of its time. The silent monitor consisted of colored wooden blocks at each worker's station that were rotated daily to measure conduct (white for excellent, yellow for good, blue for fair, black for bad).[22] Unlike the harsh discipline common in factories of the era, this system respected workers' dignity while providing immediate feedback—a precursor to modern approaches. It contributed to extraordinary loyalty and productivity. While other mills faced theft, sabotage, and high turnover, New Lanark's stable, skilled workforce helped maintain exceptional quality.

After reading Sol Price's story, you already know where this is headed.

THE MISCALCULATION

Owen understood his ideas were radical and anticipated they would be met with fierce resistance, writing that "attempts may indeed be made by individuals, who through ignorance mistake their real interests, to retard the progress of this knowledge."[23] He was right.

He also believed that if he could put these ideas into practice in an industrial setting, he could prove they were lucrative even for capital owners. He was right again.

But despite his prescience, Owen made one crucial miscalculation. He expected that his discovery of "enlightened capitalism" would make him a hero among his fellow industrialists. After all, he'd proven his reforms generated spectacular returns—"fifty, and in many cases a hundred per cent"[24]—compared to conventional methods. Following the core logic of capitalism, he expected other manufacturers would be eager to adopt more profitable methods. Anyone who refused would, in their stubbornness, put themselves at a competitive disadvantage—and add yet more evidence to accelerate the change. As he confidently predicted, his principles would "by their irresistible truth pervade society" and even "opposition will give increased celerity to their movements."[25]

Here, he was oh so wrong. Nobody was more surprised than Owen when the opposite happened instead.

By 1809, Owen's partners had grown tired of his prioritizing of worker welfare. They attempted to remove him, forcing Owen to find new investors. He faced the same scenario again in 1813, when this new group also objected to his "expensive" social programs.[26] Though Owen managed to buy them out, the constant battles with shareholders continued.

In 1828, a third set of investors finally wrested control of the company from Owen and ended his reforms.[27] The return to standard practices led to declining quality and productivity. Unlike FedMart's rapid collapse, New Lanark didn't immediately fail. Instead, it coasted along as a "cash cow," extracting value from the infrastructure and reputation Owen had built. When disruptions like mechanized weaving and steam power came along, the old-fashioned mill was left completely vulnerable.[28]

Owen died essentially bankrupt. After his betrayal by investors at New Lanark, like so many contemporary billionaires, he became increasingly enamored of utopian and mystical ideas. He gave up on reforming capitalism altogether. His utopian and spiritual experiments consumed what remained of his fortune. When philosopher Ralph Waldo Emerson asked Owen in 1841 how many in his position would follow his example, Owen replied, "Not one."[29]

Separated by 175 years and an ocean, Price and Owen independently discovered the same essential insight: Treating employees, customers, and communities well could create exceptional financial results. And both were betrayed by their own investors.

TWO HUNDRED YEARS OF "ENLIGHTENED CAPITALISM"

This pattern is so common that it has a name. Building on the work of business author James O'Toole, I use the term "enlightened capitalism"[30] to describe it:

- Entrepreneurs like Sol Price and Robert Owen repeatedly discover that an "enlightened" approach to business can create exceptional value.
- They assume the market will therefore reward and protect what they have built.
- Then they watch helplessly as what they've built systematically unravels. The cruel irony is that these companies don't fail in the marketplace; they're often thriving at the very moment they're dismantled.

This fallacy is one of the biggest market inefficiencies of all time. The more golden the goose, the stronger the temptation to butcher it.

I want to be precise about what is true and what is not. Building on enlightened principles doesn't guarantee success, and lacking them doesn't prevent it. But if the market rewards value creation, this fallacy should be exceedingly rare. And yet we see it routinely, practically every day.

Price and Owen proved their philosophy worked. They just couldn't protect it. And they're not outliers.

THE GRAVEYARD OF GOOD INTENTIONS

Everyone in business knows failures happen. Competition in the marketplace. Creative destruction. Replacement by a superior form of value creation. These are *ordinary failures*. But look closely, and you'll see the stories in this chapter don't fit that narrative. Instead, we see what I call *unusual failures*—companies whose success, paradoxically, caused their failure.

Sears

Founded in 1892, **Sears** grew into America's largest retailer through employee profit sharing and ownership plans that created extraordinary loyalty and customer service.[31] Under Robert E. Wood's leadership, Sears employees owned about 33% of the company, aligning their interests with its long-term success.[32] But Sears had no institutional protection beyond Wood himself. When Wood died in 1969, the company lost its champion. New leadership faced no structural barriers to abandoning his ethos. Employee ownership declined, and so did customer service and innovation. In 2005, hedge fund manager Eddie Lampert took control, appointing himself chairman, landlord, and lender (and CEO, too, in 2013).[33] He sold 235 profitable Sears stores to a real estate company he controlled, then charged Sears rent on buildings it once owned.[34] While the company lost $11 billion, Lampert extracted nearly $1.4 billion in fees.[35] The once-mighty retailer filed for bankruptcy in 2018.[36]

Polaroid

When Edwin Land founded **Polaroid** in 1937, he created more than just a camera company.[37] He built an R&D powerhouse at what Steve Jobs memorably called "the intersection of art and science and business." Jobs admired how Land "built an organization to reflect that" ethos.[38] His approach produced the revolutionary instant camera and countless other innovations, building Polaroid into one of America's most admired companies, with over one thousand scientists and engineers working on innovative new research. But Land's board was under no obligation to protect him or his ethos, and in 1982 the company directors forced him into retirement.[39] Steve Jobs called it "the dumbest thing I've ever heard," adding, "This man is a national treasure."[40] New leadership systematically dismantled Land's culture of innovation. Within just a few years, Polaroid's research facilities atrophied, key scientists departed, and R&D spending plummeted. The company began a slow decline and filed for bankruptcy in 2001.[41]

Cadbury

In 1878, the sons of Quaker businessman John **Cadbury** created a moral enterprise that endured for generations.[42] Their model employee village, Bournville, featured housing, healthcare, and gardens for workers, plus pension plans and profit sharing. Cadbury's approach generated extraordinary returns for more than a century, built on a foundation of fierce employee loyalty and brand devotion. By 2009, Cadbury was the second-largest candy company in the world, with solid growth, sales, and profit.

But Cadbury lacked the means to resist a hostile takeover by Kraft in 2010.[43] Kraft immediately broke faith with the Cadbury ethos. They closed factories they'd pledged to keep open, eliminating four hundred jobs. They changed the Cadbury Creme Egg recipe, in what customers and the press dubbed "the great chocolate betrayal."[44] Sales plummeted as outraged consumers abandoned the iconic product.[45] The company lost its Royal Warrant (the British monarchy's mark of excellence) after 170 years of continuous service to the Crown.[46]

By conventional metrics, this betrayal "worked" as Kraft extracted $800 million in annual savings. But this only proves how valuable the trustworthiness of Cadbury had been. As a UK Parliament investigation put it, "Some of the soul of Cadbury has already been lost."[47]

Toys "R" Us

Founded in 1948 as Children's Supermart, **Toys "R" Us** revolutionized toy retail with vast warehouse stores that felt like wonderlands to children and families.[48] But its ownership structure made it vulnerable to leveraged buyout. When private equity (PE) firms acquired the profitable company in 2005, they saddled it with the $5.2 billion debt that had financed their buyout. Toys "R" Us had to use its profits to pay off the PE firms' loans instead of investing in e-commerce or store renovations, precisely when retail was being transformed by digital competition. The debt payments consumed resources that would have gone to customer experience and innovation. By 2018, unable to service the artificial debt load, all US stores were liquidated, eliminating thirty-three thousand jobs and destroying a beloved American institution.[49]

Shall I continue? I could do this all day. A. P. Giannini founded Bank of Italy in 1904, pioneering lending to immigrants and working-class families; a century later, renamed Bank of America, it required a $45 billion bailout in the 2008 crisis after targeting those same communities with predatory loans.[50] Circuit City, founded in 1949, came under activist investor pressure in 2003. Management spent $1 billion on buybacks while gutting customer service, culminating in the 2007 firing of 3,400 experienced salespeople.[51] It filed for bankruptcy a year later. The casualties go on and on: Boeing's engineering culture,[52] Wells Fargo's fake accounts scandal,[53] Silicon Valley Bank's (SVB) collapse,[54] GE's industrial leadership. In fact, I had a front-row seat when activist shareholders pressured GE to authorize spending nearly $50 billion on share buybacks, money that could have gone to innovation and new product development instead.[55]

THE SAME ENDING, TWENTY DECADES IN A ROW

FedMart and New Lanark and Sears and all the rest are not merely anecdotes or cherry-picked examples. They are symptoms of a chronic disease that has afflicted our economy for centuries. For these companies, achievements became liabilities. Skim Table 1.1, and watch the damage tick by, decade by decade, with unnatural consistency. Even Frederick Winslow Taylor's reforms at Bethlehem Steel—the case study that launched the entire field of management science—were eventually undone by investors![56]

Table 1.1. A catalog of "unusual" failures

FRIENDLY FIRE **Shareholders dismantle the ethos that laid the golden egg.**	
Filene's (1881)	Department store where the founder's son, Edward Filene, instituted profit sharing, a minimum wage for women, a forty-hour work week, health clinics, and paid vacations. He invented "a profit-sharing plan that included limited voting rights for employees," called the Filene Cooperative Association (FCA), which he saw as "an opening step to the eventual establishment of a cooperative enterprise owned by its employees." Fear of this vision led other stockholders to oust him from management in 1928 and then merge Filene's into Federated Department Stores in 1929 over his objections. The brand was eventually absorbed by Macy's in 2006.
People Express (1981)	Low-cost airline where every employee was an "owner-manager" with significant stock ownership and profit sharing. The model worked brilliantly at first, but the stock price became tied to morale: "We used to post the stock price every day. It had a tremendous effect on how people did here." Pressure to keep the stock rising pushed CEO Don Burr to acquire Frontier Airlines for $305 million in 1985, abandoning the low-cost model. By 1986, service had collapsed, and the company was sold to Texas Air Corp, which retired the brand in 1987.
See Also	Circuit City, Twilio (Chapter 9), FedMart, New Lanark, Kellogg's (1906), Hanesbrands, Inc. (1914), IBM (1924), Bed, Bath & Beyond (1971), Quiznos Sub (1981)
HOSTILE TAKEOVER **Outside actors breach the walls and redirect the company from its mission.**	
Jo-Ann Fabrics (1943)	Founded as the Cleveland Fabric Shop by two German immigrant families whose vision was a chain of fabric and craft stores that felt local and were places for community, classes, and extensive selection, it was the largest craft brand in the US in the late 1990s. In 2011, private equity company Leonard Green took Jo-Ann private for $1.6 billion in a leveraged buyout that saddled the company with significant debt. After a brief comeback during the 2021 pandemic, its value plunged 99% by 2024. Filed for bankruptcy in 2025 and liquidated all stores.
Gymboree (1976)	Founded by Joan Barnes in 1976 as a place for new moms to connect while supporting their children's development, Gymboree expanded into children's apparel and by 1991 had revenues of $48.5 million and went public on NASDAQ in 1993. It was bought by Bain Capital in 2010 for $1.8 billion, which piled on $1.2 billion in debt and overexpanded in search of growth. Sales nose-dived, and Gymboree filed for bankruptcy in 2017 and again in 2019, closing its stores and selling off assets.
See Also	AND1 (Chapter 13), Cadbury, Honest Tea (Chapter 13), Toys "R" Us, Neiman Marcus (1907), Hertz (1918), Claire's Stores (1961), iHeart Media (1972), J. Crew (1983)

BOARDROOM BETRAYAL Directors are more loyal to "best practices" than to the mission.	
Snapple (1972)	Founded with an outsider, noncorporate ethos including branding and a grassroots business style, by 1994, Snapple had $674 million in sales and was the fastest-growing soft drink in America. It was sold to Quaker Oats for $1.7 billion in 1994, and their strategy was overridden: Branding was changed, and Snapple grocery store sales were substantially expanded. Sales sank by more than 20%. In 1997, Quaker sold Snapple at a $1.4 billion loss. Analysts calculated that Quaker had destroyed $1.6 million of value for every day it owned Snapple.
Men's Wearhouse (1973)	Founded by George Zimmer on two principles: "serve customers by delivering value" and "embody servant leadership by trusting and empowering employees." Zimmer built a multibillion-dollar company famous for his personal guarantee: "You're going to like the way you look. I guarantee it." In 2013, the board fired him after he raised concerns about the company's direction. Zimmer warned the board was "eroding the principles and values" that made the company successful. The board then approved a $1.8 billion merger with Jos. A. Bank that Zimmer had opposed, taking on $1.6 billion in debt. The company filed for bankruptcy in 2020.
See Also	Vectura (Chapter 4), Whole Foods (Chapter 3), Kroger (Chapter 9), AND1 (Chapter 13), Polaroid, SAIC (Chapter 9), A&P, Lehman Brothers (1847), Olympus (1919), Hewlett-Packard (1939), Fairchild Semiconductor (1957), Parmalat (1963)

SUCCESSION FAILURE Even the greatest leaders are mortal. Without institutional safeguards, leadership change becomes mission abandonment.	
Zenith Radio Corporation (1923)	Founded by Navy veteran Eugene McDonald, known as "The Commander," who built a quality-first culture around the slogan "The quality goes in before the name goes on." During the Depression, employees took less pay to keep the company alive; when profits returned, McDonald rewarded them with shares and profit sharing. His willingness to take risks produced breakthrough innovations: the first portable radio, the first wireless TV remote, and even pay-per-view television decades before its time. After McDonald died in 1958, later managers could not maintain his ethos. Although the company kept growing through the 1960s, it ceased to innovate. By the 1980s, Zenith fell to Japanese competitors with lower prices. It filed for bankruptcy in 1999 and was acquired by LG Electronics.
Howard Johnson's (1925)	Founded by Howard Johnson on the philosophy "quality sells" and "there's no substitute for quality." He spent an industry-high 48% of revenues on food, performed surprise inspections at franchises, and built the largest restaurant chain in America by 1965. Johnson passed the company to his son Bud in 1959 but remained obsessively involved until his death in 1972. Bud then cut costs and lowered food quality to compete with fast-food chains. As chef Jacques Pépin observed, "After Howard D. Johnson's death, his organization lost its raison d'etre." Bud sold the company in 1979; the brand passed through multiple owners, and the last restaurant closed in 2022.
See Also	Bank of Italy, Sears, SAIC (Chapter 9), A&P, Steinway & Sons (1853), Arnold, Schwinn & Company / Schwinn Bicycle Company (1895), Seagram Company (1924), Commodore (1954), Atari (1972)

TEMPTATION TO HARVEST **It's easier to spend down trust than to keep earning it. Once leadership starts, they find it hard to stop.**	
Kodak (1888)	Founded by George Eastman, who believed "the prosperity of an organization was not necessarily due to inventions and patents, but more to workers' goodwill and loyalty." In 1899, he gave $178,000 of his personal profit to nearly three thousand employees—one of corporate history's first bonuses. In 1919, he gave one-third of his stock holdings ($10 million) to employees. His slogan, "You press the button, we do the rest," made photography accessible to all. After Eastman's death in 1932, later generations of managers saw "the relationship with employees change over time, particularly as shareholder value became the only measure of company success after the 1970s." This is why, when a Kodak engineer invented the digital camera in 1975, leadership refused to commercialize it, fearing it would cannibalize the lucrative film business. Kodak filed for bankruptcy in 2012.
Blockbuster (1985)	Video rental chain founded on a family-friendly, no-pornography ethos that made movies accessible to all. At its peak: 9,094 stores and 84,300 employees. But late fees brought in roughly $800 million annually—and massive customer resentment. As one analyst put it, "Blockbuster was addicted to this source of income and couldn't envision a model without it." CEO John Antioco tried to break the addiction: He launched "No Late Fees" plus an online platform that was winning customers from Netflix. But activist investor Carl Icahn opposed eliminating the lucrative fees and forced Antioco out in 2007. His replacement reinstated late fees. Blockbuster filed for bankruptcy in 2010.
See Also	Boeing (Chapter 2), Enlitic (Chapter 6), A&P, Firestone Tire (1900), Craftsman (1927), Hostess (1930), Friendly's (1935), Xerox (1961), Linens 'n Things (1979)

MISSION DRIFT **Companies gradually abandon their ethos, one compromise at a time.**	
A&P (1859)	Founded to make food affordable to all, including money-back guarantees. With sixteen thousand stores, it was the world's largest retailer by 1930. The founder's sons continued the original mission, reinvesting profits into lowering prices. When they died in the 1950s, their shares passed to the Hartford Foundation, a charity they had created in 1929. The foundation became A&P's largest shareholder but saw its mission as funding charitable grants, not protecting the company's ethos. It pressured management for high dividends rather than reinvesting in the business. While competitors moved to the suburbs, A&P's stores stagnated. It filed for bankruptcy in 2010 and again in 2015 when it was liquidated.
Merrill Lynch (1914)	Founded on the principle of "Bring Wall Street to Main Street" to serve middle-class investors with radical transparency. Founder Charles Merrill paid employees' salaries instead of commissions, insisted on full disclosure, and invested in customer education. The company's five principles—client focus, respect for the individual, teamwork, responsible citizenship, and integrity—made it the world's largest brokerage by the 1970s. Merrill led the company until his death in 1956, but later managers abandoned these principles in favor of proprietary trading and debt products. By 2008, the firm held more than $46 billion in toxic assets; its stock plunged 80%. It was sold to Bank of America in 2009.
See Also	Google (Chapter 7), Enron (Chapter 8), Bank of Italy, Bethlehem Steel (1904), Arthur Andersen (1913), Radio Shack (1921), Pier 1 Imports (1962), Borders Books (1971)

EVEN MORE "UNUSUAL" FAILURES: Believe it or not, this chart is only the tip of the iceberg. To see the expanded chart, plus citations for this one, scan the QR code or go to incorruptible.co/more-failures.

Every story has its own unique villain. A greedy investor or a delusional founder or a feckless board. But just as we saw with Sol Price, it simply doesn't add up to pin this on individual shortcomings alone. Robert Owen counted the famous utilitarian philosopher Jeremy Bentham among his investors—would you really say he was not smart enough to understand Owen's ideas?[57]

These individual dramas distract from deeper causes. If the actors change but the play remains the same, there must be a reason why.

CORRUPTION, DEFINED

Not all forms of making money are equal. Some create wealth; others merely redistribute or destroy it.[58]

Over the centuries, when people have gone searching for the moral logic of capitalism, they always hit this same bedrock principle: Fully informed, uncoerced, voluntary transactions create surplus value because both parties end up better off.[59]

Think about your last genuinely good purchase. You valued the product more than the price you paid, so you are better off. But the seller, too, is better off (otherwise they would not have sold). Both parties are wealthier. When this happens, it's a bit of a magic trick. In an instant, new value exists that did not a moment before. This wealth was not stolen; it was generated.

But this only works when the exchange is truly voluntary and informed. Remove any of these conditions and the mechanism breaks.

This is why embezzlement, coercion, fraud, bribery, and deception are wrong. It's not only because they are illegal or even immoral. It's because they corrupt the fundamental premise of our entire economic system. They transform transactions meant to create value into ones that destroy it.

This trajectory is so common these days that we hardly know what to call it. The answer is simple. Since every version of it shares the same value-destroying logic, regardless of whether the violation is illegal or even immoral, we should use the same word to describe them all: corruption.

Our modern sense of "corruption" has become catastrophically narrow. What I'm talking about is something much broader than bribery or embezzlement. (After all, the Latin *corrumpere* means "to break completely."[60]) Corruption breaks the logic of capitalism itself.

Every Ponzi scheme, every hidden externality, every unit of extracted value is a drag on our whole economy's potential. These corruptions don't just harm their immediate victims; they erode trust, increase transaction costs, and destroy the civic infrastructure that makes efficient markets possible. The hidden economic costs, as we'll see, are staggering. The truth is that capitalism succeeds not because of these widespread violations but despite them.

When builders express disgust at these betrayals, they aren't questioning the logic of capitalism. They are trying to defend it.

"ERIC IS SUCH A DOWNER"

A decade ago, the CEO of a high-flying startup with a multibillion-dollar valuation came to see me for advice on taking the company public. When I outlined the weak points in his governance structure, he was alarmed. But by our next conversation, his bankers and lawyers had reassured him, "Eric is such a downer. That won't happen to you. You're a visionary. If Eric really believed in you and your business, he wouldn't be so negative."

What they didn't tell him is that, according to Harvard Law School research, among venture capital (VC)–backed startups without appropriate protections, only 20% of founders survive even three years as CEO after going public.[61]

Can you already guess what happened next? Five months after the IPO, a larger company acquired one of their competitors. Investors panicked. The stock plummeted 70%. The board removed the CEO before the six-month mark. Did he make mistakes? I'm sure he did. Was the business perfect? Probably not. But had the founder really earned so little grace after building the company up from nothing?

The irony is that it didn't even work. The company never recovered; within five years, it was sold in pieces.

Of course, the people who told the CEO not to worry made plenty of money from the carnage. The company generated commissions, trading fees, and IPO pops on its way up—and its way down. Its employees and customers were not as fortunate.

THE EXCEPTIONS THAT PROVE—WHAT?

Confession time. I used a little sleight of hand when I presented the case studies from FedMart to Toys "R" Us. I deliberately picked each of them because for every one, there exists a counterpart that successfully protected itself from similar dangers.

While FedMart collapsed after investors ousted Sol Price in 1975, Costco has thrived for decades with a similar low-margin, high-quality model, maintaining its founding principles despite intense market pressures.[62]

Though New Lanark Mills abandoned Robert Owen's reforms, Spain's Mondragon Corporation has sustained its worker-centered approach since 1956, weathering multiple economic crises without compromise and preserving a vision directly parallel to Owen's, but with protections he never implemented.[63]

Sears abandoned its employee profit sharing and paid a heavy price, but British department store John Lewis formed the John Lewis Partnership (JLP) and took the opposite path.[64] Established in 1929, JLP has maintained its constitutional governance system through economic upheavals that destroyed many competitors.

Polaroid dismantled its innovation culture after Land's ouster, but German optics pioneer Carl Zeiss has preserved its commitment to advancing science both inside and outside the company since 1846. The non-profit Carl-Zeiss-Stiftung has protected the firm's scientific mission since 1889, overseeing highly profitable private and publicly listed subsidiaries.[65]

Bank of America drifted from Giannini's community focus, but Vanguard Group created a structure that has maintained its low-fee, client-first approach since 1975, resisting the pressures that corrupted many financial institutions.[66]

While British confectioner Cadbury's mission was diluted after its hostile takeover by Kraft, the Hershey Company, founded in 1894, is protected by Milton Hershey's foresight in establishing governance structures that have repeatedly fended off takeover attempts.[67]

While Toys "R" Us was vulnerable to the leveraged buyout that destroyed it, outdoor retailer REI has thrived since 1938 as a consumer cooperative, its structure making it immune to the private equity raids that have decimated so many retailers.[68]

ARE YOU SURE YOU ARE SMARTER THAN A NOBEL LAUREATE?

One last company deserves our attention.

Picture a physician, Marie, who has just been diagnosed with an incurable illness. Her husband has just won the Nobel Prize in Medicine. Despite her fatal diagnosis, she agrees to accompany him on a lecture tour of America.

During a dinner on the tour, she hears rumors of a miraculous new medicine being tested in Toronto. She convinces her husband to extend their trip to see the breakthrough for themselves. Realizing its profound potential, they decide to found a company to commercialize it in their home country.

The cure works. Marie will live another twenty-one years.

But Marie and her husband want more than just to save one life. They see scientific discovery as a public trust and seek to prevent anyone from using control of lifesaving medicines as leverage to enrich themselves. They agree that their new company, Nordisk Insulinlaboratorium, will work primarily for the benefit of humanity.

Like Sol Price, they have a clear set of priorities: serve patients first, advance scientific knowledge second, and generate returns for shareholders third—in perpetuity.[69] They establish the company as a for-profit business under the control of a non-profit foundation. By making this ironclad arrangement from its infancy, they ensure the company will never stray from the principles on which it is founded.

The year was 1922. The physician was Marie Krogh, one of Denmark's first female medical graduates. Her terminal illness was diabetes. The miracle drug was insulin. Her husband was Nobel laureate August Krogh.

If the name Nordisk Insulinlaboratorium sounds familiar, it should. It eventually became the company we know today as Novo Nordisk.[70]

Novo Nordisk seems to defy every expectation you might have from reading this chapter. For more than a century, it has endured the exact same threats that have led to so many of the "unusual" failures in this chapter. It is a public company with millions of outside shareholders, listed on the New York Stock Exchange (NYSE). It follows governance "best practices" including the appointment of independent directors.

And as you'd expect, it has faced almost every kind of attack we've seen in this chapter. Time and again, the directors of its non-profit foundation intervened—creating literally hundreds of billions of dollars in shareholder value. (This may sound like an exaggeration, but you'll have the chance to judge for yourself when we encounter the full story in Chapter 11.) Today, that foundation controls 77% of the voting shares through an unbreakable dual-class structure.[71] And thanks to the success of the scientific research it oversees, it has become the largest charitable foundation in the world.

When leaders today consider their organizational structure, they're typically guided by lawyers, MBAs, and investment bankers who confidently prescribe "best practices" that sound good on paper but are quite weak in practice. These advisors seem impressively credentialed and speak with absolute certainty about what's required for success.

But before someone listens to this advice, I always ask: Are you sure you're smarter than a Nobel laureate?

Because the Kroghs worked out an organizational solution a century ago that has demonstrably succeeded through every economic cycle, war, technological disruption, and market pressure imaginable. Meanwhile, many of the "best practices" everyone eagerly adopts are younger than the trees in your local neighborhood park.

THE ARCHITECTURE OF INSTITUTIONAL LONGEVITY

Every founder in this chapter—from Sol Price to Robert Owen—built an organization with an ethos worth protecting. But only a few were able to *make it stick* for the long term. Why?

When a bridge collapses, it is facile to say that gravity caused it to fall. No kidding. Gravity may be universal, but that does not leave us helpless to build strong bridges. Instead of throwing up their hands, engineers study the factors that led to the collapse: wind shear, tensile strength, load factors, material fatigue. They ask, Why was the bridge built in a way that couldn't withstand the forces acting upon it? And only then do they move to, How can we do better next time?

Similarly, when we see an organization fall, external forces are often the proximate cause. But there is a deeper question: why was the organization built in such a flimsy way in the first place? Why did it lack the structural strength to resist?

Before we can build organizations that resist corruption, we need to understand the forces acting upon them. What are the organizational equivalents of the problems of wind shear, load factor, and tensile strength? Only then can we design structures strong enough to resist. What we need is not better intentions but better *architecture*.

Each of the "exceptions" we saw earlier has confronted these problems successfully:

- Successful organizations eventually outlive their founders and so require institutionalized succession; they must have an internal character strong enough to bear this legacy through multiple generations of leaders.
- In our highly financialized economy, all organizations face financial pressures that can overwhelm the mission; they need mechanisms to survive the tension between the two without being torn apart.

- Thanks to modern "best practices," short-term and extractive thinking has come to dominate too many boardrooms; organizations need a constitutional foundation with the tensile strength to maintain their structural integrity.

Think about whatever organization you hold most dear. Whether you're its founder, its leader, an employee, or simply someone who cares about its mission, take a moment to honestly reflect: Is it giving in to temptation right now? Is it being pressured to abandon its essential purpose? Is its commitment to its mission strengthening or weakening, day by day?

In the chapters that follow, we are going to probe these questions deeply in order to discover solutions that enable organizations to stay true to an ethos across generations, not just quarters.

We begin with the first, most fundamental obstacle to making an ethos stick: Like Frankenstein, leaders are prone to losing control of their creations.

CHAPTER TWO

WHO IS THE BANK?

> But—you see, a bank or a company can't do that, because those creatures don't breathe air, don't eat side-meat. They breathe profits; they eat the interest on money. . . .
>
> The bank—the monster has to have profits all the time. It can't wait. It'll die. . . .
>
> We're sorry. It's not us. It's the monster. The bank isn't like a man.
>
> Yes, but the bank is only made of men.
>
> **—John Steinbeck**
>
> *The Grapes of Wrath*
>
> 1939

I RECENTLY HAD A CONVERSATION with the CEO of a multibillion-dollar company who'd come to see me for help with a baffling problem. He had made a bold new bet on the promise of AI to revolutionize his business. He'd personally overseen the development of a new AI product and tested it with customers. They loved it. Satisfied that he had created something amazing, he turned it over to the rest of his team to commercialize and scale.

Six months later, this new product was going nowhere.

The sales team wasn't selling it. Developers were loath to work on it. Marketing would not promote it. When confronted, the executives would insist that the product was part of their quarterly priorities.

Each of them was telling their teams to focus on it. Yet, somehow, line employees and middle managers were consistently avoiding the AI product. It was a pattern throughout the organization.

When the CEO personally intervened, he could easily get individual customers to adopt the new product. But he could not get his team to do the same, even after investing extensively in training, performance bonuses, and top-down directives. He couldn't identify any one person or group actively blocking the AI initiative. He even replaced several key executives with new ones explicitly chosen for their enthusiasm for this new direction. And yet, within months, the uneasy *status quo* prevailed.

He shook his head. "You know what's driving me crazy? I founded this company fifteen years ago. When I first proposed the core idea, everyone thought I was nuts. Investors, potential employees, even my family.

"Now that we're successful, when I suggest we need to pivot, many of the same people, including my own leadership team, resist because 'we can't risk what we've built.'" He threw up his hands. "They're protecting something that exists only because I took the 'crazy' risk they all thought was impossible. Now they think I'm reckless and can't seem to appreciate how many times they've benefited from my pushing through the impossible to get us to new success."

He could feel the stress his insistence was putting on his employees, he told me, as if they were being torn between two authorities. But who, exactly, was this other authority?

Like so many founders, he had assumed that being in charge meant the organization would reflect his values. How could it be that he had all the control on paper but so little in daily practice? And if he wasn't in control, *who was*?

THE POWER OF ETHOS

We've already seen the answer to this question, though you may not have realized it at the time. Sol Price figured it out.

What separated Sol Price from most founders wasn't just his business acumen or his work ethic. It was his *ethos*. Every organization has a culture; every business has a strategy; every founder has a vision.

Price built something deeper: a consistent organizational *character* that shaped every decision. I use the ancient Greek word *ethos* to describe this quality. Aristotle used it to mean the "habit" or "character" that defines a person.[1] At FedMart and again at Price Club, this ethos reliably aligned strategy, business model, and culture like interlocking pieces of a high-performance engine.

The CEO who opened this chapter has a strong *personal* ethos. But his organization doesn't reflect it. Somewhere along the way, it developed a different character: cautious, self-protective, resistant to change. He's on track to lose his company just as surely as Sol Price did when investors forced him out of FedMart.

Both pathways lead to the same destination. You can lose your company to outside forces, or you can lose it from within.[2] Either way, what you built stops being yours.

But to understand why, we need to reckon with what it means to apply a word like *ethos*—which, after all, Aristotle applied to human beings—to a creature that breathes profits instead of air.

EMERGENT INTELLIGENCE

In a 2024 study, researchers at the Weizmann Institute of Science set up what they called the "piano mover puzzle," a deceptively simple challenge of moving a T-shaped object through narrow slits.[3] Take a look at Figure 2.1 and imagine how you would move the object through the passageway.

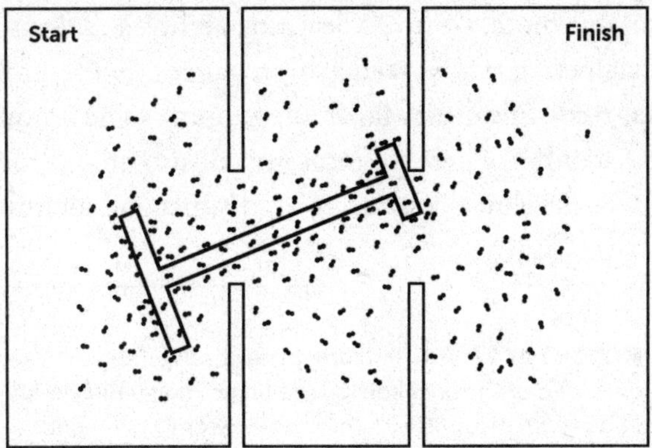

Figure 2.1.

The researchers asked individual humans to perform the task. They solved it easily.

Then they gave the same challenge to . . . ants. Individual ants were terrible at it. But when the researchers tried larger groups of ants, they witnessed—and measured—a brand-new capability.

The ants began to move differently. Not faster—differently. If you watch the video of the experiment, you'll see individual ants swirling and shifting around the puzzle, and suddenly the object is through the gap.[4] The swarm finds solutions no individual ant could discover, exhibiting collective memory, learning from failed attempts, and persisting in productive directions while avoiding repeated mistakes. Some groups of ants even outperform individual humans.

Scientists call this *emergent intelligence*—a new intelligence that doesn't exist in any single ant.[5] The Weizmann experiment is a particularly elegant demonstration, but the underlying science is well established, backed by decades of empirical research.

And most importantly for our purposes, these emergent properties have been studied extensively in groups of humans too. MIT researchers Anita Woolley and Thomas Malone discovered that teams develop measurable "collective intelligence" only when specific structural conditions are met.[6] When humans were placed in groups to solve the piano mover puzzle without structured communication or clear coordination methods, their performance actually worsened as the size of the group increased. They defaulted to self-centered short-term solutions that proved counterproductive.

But when the right structural conditions align, human groups take on emergent properties just like ant swarms do. Groups develop their own measurable moral compass, learning ability, and decision-making patterns that persist across leadership changes. Some groups consistently prefer risk while others favor safety. Some value innovation while others prize stability. These patterns are consistent and measurable—human groups develop a "character" as distinct and identifiable as any

MOVERS AT WORK: To learn more about emergent intelligence and see the video of the ants solving the piano mover puzzle, scan the QR code or go to incorruptible.co/movers-at-work.

individual's. (In some studies, scientists have even found ways to measure how ethical the resulting character is.[7])

As we scale up from teams to entire organizations, these emergent properties become more pronounced. Good organizational structures can amplify the group's intelligence far beyond any individual. But bad structures can actually inhibit human ability—just as we saw in the piano mover puzzle. An organization might develop collective intelligence for problem-solving while simultaneously developing blind spots. Or it might exhibit rapid learning in some areas while becoming rigidly stuck in others.

WHO IS THE BANK?

This CEO's plight reminded me of the famous Steinbeck passage that opens this chapter. Tenant farmers are being evicted from their land during the Dust Bowl, but when they confront the men carrying out the evictions, they can't get a clear answer as to who is making the decision to devastate them. The men sent to do the dirty work answer to the bank manager, who answers to distant owners, and those owners answer to shareholders. Each of them has a role in the organization, but somehow none of them is in charge. This leads to the farmers' bewildered question:

Who is the bank?

Steinbeck portrays it as a faceless system in which no individual can be held accountable, even though real people are losing their homes and livelihoods. He calls the bank "the monster. Men made it, but they can't control it."[8]

My friend the CEO, grappling with resistance he couldn't locate, experienced the same bewilderment. If the person at the top is not in charge, who is?[9]

The CEO I was counseling wasn't fighting his own people on the AI initiative. He was wrestling with a different kind of living being—one that had developed its own character, its own preferences, and its own will. His personal ethos of innovation was at war with the organization's emergent character, which craved safety, certainty, and predictability. The fact that he had created it mattered very little.

Life is defined not by flesh and blood but by specific properties. Living things maintain boundaries between themselves and their environment. They metabolize resources into energy. They grow, adapt, and reproduce. They exhibit behaviors that emerge from their parts but can't be predicted by studying those parts in isolation. Most importantly, they display a will to survive that shapes every action they take.

Organizations exhibit every one of these properties. They maintain legal and cultural boundaries that define who's inside and who's out. They metabolize capital, talent, and raw materials into products and services. They grow through hiring, adapt to market pressures, and spawn subsidiaries or merge with others. A company's "culture" emerges from thousands of daily interactions but can't be found in any employee handbook or org chart. And when threatened, organizations exhibit a tenacity that can override the preferences of any individual within them—even their nominal leader. Each one is a *superorganism* unto itself, operating according to its own rules of existence.

Now we can answer Steinbeck's question, *Who is the bank?*

An emergent intelligence, every bit as alive as you or me. A superorganism.

This is who the bank is.

WHEN ETHOS STRIKES BACK

The fact that organizational ethos can override leadership intentions is neither good nor bad, intrinsically. We opened this chapter with a CEO who found it infuriating. But other times, a strong organizational ethos is just what is needed to resist corruption.

Consider 3M, founded in 1902.[10] A century of research-first culture had produced products like Scotch tape and Post-it notes. In 2001, the board imported its first outside—and first nontechnical—CEO to maximize shareholder returns. The new CEO, a protégé of legendary General Electric CEO Jack Welch, slashed eight thousand jobs, froze R&D spending, and imposed Six Sigma efficiency methods on the innovation process. It was a risky move. "If you take over a company that's been living on innovation, clearly you can squeeze costs out," one Stanford University professor warned. "The question is, what's the long-term damage?"[11]

The answer turned out to be: severe.

Unlike the losses we examined in Chapter 1, this time something different happened. 3M's organizational being fought back.

The new CEO required every research project to fill out "red books" with scores of charts justifying commercial applications. Scientists suddenly had to spend more time on paperwork than on research. The resistance was immediate and visceral. Veterans pointed out that Post-it notes—3M's accident turned gold mine—would have been killed in its cradle under this system. The famous "15% time" for tinkering, which had produced so many breakthroughs, became a battlefield.[12] Researchers who'd spent decades exploring without permission now had to justify every experiment. Some stopped innovating entirely. Others found creative ways to hide their real work. It was another case of two different authorities in conflict: 3M's historical ethos of innovation versus the CEO's new ethos of shareholder value.

But this time the outcome was different. When an organization is at war with itself, it can be hard to tell whether it is having a knee-jerk reaction to change or a healthy immune response to a dangerous pathogen. Luckily, 3M had been structured ahead of time to be able to tell the difference. This structural preparation proved decisive.

For decades, the company had religiously tracked the percentage of its revenue that came from products introduced in the previous five years (3M's famous "New Product Vitality Index," or NPVI). This metric made the organization's distress visible at the board level (a "holistic measurement" we will learn how to wield in Chapter 7). When it plummeted from 33% to barely 20% (and other metrics dropped to match), the board recognized that the CEO's treatment was killing the patient.[13]

The board changed course, elevating engineer George Buckley, who immediately eliminated Six Sigma from the research labs, increased R&D spending by 11%, and restored the company's innovation culture.[14] Within a few years, the NPVI began climbing back toward its historic levels. The organizational being had effectively rejected the transplant.

3M's ethos was so deeply embedded—and, crucially, so carefully measured—that it outlasted antagonistic leadership. Notice how similar this is to the story that opened this chapter. Both involve a CEO unable to make their own organization comply. Whether you judge this as "good" or "bad" depends on how sympathetic you are to the CEO's aims.

SAME LEADER, DIFFERENT RESULTS

You may feel you are owed a happy-ending story after so much carnage in these early chapters. At first blush, 3M seems to fit the bill. But this is not that kind of book.

For one thing, 3M's focus on innovation left it with significant blind spots. The company would later pay $12.5 billion to settle claims over PFAS "forever chemicals" that contaminated water supplies—harm that NPVI was not designed to measure.[15]

There was one more consequence.

The CEO who tried to reshape 3M was James McNerney. After leaving 3M in 2005, he was immediately hired—by Boeing.[16]

This marked a complete reversal from Boeing's historic ethos. For eighty years, Boeing had functioned as "an association of engineers devoted to building amazing flying machines."[17] Technical excellence was meant to rule every decision. As at 3M, McNerney was the first nonengineer CEO in the company's history.

However, unlike at 3M, the ground at Boeing had been softened in advance of his arrival. Boeing's 1997 merger with McDonnell Douglas had elevated Harry Stonecipher—a GE veteran—to president and COO of the merged company. Stonecipher was explicit about his intentions: "When people say I changed the culture of Boeing, that was the intent, so that it is run like a business rather than a great engineering firm."[18] As industry analyst Richard Aboulafia observed, these Welch-inspired leaders had one consistent philosophy: "Crush the workers. Share price. Share price. Share price. Financial moves and metrics come first."[19]

That's why Boeing's board wanted McNerney in the first place. Welch had been named "Manager of the Century" by *Fortune* magazine in 1999;[20] his cost-cutting gospel was, well, gospel. The company that once invested everything in engineering excellence now began the process of returning $68 billion to shareholders through buybacks and dividends.[21]

As management focused more and more on financial engineering, engineers inside Boeing watched one program after another unfold with growing horror. We have their internal records because of the investigations into the 737 MAX tragedy.

One engineer wrote, "This airplane is designed by clowns who in turn are supervised by monkeys."[22] They knew the 737 MAX was dangerous. They documented problems. They raised concerns. Management's response was always the same: costs, deadlines, stock price.

As the pressure mounted, even those who'd fought hardest began to break. Another Boeing employee later confessed, "I still haven't been forgiven by God for the covering up I did last year."[23] Psychologists call this "moral injury"—the inner damage caused by knowingly causing harm. Given the scale of the harm in this case, it should be more surprising that people went along with it. But given the choice between speaking up—only to be ignored, transferred, or fired—or staying silent, most people choose silence.

The moral compromises went deeper. In February 2018, months before the crashes, one employee asked another, "Would you put your family on a MAX simulator-trained aircraft?" The response: "I wouldn't."[24]

They knew.

They shipped it anyway.

On October 29, 2018, Lion Air Flight 610 crashed into the Java Sea. All 189 people aboard died. On March 10, 2019, Ethiopian Airlines Flight 302 crashed six minutes after takeoff. All 157 people aboard died.[25] Passengers from thirty-five nations. Twenty-one UN workers heading to an environmental conference. Four Catholic Relief Services staff. A family of six.

It can't be blamed on just one leader. In fact, McNerney had retired by the time of the crash. (*Chief Executive* magazine named him "CEO of the Year" in 2015.[26]) The same methods that 3M's immune system rejected, Boeing's culture embraced.[27]

Though their aims were quite different, McNerney (at 3M) and the CEO who opened this chapter have this in common: They couldn't make their reforms stick. But at Boeing, McNerney could—and the culture he championed endured after he left.

CAN A SUPERORGANISM SAY "I'M SORRY"?

Would you like an apology from Boeing? It's understandable. When 346 people die, we hunger for accountability. But from whom? The leaders who established Boeing's new culture are long gone. How about from the new CEO brought in for damage control? But what are his apologies worth?

Indeed, is there anything more ridiculous in modern life than a corporate apology? We've all seen the ugly spectacle of the CEO who apologizes while conducting remorseless layoffs. Steinbeck's bank lackey evicting the tenant farmer. Customer service agents who are so sorry that they can't help you. The human being on the other end of the line may feel genuine remorse, but do they have the power to do anything about it? They and we both know that they don't. So their apology rings hollow.

The problem is this: No individual person can ever—ever—make promises on behalf of a superorganism.

This may be the single most important consequence of understanding organizations as superorganisms: If someone is replaceable, they cannot be trusted to fulfill the promise they make on their organization's behalf. How can anyone be sure their successor will honor it?

The churn is everywhere. Company lifespans on the S&P 500 have collapsed from sixty-one years in 1958 to just eighteen in 2025.[28] Average stock holding periods have fallen from eight years to under six months.[29] Average CEO tenure shrinks with each decade.[30] We've entered an age of temporary operators managing temporary organizations for temporary owners.

The public has learned this through bitter experience. The word of those who lead organizations cannot be relied upon, not because these leaders are necessarily dishonest but because they fundamentally cannot bind the superorganism they temporarily steward. The person making today's promise won't be here to keep it.

The result is a worldwide collapse in trust. In the US alone, trust in government fell from 77% in 1964 to just 22% today.[31] Confidence in big business dropped from 30% in 1999 to a record low of 16% in 2024.[32] Trust in nearly every sector has declined: medical leaders (73% in 1966 to 34% by 2012),[33] news media (72% in the 1970s to 28% in 2025),[34] and organized religion (60% in 2001 to 32% in 2024).[35]

We're left with organizations that can't keep promises, run by executives who can't control them, protected by governance that accelerates rather than resists this drift. No wonder the public has stopped believing. The following two chapters will explore the forces behind this decline: market incentives that bend organizations toward extraction rather than creation and governance structures that amplify rather than resist the drift.

The CEO whose impasse opened this chapter learned this the hard way. He had a strong personal ethos of innovation, adaptation, and risk taking. He assumed this would naturally become the company's ethos. But personal ethos doesn't automatically transfer to organizational ethos.

He doubled down on what he knew: directives, bonuses, training programs. It worked in the short term. He launched into founder mode, personally overseeing new product launches, replacing key executives, conducting skip-level meetings (bypassing senior managers) to align junior staff. He did put the organization on a new course. But the constant pushing, convincing, and explaining—to his team and to skeptical Wall Street analysts—exhausted him. He was fighting the organism's nature every single day. Within two years, he had resigned from the job he'd previously vowed he would hold for life.

"FOUNDER MODE" EXPLAINED

The CEO's predicament exemplifies a pattern I've seen countless times. Founders cannot understand why their past success doesn't give them credibility to try something new. Yet their executives aren't quite so sure the founder deserves the credit for everything they created.

When pressed, executives acknowledge the founder's role intellectually. "Of course, we wouldn't be here without her," they'll say. But there's another story that lives in the back of their minds: Maybe the company succeeded because it served a market need. Maybe it would have succeeded even without this particular founder. As companies scale, this way of thinking becomes more common. The percentage of current employees who can remember those early underdog days inevitably shrinks. New managers and executives act as if the company's existence was inevitable.

These two competing stories have diametrically opposed views of cause and effect. Was the founder a visionary genius without whom none of this would be possible—in which case, executives had better follow their new vision? Or was the founder just in the right place to exploit a market need—in which case, they'd better not?

This mutual incomprehension between founders and their organizations has given rise in recent years to the concept of "founder mode"—a term that describes the effort by founders of successful companies to reassert control over their own organizations.[36] When companies drift from their ethos, founders often respond with dramatic interventions: firing managers, dismantling procedures, and orchestrating cultural reboots that only they can accomplish. When it works—and it doesn't always—it's because the original founder has the moral authority to demand drastic changes that others simply could not.

Founder-mode stories make for compelling business narratives, but they leave a curious question unexamined. Who hired all those bad managers and established flawed procedures in the first place? I've known successful founders who have gone through this cycle more than once, breaking down their own organizations and building them back up, only to discover that similar problems have grown back too. Somehow, experiencing this painful cycle once never seems to immunize a company against the need to repeat it.

That's because an organization's emergent intelligence is powerful enough to defeat the efforts of smart, well-intentioned leaders again and again. This is not unique to founders. CEOs, university presidents, and non-profit directors can all fall prey to this pattern, too. Boards of dysfunctional organizations can cycle through CEOs like teenagers chasing fashion fads—Yahoo had five CEOs in just five years[37]—while customers still experience the effects of the same old bureaucratic culture.

THE PATH FORWARD

We birth organizations; we do not own them. Like children, they develop their own character, inevitably absorbing ideas and values from the environment around them.

Yet some leaders do manage to bind their organizations to purposes that outlive them. Remember the exceptions from Chapter 1: organizations that maintained their ethos for decades, even centuries. This cannot be the act of a single person, no matter how charismatic or brilliant.

Emergent phenomena cannot be directly commanded, but this does not mean leadership doesn't matter. Like physical health, ethos requires daily practice and constant discernment. Every day, ethos either strengthens or decays. There is no steady state.

This discipline matters now more than ever. As writer Ted Chiang has observed, "Most fears about A.I. are best understood as fears about capitalism."[38] When we imagine rogue AI systems optimizing the world to death, we're actually describing what many corporations already do. If an organization's ethos is misaligned, any technology platform it creates will amplify that misalignment.

Take a moment to reflect on the organization you hold most dear: Does it have an ethos, or is it drifting without one? Does it fight for human flourishing or against it? Is it creating value or extracting it? Are you shaping its ethos, or is it shaping yours?

No matter your formal title, you have influence over this organization. Yet if you cannot answer these questions with confidence, you are not in control. You are a passenger in a vehicle you think you're driving.

But if nobody is consciously driving, where is the organization going? If the behavior of superorganisms were random, we would see as many evolving toward flourishing as toward corruption. Instead, the vast majority wind up in the same place, with indistinguishable values. Steinbeck's bank is the rule, not the exception.

This uniformity suggests a deeper force at work. It is to this force that we next turn our attention.

Chapter Three

GRAVITY

> **GEOFFREY:** Why, you chivalric fool—as if the way one fell down mattered.
>
> **RICHARD:** When the fall is all there is, it matters.
>
> —**James Goldman**
> *The Lion in Winter*
> 1966

For most of human history, the idea of human flight seemed like a ridiculous fantasy. Not just unlikely but physically impossible. After all, everyone knew that everything falls down. Always has, always will.[1]

Then, in 1666, Isaac Newton had his famous encounter with the apple. By 1687, he had unraveled the universal laws of gravity. People sometimes say that Newton discovered gravity, but this is not quite correct. Everyone on Earth experiences gravity every day of their life. What Newton discovered was the mathematics behind the invisible force that makes things fall. Then he wrote down its laws and gave it a name.

To anyone dreaming of human flight, this must have felt like terrible news. Mathematical proof that everything, absolutely everything, is pulled inexorably downward.

But in retrospect, Newton's discovery was the foundation that made modern aviation possible. By understanding exactly how gravity works (its laws, its properties, its predictable effects), we eventually figured out how to defy it. What seemed like the final word on the impossibility of flight became the first step toward making it inevitable.

And just as surely as physical gravity pulls an apple, organizations face their own invisible force that pulls them down. Understanding it is the only way to understand three otherwise inexplicable phenomena.

First, we saw in Chapter 1 how investors routinely kill the golden goose, even when companies are worth far more intact. These betrayals seem irrational when viewed simply in terms of profit and loss. It's natural to chalk them up to individual greedy actors, but this is insufficient as an explanation. The consistency of the pattern indicates that a deeper force is at work.

Second, if I tell you that a certain company has succumbed to "BigCo disease" (as we call it in Silicon Valley), you already know what I mean. The symptoms are bureaucracy, short-term thinking, hollow culture, and issuing the same anodyne press releases as everyone else. These symptoms are not random. Despite starting in different industries, with different missions and characters, the uniformity of their end state suggests something must be aligning them behind the scenes.

Third, companies routinely hire outside experts to advise them. They seek out people with deep experience to serve as counselors or independent board members. As we will see in later chapters, these advisors are far more likely to push "best practices" rather than try to protect a company's distinctive mission and ethos. This happens even when they are being paid by the company or have a fiduciary duty to it. They're more loyal to the financial system than to their actual clients. They've clearly been captured. But by what?

FINANCIAL GRAVITY

I call the force behind these phenomena *financial gravity*. It's the psychological pressure that shapes behavior and, eventually, values based on the desire to succeed at future transactions.

This pressure is real, not imagined, and it emerges from actual resource imbalances that are easy to name and quantify. Investors control capital, employers control livelihoods, and markets control valuations. These imbalances create genuine incentives that, over time, change the way people and companies act.

Financial gravity has deep evolutionary roots.[2] For millions of years, humans and their ancestors survived by tracking who controlled resources and adjusting their behavior accordingly. Those who didn't track didn't survive. In other words, we inherited minds that are tuned to read status and coalition signals. These reflexes aren't running every moment, but they're easily triggered and hard to resist. They lie waiting in the background of every transaction or potential transaction. You cannot turn them off any more than you can stop your pupils from dilating in the dark.

Modern life is full of transactions: getting the job, landing the plum assignment, raising the money you need, earning the promotion. Our reflexes kick in automatically in the face of money, power, or status disparities, which, in our hyper-financialized world, have become interchangeable. It's why politicians get rich and why the wealthy become politicians. It's why celebrities become investors and investors become celebrities.

We've all felt this force at work. That tightening in the chest before disagreeing with someone who controls a resource we need. That moment of nodding along, in a pitch meeting or board meeting or strategy session, to ideas that deserve challenge, because the person speaking might be useful someday. We've all felt the sinking realization that the promotion might go not to the most deserving but to whoever understands the "real rules" better.

The real rules. The ones no one writes down, no one explains, but everyone somehow knows. These are the rules of financial gravity that organizations unconsciously obey. And before long, they begin to drift.

Consistently enacted behavior eventually becomes internalized as values, which gravity transmits across great distances. For example, the stock trader obsessing over quarterly earnings and the line worker may never meet, but over time, the line worker adopts the trader's worldview: Numbers matter more than craftsmanship, efficiency trumps everything, the stock price is the score. If this were merely about incentives, sometimes it might work the other way; the trader might need to learn from line workers too, since such understanding might make the trader a better investor. Instead, that kind of "upstream" influence is practically unthinkable. Gravity is a one-way arrow that always transmits the values of those who control resources. This transmission may be unconscious or even inadvertent, but that doesn't make it any less real.

Multiply these small individual transformations across thousands of people, and it's clear how powerful financial gravity truly is. It doesn't respect company boundaries or even industry boundaries. When I ask CEOs who've taken companies public to identify the biggest change they notice before and after, I always get the same answer: Every employee starts watching the stock ticker. And so a company might preach quality, the CEO might genuinely believe in craftsmanship, and the company may strive to reward great work. But when employees see the stock price crash because of a competitor who ships junk, the temptation is overwhelming to compromise "just this once." If this juices the stock price, even for a short time, it's only a matter of time before employees are teaching each other that quality is an unaffordable luxury. We become what the gravitational field rewards, then forget we ever wanted anything else.

Over time, this subtly changes the company's values. People become extremely wary about whatever *might* make the stock price go down. Notice the "might" in that sentence. This is different from interrogating investors to discover what they actually want. That would be a healthy dialogue. No, this is allowing the ghost of "the market" to be a silent participant in every strategy, product, and board meeting. It's no different from a startup wondering what "investors" want them to do or a non-profit slowly conforming to the perceived preferences of the donor class. In every case, it's an automatic, sometimes even unconscious, response that may not even reflect the true preferences of the partners in question.

THE LAWS OF GRAVITY

Like physical gravity, financial gravity follows specific laws that operate whether we acknowledge them or not.

First Law: Gravity overrides direct authority

A National Bureau of Economic Research study of 401 CFOs found that 78% would intentionally cancel profitable projects if it meant hitting analyst targets.[3] When people say Wall Street makes companies act short term, this is what they have in mind. These executives are knowingly destroying the value they were hired to create. The board and the CEO may direct the CFO to allocate resources to R&D, but the CFO's priorities are shaped by gravity. I once asked a CFO to explain it, and he put it this way: "My board might be disappointed in the long run. But Wall Street will definitely destroy me if we miss earnings. Once you get that reputation, your career options vanish."

Stanford's Jeffrey Pfeffer documented this as a "social contagion."[4] When competitors announce layoffs and their stocks rise, executives make matching cuts despite knowing they're harmful. As one confessed to Pfeffer, "[I know] layoffs are harmful to company well-being, let alone the well-being of employees, and don't accomplish much, but everybody is doing layoffs and [my] board is asking why [we] aren't doing layoffs also."[5]

I see this constantly in startups. I remember as a founder how frustrating this pressure was. When a competitor would raise capital to aggressively expand at all costs, the board would immediately ask for dramatic measures for us to do the same. Discipline evaporated. In most cases, the free spender would be dead within two years. Chasing it would make us little more than lemmings going over the cliff with them. Yet the pressure to chase was immense because "the market has spoken."

Second Law: Gravity works through perception

When I first teach leaders about gravity, they are heartened. They feel like they will be able to use it to amplify their influence. Managers think they can harness it to instill their values. Investors believe they can shape portfolio behavior. But this often backfires in ways they find surprising.

A manager might preach work-life balance in every meeting, write it into policy, and genuinely believe in it, but if employees see midnight emails and only workaholics getting promoted, that's the message that gets through. Individual investors may praise long-term value creation, but ask most executives what "the market" wants, and they'll say the opposite. This happens even when the long-term investor is one of their own shareholders.

I once intervened to save an innovation team that ran Lean Startup experiments for less than $100k, saving their company as much as $900k each time they proved a concept wasn't viable. Management praised the new "FastWorks" innovation culture publicly. But the team got negative reviews for "poor budgeting" and "failure." Every employee learned the real rule: Don't take risks, no matter what leadership says. Gravity doesn't care about your intentions. It makes its point through the concrete consequences—the falls and bruises.

Third Law: Gravity is a function of size imbalance

The larger the resource disparity, the stronger the gravitational pull. For example, I advised a B2B startup that had a solid roadmap and a happy team—until their biggest enterprise client, 40% of their revenue, "suggested" new features. Not demanded; suggested. Six months later, the product was unrecognizable. The sheer mass of that one client warped everything around it.

Even when they weren't actively making requests, every product decision was made with them in mind. "What would Company X think?" became the unspoken filter. The team that once valued elegant design now celebrated whatever might please the entity controlling their survival. The client never asked them to change their values. Gravity did it automatically.

It's important to see how this leads to a nested-dolls situation. The big enterprise client was itself being shaped by the gravity of the public markets. Its executives were shaped by their shareholders, who were shaped by their limited partners (LPs), who were shaped by their own need to compete for capital. Each level feels the weight of the resources above it, even when those resources aren't actively being deployed. The anticipation of future failures or successes shapes present values.

These three laws explain why organizational life feels so predetermined—why almost every company ends up in the same place and why fighting for your mission feels like swimming upstream.

What feels inevitable, like it's just "how things work," is really the gravitational wake of something bigger than you.

So although executives love to blame "Wall Street" for the pressures they feel, if you spend time with the investors, traders, analysts, and bankers who make up Wall Street, you'll find they are all themselves trapped in gravitational fields. The powerful CEO obsessing over quarterly earnings is just as trapped as their entry-level employee.

It's gravity all the way down.

THE COWS DON'T CARE

I once met a quantitative trader at a conference who opened my eyes to how disconnected financial governance has become. At the hotel bar, I asked about his best day at work. His eyes lit up as he described engineering a synthetic short against a mid-cap company, betting the stock would fall. "The stock dropped eighteen percent in two hours," he said, practically bouncing. "Beautiful execution."

I asked if he realized he was now part of that company's governance.

"What do you mean?"

"Right now, every manager at that company is in crisis mode. Emergency meetings, questioning strategies, people getting fired. Your trade just threw hundreds of lives into chaos."

He stared at me for a long moment, then said something I'll never forget: "But the stock movement has nothing to do with them. Their behavior is totally irrational. When I short cattle futures, the cows don't care. Companies should be the same."

I tried once more: "But companies are made of humans, not cattle."

"That's their design flaw." He shrugged, returning to his drink.

The awful part? He was right, just not in the way he meant. Most organizations today have severe design flaws that do not account for the gravitational forces that will inevitably act upon them. They're like buildings designed without considering wind load. When the pressure comes, they crack.

WHOLE FOODS: WHEN ETHOS MEETS GRAVITY

In 2017, John Mackey found himself sitting across from Jeff Bezos in a boathouse, contemplating the unthinkable. After forty years building Whole Foods from a single Austin storefront into a $13 billion company, Mackey found himself in an impossible situation.

"I had nurtured Whole Foods, my proverbial child, my baby, from her infancy. . . . Was I now ready to let her go?"[6] That fateful meeting would end Whole Foods' independence forever.

How does a company built on love end up for sale to the highest bidder?

In 1978, Mackey was a twenty-five-year-old college dropout who'd borrowed $45,000 from family and friends to open a natural foods store. When he and his girlfriend Renee got evicted from their apartment for storing food products, they moved into the store, bathing with the dishwasher hose.

Their initial *minimum viable product* (MVP) may have been scrappy, but their ambition was expansive. Mackey said his goal was to create "the happiest workplace in America—a workplace based on love."[7] This love, he envisioned, would radiate through everyone the enterprise touched.

In 1981, Memorial Day flooding left Austin underwater. Eight feet of muddy runoff sluiced through the Whole Foods store, destroying $400,000 in inventory and ruining everything they'd built. The store should have died that day. Instead, customers and neighbors showed up with buckets and mops. They weren't there to shop but to rescue something they loved. Suppliers extended credit. Their banker personally guaranteed the loan they desperately needed. "Whole Foods Markets would not have survived," Mackey later wrote, "had it not been for so many people who loved the business and believed in us."[8]

For decades, this love-based approach drove Whole Foods' extraordinary success. Store teams were free to reject products they felt didn't fit their community; employees voted on new hires after a trial period; salary information was transparent to all. Customers paid premium prices not grudgingly but gladly, knowing they were supporting something meaningful.

This mutual devotion drove decades of profitable growth—right up until the end.

In 1988, Whole Foods took $4.5 million in venture capital (VC)—a 34% stake in the company—giving the VC firms three seats on the board.[9] "I knew that we had entered a different phase of business life," Mackey recalls. "The new directors wanted to see the company succeed, but their incentives were different."[10] As time went on, Mackey came to think of their VC partners as "hitchhikers with credit cards—they were along for the ride and benefitting from our forward progress, and as long as they felt we were going where they wanted to go, they'd help pay for gas. But they did not have the same level of commitment to stay in the car for the entire journey."[11]

The same VCs who had once dismissed Whole Foods as "just a bunch of hippies selling food to other hippies"[12] now controlled a third of the company, and they wanted more. The pressure manifested in expansion. Where Whole Foods had grown organically in Texas for its first decade, now growth meant acquisition, standardization, and private-label products.

"We never had enough money," Mackey would later admit of those years.[13] But when the VCs proposed another financing round that would have given them control of the business, Mackey realized it wasn't about money anymore. It was about who would determine Whole Foods' future. To escape VC control, Whole Foods went public in 1992 at a $100 million valuation, raising $28 million. "Honestly, the day we went public was one of the happiest days of my life," Mackey later said, "not just because the venture capitalists were moving on, but because all those people who had shown faith in us and invested back in the early days, we delivered for them."[14]

For years afterward, the model held. By the end of 2006, Whole Foods had expanded to 186 stores. But public markets brought different gravitational pressure. That year, at the height of success, Mackey reduced his salary to $1 and donated his stock options to charity. "I no longer want to work for money," he announced, "but simply for the joy of the work itself."[15] Then came 2008. The financial crisis sent Whole Foods' stock plummeting 90%.[16] In the years that followed, Mackey worked hard to push the stock price higher but held to the company's premium pricing, defending their 35% gross margins. The stock rebounded spectacularly, recovering the 90% it had lost and then rising fivefold by 2010 and nearly tenfold by 2012.[17] Looking back, Mackey would call this his "single biggest regret as the CEO." As he explained, "We missed the best opportunity we ever had in the history of the company to lower our prices. Our stock wouldn't have gone as high. We wouldn't have created as much short-term shareholder value. We'd still be an independent company today, I think, if we'd done that."[18]

Why couldn't he make this obvious move? Mackey was blunt about the constraints: They were never "able to make such price investments under the tyranny of quarterly earnings pressure. With Wall Street clamoring for short-term profits and rising same store sales," the right long-term decision felt impossible.[19]

THE GRAVITATIONAL COLLAPSE

I want to really drive this point home. Whole Foods was profitable every year (even 2008!) and every quarter, right up until the end. They didn't need to raise capital. They didn't need a high stock price to run the business. And yet the need to keep the stock price high drove decisions that led them, inexorably, to lose their independence.

Why?

You would think Mackey would be the kind of visionary leader who would find it easy to ignore the stock ticker. Remember, he had donated his own stock options to charity back in 2006, so this was certainly not about greed. Nor was it a complicated strategic bind. The main challenge the store faced was its "Whole Paycheck" reputation, caused by high prices; growing competition from other organic food stores led to declining foot traffic. The biggest mystery of the Whole Foods saga is that this problem had an obvious solution: cut prices. But Mackey could not bring himself to do it. He was too worried that the stock price would go down.

Again: Why?

Mackey had given almost every Whole Foods employee stock options to share in Whole Foods' success.[20] This created tremendous alignment and loyalty to the company, but it also meant thousands of workers had their retirement savings and college funds dependent on the stock price. If Mackey cut prices and the stock fell, even temporarily, his own team would watch their net worth shrink. The company had lived through that kind of trauma in 2008, and the psychological scars ran deep. No one wanted to repeat it.

The internal pressures were magnified by how our modern stock market works. After its post-2008 recovery, Whole Foods had several episodes when market sentiment turned sharply against the company after it failed to meet analysts' targets for growth or margins.[21] Each time, Mackey watched employees grow anxious, suppliers tighten terms, and media narratives spiral. Throughout this period, hedge funds and activist investors hounded him to change the way he ran the company, and he was aware that the lower the stock fell, the cheaper it would be for one of them to buy a larger stake in the company or take it over entirely. In fact, the more the market irrationally undervalued Whole Foods, the more profitable it would be for an acquirer to take it over, as Amazon eventually did.

Each of these problems had a fix, but each solution would have required different choices years earlier. Don't rush the recovery from the 2008 crash; let the stock grow slowly while cutting prices. Don't distribute short-term stock options and then act surprised when employees want the stock price to rise. Don't go public without the protective provisions necessary to shield the mission. It is facile to call these "mistakes" on Mackey's part, but at the time, each one was a "best practice" cheered on by experts and (most likely) by his own highly compensated advisors. In many ways, the danger began decades earlier, when he first decided to put "hitchhikers" on his board.

None of this would have mattered, however, if not for the governance structure of Whole Foods. It was built according to governance "best practices" in our era of shareholder primacy—which left the company defenseless against these pressures.

And as the company aged, more and more of its executives and board members were themselves captured by the allure of those "best practices." Mackey put it this way: "I think this is a problem most successful companies eventually face, as the leaders who created and built the organization grow older and retire. They are gradually replaced by 'business professionals,' who are very smart and capable but ultimately more loyal to their own careers than they are to the company."[22]

Ironically, this vulnerability repeatedly earned Whole Foods the highest ratings from governance experts. (One such agency, ISS, consistently rated the company a 1 on its 1-to-10 risk scale for "shareholder rights," where 1 represents the best possible score.)[23] In practice, this meant Whole Foods had no ability to resist a hostile takeover. As the stock gradually declined from its peaks, that same "good governance" gave hedge fund Jana Partners their opening.

In 2017, what Mackey had long dreaded finally happened: Jana Partners took an 8.3% position in Whole Foods.[24] "Like most public company CEOs," Mackey later wrote, "I feared few things more than shareholder activists—calculating speculators who buy up shares in a company with the sole intention of engineering short-term increases in the stock price so they can cash out at a quick profit." He compared them to "predatory sharks—attuned to vulnerability in a company like the smell of blood in the water. And on that spring day in 2017, I learned that the sharks had their teeth in Whole Foods."[25] In their Securities and Exchange Commission (SEC) filing, they said the shares were "undervalued and represent an attractive investment opportunity" and promised to address the company's "chronic underperformance."[26] Jana's analysts weren't wrong about the symptoms; seven quarters of declining same-store sales had depressed the stock price. But remember why this "underperformance" existed. The market's gravity had created the problem that Jana now arrived to solve.[27]

Mackey was livid: "They're greedy bastards. They just want to sell us because they think they can make 40 or 50 percent quickly."[28] It turns out he estimated their profits pretty accurately.

"This kind of predatory investor strategy was exactly what gave capitalism a bad name," he later wrote. "It had no concern for any stakeholder other than the shareholders—and even that was a short-term concern focused on quick profit, not long-term value creation. It had no loyalty to our higher purpose, no care for our culture, and no long-term leadership vision." For Mackey, the fight for Whole Foods was "a morality play to see which version of capitalism would prevail: the Conscious Capitalism that had guided us so well up to this point, or the short-term, narrow-minded financial capitalism represented by Jana and others like them."[29]

Even worse, Mackey couldn't count on his own board for support: "As a founder and iconoclast, I was simply an obstacle to be removed." One advisor warned him, "I know you think your new Board is a friendly one. . . . But I suspect they're still going to vote you out, and quickly. The lure of those longer-term relationships with private equity players, the promise of future Board positions—they can be powerful motivators. They'll apologize, say something about 'fiduciary responsibility' and 'professional management,' and cast their vote against you."[30]

Facing Jana's assault, Mackey confronted a devastating reality: He could not figure out how to solve the fundamental problems facing his company. But once again, I want to emphasize: These were not business problems in the conventional sense. Customers still loved shopping at Whole Foods. Employees still loved working there. The company was profitable every quarter. After decades of building something beautiful, Mackey found himself reduced to a single, heartbreaking choice: not whether to sell but whom to sell to.

He hoped that Amazon's commitment to long-term thinking would make them a more sympathetic acquirer than the alternatives. The fall was all that was left.

That's how he wound up in the boathouse with Jeff Bezos.[31]

The bitter irony came immediately. On the day Amazon closed the acquisition, they slashed prices on organic staples by as much as 43%.[32] Foot traffic jumped 25%.[33] Amazon did in one day what Mackey had known was necessary but couldn't bring himself to do.

Jana made about $300 million for their six months of work, more than one hundred times what the typical Whole Foods employee would make in a lifetime.[34] Jana advertises itself as a firm that "leverages shareholder engagement with the goal of creating substantial value for both our investors and stakeholders"[35] and boasts of "improving governance at public companies."[36] From the traditional view of governance, this whole story counts as a victory. Whole Foods had "best practice" governance the entire time. Jana made money for themselves and their investors.

The aftermath for everyone else was pretty much in line with the grim stories we heard in Chapter 1. Whole Foods fell off *Fortune*'s list of "100 Best Companies to Work For" in 2018;[37] customers complained about empty shelves and disappearing products.[38] Today, the Whole Foods ethos of love is all but lost.

"I had some small hope that our culture might have some influence on the innovative but more transactional business culture of Amazon," Mackey reflected before his forced retirement. "But not only did they largely ignore our culture, they unconsciously began to make decisions that damaged it."[39]

Was it at least a victory for Whole Foods in purely financial terms? Not really. By all accounts, adding grocery know-how and distribution to Amazon's retail empire has helped Amazon. But in terms of Whole Foods itself, Amazon's deep pockets have grown the brand only modestly. The initial price cuts did lead to a surge of foot traffic, but overall, Whole Foods' market share today is roughly the same as it was at the time of the acquisition.[40]

So in the end, did Jana Partners' investment create value? Their $300 million was transferred from the company's future to Jana's accounts. We call this "investment" today, but Adam Smith would have called it extraction: harvesting what others planted. Nor is Whole Foods an outlier in this respect. Research on hedge-fund activism finds no conclusive evidence that it creates long-term value.[41] Often, the value is moved from one pocket to another without creating anything new.

When asked if he regretted selling to Amazon, Mackey gave an answer that captures the heartbreak of leadership under financial gravity: "The most honest answer I can give is that I regret the circumstances that made it the best option. I still believe it was the best strategic choice available at that time."[42] Here was a leader who had done everything right—built a beloved company, created genuine value, inspired fierce loyalty—yet found himself powerless to save what he had created. In the end, even his victory was a form of defeat.

THE SYSTEMIC TRAP

After the sale, economist Owen Davis published an article titled "The Greedy Bastards Won," charging that "Mackey wanted to have it both ways, to rhapsodize warm-and-fuzzily about being a different sort of 'conscious' company while still operating legally as a standard-issue publicly traded corporation."[43]

Davis, like most observers, saw only the high drama of "Jana versus Mackey." Would conscious capitalism or the greedy bastards win? Which side is the more savvy? In that story, Jana Partners was the winner; Mackey's ethos, the loser. But there is another way to look at this story. The real winner was financial gravity. Jana Partners was merely the instrument.

Davis was right that being a "standard-issue publicly traded corporation" was not compatible with Mackey's ethos.[44] But why should Whole Foods have been embodied in such a structure? If the company had been built with different governance structures, there would have been no insoluble conflict between Mackey's ethos and shareholder value. This is financial gravity's most insidious effect: The gravitational field has become so strong that we've forgotten that other organizational forms are possible.

That's why we're about to get into the specific alternatives to being gravity's victim. Because if even John Mackey—after forty years of fighting—still lost, then fighting harder isn't the answer. Building differently is.

THE TURN OF THE TIDE

I once talked to a founder who had led his company to tremendous success, making millions of dollars in returns for his investors, before being summarily forced out by some of his investors. Within months, the company began cutting R&D, raising prices, and squeezing suppliers.

And yet talking about his experience, the CEO blamed mostly himself. “I should have chosen better board members,” he said. “I should have maintained more leverage with investors.” As he was starting a new company, I asked what governance changes he was considering. He looked at me blankly. “Like what?”

It’s time to start answering his revealing question.

Some organizations have figured out how to defy gravity. You’ve seen glimpses of them already. They’ve built the kind of strength that allows them to resist corruption. Other organizations, despite the best intentions, fall due to the design of their organizational structure. The approaches that save companies are not only proven, with long track records of success, but also learnable. Some require no more than a two-page legal filing—and the courage to use it.

In order to build organizations that are truly strong, we need to pay special attention to the exoskeleton that separates inside from outside. Fortunately, there is already a discipline that specializes in the design of this most essential semipermeable membrane. I like to think of it as the art of organizational soulcraft, designing the deep structural foundations that give organizations strength. It is called governance, and it is the subject of the next chapter.

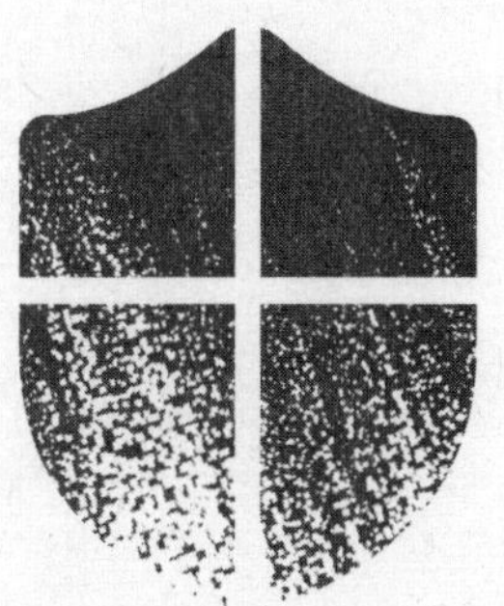

Chapter Four

THE NEW GOVERNANCE

When plunder becomes a way of life for a group of men in a society, over the course of time they create for themselves a legal system that authorizes it and a moral code that glorifies it.

—Frédéric Bastiat
Economic Sophisms
1848

Managers not only may but should violate the rules when it is profitable to do so.

—Frank H. Easterbrook and Daniel R. Fischel
Michigan Law Review
1982

Let me ask you a question: Who do you think is the most evil company in the world?

I've asked this question in settings all over the world. It's fascinating to me how many different answers I get. They've changed over time too. As of this writing, common answers include armed mercenaries, certain bioengineering companies, oil or mineral extraction companies, and, lately, the largest tech giants—pretty much anyone that could (with some creative license) be cast as the villain of a dystopian sci-fi movie.

As you read this chapter, ask yourself the same question. You don't have to share your answer, but most people have a pretty good idea who should be on the world's largest most wanted poster.

My father is a pulmonologist, so I generally use Philip Morris as my hypothetical example. But I acknowledge that your values may be different from mine, so you should feel free to silently substitute someone else as you read along.

My next question is always the same: Imagine you've started a company. If Philip Morris (or your own personal corporate demon) offers to buy your company for one dollar per share more than it's currently worth, would you sell it?

I've been using this quiz for many years now, and I have never had anyone answer yes. "Hell, no!" is the most common answer—the rest are unprintable.

Someone did once ask me, "Well, what are they going to use it for?"—which is fair. "To sell cigarettes to children," I told them. "Does that affect your answer?" They went straight to "Hell, no!"

Now keep in mind that I have done this exercise with hundreds of people who have actual, existing, operating companies. So for them, this is no hypothetical. Next, I ask them if they are aware that most governance experts believe that if Philip Morris offers that extra dollar per share, they are legally required to say yes. In fact, according to their own corporate charter, they have what's called a fiduciary duty to say yes.[1] It's an ironclad legal requirement. Remember when Elon Musk bought Twitter? After he tried to back out of the deal, fiduciary duty required Twitter's board to *sue him in order to force him to complete the transaction*, even though they had misgivings about what his ownership would mean.[2]

This is not an uncommon occurrence, as we saw in Chapter 1. And this is before we even get to famous cases of companies acquired in order for their products to be shut down, as happened with electric cars in the early 1990s.[3] According to the rules that most governance experts uphold, it doesn't matter who the acquiring company is or what they intend to do. The bottom line is that today's governance "best practice" is that if investors demand it, any company can be destroyed at will.

Does this strike you as sane?

WHY GOVERNANCE SEEMS BORING

I understand if you find corporate governance boring. When I bring it up, so many people look at me like I just changed the subject to tax returns or folding laundry. Eyes glaze over.

It's no wonder. The rise of financialization has led to the professionalization of governance jobs. These professionals have developed their own esoteric and convoluted terminology that most builders find incomprehensible. (Pop quiz: Would a "classified board" lead to greater "entrenchment" or less?[4]) As a result, it's common to think operations, strategy, and vision are entirely separate from governance. Many assume it's something drab, a matter for lawyers and bankers to fuss over—compliance, filing deadlines, and reporting accurately.

But here's what happens when that assumption meets reality.

For many of the founders I meet, I am the first person to ask about the implications of their own governing documents. "My what?" is a common response. I know some readers may find this hard to imagine. How can people with an existing operating company—with customers, investors, employees—not know about their own governance? The truth is that most leaders treat their governing documents—the constitution that determines their company's future—like a building permit or terms of service agreement.

(This disconnect between builders and their own legal reality is so common that it was expertly parodied in the HBO show *Silicon Valley*, where founders routinely agree to terms without understanding them. In one episode, an investor can't contain his incredulity: "You don't know how your own f—ing company works?" he asks a naive founder.[5] No, Russ, he does not.)

So when I actually walk them through the consequences of their governance choices, they are invariably shocked. Told that their own charter requires them to sell to the highest bidder, they assume I've made a mistake. "Surely," they say, "my lawyer would never do this to me." I always invite them to call their counsel, ask, and then call me back. On occasion, I have actually had their lawyer pull a copy of their charter from the State of Delaware so they can see with their own eyes what they signed. It makes me feel like Perry Mason: "Is this your signature right here on this document?"

They go quiet. I've seen it a hundred times, the total look of incredulity. Meanwhile, their lawyer never understands why they feel betrayed. They got the very "best practice" documents available: the ones that get deals closed quickly, the ones investors never question. The default documents are designed to be investor favorable, optimized for the next round, not the next decade.

After all, what could be more important to an entrepreneur than the ability to raise money?

This is the reality of what passes for "governance" in countless board rooms around the world today. It's not a conspiracy. It's just the way it is. They do it right out in the open.

A leader can sell their company for many valid reasons. Not every transaction is a tragedy. Unfortunately, I've also watched successful founders lose control involuntarily, winding up with plenty of wealth—and regrets.

To put it as plainly as possible, if you don't get governance right, nothing else you do when building your products or your company will matter for the long term. Any company can be bullied into submission by anyone who has enough money to mount a takeover or activist campaign. This isn't just rule by whoever is richest (which would be bad enough). It's also rule by whoever can borrow the most money.

This has massive consequences for product, strategy, and culture. After all, how can you trust an organization that might be forcibly acquired by anyone at any time, practically overnight?

THE FIFTEEN-CENT BETRAYAL

Did you think I was exaggerating when I gave my "one dollar per share" hypothetical? Before you dismiss it as an abstract thought experiment, I'd like you to consider it from the point of view of the founder-scientists of Vectura.

Vectura was founded in 1997 as a research spinout from the

University of Bath.[6] Professor of pharmaceutical technology John Staniforth and his team of researchers had dedicated their careers to improving inhaled medicines for respiratory diseases like asthma and chronic obstructive pulmonary disease (COPD). Vectura became the vehicle for their work, and the company's mission was to bring these lifesaving medicines to patients. By 2021, Vectura was an independent public company trading on the London Stock Exchange, with more than a dozen approved therapies on the market.

Philip Morris International (PMI) attempted to acquire Vectura for £1.1 billion.[7] (At the time, PMI was in the midst of an ill-fated strategy of diversifying "beyond nicotine" by investing in e-cigarettes and inhaled therapeutics.)[8] This headline number sounds impressive, like the classic "offer you can't refuse." But it was actually only 165 pence per share.[9] A private equity firm had also bid for the right to acquire the company, offering 155 pence per share. To prevent further bidders, PMI had declared their intention to outbid any rival. (As we'll see in the next chapter, they can afford such moves because their $7 billion in annual net income doesn't account for their portion of the $600 billion in annual costs the tobacco industry imposes on the US economy alone.[10])

Vectura's board of directors had to make a choice. Stay independent, sell to private equity, or sell to Philip Morris International and earn an extra ten pence per share.

See, the "dollar per share" premium in my example *was* an exaggeration. In real life, it was closer to fifteen cents. Care to guess what happened next?

Health charities begged them to say no. The British Thoracic Society called the potential deal "unethical."[11] The broader British public was outraged at the idea that a healthcare company would be owned by Big Tobacco. But Vectura's board? They unanimously accepted the bid from Philip Morris International, claiming that their fiduciary duty to shareholders left them no choice. After a mere four months of deliberation, the deal closed in September 2021.

The fallout was swift and predictable to everyone except those bound by law to ignore it. Partners fled. Executives quit. Within three years, PMI had taken a $680 million write-down on its investment and sold the company's assets for a mere £150 million.[12] It was an incredible act of value destruction.

It's true that some investors made some money, especially those who sold quickly to capture the 40% premium PMI paid over the pre-takeover trading price. But was this transaction as a whole profitable? For Vectura, the corporation, it was a death sentence.

All for ten pence per share.

This was my hypothetical made real: a company that helped people breathe, sold to a company that profited when they couldn't.

GOTTA SERVE SOMEBODY

Vectura's board claimed they were obligated to sell to PMI because they were in the grip of a particular idea about the "purpose" of the Vectura corporation: to maximize shareholder returns.

Now a good many people think talk of corporate "purpose" is either fuzzy ESG nonsense or a manipulative smokescreen designed to deflect blame from executives. And I understand why.

Investors frequently complain to me about leaders who use noble-sounding language about "stakeholders" and "social responsibility" to evade accountability while extracting massive compensation for themselves. They fear these executives will underinvest in performance while getting distracted by what they see as unrelated social issues.

But there's plenty of absurdity in the other direction too. The recent debates about ESG and corporate purpose have taken on the tenor of a surrealist play. For example, a major investor recently spoke derisively of British multinational consumer goods giant Unilever's attempt to infuse "purpose" into all of its products: "A company which feels it has to define the purpose of Hellmann's mayonnaise has in our view clearly lost the plot."[13] On the one hand, I am sympathetic. A lot of corporate rhetoric about "purpose" is frankly ridiculous. Fair enough. But what's so amazing about this quote is that, humble though the product may be, Hellmann's mayonnaise is *food*. Its purpose could not be clearer: to nourish and delight those who eat it.

This is no abstract concern. Think how easy it would be for an efficiency consultant to suggest that the company replace one of the ingredients in the mayonnaise with an inferior chemical that is cheaper but more addictive (or even damaging to long-term health). The recipe change may damage the company in the long term, but likely long after the efficiency consultant is gone and the product manager's stock options have vested.

Product managers face these kinds of trade-offs every day. How they see themselves and how they see their organization's purpose matters a great deal. There is nothing vague about purpose.

Purpose is not a mission statement or a marketing slogan. It's the specific legal obligation that tells companies what they have to maximize and optimize for. Every US corporation has a legal charter in the form of a founding document filed with a state government. This charter declares what the company exists to do.

Check your charter. You already have a purpose, whether you realize it or not. So did Vectura—right up until the end.

Many people claim that today's standard charters are neutral on the question of purpose. This is understandable, as most corporate charters these days use a standard formulation: that the corporation exists to "conduct or promote any lawful business or purposes." Sounds pretty open-ended.

But there is no neutral position. Every organization serves something.

As we will see, in today's world, this "neutral" charter is widely interpreted to mean that the company is obligated to maximize returns for shareholders. That means that the company's purpose—its legal, actionable "goal in life"—is often out of alignment with the desires of its founders, employees, and customers. It may not even be what the investors want. Which seems like a sad state of affairs.

So the next question is . . .

HOW DID WE GET HERE?

Most founders assume that the way governance works today is "just the way things are"—the way they've always been. But the dirty little secret that every builder needs to understand is that our current system isn't a necessity, isn't ordained by natural law; it's a recent invention. Once you see how we got here, you'll understand why Vectura's board felt they had no choice.

The concept of *general incorporation*—that a company can be legally incorporated for any purpose—dates only to the late nineteenth century. (Delaware didn't join the party until 1899.)[14] Before that, corporations had to prove they served a defined public benefit to form at all.

For example, the Philadelphia Contributionship for Insuring Houses from Loss by Fire received its charter in 1768 by declaring its purpose was "for our own mutual security, as for the common security and advantage of our fellow-citizens."[15] The Union Pacific Railroad was chartered specifically "for the purpose of constructing the transcontinental railroad."[16] Purpose was paramount. Courts were rigid about this. If a corporation took any action beyond its stated purpose, the courts would void its charter. (This doctrine was called *ultra vires*—beyond legal authority.) Under that framing, it would have been absurd to claim a corporation existed only to enrich its stockholders.

It's this earlier corporate history that gives us our modern idea of "fiduciary duties." The original conception of the corporation was a three-legged stool:

1. First, corporations were incorporated only for a specific beneficial purpose.
2. Second, boards had a duty to the corporation itself: a positive duty to pursue the company's chartered mission without self-dealing.
3. Third, corporations had a duty to their stockholders: a negative duty not to misappropriate their funds for some other use. As Angell and Ames stated in 1832, "The funds of a corporation are intrusted to the management of its directors for specific purposes, and to divert them from their proper use would be a fraud upon the stockholders."[17]

These three legs supported each other and produced a stable, logically coherent structure. In this context, fiduciary duties made sense because any deviation from the stated purpose would be defrauding the shareholders who had invested in that mission. In exchange, shareholders began to enjoy the special protection of *limited liability*: they could lose their investment if a company failed, but they couldn't be held personally responsible for the corporation's debts or actions.[18] This was sensible in a context where corporations were free to operate largely independent of investor oversight. When Cornelius Vanderbilt tried to take over the Erie Railroad in 1868 with his nearly unlimited wealth, the board fought him off. They felt no obligation to accept his money.[19]

Coherent though it was, this system had serious flaws. Gaining permission to form a corporation from the state legislature was cumbersome and prone to cronyism. A modern economy required a more democratic approach. So over the course of the nineteenth century, reformers pushed the concept of general incorporation. The idea was to allow anyone to form a corporation for any purpose without requiring a special legislative act. It was so controversial that it had to be fought statehouse by statehouse. The whole project took decades. But general incorporation prevailed in almost every state in the US by the late nineteenth century (the key date for our purposes was Delaware's adoption in 1899), allowing companies to form for "any lawful purpose."[20]

However, this kicked out one of the legs of the stool. Things began to wobble.

As more corporations formed, more controversies arose. Courts were frequently required to step in and interpret what was and was not permissible in pursuit of "any lawful purpose." To do so, they drew on two important common law traditions:[21]

1. The first tradition came from trust law, where *trustees* manage property for *beneficiaries*. In this model, the board was seen as a trustee of the corporation itself. Directors were obligated to pursue the corporation's long-term prosperity and survival, avoiding self-dealing or conflicts of interest.

2. The second tradition came from agency law, where *agents* act on behalf of *principals*. In turn, those principals were held liable for the actions their agents take on their behalf. In this model, directors were seen as agents of the shareholders who elected them. Their duty was to carry out the wishes of the principals who had entrusted them with capital.[22]

These two traditions share the notion of trusted stewardship but pull in opposite directions. A trustee protects and preserves; an agent maximizes and delivers.[23]

Table 4.1. The three-legged stool of purposeful incorporation

PILLAR	DEFINITION	LEGAL ORIGIN	WHAT IT MEANS
Specific beneficial purpose	Corporations were incorporated only for a specific beneficial purpose (e.g., building a railroad, providing fire insurance, constructing a bridge)	Legislative charter system (1790s in the US)	Any deviation from the stated purpose would be defrauding the public, whose interests had to be served in chartering the corporation.
Duty to the corporation itself	A positive duty to pursue the company's chartered mission without self-dealing	Trust law: Trustees manage property for beneficiaries; the board was seen as a trustee of the corporation itself (roots in twelfth-through thirteenth-century English common law; Magna Carta 1215)	Directors were obligated to pursue the corporation's long-term prosperity and survival, avoiding self-dealing or conflicts of interest. *A trustee protects and preserves.*
Duty to stockholders	A negative duty not to misappropriate their funds for some other use	Agency law: Agents act on behalf of principals; directors were seen as agents of the shareholders who elected them (roots in Roman "mandatum"; developed in English common law, formalized in the eighteenth century)	Shareholders invested in the stated mission and boards owe them the best effort to see it done; diverting funds from that purpose would be *ultra vires* and void the charter. *An agent maximizes and delivers.*

Over time, these two distinct duties were condensed into a single formulation: directors standing "in a fiduciary relation to the corporation and its stockholders," as the Delaware Supreme Court stated in *Guth v. Loft, Inc.* (1939).[24] But notice how fundamentally different these two concepts are! What are directors supposed to do if what is best for the corporation is at odds with what shareholders want? The wobbling increased.

This two-legged stool couldn't withstand the mounting pressures of financialization over the course of the twentieth century. As financial markets grew, the agency model gradually came to dominate. Today's financial gravity overwhelmingly rewards those who pledge fealty to maximizing returns. Effectively, we are down to a one-legged stool.[25]

By the 1960s, thinkers like Milton Friedman were declaring that "there is one and only one social responsibility of business—to use its resources and engage in activities designed to increase its profits . . . without deception or fraud."[26] (Delaware courts enacted this into law over the course of the 1980s in cases like *Revlon, Inc. v. MacAndrews & Forbes Holdings, Inc.*)[27] This reductive view treats the corporation not as an entity with a mission that needs to be tended to and maintained but merely as a financial instrument for generating returns.

In elite circles, this idea is called *shareholder primacy*. We've been living in the world it created ever since.[28]

SHAREHOLDER PRIMACY: THE ARGUMENTS FOR AND AGAINST

Here's the wild thing. This fundamental shift in corporate purpose has never—not once—been enacted by any legislature or approved by any referendum. While general incorporation required state-by-state legislative approval, shareholder primacy has no such democratic legitimacy. In fact, the most prosperous period in our nation's history was during the brief interregnum after state legislatures switched to "general incorporation" and before "shareholder primacy" took root in the twentieth century. This is not a coincidence.

This monumental shift in the nature of the corporation was

enacted by a small cadre of judges, lawyers, and academics without seeking democratic consent.[29] We live under this dominant idea only because their arguments proved persuasive to those who controlled business education, law, and practice. Let's examine what made these arguments so compelling.

Why should corporations seek only to maximize shareholder value?

First, there is the moral claim. Without the resources investors provide, the company wouldn't exist in the first place.

This argument has some truth to it. But it cuts any number of ways. No company could operate for even one day without its customers, employees, suppliers, or communities. Their moral claims are just as strong. What investors put into any one company is generally much lower stakes and more replaceable for them than the human resources—time, energy, talent, trust—that others invest.

Second, shareholders are "residual claimants." They only receive returns after everyone else has been paid.

This assumes shareholders are passive recipients of whatever remains. In reality, when shareholders pressure companies to cut salaries, squeeze suppliers, or reduce product quality, they're actively shrinking everyone else's share to increase their own "residual." Moreover, shareholders can exit their positions at any time by selling their shares. Meanwhile, employees who've dedicated years to a company can lose their livelihoods overnight. Communities can be devastated when a company relocates. Who truly bears the residual risk?

Third, shareholders face unique agency problems. They must trust managers to treat them fairly and not exploit their information asymmetry for self-enrichment.

This issue is real but, once again, hardly unique to shareholders. Employees trust companies with their careers. Customers, with their data, or in the case of many products, with their lives. Communities, with their economic and environmental health.

The company may not be their "agent" legally speaking, but they are worthy of protection too.

Luckily, we already have strong securities laws, disclosure requirements, and auditing standards that protect investors. Just as in the case of consumer and employment protections, these don't require giving shareholders supreme authority.

Finally, a single metric—maximizing shareholder value—supposedly makes business straightforward and creates clear accountability.

This one is problematic not because it is false but precisely because it is true. It's a trap. Being customer centric is not the same as obeying every request from a random customer. Similarly, being accountable to shareholders shouldn't mean obeying their every short-term demand.

This simplistic interpretation drives otherwise inexplicable phenomena.

Walk into almost any business school, and here's what you'll see. In the morning, students learn that companies aren't morally responsible for their actions so long as they follow the rules. This encourages students to trust governments and society at large to set the rules, absolving companies and investors of the need to consider the broader impacts of their actions.

In the afternoon, those same students learn that it is part of their fiduciary duty to press the government to pass laws more favorable to companies—that is, to influence those rules as much as possible. As a result, in many industries, "regulatory capture" is a fact of daily life, as companies effectively set the rules by which they themselves will be judged.

So which is it? Are the rules set by the government (in which case companies do not bear moral responsibility for their actions) or by the companies themselves (in which case they do)?

This contradiction is why the CEO of SVB lobbied Congress to weaken the very rules that would have prevented his bank's collapse.[30] At the time, because these changes maximized the bank's short-term profits, this lobbying was considered a governance "best practice." With the rules changed, the bank was able to take risky financial bets that would otherwise have been prohibited.

These risky bets had nothing to do with serving customers. They were only designed to extract more profit from depositor funds. The bank's claimed mission—"to help innovative companies move bold ideas forward"[31]—would not have benefited, even if every bet had paid off.

But as you probably guessed, the bets did not pay off. Five years after the lobbying campaign, the bank failed due to the very recklessness it had lobbied to legalize. Its shareholders lost everything. In the name of shareholder primacy, SVB killed their own golden goose.

The ultimate irony is that shareholder primacy is bad for long-term shareholders too. Companies that manage to the quarter consistently underperform those with longer time horizons.[32] This creates a prisoner's dilemma; each shareholder feels they must extract value quickly lest another investor beat them to it. When everyone does this, all shareholders lose.

As a result, advocates for shareholder primacy are undermining the investors they claim to support. They insist that fiduciary duties require corporations and boards to act as agents of shareholders, maximizing their returns. But for hundreds of years the law has understood that an agency relationship requires liability for the principal. This is logically incompatible with limited liability—the very protection shareholders value most.[33]

The victims aren't just the wealthy. They're pension funds and university endowments that need companies to thrive for decades, not quarters. They're teachers, firefighters, and retirees whose futures depend on genuine long-term value creation. As legal scholar David Berger points out, "Corporations have perpetual lives and shareholders (especially of public companies) have very short-term interests."[34]

This extractive mindset may seem like a collapse in governance norms affecting only corporations. But researchers across disciplines have reached the same conclusion: When ownership shifts from stewardship to extraction, institutions fail. If your favorite sports team has ownership that drives you crazy, you're not alone; researchers have demonstrated that "profit-maximization produces the lowest quality team and the smallest fan attendance."[35] Modern political parties have similarly weak governance, "subject to hostile takeovers," as political scientists have warned.[36] When private equity firms acquire hospitals, they cut clinical staff to boost profits—and emergency room death rates rise 13%.[37] Increasingly, we're not citizens, fans, or patients anymore; we're a resource being mined.

But suggest shifting fiduciary duties away from shareholder primacy today, and people react as if you're proposing the end of capitalism itself. The older conception—a holistic responsibility to the corporation—has been erased.[38]

WEATHER CONTROL

So what does shareholder primacy look like when taken to its logical conclusion?

Consider a startup I met in the emerging field of geoengineering, developing technology to control weather patterns, to bring rain to drought-stricken farmers and deliver snow to struggling ski resorts. Their long-term vision is to turn deserts into farmland and dissipate hurricanes before they make landfall. It's a company with transformative potential.

What constitutes "good governance" of a technology that could reshape the world?

Imagine this company succeeds. They're making the pivot from early trials to global deployment. Then the story turns tragic. In Chapter 1, we saw how this is often due to a hostile outside actor. But we don't need that here. Imagine instead that the board, bound by their fiduciary duty to maximize shareholder value, seeks a faster path. Product, growth, quality—maybe these methods for maximizing revenue are too slow.

Perhaps they could become the weather arms dealer to the world.

Every city, town, resort, and farm gets the same offer: Pay us to optimize your rainfall, or watch us do it for your rival instead. If they pay and you don't, well, you may find the rain falls mainly on the plain next door.

Immoral? Certainly. Illegal? Hardly. But even if it was illegal, what if the company made so much money that it could afford to lobby to have the laws changed?

When I shared this scenario with the founder, he was horrified. He could see that no amount of "founder mode" would be enough to prevent it. Under current governance norms, if the board believes a certain strategy maximizes shareholder value, they're not just allowed to pursue it; they're arguably required to.

And even if they weren't required to, they might do it anyway. Board members might correctly calculate that betraying this one company would lead to career advancement in the future. In fact, as we will see in Part II, this kind of *career equity* often matters more than actual equity.

There's simply no reason for transformative technologies to be governed this way. The solution isn't to abandon traditional governance; it's to complete it.

A NEW VISION FOR GOVERNANCE

I've watched so many amazing companies be surgically deboned year after year, the very qualities that made them unique gradually removed. We rationalize these surgeries as necessary compromises to raise money or as what "the market" demands. If you've ever wondered why so many large companies look and behave indistinguishably, this is the reason. They were left too weak to preserve what made them distinctive. If a company cannot control its own destiny, it cannot be a trustworthy counterparty. Not to customers, not to employees, not even to the investors it supposedly serves. Builders act like they run the show, but as the long, painful history in Chapter 1 showed, it's really the governance class who has the final say.

It is time to recognize that operations and governance are two sides of the same coin. Builders create the value that governance is meant to protect. They deserve a much more robust seat at the governance table, not to take over governance, but rather to create a synthesis. Builders need to understand how governance shapes their organizations' destinies. And the governance class needs to deeply understand operations, not just financial metrics and legal liabilities.

Current governance teaches boards their job is simple: maximize shareholder returns (that's what passes for "purpose") and don't break any laws while doing it (that's "compliance"). Whether Vectura gets destroyed, whether the weather company becomes a protection racket, whether their company's mission dies—that's not their concern. They did their "fiduciary duty."

Every board that forced a sale to a predator, every board that gutted a company's mission in order to make a quarter, every board that betrayed the trust of customers and employees—none of them thought they were failing at their job. They were doing exactly what they'd been taught to do.

The scandal is that destruction is built into the job description.

But real governance—complete governance—requires building an exoskeleton with four load-bearing responsibilities:

Compliance

Following laws, preventing self-dealing, reporting accurately, and holding management accountable are essential oversight skills. The governance class has developed tremendous skills in the past century in these areas, and we should build upon them. The problem is that they can become runaway systems, like a metabolic disorder or autoimmune disease. What starts as a healthy immune response—proper oversight and controls—can spiral into an obsessive focus on procedures that actually weakens the organization it's meant to protect.

Purpose

The legally binding commitment that defines what a company exists to maximize. Not a mission statement but a charter-level choice. Remember, there is no neutral here. Choose wisely. Lawyers may advise building a company to pursue "any lawful purpose." But most builders aspire to create organizations designed to pursue a long-term mission aligned with human flourishing, backed by a principled ethos like that of Sol Price. This powerful combination unlocks magnetic powers of attraction that are stronger than gravity (covered in Chapters 5–6).

Coherence

The degree to which an organization's systems, functions, and departments pursue a singular, unified direction. This requires an aligned business model so that it can only profit and grow via mission attainment. But it also requires consistent alignment between a company's stated principles and its cultural realities, so that its deep character—its ethos—reflects its purpose even when nobody is watching. Coherence protects against internal forms of corruption, which, like a cancer, cause parts of the organization to turn against itself (covered in Chapters 7–8).

Integrity

The degree to which an organization is protected from external forces that can force or tempt it to act in ways counter to its purpose. This is the domain of boards, partnerships, and investors. The board of directors in particular has a special responsibility here, as both the highest authority and the guardian of the border with the outside world. I use the word *integrity* both in the sense of *being able to keep a promise* and in the sense of *structural integrity*, the ability to resist external pressure. Integrity turns governance into a semipermeable boundary that allows beneficial exchange while filtering out corrupting influences (covered in Chapters 9–11).

Under traditional governance, board meetings are dry affairs, often significantly divorced from the daily realities of employees, customers, and the communities they inhabit. But expand governance to include *coherence* and *integrity*, and the board's job becomes protecting and fulfilling the organization's true long-term purpose. It's frankly a lot more meaningful.

Boards become guardians, not liquidators.

This is the difference between companies that betray their promises and companies that endure long enough to keep them. Between the weather company that becomes an extortionist and one that saves the world. Between Vectura dying for fifteen cents a share and a company that would have said "Hell, no!" to PMI.

Either we fix governance, or every breakthrough becomes a breakdown and every transformative company becomes the next cautionary tale.

LEARNING TO FLY

This marks the end of Part I. Think of how far we have come. We began with the grim history of "enlightened capitalism" and the corruption that has, generation after generation, defeated it. Then, chapter by chapter, we have explored the obstacles our movement will face, one after the other.

In physics, gravity seems like the strongest force in the universe. That's why, of the fundamental forces, humans discovered and explored it first. But gravity is actually the weakest physical force. It only feels so powerful because the planet you are standing on is so large.

When you do something as simple as stand up, your body generates a force so powerful, it defies the pull of a planetary body 10^{23} times more massive than you: the Earth itself. Organizations possess a counterforce as well, though it's rarely harnessed properly. This force makes it possible to build companies with the strength and integrity to stand up. We urgently need to learn to master it.

Remember: Gravity itself doesn't keep us from flying. Understanding gravity makes flight possible. The same force that pulls organizations down can be harnessed to lift them up. It's time to learn how to fly.

Part II

ESCAPE VELOCITY

Chapter Five

THE BLUEPRINT

> For what shall it profit a man, if he shall gain the whole world, and lose his own soul?
>
> —**Mark 8:36**
>
> *King James Bible*
>
> 1611

"She's my guardian angel."

Dwuane was describing her health insurance representative. Not her doctor. Not a nurse. Her insurance rep. The person most of us dread calling, if we can even reach them at all.

The rep's name was Amanda, and she had helped Dwuane find new housing when she discovered that toxic mold in Dwuane's apartment was undermining her medical treatment. A traditional insurer might think, "Not our problem; we just process claims." Amanda's employer, Devoted Health, knew that helping Dwuane move to new housing was a way to prevent future hospitalizations at the cost of $15,000 or more each. But that isn't the reason they did it. The economic benefit is just a side-effect of their actual mission: to treat every member of Devoted like their own family member.[1]

I learned about Dwuane thanks to Todd Park, the founder of Devoted Health. It was just one of many stories he shared that reveal what "guardian angel" truly means. For example, the time a member called their Devoted Guide and said, "I want to let you know that I've just lost my second husband, and I just can't be here anymore, and I have knives in the kitchen, and I have a plan." The Devoted Guide kept her on the phone while another guide called for help, Todd explained. "And then we stayed with her until we were sure she was okay and we connected her to longer term behavioral health help."[2]

As another member told their Guide, "My life has been filled with hate, and so I therefore have been filled with hate. I'm working to turn that around and become a more positive person because y'all listen to me and you care for me and you remind me what it was like to be loved." Another called just to say, "I just want to let you know I got home safely. Because I thought you'd want to know." This kind of relationship goes far beyond what we usually think of as "healthcare."

Todd and I have been longtime collaborators, stretching back to his time as Chief Technology Officer of the United States. Sitting in my living room one day soon after he finished his tour of duty in government service, he described his plans for a revolutionary healthcare company that would tackle the entire broken system rather than just one small piece of it.

I found his vision dizzying. Frankly, it sounded impossible. The same old knee-jerk instincts we've all been conditioned to kicked in, and I peppered him with questions. Isn't tackling everything everywhere all at once making the problem much harder? Why attempt to bite off such an unreasonable chunk of a dysfunctional system? His reply reframed everything: "You have it backward. This is the only possible way to solve this problem. It only works because it's so hard."

Todd had already been a successful healthcare entrepreneur, having cofounded Athenahealth (which went public in 2007 and reached a $5.7 billion valuation by 2018)[3] and launched Castlight Health to bring price transparency to healthcare.[4] He'd succeeded with incremental improvements. But Devoted Health was different. Part of the reason modern healthcare is so expensive is that it's a Frankensteinian assembly of thousands of partial solutions. Fix one part, and the dysfunction just moves elsewhere. At its core are people who are sincerely dedicated to human well-being: the doctors, nurses, and scientists who make healing possible. But economically speaking, they represent only a small fraction of an overall system of immense complexity. And feeding off this massive, dysfunctional body are countless other financial and administrative actors—some parasitic, others symbiotic—all adding layers of cost and complexity.

So Devoted set out to build an "alternate universe, full-stack, American healthcare system as a service." This was necessary to "guarantee the ability to deliver on our mission" because "anything short of that was going to fail at hyper-scaling, to everyone, the kind of care you want for your family."[5]

This meant building a *constellation* of three interlocked companies simultaneously:[6]

1. An *insurance company* serving seniors, one of the most heavily regulated sectors in America, requiring state-by-state approvals, massive capital reserves, and compliance with thousands of pages of rules.
2. A *technology platform* called Orinoco that is not just software but an entire healthcare operating system built from scratch to coordinate care, process claims, and predict health needs.
3. A *medical practice* called Devoted Medical, which recruits doctors burned out by the current system to provide virtual and in-home care, essentially creating a new kind of healthcare delivery that works to prevent hospitalizations rather than just treat symptoms.

You can see why I was concerned. Most startups die trying to build one company. Todd felt called to build all three. At once. Think about the sheer operational challenge. Debugging code while negotiating with state regulators. Training doctors while building provider networks. Raising capital—$2.2 billion to date[7]—to cover insurance reserves while trying to change fundamental assumptions about how healthcare should work. The economics are easy to understand but require solving a massive multivariate problem. Devoted has an aligned business model—they only profit if their members stay healthy—so they have to be relentless about driving down costs. But their members also have other options, so their member experience has to be best in breed. And besides, their ethos and their mission "to build a healthcare solution good enough for Mom" wouldn't allow them to do it any other way.[8]

I asked him what makes this all possible. Exceptional execution?

IN THEIR OWN WORDS: To hear from Todd Park and others featured in this book in their own words, scan the QR code or go to incorruptible.co/their-own-words.

A brilliant strategy? World-class technology? His experience building other healthcare companies? He thought for a moment, then replied with one word: "Love."

THE INCORRUPTIBLE BLUEPRINT

In Part I, we saw the common ways corruption comes for organizations as they scale. FedMart, Boeing, Whole Foods, and Vectura each represent one such archetype. Notice how each story ultimately boils down to a form of inner conflict or outer pressure.

And yet Devoted Health does not seem to experience either. Customers repeatedly say they feel like Devoted Health literally loves them. Their employees love working there. And as we'll see, investors are pretty happy with the results too. Its founders have been able to scale their unique ethos—financed by traditional venture capital—without seeming to be bothered by gravity in the slightest.

In the chapters ahead, we will see this same pattern repeatedly. The leaders of these organizations do not seem to see "trade-offs" the way their conventional counterparts do. I've asked many of them about the necessary compromises required to work this way, and they often stare back with incomprehension. It's as if I'd asked them about the trade-offs between eating food and eating poison.

And yet when you ask them directly how they have accomplished such incredible feats, they answer in ways that most leaders find cryptic or confusing. They talk about "love" and "provenance" and even "soulfulness"—and so their insights are often misunderstood.

But if you know where to look, you'll see that they are following the principles of the *incorruptible blueprint* I laid out in the Introduction:

> **First, they create something worth protecting.** Resisting gravity requires activating an even stronger counterforce. I call it the *force of magnetic alignment*. It generates a level of trust and loyalty that many readers will find almost unbelievable. But its power is not mysterious. It can be understood and mastered with the right tools.

Second, they build with structural integrity. Profits attract predators, including sometimes investors and board members, who are themselves captured by financial gravity. Strong organizations are architected in such a way that they protect their ethos and preserve their commitment to the mission. Without this, every organization is destined to become just another tragic case study in some future book on "enlightened capitalism."

In Part II, we'll flesh out this blueprint chapter by chapter, moving steadily outward: from the inner choices leaders make about purpose and mission, to the organizational systems that embed those values in business models and culture, to the governance structures that preserve them even if leadership changes—and ultimately to the legal vehicles that can lock a mission in place permanently. At each step, we'll see how real companies have put these ideas into practice.

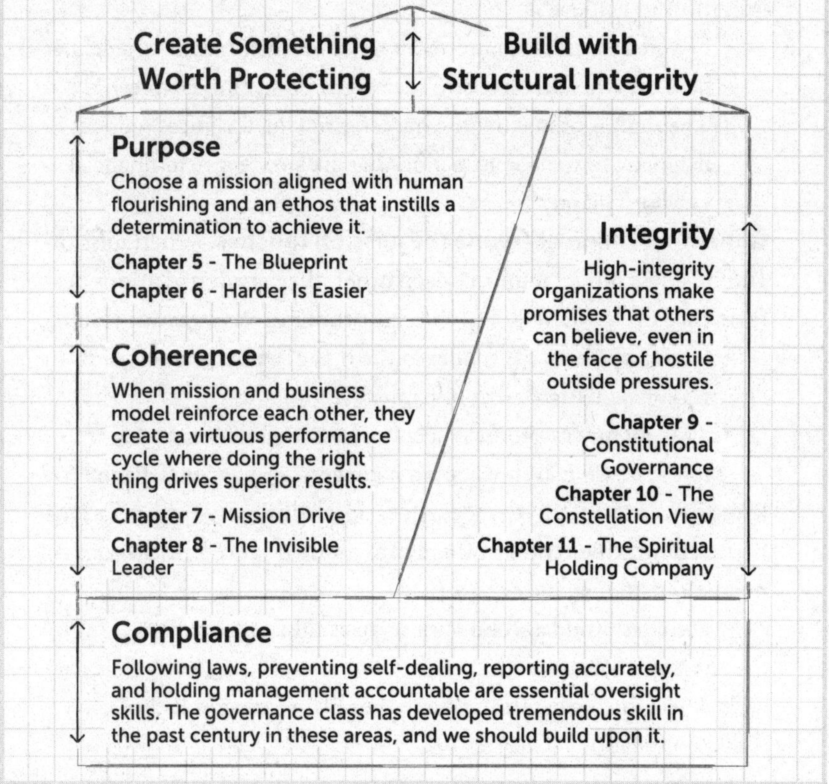

Figure 5.1.

To illustrate how this blueprint encompasses all four responsibilities of the "new governance," let's look first at how Devoted Health tackles each one. This will also provide a roadmap for the chapters that follow, where we'll meet organizations that have mastered each dimension.

Compliance: Lay an essential foundation. Recall that, today, most people think that compliance—following laws and regulations—is the main (or only!) responsibility of governance. They're not wrong that it's essential; compliance is table stakes for any successful company. Devoted has this challenge in spades: It operates in one of the most regulated industries in America. As compliance is well covered elsewhere, we'll focus on the other three responsibilities in the chapters ahead.

Purpose: Build something worth protecting. Choose a mission aligned with human flourishing and an ethos that instills a determination to achieve it.

- Devoted Health's commitment to "love" their members redefines how the whole enterprise understands profit (this chapter).
- Their ethos of making the harder, principled choices unlocks magnetic powers of attraction that are stronger than financial gravity (Chapter 6).

Coherence: Align everyone the mission touches. When mission and business model reinforce each other, they create a virtuous performance cycle where doing the right thing drives superior results.

- Design the business model so the organization prospers only via mission attainment (Chapter 7).
- This alignment produces a culture where individuals stay true to the mission even when no managers are present (Chapter 8).

Integrity: Stand up to pressure. High-integrity organizations make commitments that others can count on, even in the face of hostile outside pressures.

- Founders Todd and Ed Park serve as mission guardians (Chapter 9).
- Their three separate entities exemplify a "mission-locked constellation" (Chapter 10).

- Beyond conventional structures lie advanced organizational forms that transcend the false dichotomy of non-profit and for-profit (Chapter 11).

With that, you've got a good preview of how we're going to learn to build an organization whose success includes, and even depends on, staying true to the meaningful mission that made it worth building in the first place.

One note before we dive in. The naive observer might say that Devoted Health's structure is "too complicated," but as we'll see, it's actually simpler in the long term. Complexity in structure enables simplicity in operations.

Therefore, the first step in establishing this blueprint is to commit to a definition of success that transcends "shareholder primacy" and its obsession with extraction. In Devoted's case, this intention has informed every decision that has led to the company's success. In fact, if you ask Todd what Devoted's product is, his answer will surprise you: "We're not a health insurance company. We're not a medical group. We've certainly built those things, but those are just channels through which we deliver what we really are, which is love."

CAN A SUPERORGANISM SAY "I LOVE YOU"?

This idea of "love" as the animating force of Devoted is an operational framework.

Most companies need hundreds of pages of policies, procedures, and training manuals to tell employees how to make decisions. Devoted has it much easier. This is Todd's verbatim directive to everyone at Devoted: "When making any decision, visualize the faces of your own family members and loved ones, then ask yourself: If this decision impacted them, what would you do? Then go do that thing, big or small."[9]

That's not a motivational poster. That's their actual decision-making process.

This simplicity is deceptive. The Devoted ethos answers thousands of complex questions instantly:

- Should we spend more time with this confused member? (Would you rush your mom off the phone?)
- Should we cover this edge case? (Would you want your dad to have this treatment?)
- Should we invest in this new capability? (Would it help you take better care of your family?)

The genius is that love isn't vague; it's the most specific instruction possible. Everyone knows what love looks like in action. It means staying on the phone until the problem is solved. It means noticing what's not being said. It means fighting for someone who can't fight for themselves.[10]

I feel your skepticism all the way on the other side of this page. I know. But there's a big difference between Devoted and companies that hypocritically claim to love customers or treat employees like family: aligned incentives. Devoted only profits when members stay healthy. When love says "Help this member" and traditional business logic says "That's expensive," there's a conflict for most companies. But not for Devoted: Keeping members healthy *is* the business logic. Now imagine this from a competitor's point of view. You're running a traditional insurance company. You do things the "serious" way. You've got competitive premiums, decent coverage, a solid network. You spend millions on marketing to win customers like Dwuane. But when you call her during open enrollment, she's not even willing to hear your pitch. You're asking her to switch away from her "guardian angel." Good luck with that.

I asked you to imagine feeling loved by your insurance company. Now imagine being the company trying to compete with that love. Customers won't churn!? What a nightmare! When you develop a true, lasting bond with a customer based on genuine care, you literally shrink the total available market for your competitors by one. Loyalty is a boa constrictor inexorably shrinking opportunities for competitors.

THE BUILDER'S INTUITION

Devoted's "love" framework might seem unique, but it's actually just one expression of a common desire. Many of the founders, executives, and investors I have worked with over the years have tried to build something extraordinary. But unlike Todd and Ed, they consistently struggle to reconcile that longing with the nature of being a for-profit company.

We have all been taught a very narrow definition of what it means to make a profit. And yet we also instinctively feel that something is missing from this definition. Its very narrowness is what leaves us all vulnerable to the kind of corruption we saw in Part I.

When most people in business talk about profit today, they mean something simple: revenue minus operating costs. In other words, what's left over after paying expenses. This accounting definition has served us well for measuring performance and comparing companies. Remember The Professor from the Introduction? I still recall the way he scoffed when I asked him if he knew what it means to be a for-profit company. "Everyone knows that. It's one that makes money," he said with the confidence of someone who'd just sat through countless investor meetings.

As I have with many others over the years, I took him through an exercise to interrogate this breezy definition.

Now it's your turn:

A Ponzi scheme makes money. Is that profitable?

If you're like most builders, you'll immediately say no, but it certainly seems to make plenty of money. After all, Charles Ponzi's original scheme vacuumed up $15 million in just eight months.[11] That's about $240 million in today's dollars.[12] But calling this "profitable" requires myopically focusing only on this minuscule time horizon.

Having done this exercise many times, I can assure you nobody wants to admit that a Ponzi scheme is profitable. We know Charles Ponzi frantically kicked the can down the road, cheating a lot of people along the way, and that collapse was inevitable. Surely that's not profit.

But then how about a chemical company that generates revenue but creates a secret toxic waste dump in its backyard? We know it will have to spend millions cleaning up later, costs that could easily bankrupt the company. Is that really any different from Charles Ponzi? The money it brings in is more than offset by the value it destroys down the road. It will also kill or sicken a lot of people along the way.

In economics, both of these scenarios are covered by the accounting term *deferred liabilities*.[13] This means a company has generated a "profit" in the current period by skewing the revenue minus expenses formula over time. The revenue is received today, but the expenses are deferred (but still owed) into the future. In effect, the value is being borrowed from the future, not created in the present. You don't need an economics degree to see that these profits are not real.

Let's keep going. What about a factory that dumps waste into a river, forcing downstream communities to pay for water treatment and deal with poisoned fish? Imagine the factory managed to keep the cause and effect a secret, so nobody knew who was responsible. That's different from our first example, because the bill may never come due for the factory. But someone else still gets stuck cleaning up the mess. Is this really profitable? No, since it just shifts the costs in "revenue minus costs" elsewhere.

This pattern is also common enough to have a special name in economics: *externalities*.[14] Externalities are economic actions that affect people beyond those directly involved in a transaction. So-called *negative externalities* are costs that economic actors impose on third parties without paying for them.

Consider cigarettes. They generate "profits" for tobacco companies while imposing costs on everyone else: secondhand smoke, increased health insurance premiums for nonsmokers, and hundreds of billions in healthcare costs we all bear. Similarly, financial institutions privatize gains in good times but socialize losses when their risky bets fail, like the banks that needed taxpayer bailouts after the 2008 crisis. They keep the money, someone else pays the price.

Pushing costs onto others doesn't really create value; it just moves it around.

Now here's the example that makes everyone squirm. What if I told you I was going to create a startup marketplace for hit men who kill for the highest bidder? The idea repulses most people.

Ridiculous? Sure. But indulge me.

Most people recoil from calling this profitable. Luckily it's illegal. But what if I managed to make so much money that I could successfully lobby the government to make it legal? Would that make it profitable?

I've done this exercise countless times, and especially for founders who aspire to use their products to save lives, it's a shock when I mention a hit man. They absolutely do not want to call murder-for-hire profitable. But by the formal definition they carry around in their head, it is.

Some people, at first, insist to me that this is "profitable but unethical" or some other dodge. But this falls apart if we probe: If profit is revenue minus costs, where is the profit? Is the cost of a person's life truly worth so little?

But then what about a company that sells products it knows are damaging to its customers' health?

This upends yet another economic concept. Profit is supposed to be a signal that a company has created new value in the world, what economists call a *positive margin* transformation. Companies take "inputs" like raw materials and labor and transform them into products, which, when sold, are worth more than the sum of those parts. A carpenter turns $50 of wood into a $200 table. A software company transforms engineering hours into a product millions can use. Standard economic theory says that this surplus, called "value added," is why society benefits when businesses maximize profits.[15]

But can human lives ever legitimately be considered an input factor of production?

This is where conventional profit accounting breaks down completely.

The pattern is everywhere, once you know to look for it.

Tobacco companies profit from the deaths of their own customers.[16] Insurance companies boost margins by denying legitimate claims on technicalities.[17] Private equity firms buy nursing homes and cut nursing staff to boost returns.[18] Monopoly rents act as a tax on whole sectors of economic activity.[19] Some "investors" push companies to do things that are bad for them in the long term but boost short-term returns, then sell before the bill comes due.[20]

All of these are examples of the same thing: ways to make money without creating value.

If you feel discomfort with this behavior, you need not apologize.

Your discomfort is, among other things, a sophisticated form of business wisdom. You're simply recognizing that companies that extract value rather than create it have structural weaknesses that lead to real problems in the long run. Deferred liabilities eventually come due. It may not come due for your executive team or in your lifetime. You might be able to get out by dumping them on someone else. But is that really something to be proud of?

In my experience, those with the deepest conviction about what real success looks like, even when they struggle to put it into words, consistently build the strongest companies. They instinctively reject calling a Ponzi scheme "profitable." They aren't inspired by the idea of extracting value from the world. When they visualize their future success, they're not picturing a hollowed-out cash cow. They're envisioning a future where their own success aligns with making the world genuinely better off.

Call this idealism if you wish. I call it the *builder's intuition*: the instinctive understanding that the best way to prosper is to create net new value. It's the same recognition you had when confronted with the hit-man scenario. Real competitive advantage comes from value creation, not extraction.

HUMAN FLOURISHING

The conventional definition of *profit* has fatal blind spots. If it can't see externalities, if it ignores human costs, if it's at odds with the intuitions of most builders—what good is it? We saw in the previous chapter how advocates for "shareholder primacy" gradually redefined the purpose of a corporation to a new, more narrow view. Notice they did not invent their own parallel terminology. Instead, they redefined the core conceptual vocabulary of business to align with their ideas.

So the first step in building an incorruptible organization is to reject this narrow thinking. Each organization must reclaim its power to define its own purpose. This begins with declaring clearly what it means to be a for-profit company.

Yet for so many builders, their intuitive insight is buried beneath an internalized and outdated formal definition. Rather than continuing to suppress this wisdom, builders should embrace a different approach:

Profit is the maximization of human flourishing.

To be precise, profit itself is the surplus of human flourishing that an organization creates. By surplus, I mean what remains after accounting for all the organization's impacts on human lives. This accounting spans immediate and distant, measurable and not, today and decades from now. A "for-profit" company, properly understood, is one that seeks to maximize this surplus.

This definition is not a rejection of financial success. In fact, organizing around human flourishing allows companies to achieve tremendous financial results, as we'll see. But I do want to be clear that adopting it won't guarantee financial riches. Extractive companies often accumulate vast wealth; tobacco executives collect bonuses while their customers die. My claim is simply that we should stop calling that behavior profitable. It is closer to theft than value creation.

Changing how we think about profit changes how we build, measure, and govern organizations.

WHY "HUMAN FLOURISHING"

I have been chiseling away at this definition for years, trying to find the most concise, memorable, and effective phrase that works in the real world. Every element is deliberately chosen.

Maximization is important because it preserves what was valuable in the conventional understanding of profit. The strongest organizations are those that are good stewards of the resources under their control. Efficiency still matters. Accountability is essential. For all its flaws, capitalism has lifted billions out of poverty and unlocked the abundance that gives us the luxury to contemplate these higher aspirations. Our goal should be nothing less than harnessing the awesome power of the engine of capitalism redirected toward a worthier goal.

Why *human flourishing*? It's the only phrase honest enough to capture the true scale of what we're after. *Happiness* is subjective and easily confused with dopamine hits. *Sustainability* might connote a miserable, bare existence. *Well-being* is too easily misinterpreted as mere physical health. *Human dignity* isn't really something that can be maximized, only protected.

Flourishing—real human flourishing—means people growing into their potential, physically, emotionally, spiritually.

This is the moral foundation of capitalism, the fuel that drives the engine.

This is why our definition of profit matters so much. Our current financial metrics can't distinguish between genuine value creation and clever extraction.[21] They create the illusion of profit whether customers are delighted or deceived, whether employees are thriving or suffering, whether communities are enriched or poisoned, and whether loyalty stems from satisfaction or addiction.[22] We'll explore how to measure this properly in Chapter 7. As we'll see, organizations that create genuine human flourishing routinely outperform those that merely extract value.

Metrics aligned with human flourishing consistently drive tomorrow's financial indicators. Let's look at how Devoted Health uses them.

THE VIRTUOUS PERFORMANCE CYCLE

Todd Park explained to me the mechanism that powers Devoted's success. "There's something that we call the *virtuous performance cycle* that lives at the heart of our solution," he said. "It is, I think, a great way to understand why love can power enormous business success and why it is in fact the key."[23]

He walked me through each step: "Because we deliver spectacular, loving service to you, you trust us. Because you trust us, when we reach out to you to offer you help, you accept the help. Because you accept our help and we can help you, we keep you healthy and well. Because we keep you healthy and well, our costs are the lowest in the industry. Because our costs are the lowest in the industry, we can invest in the best benefits and the best service, which enables us to grow super fast."[24]

This cycle reinforces itself, getting stronger with each revolution. "That is a cycle that we're able to uniquely do in our industry," Todd emphasized. "And it is powered by love."

The linchpin that makes it all work is trust, which Devoted measures obsessively. After every interaction, they text members asking, "Based on the interaction you just had, do you trust Devoted to keep its promise to you to get you the care you truly need?" Their overall trust score is 94%.[25] After seeing a Devoted Medical clinician, the trust score jumps to 99%. As Todd put it, "We're talking about American seniors. They don't trust anybody, often for very, very good reason, right?" Yet they trust Devoted almost completely. Because members trust Devoted, they "accept our help at rates that are a multiple of what's normal." Trust directly enables the health interventions that drive the entire business model.

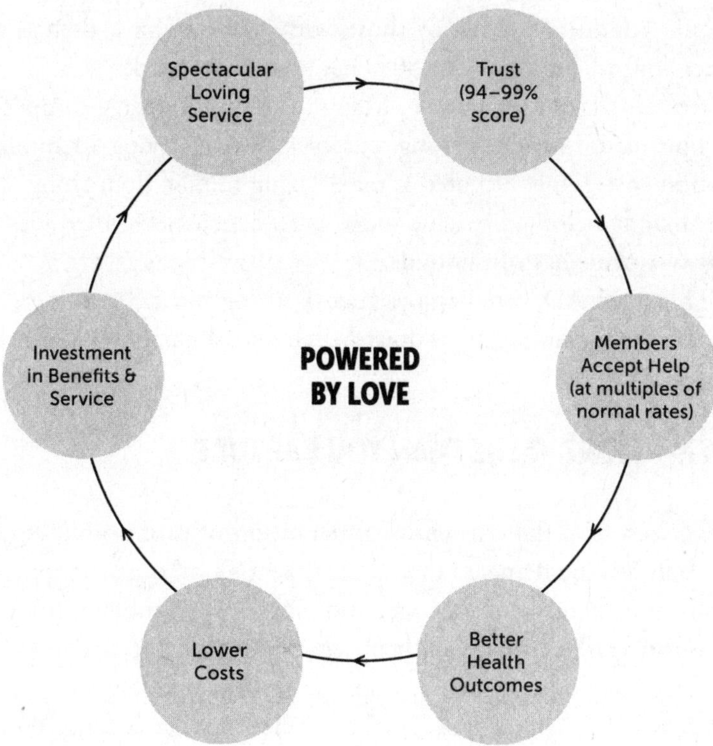

Figure 5.2.

The virtuous cycle creates moments of grace that ripple outward. A single member in Houston has referred three hundred other seniors to Devoted over four years. He leads a prayer for Devoted at his church every Sunday. Sol Price would be smiling at this "unsolicited testimonial of a satisfied customer."

This only works because Devoted's business model profits by keeping people healthy, not by denying claims. Customer service isn't just a nice-to-have; it's what allows Devoted Medical's doctors to deliver actual care in members' homes, using technology custom-built to coordinate treatment. As Todd puts it, "The best care is the right care, both clinical and non-clinical, delivered at the right place, at the right time. If you do that it's axiomatic that it will cost a lot less money."[26]

The virtuous performance cycle has powered Devoted's hypergrowth, expanding to 20 states and serving over 215,400 members with revenue surpassing $3.3 billion in 2025.[27] Their Net Promoter Score of 79 towers above the industry average.[28] Of members with chronic conditions, 85% of those with diabetes have their disease under control, far above the 50% national benchmark.[29]

You can't fake love at scale. Many insurance industry competitors are optimizing for the wrong variable. They're trying to minimize medical costs while Devoted is maximizing human flourishing. They see Amanda helping Dwuane move as an expense. Devoted sees it as an investment that compounds.

This is why Devoted enjoys such a strong moat. Customers who call you their guardian angel don't switch for a slightly lower premium.

CREATE MORE VALUE THAN YOU CAPTURE

We've seen how the conventional definition of profit omits *negative* externalities, the damages that don't appear on an organization's own books. But there's an even larger and more costly problem. It is blind to *positive externalities*. Like their negative cousins, positive externalities accrue to others but don't appear on the company's own profit and loss (P&L) statement. They are called *positive* because they are benefits, not costs. This accounts for the blindness. When a company invests in a positive way—in quality, relationships, or anything that builds trust—the costs of these investments show up on the P&L. The benefits don't. For an organization optimizing for return on investment (ROI), these actions score negatively, despite being the biggest sources of wealth creation in the world.

Tim O'Reilly put it simply: "Create more value than you capture."[30] As we'll see, many extremely valuable companies succeed precisely because they see generosity as a moat, not just a cost.

But here's what makes this principle so hard to follow: Our measurement tools are designed to miss it.

Costco's generous supplier payment terms cost millions annually. The company pays within thirty days, while competitors take sixty to ninety, maintaining decade-long partnerships versus typical two- to three-year contracts.[31] Irrational? The spreadsheet says yes. But when shortages hit, Costco gets first access to premium products no competitor can touch. That loyalty has no ledger entry. (We'll explore this in Chapter 6.)

GitLab built a $7 billion company by being transparent to a degree that would make most executives squirm.[32] Their source code is open source, and so is their complete employee handbook. Yet even their competitors' employees debug GitLab's code for free. They can't help themselves; they see problems and fix them. Try putting that on a balance sheet. (Chapter 8 has the full story.)

As one CFO told me, "I can calculate the cost of raising wages to the penny, but the spreadsheet can't capture what happens when employees stop viewing us as the enemy."

This asymmetry between measurable costs and unmeasurable benefits explains why conventional business analysis systematically misses the most profitable opportunities.

Nearly a century ago, W. Edwards Deming showed Japanese manufacturers that quality investments looked like pure cost on any P&L. Then he showed them the invisible returns, including system-wide improvements, customer loyalty, and worker pride. Those "costs" helped Japan dismantle Detroit's dominance.[33]

We will see many examples of this paradoxical truth in later chapters. The logic is straightforward. Companies that grab every dollar force customers, employees, and partners to protect themselves. The pie shrinks. Those who take the harder path and risk leaving money visible on the table invite others to invest in mutual success.

By creating more value than they capture, they don't just get a smaller slice of a much larger pie. They become the table on which the pie sits, needed by everyone else.

MISSION CONTROL

Committing to human flourishing does more than create competitive advantage. It resolves three conceptual contradictions that have plagued business for generations.

First, there's no such thing as a "double bottom line" or "triple bottom line"[34] when profit is properly understood. We don't have "good profits" and "bad profits."[35] We regain the simplicity of one clear objective: human flourishing.

Second, it also upends our existing ideas about "non-profit" versus "for-profit." The Smithsonian Institution is extraordinarily profitable. It's creating immeasurable value in preserved knowledge, scientific advancement, and education for nearly seventeen million annual visitors,[36] with $275 million net income annually to boot.[37] Similarly, "non-profit" Goodwill Industries earns $8.2 billion in annual revenue[38] in competitive retail markets while serving 2.1 million people, including providing career training to 142,000[39] of them and diverting billions of pounds of clothing from landfills.

By contrast, as we have seen, Philip Morris has $7 billion in annual net income,[40] which sounds impressive until you realize that the tobacco industry imposes over $600 billion in healthcare and productivity costs annually in the US alone.[41] Such companies destroy far more value than they create. They are profoundly unprofitable. Oh, and that's before we get to the killing of customers or environmental destruction.

These examples reveal that our "for-profit" and "non-profit" labels are deeply confused. We should be using labels relating to who controls the organization instead. In practice today, "for-profit" usually means *investor controlled* (the board is accountable to outside shareholders), while "non-profit" typically means *self-controlled* (the board is accountable only to itself).[42] Using human flourishing as our guide, we can build what I call *mission-controlled* companies. (In fact, as we will see in Chapter 11, this even enables new hybrid corporate forms that combine the best elements of both for-profit and non-profit entities.)

Third, this redefinition dissolves capitalism's most frequent critique: It puts profits over people. When profit is understood to be about flourishing, not just money, this criticism is rendered incoherent. So are many of the targets of that critique: Their exploitative business practices are revealed to be value destroying, a bug in the system of capitalism, not a feature.

Of course, this clarity doesn't eliminate the difficult choices leaders face every day. Does a layoff serve human flourishing? That depends. If it preserves the organization's ability to serve for decades, it does. If it merely gooses the stock price, no. Recognizing the true nature of profit does not magically eliminate these tensions; it simply makes them evident. As we'll explore in Chapters 6 and 7, resolving these knots actually provides a hidden fuel that can create a significant competitive advantage.

After all, organizations require financial performance to survive, but mere survival is not their purpose. The human body needs oxygen to survive, but nobody would say the purpose of a human life is to consume as much oxygen as possible—"as tho' to breathe were life."[43] Those who attempt to put "profits over people" reveal nothing but their own confusion and therefore their unfitness for positions of leadership.

THE BUILDER'S CHOICE

I've told Todd's story to many leaders over the years. A common reaction sounds like this: "Sure, this would work for Todd. He's extraordinary. He was the US CTO. He's had multiple successful exits. He's raised billions. Everyone loves the guy. Of course he can afford to have an ethos."

The implication is that this path is open only to special people. But notice the fallacy: They're pointing to Todd's results as though he achieved them using conventional methods. Only after having such success, they claim, could he pursue the ethos that powers Devoted today.

They have it exactly backward. What if his prior successes *are the result* of his ethos? What if he became special because of what he chose? Think about Amanda helping Dwuane find new housing or the other stories we've seen that transform cost centers like "customer support" into "guardian angels." None of that required billions of dollars. Devoted was helping heal people long before it became one of the fastest-growing companies in America.

Devoted didn't choose this path because they had the luxury of billions in funding. They raised billions because "love" as a strategy made them the kind of company investors dream of finding. This way of working isn't reserved for the special few. It's available to anyone with the courage to choose it.

The mission didn't follow the money. The money followed the mission.

No matter what stage you're at, you already have everything you need to start building this way. It starts with one hard choice.

CHAPTER SIX

HARDER IS EASIER

> If you raise the f—ing hot dog price, I will kill you. Figure it out.
>
> —**Costco CEO Jim Sinegal**
> to then-COO Craig Jelinek
> circa 2008

I LOVE TELLING THIS STORY.[1] Today, Costco is a giant of modern retail. With a market cap of over $400 billion,[2] you'd think their market power would afford them the luxury to charge whatever they want for their signature hot dog, available in every store's food court. Certainly then-COO Jelinek thought so when he approached Sinegal about a price increase, complaining, "We can't sell this hot dog for a buck fifty. We are losing our rear ends."[3] But he was wrong.

Remember Sol Price from way back in Chapter 1? I promised his story had a happy ending. Price reshaped the face of modern retail. Have you ever wondered why Walmart is called Walmart? The name was inspired by FedMart. Sam Walton credited Sol Price as his inspiration, saying, "I guess I've stolen—I actually prefer the word 'borrowed'—as many ideas from Sol Price as from anybody else in the business."[4] And yet despite all his success, Price's most lasting legacy would be shaped by an unlikely protégé.

In 1954, an eighteen-year-old college student named Jim Sinegal was stocking mattresses at the brand-new FedMart when he heard a gruff voice boom out, "Put that damn thing down before you break your back, or worse yet, break something in the store!"[5] That voice belonged to Sol Price, and that chance encounter began a mentorship that would shake the foundations of modern business. Years later, when a reporter noted that Sinegal must have learned a lot from Price, Sinegal corrected him: "That's inaccurate. I learned everything."[6]

Sinegal worked his way up from stockboy to founder. After FedMart failed, Sol Price went on to create Price Club in 1976, pioneering the warehouse membership model.[7] Sinegal went with him. In 1983, Sinegal founded Costco.[8] A decade later, Price and Sinegal were reunited when Price Club merged with Costco, creating the retail behemoth you know today.

Shortly after Costco's founding, they began selling a hot dog and soda combo from a cart outside their San Diego warehouse. It cost \$1.50.[9] Around that same year, a McDonald's Big Mac cost \$1.60. Today, that same Big Mac costs around \$7.[10] Care to guess what Costco's hot dog combo costs today? That's right—\$1.50.

In a world of shrinkflation, hidden fees, and subscription traps, that unchanged price is a rare promise kept. The hot dog combo is Costco's way of saying, "We will never betray your trust to improve our own bottom line." In response, customers have developed an almost religious devotion to this humble hot dog. The combo has achieved meme status online, celebrated as an "inflation-proof icon."[11] Fans have made a T-shirt—it went viral—featuring Sinegal's famous threat.[12]

Cheap hot dogs may not be your vision of human flourishing. I get it. My good friend Clark, a longtime vegetarian and environmentalist, finds this story appalling every time I tell it. "Processed beef is one of the worst possible products for both the environment and health." People's values differ widely, and no organization can please everyone—nor should they. The beauty of a market economy is that every organization can declare what it stands for and bear the consequences, good or ill, of that choice.

I've told this story of Costco's refusal to raise the hot dog price many times. Most people find it surprising. They ask, Does Costco treat the hot dog as a loss leader? How do they deal with inflation? Don't they have a fiduciary duty to their shareholders? But what I find most interesting is the question nobody ever asks: Why did the COO suggest raising the price in the first place?

Because of course he did! The conventional business playbook has taught us to raise prices whenever we can. Sinegal understood this temptation intimately. As he once explained, "You could raise the price of, say, a bottle of ketchup to $1.03 instead of $1, and no one would know. Raising prices just 3% per product would add 50% to your pretax income. Why not do it? It's like heroin: You do a little and you want a little bit more. Raising prices is the easy way."[13]

In 2023 alone, Costco sold nearly two hundred million hot dog combos, almost ten times as many as every Major League Baseball (MLB) stadium combined.[14] That's a staggering number. Put another way, for every dollar they could get away with raising the price of the hot dog combo, they would add an easy $200 million to the bottom line as pure profit. No wonder the COO suggested it. No wonder most companies can't resist.

Instead, Costco took the harder road.

As inflation drove up meat prices and supply costs over the decades, the company refused to budge on that $1.50 price point. To make it work, they had to embrace complex solutions that required significant capital investment and operational expertise. In 2008–9, they built their own hot dog manufacturing plants in Los Angeles and later Chicago, vertically integrating their supply chain rather than accepting price increases from vendors.[15] They've switched soda suppliers to secure better deals.[16] They've accepted lower margins on the hot dog while refusing to compromise on quality. All this extraordinary effort just to keep that promise.

When asked in a 2009 interview what it would signal if the hot dog combo price ever increased, Sinegal quipped, "That I'm dead."[17] And, in fact, the hot dog has transcended legend and passed into corporate lore. It has survived two CEOs in succession—including Jelinek, who originally suggested raising the prices and succeeded Sinegal in 2012. In 2023, Costco's CFO even felt compelled to publicly address rumors about a price increase, vowing, on an earnings call, that Costco would hold the hot dog combo price "a little longer"—then slyly adding, "forever."[18]

THE VALUE OF TRUST

Today, Costco stands as a retail powerhouse, beloved by customers and admired by investors. Whatever time horizon you choose, Costco has outperformed: up 28,070% versus the S&P 500's 877% since 1987,[19] a ten-year return of 773% versus the market's roughly 250%,[20] and a five-year return of 233% versus 137%.[21] Its membership renewal rates hover around an astonishing 90%.[22] And yet it could make even more money in any given year by making slight changes to the prices of everything it sells, including the two hundred million hot dog combos. Costco doesn't because Sinegal understood that being a trustworthy partner to members, employees, and suppliers is far more valuable over the long term. The results speak for themselves. (But I'm still going to give you one more figure: Its store brand, Kirkland Signature, generates $86 billion in annual revenue.[23] That's more than all of Procter & Gamble's brands combined. If Kirkland were a standalone company, it would be bigger than Nike, Coca-Cola, or United Airlines.)

Remember the mutually reinforcing elements of Sol Price's ethos? They still guide Costco's decisions in good times and bad. The hot dog is just the visible tip of an entire integrated iceberg. Costco has kept Sol Price's capped gross margins of 14% (compared to 25% at other discount retailers) and his "intelligent loss of sales."[24] Their employees know what they stand for too. During the 2008 financial crisis, when most retailers were freezing wages or laying off workers, Costco gave hourly workers a $1.50 an hour raise to be split over the next three years. Doing it in three fifty-cent increases rather than smaller ones over a longer time cost the company an extra $20 million, but Sinegal didn't care. As he said at the time, "This economy is bad. We should be figuring out how to give them more, not less."[25] That's character.

When challenges arise, be they inflation, supply chain disruptions, or pressure from Wall Street, company leadership doesn't complain that it's too hard to stick to their values. They "figure it out." This is what it means to be a fiduciary to the customer.

These commitments are difficult to architect and to execute. But once they are in place, they make everything else about business so much easier. Here's what that looks like for Costco at a high level:

Vision. "To continually provide members with quality goods and services at the lowest possible prices"[26]—not just today but forever.

Mission. Act as fiduciaries for members, treating every stakeholder—employees, vendors, shareholders—as if they were family because mutual trust creates mutual prosperity.[27]

Strategy. Accept lower gross margins (that 14% cap) to deliver unbeatable value. Build warehouses, not stores. Sell memberships, not just products. Choose quality over variety. Say no to Wall Street when financial gravity conflicts with member interests.[28]

People. Pay $26 per hour on average (versus $17 retail average). Promote from within (85% of warehouse managers started as hourly workers). Provide health benefits even to part-timers. Create careers, not jobs. The results: 8% turnover versus the industry's 60%.[29]

Business model. Membership fees provide profit cushion, allowing aggressive pricing on goods. Limited SKUs mean massive volume per item, creating negotiating power. No advertising means those savings go to members. The warehouse format keeps costs minimal.[30]

As a result of this alignment, everyone from customers and employees to suppliers and investors knows exactly what Costco stands for. Its commitment to its ethos enables deep trust, and that trustworthiness is the compounding asset that creates Costco's incredible magnetic attraction of partners, capital, and customers. As legendary investor Charlie Munger, who served on Costco's board, put it, Costco is "one of the most admirable capitalist institutions."[31]

FIGURE IT OUT

There's one more thing about that Sinegal story that nobody ever asks me about. Not the threat to kill Jelinek. Not the profanity. But those three words at the end: "Figure it out."

"Figure it out" is what great leaders say when they realize that impossibilities are opportunities in disguise. They don't accept the lazy defaults. They recognize that solving the genuinely difficult problems that everyone else avoids creates the trust and loyalty that makes everything else easier.

As we saw with Devoted Health, it's a gift that an ambitious mission creates these extra obstacles and difficulties on the regular. Overcoming them leads to repeated breakthroughs.

In fact, I would go further. The best leaders welcome these challenges, seeing them as an opportunity to teach. This is how ethos is built, brick by brick. Todd Park fundamentally changed how I think about business when he taught me this pattern. I call it "harder is easier."

From here on out, I'll use the shorthand of a *harder-is-easier mission* to mean this specific combination I've witnessed in the very best companies:

1. An ambitious mission to maximize human flourishing, aligned with the business model so the company only makes more money by accomplishing more mission. This rejects "making money by any means necessary" in favor of *making money by doing as much mission as possible.*
2. An ethos that includes an unwavering commitment to principled decision-making. A team on a harder-is-easier mission is willing to face the full consequences of its principles, no matter how difficult.
3. A commitment to "figure it out" when challenges arise. They find solutions that are both economically sustainable and mission maximizing.

These companies are just as greedy as any traditional for-profit business. They're just greedy for mission. The fact that this approach also generates enormous profits is a fortuitous side effect.

Costco went to outrageous lengths for a $1.50 hot dog. Now let me tell you about a company that figured out how to give their most profitable product away for free and made billions doing it.

THE CLOUDFLARE STORY

Every company must define its own vision of how it advances human flourishing. But not all definitions are equally good. Matthew Prince, CEO of the internet infrastructure company Cloudflare, told me how they found theirs.

They'd started in 2009 with a practical business idea: put firewall functionality in the cloud.[32] Not every mission-driven founder has a high-concept mission ready to go on day one. Matthew Prince and Michelle Zatlyn, Cloudflare's cofounders, certainly didn't. "I thought missions were those things that marketing teams came up with and painted on the walls," Matthew told me.[33] He focused instead on building the company: "You've got to start with the business, then figure out how it could get bigger and bigger. The mission will emerge from that."

And emerge it did. About two years in, the team was having lunch in Palo Alto. No agenda, no strategic planning session, just eating and talking. That's when one engineer said something unexpected: "I've never worked somewhere where I feel like I'm really helping build a better internet."

The table went quiet for a moment. Then others began echoing the sentiment, almost in unison: "Yeah, that's exactly it" and "That's why I'm here."

Matthew was skeptical. "I was like, that's marketing gunk." But the engineers pushed back: "No, no, this is important. This actually resonates."

The phrase wouldn't go away. Week after week, in different contexts, people kept returning to it: building a better internet. They didn't need a focus group. It had emerged, organically and persistently, from the work itself. Eventually, the founders recognized what their employees had been trying to tell them. This was their mission.

Years later, that mission would be tested. At the time, web encryption was Cloudflare's flagship premium feature, one of the main reasons customers upgraded to a paid subscription. This made sense, as encryption incurs real costs. Then a young French engineer asked during a team meeting, "Our mission is to build a better internet, right?" Matthew nodded. "Isn't an encrypted internet a better internet?" Matthew agreed again. "So why are we charging for encryption?"

Picture this moment. An employee just suggested giving away their most valuable premium feature. The one that, as Matthew later told his board, was "one of the reasons people upgrade to a paid plan." You probably visualize the CEO responding like this: "Of course we're not going to do that. We'll lose significant revenue. Plus, encryption costs us real money. Next question."

Except Matthew didn't say any of that.

He leaned back and was quiet for a moment. "Once we saw it, we couldn't unsee it," he told me later. For him, a better internet meant one that's harder to throttle, censor, or restrict. Instead of explaining why they couldn't do it, he echoed Sinegal's key three words: "Figure it out."

"We didn't know if we could pull it off technically," Matthew told me. For months, he drove his team to attack the root causes of encryption's high costs, including certificate fees, computational overhead, and IP address allocation. "We obsessed, just obsessed over costs." Roadblocks abounded. For example, when they approached the certificate authorities (CAs) about pricing for millions of free users, Matthew remembers, "We called every CA, and all of them said, 'No way.' "

The team had every opportunity to use these obstacles as excuses. Instead, they rallied. One engineer rewrote their compression algorithms in assembly language, freeing up enough processing power to handle encryption for millions of sites without new servers. They rebuilt their systems to share IP addresses across certificates. In fact, they built a certificate management system so robust that Matthew noted, "Twelve years later, no other company has managed to rebuild what we built back in 2014."[34]

But the breakthrough came from understanding the CAs' own economics. Cloudflare discovered that serving certificate validation traffic globally was a significant burden for the CAs. To create a win-win, Cloudflare proposed a trade (called a "contradeal") where Cloudflare would handle the CAs' bandwidth costs in exchange for offsetting the expense of millions of certificates.

Note that Cloudflare could have used these breakthroughs to increase their margins substantially. But you already know what they did instead.

"Spreadsheets still matter," Matthew emphasized. "There's a hard lesson to learn in this, which is 'We're still a business. It still has to pencil out.' There's only this much money in the bank account, and it keeps getting smaller, and we have to stop playing the game if it gets too small." He explained, "It isn't just the mission and no business. It has to be a business that supports the mission."

On September 27, 2014, they pushed the button and gave encryption away to everyone.[35]

Matthew admitted they didn't know it would work out. The costs were very clear and the benefits completely intangible: "It wasn't like we did a ton of analysis saying, 'If we do this, then our revenue will increase.' It came down to one engineer saying a better internet is a more encrypted internet. And if we really believe in our mission, that's what we're going to do."

So that's what they did. And, indeed, customer conversion rates from free to paid subscriptions did go down. Many companies would have panicked and reversed course at that point. But not Cloudflare.

From a mission perspective, it was a rousing success. Cloudflare doubled the size of the encrypted web in a single day, from two million to four million encrypted sites overnight.[36] Today, we take it for granted that almost all websites are SSL encrypted. Cloudflare's sacrifice is a big part of the reason why.

From a business perspective, Cloudflare's leap of faith was vindicated. The lowered conversion rates were more than offset by an "order of magnitude" increase in sign-ups. Beyond this immediate win, they had gained something far more valuable. They had earned the deep trust of the developer community. And where developers trust, enterprises follow. Their principled stance created a magnetic pull that continues to compound. Today Cloudflare handles 20% of all web traffic. Billions of people rely on them daily.[37] Like Costco's $1.50 hot dog, Cloudflare's free encryption became proof of character, a daily demonstration that they take their mission seriously. Proving their trustworthiness set them on a path that has propelled them to an almost $75 billion valuation.[38]

That is what I mean by "harder is easier."

CHOOSE YOUR DIFFICULTY

I've been trying to get companies, organizations, even governments to do better for more than two decades now. I'm used to resistance. But what baffles me most is when people hear the Costco, Devoted, or Cloudflare stories and say, "That's too hard. Business is already so difficult, and now we're supposed to do more?"

Has anyone stopped to ask why business is so difficult? Could it be that all that mistrust and friction comes at a cost?

Too hard? Let me tell you what's actually difficult.

What's difficult is running a company where sales fights with customer service, finance battles R&D, employees distrust management. What's difficult is sustaining motivation when people feel they're selling out their customers or themselves. What's difficult is working in dysfunctional organizational cultures that are cutthroat or highly political in ways that undermine the work itself. What's difficult is being rewarded for running on the treadmill of seeking an ever-greater margin or stock price rather than getting to focus on building a healthy business. What's difficult is the daily grind of herding everyone in the same direction through monitoring, incentives, and consequences. And then watching talent flee, customers churn, and partners defect because nobody trusts the organization. What's most difficult of all is that under this constant friction, good people lose their will to fight.[39]

When people say, "That's too hard," they're only thinking about one type of hard. But as Costco and Cloudflare show, there are two types of "hard." One hard is depleting. One hard is exhilarating. One hard makes talented people do mediocre work. The other calls forth their passion, creative thinking, and loyalty. There really isn't an easy way. The only question is which hard a company chooses.

THE MISERY OF THE CASH COW

The conventional wisdom—and I've heard it in more meetings with lawyers and investors than I can count—is to be parsimonious in defining a mission, to be narrow and incremental with aspirations. Even if a company talks a big game to investors, lawyers believe that the best way to protect it is by making sure it maintains maximum optionality for the future. They guide the discussion away from overpromising or taking too big a swing. Founders may have some grand vision for what they'll do in the future, but it remains notional because the company they end up building lacks the determination to pursue it. By design, it can only do something much smaller. Let's call it fulfilling a function as opposed to a vision.

Jeremy Howard (my cofounder at Answer.AI) experienced this firsthand in a previous startup. After years of studying the potential of machine learning, he launched Enlitic with a bold vision: to fundamentally change how medicine is practiced worldwide, making it more individualized and accessible, particularly in regions with critical doctor shortages. "Success for me was an industry-level thing," he told me. "I wanted to see everybody using this technology because it felt like it could transform humanity."[40]

His team's early breakthrough—neural networks that could identify lung tumors faster than human radiologists—was meant as just an initial proof of concept. But when they found immediate market traction helping radiologists, everything changed. The company discovered its cash cow.[41]

Immediate revenue validation made the "easier" path seductive ("Look, we're making money!"). They had a clear product-market fit with no need to explain the bigger vision. A simple story for investors. A proven business model, less operational complexity, and one product instead of a platform. It all added up to reduced risk.

When investors pushed to focus solely on this narrow application, Jeremy fought back. But one by one, his allies fell away. "I felt pretty disappointed to realize I was literally the last man standing. I was the only one of all the stakeholders still interested in the big vision."[42] The experience was heartbreaking for him.

By conventional measures, Enlitic's initial public offering (IPO) was a success. But at what cost? Beyond Jeremy's disappointment and the demoralized team who signed up to transform healthcare, the real tragedy was the opportunity cost—all the lives that could have been saved, all the innovation that never happened, all the potential that was never even attempted. "What amazes me," Jeremy says, "is today Enlitic is a publicly listed company, and it still just does radiology workflow processes."[43] Jeremy learned from this experience. His subsequent ventures have all been characterized by a strong ethos and, particularly for Answer.AI, a strong governance that ensures the vision can't be so easily abandoned.

Enlitic is just one example of a big vision falling by the wayside. All across our economy, these silent losses hide in plain sight, masked by the appearance of success. The tragedy isn't having a cash cow; it's having nothing else. The term "cash cow" originally described one quadrant in a balanced portfolio, the profitable, mature product that funds investment in future growth. Today, many consider it a best practice to discover one thing that makes money and abandon everything else. They call it focus. But real focus comes from mission clarity, not narrowness. Stories like Enlitic create a false impression that founders must choose between idealism and pragmatism, which is exactly backward. What seemed like the pragmatic choice—focusing on the sure thing—ultimately led to hollow success. The "easier" path created its own form of difficulty: talented people leaving, vision evaporating, and a company trapped in its first win.

On the other hand, the moment a company refuses to compromise its commitment to a higher principle—whether in product quality, design excellence, ethical standards, or exceptional service—it has chosen the harder road. This puts it at odds with the dominant business culture, but as we're about to see, this harder road unlocks advantages that make everything else easier.

THE MAGNETIC POWERS

I remember telling Todd Park that his vision for a new love-centered healthcare system sounded almost too good to be true, like a utopia impossible to reach. Real Robert Owen stuff. But as I watched him execute each step, consistently refusing to compromise, I began to see it differently. And this filled me with a desire to understand why it works.

Because at every step, conventional business thinking would say that what Todd is doing is impossible. He's partnering with some of the world's largest investors and most legacy healthcare players. But instead of Todd being warped by their gravity, they are buying into his vision. He's able to attract true believers from the ranks of some of the most cynical professions on Earth. How?

At first, I thought it was simply the power of his consistency. But that can't be right. After all, a drug addict is remarkably consistent too. Remember Sinegal's warning that raising prices is like heroin? He was describing how companies become addicted to short-term rewards, predictably self-absorbed in their need for the next fix.

Eventually, studying Sol Price, Jim Sinegal, Todd Park, and other leaders like them, I came to understand that when a company's mission is genuinely aspirational, people think, "I want to be part of that world." When its actions are principled and consistent, they realize, "I can count on them." When these combine, a new asset is created, one of the most valuable and underrated assets in the world: trustworthiness.

In a world of broken promises and corporate betrayals, trust powers magnetic attraction. People desperately want to work for, invest in, and buy from organizations that stand for something aligned with their most fervent dreams. This magnetism manifests in four specific powers that make the "impossible" suddenly achievable.

The talent power

Amazing things happen when employees trust that their work will genuinely matter. As Matthew Prince revealed, "Last year we had 1.5 million people apply for a thousand jobs."[44] Their harder-is-easier mission is the magnet. This is not just about paying higher wages. In fact, research consistently shows employees will accept lower wages to find more meaningful work. MIT research found that culture predicts turnover ten times more than compensation.[45] Another study found that workers at mission-driven companies, where they "agreed with the statement 'My work is meaningful,' were 2.7 times more likely to stay with their organization. Purpose revealed itself as the top driver of employee retention."[46] When people trust that the organization's mission is real and that their effort won't be betrayed, they bring their whole selves to work, including their creativity and passion. That trust transforms a job into a calling.

The alliance power

Harder-is-easier missions naturally have few competitors because so few organizations can sustain the commitment required. And that scarcity creates another advantage: It magnetically attracts sophisticated allies from every sector. Devoted raised $2.2 billion not despite the difficulty but because of it.[47] I've witnessed even hardened venture capitalists (VCs) be moved by Todd's vision for healthcare delivered with love. They recognize what Charlie Munger saw in Costco—an "extreme culture where everybody's bought in"[48] that creates competitive advantages others simply cannot replicate.

The magnetic force can transform even sworn enemies into allies. Consider the eternal struggle between health systems (who administer care) and insurers (who pay for it). Frequently, they treat this like a zero-sum hostage situation, each holding the other's economics at gunpoint. When new insurers try to enter a market, health systems typically block them at every turn, protecting their existing relationships and negotiated rates.

Todd Park once told me the story of meeting with executives from a major health system that had the ominous nickname "Darth Vader" because of its tenacity in battling other insurers. In that meeting, Todd explained Devoted's radically different approach: the guardian angels who answer every call (even from health systems!), the commitment to pay claims fairly and fast, the focus on keeping members healthy rather than denying care.

The response was immediate. "These senior executives melted in front of me," Todd recalls.

Darth Vader took off the helmet. Instead of blocking this new entrant, they offered "really advantaged unit costs." They encouraged their patients to try Devoted. They enlisted in the Devoted vision, becoming yet another segment of the virtuous performance cycle. As their economics and patient outcomes improved, they even evangelized to other health systems, who have since invited Devoted into their own markets. By choosing the harder path of genuine care, Devoted transformed what could have been its most adversarial relationship into a most powerful alliance.[49]

The alignment power

When employees trust that ethos is genuine, alignment is a natural consequence. Strategy textbooks are full of disdain for companies that fail to execute because they cannot get their employees to pursue a unified strategy. It's also one of the most common complaints I hear from leaders at all levels. Endless millions are spent each year on "employee communications" that utterly fail to get everyone rowing in the same direction. Much of this problem stems from the fact that:

- people don't understand a complex plan that doesn't intuitively resonate and
- employees don't trust leadership to follow through on their commitments.

At Devoted, the endless debates and silent pushback are eliminated by one simple question that employees are asked to keep in mind: "Would this be good enough for Mom?" Similarly, for Costco, when the 2008 crisis hit, management didn't debate whether to raise wages. The "Costco way" made the decision obvious.

Trust creates alignment. Alignment enables speed. Speed leads to ferocious execution that leaves competitors scrambling to understand what happened.

The loyalty power

When customers trust their "guardian angels" to fight for them even when it's costly, they tend to stick around. As one Devoted member explained, "This is like going back to the '60s or '50s where there was [actual] customer service."[50] Costco's 90% renewal rate year after year tells the same story. Satisfied customers have been converted into true believers. This loyalty creates an unassailable competitive advantage. Customers with high trust are three times more likely to stick with a company through mistakes, and 62% of them buy almost exclusively from that brand.[51] And for attracting new customers, money can't buy "the unsolicited testimonial of the satisfied customer."[52]

A WORD OF WARNING

I want to end this chapter with a word of warning.

Sol Price died a wealthy and respected businessman. But remember that Costco was his *third* try. His own investors betrayed FedMart, expelling him from the company and driving it into bankruptcy. Ultimately, it was his disciple, Jim Sinegal, who built Costco into the behemoth it is today.

Price had figured out "harder is easier" back at FedMart. He just couldn't protect it.

Financial gravity constantly pulls organizations toward exploiting the trust they've built and milking it for short-term gain. Remember Sinegal's warning that raising prices is like heroin? Modern organizations live with the ever-present temptation to go down this addictive path. (Tech critic Cory Doctorow calls it "enshittification"—the ubiquitous pattern of companies that lock in customers and then gradually make their products worse.[53]) Without comprehensive alignment of mission and ethos—and the structural integrity to defend them—even the best companies eventually succumb.

The first step of the blueprint is to build something worth protecting: Costco's $1.50 hot dog. Cloudflare's free encryption. Devoted's healthcare delivered with love. Each company chose the harder path and unlocked the magnetic powers that made everything else easier.

But these magnetic powers attract more than just customers and talent. They also attract predators. I mentioned earlier that trust is the most underrated asset in the world today. That's why people will try to steal it from you. The more successful the organization, the more tempting a target it becomes. Sol Price learned this too late. The next generation of builders can't afford to repeat his mistake.

The remainder of Part II covers instilling defenses into the very foundation of an organization. Not lame posters about company values but actual structural safeguards: the business model that only makes money by fulfilling the mission, the coherent culture that executes even when nobody's watching, the governance structure that makes betrayal impossible.

Next, we turn to how to install this "mission drive" and make it permanent.

JUST GIVE THE PEOPLE WHAT THEY WANT

I've been called a lot of things over the years. The same people who complain to me night and day about how hard it is to run their own business consider me too radical. And from a certain point of view, I get it. The prescriptions in this chapter may sound radical.

But from a different point of view, this is one of the simplest and most obvious ideas I have ever had: Instead of bending ourselves into pretzels trying to advance some galaxy-brained strategy, why don't we just give the people what they want?

Where do people want to work? Employees at high-trust organizations report 74% less stress and 50% higher productivity[54]—numbers that should make any CEO take notice. We all know this to be true: People want to work where they can trust leadership and feel trusted in return. Another survey found that "79% of employees who highly trust their employer feel motivated to work."[55]

What do people want to invest in? Trust powers superior investment returns. A World Economic Forum study found that trusted companies have consistently beaten the market by 5% in times of growth and 11% in times of crisis.[56] A thirty-year analysis of US firms found that companies more trusted by investors could raise money more cheaply and enjoyed a significantly lower cost of capital.[57] A new generation of investors increasingly looks to find companies that align with their values. Companies that treat their investors in a trustworthy way benefit too. A study from April 2025 reveals that almost 73% of younger individual investors, including millennials and Gen Z, prioritize aligning investments with their social values.[58]

What do people want to buy? Products from companies they trust. Research shows that 59% of adults are more likely to purchase a brand when they trust it, while 71% of consumers will stop purchasing from a company altogether if their trust is broken.[59] And they put their money where their mouth is: Consumers who trust a brand are twice as likely to be first to buy new products and twice as likely to stay loyal even when facing trendy or innovative competitors.[60] This is why lifetime value is higher, why retention is stronger, and why word of mouth flourishes. As business strategist Fred Reichheld puts it bluntly, "Without trust, there can be no loyalty—and without loyalty, no true growth."[61]

What do partners want? Trust's economic impact extends far beyond customer relationships. Think about supply chains: When organizations can't trust their partners, they create costly redundancies—multiple vendors for the same component, quality inspections at every handoff, elaborate contracts with enforcement mechanisms. These inefficiencies compound exponentially as supply chains lengthen, creating enormous waste—all because companies can't trust each other. High-trust business relationships require up to 40% less contractual complexity and monitoring costs.[62] We all know it instinctively: People prefer to partner with those they can trust.

The irony of all of this is that, despite the claims of conventional thinking, this approach is more profitable too. Again, trustworthiness is the reason why. It compounds over time. Companies with high levels of customer trust grow revenues at more than twice the rate of their industry peers and deliver two to five times the returns to shareholders over a ten-year period.[63]

Chapter Seven

MISSION DRIVE

> I have come to the conviction that once one embarks on a concept for a building, this concept has to be exaggerated and overstated and repeated in every part of its interior, so that wherever you are, inside or outside, the building sings with the same message.
>
> **—Eero Saarinen**
> *Some Thoughts on Modern Architecture*
> 1959

So there I was, living a scene right out of a dystopian science fiction novel.

Almost every day, founders of startups large and small seek my advice. Today, all I knew ahead of time was that we'd be talking about "a new technology meant for agricultural monitoring." Sure, I'll take the meeting.

It started with a pretty normal startup pitch. Slides, diagrams, demos, and videos of the product in action: autonomous drones that can roll, float, or even fly across difficult terrain. I tried to focus on the founder's business, but I was distracted. Every video of these spherical robots gently wafting over the ground had me looking over my shoulder. All I could think of was how sinister they looked and how easily they might be repurposed for warfare. Finally, I asked the founder directly, "Is there any chance at all that these could be used as weapons?" His shoulders sagged. He rubbed his temples with both hands. "I really don't know why, but I get that question all the time." Then, leaning forward with sudden intensity, he exclaimed, "I'm not trying to create doomsday murder robots! I swear!"

You've heard a bit about what this technology is for. You've had a moment to share my worry about what these drones might become. Now that you've heard that the founder pinky-promised not to create doomsday murder robots, do you feel any better?

I don't know about you, but I certainly didn't.

When I asked what would prevent a future pivot to weapons, he seemed puzzled. "Why would we do that? We're an agtech company." He proudly pulled up his metrics dashboard. "Customer acquisition cost, drone utilization rates, recurring revenue per farm. We're crushing it." Then, brightening, he added, "Plus, we just added this amazing board member. Ex-Raytheon. Really gets autonomous systems."

He had just described exactly how it would happen, and he had no idea.

Leaders can make all the promises they want, but we all have long experience watching organization after organization be pushed off course by financial gravity, regardless of anyone's good intentions. Intentions belong only to individuals, and as we saw, individuals can be replaced. The organization endures (or doesn't).

This founder wanted desperately to be trusted so that he could activate the magnetic powers that trust makes possible. He needed future employees, customers, and investors to believe that he was truly committed to his mission. He wanted to be seen as what we colloquially call mission-driven. But wanting isn't enough. Most companies are, at best, *mission-hopeful.*

To be actually mission driven requires something more deliberate. We've already seen an example of this with Devoted Health's virtuous performance cycle: "The healthier we keep people, the more money we make," Todd Park pointed out. "That's the simple truth of our business model."[1] This may sound simple, but creating this alignment requires relentless effort and singular focus. I call this *mission drive*: the management discipline that ensures an organization only profits via mission attainment.

MISSION DRIVE AT PATAGONIA

Walk into any Patagonia store. Within thirty seconds, you'll know what they stand for. The recycled materials, the repair station, the climbing photos, the employee who actually uses the gear—everything tells the same story. This is a company founded by climbers who once hand-forged their own carabiners because the existing ones weren't good enough.[2] The obsessive commitment to craft and love of wild places radiate from every corner.

This immersion is similar to the experience customers have entering Costco, where concrete floors and steel shelving continue to palpably embody Sol Price's ethos of eschewing decor in favor of passing on the best prices to shoppers. Obviously the similarity isn't about brand or design; the two stores are aesthetically quite different. What they have in common is that both organizations know exactly who they are.

Patagonia was founded by Malinda and Yvon Chouinard, who guided its ethos for decades. I studied their approach with David Gelles, who has chronicled their story for many years. He explained the company's deep sense of self this way: "Yvon was using the same phrases, coming back to the same values, understanding the world in the same way 50 years ago as he still does today."[3] For decades, Patagonia has obsessively aligned its business model with its mission. The result is a company that's coherent inside and out.

For example, instead of dusty corporate seminars, Yvon for years taught philosophy classes exploring questions like "What does it mean for an object to be of high quality?"[4] He'd place a bag of Peet's coffee beans on a table and ask, "Is that a quality coffee bean?" His students were bewildered as he pressed for an answer. When some protested that quality was a matter of taste, Chouinard would dig in his heels. "No. It's about consistency. It's about a product fulfilling its function." Next, he would challenge them to name the highest-quality piece of clothing in the world. Someone would offer up a custom-tailored Italian cotton dress shirt as the ideal, and Chouinard would pounce. "How would it hold up in a washing machine? How long would it last?"[5] For all it made his students squirm, Chouinard insisted that quality is an objective standard, not merely what customers would accept but what the product deserves.

Today, Patagonia is widely known for its activism in environmental and social causes. This is an outgrowth of its original obsession with quality, which required supporting the health, safety, and welfare of its customers. What began with lifesaving gear for climbers led naturally to the rest. After all, every one of their customers lives on the same planet.

This approach was, paradoxically, bad for the bottom line—at least in the short term. Durability means less need to repurchase. And educating customers about the negative externalities of apparel production risks turning them away from the brand. "Everything we make pollutes," their 1991 catalog bluntly informed customers. Patagonia's radical solution? "Buy fewer items and buy things that last."[6] They were literally telling customers not to buy replacements. But whatever customers were alienated by this authenticity were more than offset by thousands more who embraced the company's honesty and passion.

MISSION TESTED

Patagonia's harder-is-easier mission activates all the magnetic powers of attraction we explored in Chapter 6. In the early 1990s, L. L. Bean, one of their biggest customers, wanted to buy three thousand pairs of shorts to sell at a small discount. Keep in mind that L. L. Bean would pay full wholesale price, and Patagonia would make the same amount of money on each pair of shorts. The order would have "made their year." Nonetheless, Patagonia refused. They felt that discounting—even the tiny 3% price break that L. L. Bean proposed—would weaken their promise to customers: "Patagonia's whole ethos was built around quality, and allowing L. L. Bean to undercut its suggested retail price would have undermined that message."[7] I don't want to paint too rosy a picture. Patagonia made plenty of mistakes along the way, at times behaving in ways Gelles calls "ad hoc, messy, even contradictory."[8] For example, aggressive overexpansion in the late 1980s brought the company to the brink of bankruptcy. Their lenders were on the verge of calling in their loans. CEO Kris McDivitt "negotiated a six-month window with HSBC that would give her a chance to turn the company around." That required a painful 20% layoff; the Chouinards were "particularly anguished" and henceforth called it "Black Wednesday." HSBC pushed for an equity sale. Chouinard refused, "convinced that doing so would ultimately destroy the company." HSBC finally agreed to the plan, but on one condition, that Patagonia cease "making environmental grants while it was working to sort out its debts." CEO Kris McDivitt refused, as "the point of this process was to save Patagonia, not change it; the grants would keep flowing." McDivitt forced HSBC to choose between calling in the loan (and getting nothing) or letting Patagonia be Patagonia. In the end, the bank relented.[9]

The company survived because customers remained loyal to a brand that remained loyal to them. As Chouinard put it, "There's two kinds of growth. One where you grow stronger, and one where you grow fat."[10] Patagonia chose strength.

Patagonia has almost six decades of stories like this. When buttons fell off products from Asian factories, operations manager Hal Harward didn't need to ask what to do. He spent $6,000 per machine on lock-stitch equipment that was slower and more cumbersome but guaranteed buttons that stayed on.[11] No one had to tell him to choose the expensive fix—the philosophy classes had made the answer obvious. This was Patagonia's business model: succeed by making products so good that customers rarely need to buy them.

This same approach to alignment showed inside the company too.

For years, they maintained a "Let My People Go Surfing" policy. When the waves were good, employees could just leave.[12] As unusual as it sounds, it makes perfect sense, once you think about it. What would be the point of a company that was dedicated to outdoor living but trapped its own people in fluorescent-lit cubicles? (The policy was so central that Chouinard later used it as the title of his book about building Patagonia.) Employees who lived the lifestyle designed the products.

Malinda Chouinard proved herself a pioneer once again when a colleague needed to nurse her colicky newborn in 1983. Malinda parked a trailer in the parking lot and invited all Patagonia parents to bring their kids. Two years of productive chaos followed—"like *Lord of the Flies*," one employee recalled—as Malinda figured out what working parents truly needed to feel supported at work. In 1985, Patagonia hired professional staff and created one of America's first corporate childcare centers. As always, the costs were tangible, but the benefits were intangible. Patagonia did it anyway. With the benefit of hindsight, we can quantify the advantages of her farsighted choice. The program costs Patagonia $1 million annually, but 100% of mothers return from maternity leave (versus 60% nationally), and parents who use it have 25% lower turnover.[13]

BEYOND FOUNDER MODE

In the early days, building a mission-driven company often requires "founder mode"[14] and having the courage to insist the company grow in a way consistent with its own values. But in order to last, this must evolve into institutional commitments. Mission drive is the approach to leadership that makes those actions systematic rather than sporadic.

Patagonia has faced this test numerous times. Try to approve a supplier who can't document their environmental practices? Impossible. The Patagonia ethos won't let you. The procurement team will block it, finance won't process it, and if you somehow push it through anyway, you won't be there long.[15] This total alignment has also allowed them to solve one of the most difficult problems that afflict mission-driven companies: succession. Although the legends about Patagonia often focus on its idiosyncratic cofounders, the company itself has had four CEOs in its sixty-year life. (And Patagonia has a succession plan designed to last beyond the eventual death of the Chouinards, a solution we'll discuss in Chapter 11.)

That same institutional strength shows in how they treat employees. In 2008, when the economy crashed and every company was cutting costs, Patagonia didn't touch their healthcare or childcare benefits.[16] It was inconceivable to them, a nonstarter. That kind of commitment acts as a talent magnet, bringing people who truly believe and creating tremendous loyalty, just as it does at Costco. Patagonia has maintained around 4% annual employee turnover for years, in an industry where it's generally much higher.[17]

Every organization develops a culture. It might be paranoid or trusting, exhausted or energized, cynical or idealistic. But not every organization reflects an ethos. While culture emerges automatically, ethos must be built through consistent action. When that happens, the culture that emerges provides a form of leadership powerful enough to operate even when no manager is in the room. As Chouinard put it, "We follow our beliefs, our customers follow us, and positive change tends to follow that."[18]

FIDUCIARY TO WHO?

When you swallow a pill, you are betting your life that the corporation that manufactured it calculated that keeping you alive serves its fiduciary duty to shareholders better than the alternative.[19] The fact that it generally works out should not obscure what a radical leap of faith this is. As we've seen, most companies today recognize primarily (or only!) their fiduciary duty to shareholders.[20] Your survival matters to them only insofar as it serves that duty. The moment the calculation changes, *caveat emptor*.[21] I can't stress it enough: This fiduciary myopia is a choice. And companies are free to make a different one.

Would it annoy you if I say that again? In capital letters?

YOU ARE FREE TO CHOOSE!

To do so, we need to explore what it means to make this choice in practice. In Chapter 5, we saw that the first step toward breaking free of this myopia is to commit to a purpose as a for-profit company beyond simply making money. In this chapter, our challenge is to transform this commitment into an operational discipline that can guide daily behavior, as Sol Price did when he conceived FedMart as a fiduciary to its customers. This is first and foremost an operational question; we will cover the legal aspect in Chapter 9.

Leaders have been grappling with this tension for generations. In 1910, Robert Wood Johnson II took an entry-level job at his father's company, Johnson & Johnson, working in the boiler room. He rose through the ranks and took the reins of the company in 1932, in the depths of the Depression. With unemployment at 25% and competitors slashing everything to survive, Johnson raised all wages by 5% and created hundreds of jobs when he opened a new Chicago factory.[22] His calculation was that quality medicines require workers focused on craft, not survival. J&J emerged from the Depression stronger, while competitors who'd sacrificed quality for savings struggled to rebuild trust.

A decade later, preparing for J&J's 1944 initial public offering (IPO), Johnson codified these proven values in what would become the company's famous Our Credo. He ranked the company's responsibilities in a clear hierarchy:

1. "We believe our first responsibility is to the patients, doctors and nurses, to mothers and fathers and all others who use our products and services."
2. "We are responsible to our employees who work with us throughout the world."
3. "We are responsible to the communities in which we live and work."
4. "Our final responsibility is to our stockholders."

Notice how similar this is to Sol Price's: "Our first duty is to our customers. Our second duty is to our employees. Our third duty is to our stockholders."

Every company must make this same choice, ordering its commitments in line with its mission. This is why the *mission-hopefuls* are so deceptive. They may earnestly want to serve customers, make a great product, or make the world a better place. But their fiduciary commitments tell a different story.

Johnson took no chances. He declared his fiduciary hierarchy before taking the company public, then had it carved in eight-foot limestone blocks at headquarters.[23]

But stone doesn't enforce itself. Johnson was "inflexible" about Credo adherence, and he had unquestioned authority. He didn't hesitate to fire his nephew from the company in 1962. A few years later, his own son was also shown the exit.[24] The message was unmistakable. The Credo was law because Johnson acted as judge, jury, and executioner. For thirty-five years, it worked beautifully.

"ALL THE BALLS ARE RED"

In 1968, R. W. Johnson died. The stone remained, but the will that animated it was gone.

By 1975—less than a decade later—J&J was at war with itself over the meaning of the Credo still carved in those eight-foot limestone blocks at headquarters. At an executive retreat that year, a senior leader stood before his colleagues to explain what he saw as the new reality of business. "We are juggling five balls," he said—one for each Credo commitment. Four were white, one was red. The red ball was profit. You could drop a white ball and survive, he explained, but drop the red ball, and it's fatal. Where Johnson had insisted patients came first, this executive was clear: Profit came first. Heads nodded around the room; this was becoming the standard orthodoxy across corporate America.[25]

From the back of the room, a voice interrupted: "My friend, I am afraid you are wrong."

The room turned to see James Burke, recently promoted to company president, standing to address his colleagues. "Today, *all the balls are red*."

Imagine the stunned silence. Burke's rebuke made clear that the coherence of J&J had fractured and that leadership no longer had a unified vision of what the Credo meant. It was a time for choosing. Within a year, the board made its choice, elevating Burke to CEO, with a mandate to restore the Credo to its rightful place at the center of the company's ethos.

He immediately instituted what he called the "Credo Challenge," in which leaders were faced with difficult hypothetical choices and used the Credo as a guide for making them. To his top managers, he declared, "If we can't live by this document together, then it is an act of pretension and we ought to tear it off the walls."[26]

Burke went further, cascading his Credo challenges throughout J&J. Managers at every level practiced on real-world dilemmas: quality versus quarterly targets, customer risk versus brand protection. He instituted the Credo Survey, assessing how well leaders implemented Credo principles in their decisions.[27] Year after year, leadership rehearsed until these principled choices became institutional muscle memory.

That muscle would be severely tested just a few years later. I'll let James O'Toole tell the story:

> When it was discovered that eight people had died from ingesting cyanide-laced Tylenol capsules (a J&J product), Burke immediately assumed full responsibility for the deaths, pulling $100 million worth of the analgesic off drugstore shelves. He then opened the company's executive suite to the media and dealt with the issue in a transparent manner that, to this day, stands as the model for corporate crisis management. His critics in the financial community said he was a fool to do so, and that his actions would cause the company to go bankrupt. He was urged to put the interests of his shareholders first: *Remember the red ball!* Later, it was discovered that a psychopath had placed the poisoned bottles on the shelves of only a few stores in one city; therefore, the company was not responsible for the deaths. But by publicly assuming responsibility before that fact was known, J&J built such a strong reputation for integrity that it recovered quickly and went on to new heights of profitability.[28]

I don't think it is an exaggeration to say that this is one of the most famous business cases in the world, taught in nearly every business school. But unfortunately, it is taught only as an example of crisis management or business ethics. Rarely do students study the years of diligent work that went into revitalizing and institutionalizing the Credo. As a result, students overlook the farsighted leadership that presaged the crisis and brought the company extraordinary profitability in the years that followed. This is mission drive in action.

But despite the fame of this story, later generations of managers ignored it—even at J&J. By 2002, CEO William Weldon was boasting about "earnings growth with double-digit gains . . . in each of the past 18 years" in his annual letter to shareholders, even as the Credo receded.[29] J&J abolished its twice-yearly compliance reviews after division presidents complained they conflicted with financial goals. Compliance head count was cut in half. Bonuses increasingly depended on hitting financial targets rather than meeting Credo-related goals.[30]

By 2009, the reversal was complete. When Motrin tablets were found defective, J&J had lost its muscle memory. It conducted a "phantom recall" by paying contractors to silently purchase the defective tablets to pull them off shelves. When the tactic was discovered and became a scandal, documents revealed that J&J had given these contractors a script, instructing them to "act like a regular customer. . . . THERE MUST BE NO MENTION OF THIS BEING A RECALL." James Burke would have been horrified.[31]

R. W. Johnson had wanted to see the company's mission and ethos protected at the board level, before the IPO. He would have been baffled by the assertion that J&J existed only to enrich shareholders. Burke strengthened that governance commitment, actively overseeing corporate culture through his Credo Surveys and compliance metrics and requiring the board to periodically review reports on how well the company was living up to its principles.

But between the Burke era and the Weldon era, J&J's board was pulled into the gravitational field of governance "best practices": independent directors, competitive benchmarking, shareholder primacy. They subtly shifted the board's focus from the Credo to shareholders. Experts applauded (e.g., governance rating agency ISS gave J&J their highest possible score in the same year J&J's McNeil division pled guilty to selling adulterated children's Tylenol and Motrin).[32] By 2012, Wharton professor Thomas Donaldson could write without irony that at J&J, managers still talked about patients first, "but there is a red ball that every manager knows about: profit—and they don't let that red ball drop."[33]

During Weldon's decade-long tenure as CEO, scandals and product recalls rocked J&J and cost the company billions of dollars. When he finally departed as CEO, he took with him more than $143 million in total compensation.[34] The company's ethical collapse wasn't merely a succession problem or operational failure. It brings up a number of much deeper questions. Why did the board choose Weldon in the first place? Why did they continue to reward him as scandal after scandal unfolded? We will revisit these board-level questions in Chapter 9. But there's another failure that runs through J&J's entire modern history. Remember 3M's NPVI, which measured innovation but not its harms? J&J suffered from the same blind spot.

For as bad as these scandals were, they are not even the worst. For decades, J&J sold baby powder that internal and external tests sometimes found to contain asbestos,[35] which scientists have shown can cause ovarian cancer.[36] Once again, we know about this because of the release of documents tied to litigation. The documents show that the company's own tests found asbestos in its talc;[37] they failed to disclose positive test results to the US Food and Drug Administration (FDA),[38] and their research director warned they needed to "protect our powder franchise."[39] By 2024, more than sixty-two thousand people suffering from cancer had sued the company,[40] and while this litigation is ongoing, the ultimate cost to J&J is likely to be in the billions of dollars (J&J proposed an $8.9 billion settlement in 2023 to resolve the claims).[41]

How could this have happened at J&J, of all companies?

FALSE PROXIES

Organizations optimize around the things they measure. In *The Lean Startup*, I introduced the term *vanity metrics*: numbers that look impressive but don't predict success. Even worse are metrics that create the illusion of progress while actively undermining the goals they purport to serve. Here I follow Seth Godin in calling these *false proxies*.[42]

Have you ever wondered why customer service seems to be collapsing across the board? In 1976, it was major news when a White

House–commissioned study found that 32% of Americans were dissatisfied with customer service.[43] Companies responded with massive investment. They professionalized customer service as a corporate function, complete with dedicated departments, toll-free numbers, sophisticated software, and rigorous metrics like average handle time (AHT) and number of complaints handled. For decades, these metrics steadily improved, and efficiency gains were celebrated in quarterly reports.

The result? By 2023, a similar survey found that—wait for it—74% of Americans were now frustrated.[44]

The metrics had improved, while the actual experience got twice as bad. How? Financial gravity had quietly transformed customer service from a human relationship into a "cost center." By measuring how long service agents talked to customers instead of how often customers ended the call satisfied, for example, they were looking in the wrong place altogether. The very metrics designed to fix the problem had become the problem.

The tendency to confuse measurement with the goal is called "surrogation" in academic research.[45] When a measure becomes the target, people forget what it was supposed to represent. Call centers optimize handle time, so agents hang up mid-sentence. Software teams maximize lines of code, creating bloated programs. The seduction works because false proxies offer the psychological relief of things like clear targets, visible progress, and freedom from difficult trade-offs. Financial gravity quietly replaces meaningful measures with convenient ones.

This explains J&J's gradual descent. Smooth, predictable growth became a surrogate for improving patient health. The phantom recall and the buried asbestos contamination each kept the numbers moving upward and to the right. The logic of surrogation even creates incentives to suppress bad news and keep it from reaching the top. The scariest part of all may be that the people making these decisions often believe they're still serving the mission. They've simply learned to keep score with whatever's easiest to count.

As we saw in Chapter 4, metrics are a governance issue, not just an operational one. If boards and leaders don't understand their own metrics, they lose control of what their organization becomes. The question isn't whether to measure but how to measure without losing sight of the mission itself.

HOLISTIC METRICS

There are two critical problems with false proxies: They develop blind spots (as in 3M and J&J), and they shortcut decision-making (as the meme says, make "number go up").[46] Both problems are solved by *holistic metrics*, a system that centers mission attainment and human judgment in everything an organization does. Mission-driven companies structure their measurements as diagnostic tools, not as automatic decision-makers. The numbers check achievement of the mission; they never prescribe how to achieve it.

The only way to know that we're creating more value than we capture is to measure the impacts (both benefits and harms) on everyone the organization has a fiduciary commitment to—whether to customers, as Sol Price insisted; to patients, as J&J's Credo promised; or to people and the environment, in Patagonia's case. Mission-driven organizations do this as rigorously as they track shareholder returns.

At J&J, even while a farsighted leader like Burke was preaching the value of the Credo, false proxies were subtly undermining the company's ethos. 3M's NPVI gave the board an early warning sign, a *fever indicator*. (Recall from Chapter 3 that NPVI tracks the percentage of each year's sales from products introduced in the preceding five years.) This indicator gave the board essential information it could use to prevent further damage.

But NPVI had its own blind spot. It measured how much the company was innovating, not whether that innovation was causing harm. As a result, PFAS contamination slipped through for decades, undetected.

J&J could articulate its values but not verify them. 3M could verify its innovation but not its consequences. Each had part of the answer, but both still fell to surrogation. To avoid this temptation requires a far more rigorous approach to measurement, a three-part framework I call *holistic metrics:*

1. **Complete value accounting.** Track all value created, not just what is captured. When Patagonia measures impact, they include worker wages, environmental restoration, product lifespan, even customer repair rates. Their Ironclad Quality Index rates every product with a combined score that blends durability, design, manufacturing, and environmental factors. Their Verified Carbon Intervention Unit applies an internal carbon price to internalize the effects of carbon emissions. These metrics capture the full ecosystem of value, not just dollars in and out.[47]
2. **Fiduciary verification.** For each fiduciary commitment, maintain metrics that track that promise. J&J's Credo declared patients came first, but their metrics tracked earnings growth, not patient outcomes. Without a *fever indicator* tied to patient health, their Credo became unmeasurable and therefore unmanageable. Costco's 92% membership renewal rate, by contrast, provides a continuous guardrail.
3. **Natural tension.** Build in metrics that fight each other. In its heyday, Southwest Airlines set its goals using a fourfold combination: lowest cost, highest employee satisfaction, highest customer satisfaction, and highest profits.[48] They couldn't just slash staff to cut costs because employee satisfaction would immediately flag the damage. They couldn't gouge customers for profit because customer satisfaction would reveal the betrayal. That sort of tension between metrics prevents any single number from becoming a surrogate.

One important caveat: Metrics can only ever bring tensions to the surface. Resolving them productively requires leadership. The best companies create *structured collision points* in the form of venues where competing priorities must be resolved through ethos, not expediency.

BUILD STRUCTURAL SAFEGUARDS

The way metrics are taught today, almost every company is vulnerable to surrogation. Patagonia fell into the trap during the outsourcing mania of the early 2000s. Pursuing lower costs, they expanded to buy from more than one hundred factories. By 2010, they admitted "we no longer knew many of the people with whom we were dealing or what conditions were like on the factory floor."[49] The cost savings looked spectacular on spreadsheets, while quality collapsed and customers fled.

This crisis caused a reckoning. Vowing never to repeat the mistake, they built *structural safeguards* to hold themselves accountable. They began with an audit process for all vendors, combined with a veto system that allowed social and environmental responsibility (SER) teams to block any sourcing deal, no matter how profitable it might seem. By the late 2000s, this system had cleaned up their Tier-1 suppliers, consisting of finished-goods factories. The company was under no obligation to go further. They did anyway.[50]

In 2011, they voluntarily extended their audits to Tier-2 suppliers, such as fabric mills and sources of raw materials.[51] That's when they found the horror: Taiwanese mills where migrant workers paid $7,000 broker fees just to get jobs, then had their passports confiscated and lived trapped in debt. At the time, one-quarter of Patagonia's fabric came from Taiwan.

The SER team's veto power meant sourcing couldn't simply promise to "work on improvements." Patagonia partnered with Verité, the global supply chain labor rights NGO; convened suppliers in 2014; and issued new standards: There would be no more recruitment fees, past broker fees would be fully reimbursed to the workers, and all passports would be returned. Comply or lose our business. Suppliers complied.[52]

Ever since, the business, quality, social, and environmental departments meet every week at Patagonia headquarters. Each has veto power over any supplier decision. Senior management backs this system completely. Overruling these vetoes in pursuit of profit is not countenanced.[53] A sourcing manager finds a factory that could save millions, with perfect margins and perfect delivery times? If SER says no, the deal's dead. No appeals. No emergency meetings. Dead. Same with quality. And business, for that matter. All four departments must agree.

The first time I heard about this, it made me uncomfortable. Many of us have plenty of scars from recalcitrant gatekeepers in standard corporations. But this is different. Because all four teams are aligned around the mission and the ethos of Patagonia, they have the tools they need for resolution when conflicts arise. And as a result, the business is far stronger than if these conflicts were resolved by meager compromise.

"DON'T BE EVIL" VS. THE QUARTERLY REPORT

Remember Google's "Don't be evil" motto? Whatever happened to that?

I vividly remember talking to a longtime Googler who had recently retired. He had watched the company transform from an idealistic startup with the motto "Don't be evil" into something sadly different by the end of his tenure. He felt this cultural erosion was almost inexplicable given how well intentioned and serious everyone seemed to be about the company's mission, from leadership on down. And yet year after year, things got gradually worse. He described it as a creeping mediocrity that infected the organization. Another Googler, Ian Hickson, an eighteen-year veteran, summarized it this way: "Decisions went from being made for the benefit of users, to the benefit of Google, to the benefit of whoever was making the decision."[54]

The mission drift eroded both their ethics and their ability to execute. He reminded me that in 2017, Google invented the transformer architecture that today powers ChatGPT. All eight authors of that breakthrough paper eventually left the company; the technology had to be commercialized elsewhere.[55] "Google may yet win the A.I. race," he admitted, "but the delayed start was incredibly costly."

In 2015, the motto was quietly changed to "Do the right thing."

By 2018, it was "all but removed from its corporate code of conduct." Ross LaJeunesse, an eleven-year Google veteran, wrote, "Beating earnings expectations every quarter became the key priority."[56]

The retired Googler I was talking to shook his head: How had all their good intentions led to this?

As we explored the reasons behind this change, I asked him to answer a hypothetical question. "What is the probability that Google will file its next quarterly report on time?" He laughed. "Certain." I asked him to quantify it. "90%? 95%?" He replied without hesitation, "100%." I asked, "As certain as the sun will rise tomorrow?" He agreed.

Then I asked another question: "What is the probability that, in the next ten years, Google's systems will contribute to someone's death, and the company will prioritize damage control over taking accountability?" He recoiled. "Come on, that's a really unfair question. I doubt they would do that on purpose."

I pressed for an answer. "Are you certain? 100%? As certain as the sun will rise?" He wanted to say it was impossible, but I could see him already thinking through scenarios. After all, Google paid $170 million for illegally collecting children's data on YouTube. It had been fined €1.49 billion for abusive advertising practices. The company had even been sued twice for betraying its "Don't be evil" pledge—once by shareholders, once by former employees. (They settled both suits.[57])

He couldn't even get himself to 95%, let alone "as certain as the sun will rise." Out loud, he mused, anguished, "What if the self-driving car hits someone?"

We treat this state of affairs as if it were a natural law. But this blinds us to how absurd it is. Are human beings somehow wired to care deeply about quarterly reports yet easily confused by questions as fundamental as manslaughter? No! That's ridiculous. The reason we can be so certain that a public company will file its reports on time is that it maintains a massive, incredibly expensive, and rigorous apparatus to make sure it does—on time, every time.

"Don't be evil" remained just a slogan. As Hickson concluded, "The deterioration of Google's culture will eventually become irreversible because the kinds of people whom you need to act as moral compass are the same kinds of people who don't join an organization without a moral compass."[58]

THEY ARE LYING TO YOU

You can decode what companies truly care about by watching what they do consistently. When a company says it's committed to something, look for the massive apparatus they've built to back up that statement. If there isn't one, they're lying, no matter what the individuals involved may feel. If a company is good at filing reports but mediocre at creating products or maintaining ethics or treating its employees and customers well, it's not an accident. It reflects which intentions have been *institutionalized* and which have not.[59]

"Lying" may sound harsh, but this is the reality of organizations that make promises they cannot keep. Without the discipline of mission drive—the systems, metrics, and safeguards that make mission attainment the only path to profit—companies are merely *mission-hopeful.* The people who lead them may sincerely want to keep their promises. But wanting isn't enough.

Managers may pat themselves on the back about their outstanding credo, but the vast majority of decisions an organization makes involve no managers at all. Watch what happens when no one's watching—that's where companies reveal their true character. Management creates the conditions. Culture is what grows in response. It may be strong or weak, healthy or malignant, credo or asbestos in the baby powder.

The companies that endure are powered by cultures more durable than carved limestone: People who've internalized the mission so completely that betraying it would feel like betraying themselves. Like health, this can be cultivated but not commanded. The question is how.

Chapter Eight

THE INVISIBLE LEADER

> Mr. Rowntree, by his vivid statement of purpose, has found a way of making all his employees share in a common purpose. That common purpose rather than Mr. Rowntree himself is their . . . invisible leader.
>
> —**Mary Parker Follett**
> describing the Rowntree chocolate factory in
> *Some Discrepancies in Leadership Theory and Practice*
> 1928

In my work as a consultant, I often spend long days running workshops and meeting with executives. After the work is done, one of the things I most enjoy is talking shop over coffee. It's a chance to learn what working at the company is really like. Some years ago, I went out to dinner with a group of employees at a company where I'd just finished a multiday workshop implementing Lean Startup practices. Everyone had seemed engaged and enthusiastic. Many of the teams had accomplished real breakthroughs.

But what happened around the table that night told a different story. One of the company's ads came on the TV over the bar. It promised it was the kind of place where your work mattered, something along the lines of "where scientists and engineers collaborate on product breakthroughs to make the world a better place." The table went quiet. Then someone laughed. Not a real laugh but that short exhale people make when they can't believe what they're seeing.

"Who do these guys think they're fooling?" someone said.

"I'd really love to work at that company," another added, stabbing at her salad. A younger engineer stared at his phone. "I sent that exact ad to my mom when I got hired," he said quietly.

I was shocked. I guess I had been taken in by the ads too. When I asked why they were scoffing, the woman with the salad put down her fork: "We all came here for that," she said, nodding at the screen, "but the people making these ads and the people who decide our promotions? Different planets."

When I asked what actually got people promoted, they all started talking at once. Hitting targets. Cutting costs. Being careful not to make waves. Market share, market share, market share.

No one seemed bitter, just tired. These were talented people who'd joined their company to do meaningful work in a place where it turned out the mission had atrophied into packaging. I left those workshops proud of everything the teams I'd coached had accomplished. But in the years that followed, I watched in horror as that disconnect slowly corroded those gains.

I call this state of affairs *incoherence*.

An incoherent organization is one where what gets rewarded contradicts what gets proclaimed. Where the values on the wall are betrayed by daily reality. Some such companies claim they value innovation but ostracize those whose experiments fail. Others promise work-life balance while ensuring only workaholics are invited to strategy meetings. Still others swear they put customers first but praise employees who engage in deceptive sales practices. Departments clash due to opposing cultures—product aspires to be Apple, but finance aspires to be Goldman Sachs. The result is a company at war with itself. And like a human body suffering from an autoimmune disease, it becomes increasingly weak and vulnerable.

A *coherent* company, by contrast, is one where the company's expressed values are in alignment with its actual practices. In the previous chapter, we explored how to install an ethos through principled management. That's a necessary foundation, but coherence lives between the lines of the org chart, in the thousands of daily choices made when no manager is present. This is the domain of culture, the "invisible leader" that guides actions, even when nobody is watching.

Most people have never experienced the flow state of working in a coherent organization. Everything clicks, like an athlete in the zone. The people who work "the right way" are the ones who get ahead. This doesn't mean that only one type of person succeeds or that the company can't evolve and change—far from it. It just means that the path to success runs through the company's actual values, not around them. Perfect coherence is difficult to achieve and requires constant vigilance, but even the pursuit of it creates a dramatically healthier organization.

VALUES ON THE WALL, CHAOS IN THE HALLS

At an incoherent company, employees stop believing that what they joined to do is possible. As that belief erodes, cynicism takes root. Passion drains away, replaced by quiet quitting and mediocre work. The best talent leaves for companies whose values they can believe in, while those who stay stop caring about the customers they serve or the products they build. The "values" become a residue of past aspirations, orphaned on the walls. Those cynical comments over dinner? They're not just venting but symptoms of an organization eating itself alive.

This disconnect between proclaimed values and actual behavior can destroy entire organizations. In 2009, Netflix published a presentation called "Culture: Freedom & Responsibility," now widely regarded as one of the most influential documents in Silicon Valley. It makes this point with a single slide that shows Enron's values, engraved in marble in their lobby: "Integrity. Communication. Respect. Excellence."[1]

Figure 8.1.

The marble was solid. The values were fiction. While "Integrity" sat carved in stone, executives were busy committing accounting fraud. And remember, at the time, Enron was America's seventh-largest company.

Why does this happen? Because values carved in marble aren't values at all. They're decoration. And as much as we might wish otherwise, people do not take their orders from decorations. Instead, they follow what Mary Parker Follett called *the invisible leader*—the "common purpose" that guides actions even when no manager is present. The Enron disaster would have been no surprise to her at all.

Follett was a pioneering management theorist of the 1920s whose ideas were at least a century ahead of their time.[2] Check this out: "Authority should go with knowledge and experience, that is where obedience is due no matter whether it is up or down the line" (1926).[3] She championed "power-with" instead of "power-over" (1924)[4] and saw workers as sources of wisdom, not just labor (1918).[5]

She wrote, "Leadership is not defined by the exercise of power but by the capacity to increase the sense of power among those led. The most essential work of the leader is to create more leaders" (1933).[6] Her work was so far ahead of its time that Warren Bennis (writing sixty years after her death) would credit her as inspiring "just about everything written today about leadership and organizations." The great management theorist Peter Drucker went even further, calling her simply "the prophet of management."[7]

Follett was a contemporary of Frederick Winslow Taylor. Yet her work receded almost entirely from public awareness, while Taylor went on to become the most famous management theorist of all time. (Follett's work was not republished until 1995.) It is perhaps the greatest what-if in the whole management canon: How might the world be different today if leaders had listened to Follett instead?[8]

What Follett understood—and what Enron missed—is that real values live in culture, not commands. Because culture is an emergent property, many leaders struggle to cultivate it actively. But although culture cannot be commanded, it *can* be fostered. To do this requires specific tools that create coherence at every level—tools that finally operationalize what Follett envisioned.

THE ALIGNMENT METHOD

The challenge with culture is that different leaders interpret it differently, creating pockets of excellence alongside areas of drift. What starts as a unified culture can fragment into departmental subcultures or outright civil war.

The *alignment method* takes what I've learned over the years about how the best organizations create consistency across every team and every decision and folds it into a clear system for avoiding the pitfall of fragmentation. It's made up of three elements:

1. **The culture bank.** A tool to make visible the intangible elements of culture building. I use the metaphor of a "bank account" on purpose. When someone makes a decision aligned with the company's ethos, they're making a deposit. When they don't, they make a withdrawal. This shared vocabulary is a powerful tool everyone in the organization can use when evaluating any decision.

2. **The leader's guide.** Since culture forms even when no managers are present, everyone—no matter their rank—needs to know how to lead within the culture. The leader's guide is a living document of real stories showing what ethos-aligned leadership looks like in practice: Here's what Sarah did, here's how it embodied our mission, and here's how she was rewarded for it. These specific examples from named colleagues can then be used in every place in the organization where standards or communication are needed.
3. **The two-way review.** Most companies harvest thousands of stories every year in their employee review process. Then they throw them away. That "one-way" review is a process aimed primarily at judging individual performance. But the two-way review recognizes that these same stories, seen collectively, also represent a judgment of the company and its culture. This surfaces problems before they become mission drift—or worse.

Like the *build-measure-learn* method described in *The Lean Startup*, these tools work as a continuous cycle. The *culture bank* defines what counts as a deposit, the *leader's guide* shows what those deposits look like in practice, and the *two-way review* ensures the people making deposits are the ones getting promoted.

HERE, EVERYTHING'S BETTER

Founded in 1905, H-E-B is a Texas grocery powerhouse with over $46.5 billion in annual revenue and more than 430 stores across Texas and Mexico.[9] During a severe winter storm in Texas in 2021, an H-E-B store in Leander lost power while hundreds of anxious shoppers were stocking up on essentials. According to Tim Hennessy, there was a "collective groan" when the lights went out. He and his wife were standing in a checkout line twenty deep. After about fifteen minutes of confusion, something extraordinary happened. The cashier started waving people through the checkout with their carts, wishing them a safe drive home. Hennessy was bewildered: "At first,

Deb and I were a bit confused, and I asked, 'How or who do we pay for our groceries?' "[10]

The answer was that they wouldn't. Unable to process payments without power, the store manager had made an on-the-spot decision to call all the customers to the front of the store and then let them leave with their full carts without paying. "And it hit us—like, wow, they're just letting us walk out the door," Hennessy recalled. Watching shoppers exit with "carts piled high with diapers, milk, and crackers—all free," the moment was so moving that many customers, including Hennessy, were brought to tears.[11]

This decision wasn't dictated by some corporate memo. It emerged from sixteen years of institutional muscle memory. Since Hurricane Rita in 2005, H-E-B had been building its emergency response capability, establishing a command center in San Antonio, and developing an explicit philosophy: "When you feed half the people in Texas, it's your responsibility to be open during times of crisis."[12] Every store manager knows that in an emergency, feeding people comes first.

This principle was battle tested during Hurricane Harvey in 2017. H-E-B arranged for planes to fly in truck drivers, reopened seventy-nine of eighty-three stores within five days, deployed mobile kitchens serving 2,500 free meals per hour, and contributed over $6 million in total relief.[13] The same values guided them through the 2022 inflation crisis, when egg prices soared from $1 to over $4 per dozen. For months, H-E-B deliberately sold eggs below cost, losing millions. As H-E-B president Craig Boyan explained, "We are trying to be a shock absorber . . . especially for low-income Texans."[14]

On that winter night in 2021, the Leander store manager didn't need permission or a manual. Years of consistent organizational behavior, from Rita to eggflation and every day in between, had long since instilled exactly what H-E-B's "unwavering belief that each and every person counts" meant in practice.[15] The philosophy had become reflex. In any crisis, when the storm passes, customers remember. H-E-B is named for the original founder's son, Howard Edward Butt, who took over as CEO in 1919, but customers often mistakenly believe it stands for "Here, everything's better."[16]

THE CULTURE BANK

That H-E-B store manager made a big deposit in the company's *culture bank*, the metaphorical accounting system I introduced earlier that tracks actions that either build or deplete organizational trustworthiness. This is a way of thinking about culture that I first learned from pioneers of strong culture companies like Devoted Health's Todd Park and Starbucks' Howard Schultz.[17] The idea is simple but powerful: Every action either builds or degrades culture. The actions that strengthen culture, leading to a more trustworthy organization, are "deposits." Opposite actions are "withdrawals." Many culture bank deposits have easily identifiable costs in terms of R&D, investing in employees, or making things right for an unhappy customer. When H-E-B absorbs losses on eggs to protect low-income families or gives away groceries in a storm, these costs show up immediately on the balance sheet. But the payback, the invisible trust inspired by the costly choice, compounds like interest. Over time, it manifests as customer loyalty that survives price increases, employee retention through tough times, and community support when you need permits for a new store.

By framing trust in banking terms—deposits, withdrawals, balances—we create terminology that can compete with financial metrics in decision-making. When faced with a trade-off between short-term gains and long-term trust, employees now have a familiar framework: Would this be a deposit or a withdrawal?

The culture bank exposes the great flaw in the modern system of objectives and key results (OKRs).[18] When given a quantitative objective, employees can willfully and repeatedly boost their personal numbers by borrowing against the company's trustworthiness. Even worse, in a competitive compensation environment, those who refuse to make these trades are at a permanent disadvantage. The OKR system rewards those who spend down the company's trust without even tracking that it's happening. The culture bank provides a counterweight. Ship buggy software to hit the deadline? That's a withdrawal. Oversell a product's capabilities to close the quarter? Another withdrawal.

The next time someone proposes damaging your company's long-term health by acting in an untrustworthy manner, you'll see it more clearly. This is not about hardheaded "making money" versus soft-hearted "caring." This person is proposing the liquidation of a critical asset. Say so.

THE TODD PARK RULE

Here's a simple rule I learned from Devoted Health CEO Todd Park: **Don't make withdrawals from the culture bank. Only make deposits.**

Everyone reacts the same way when hearing this for the first time: It sounds too difficult. Only deposits? Impossible. And yet this seemingly rigid rule actually simplifies decision-making. When a company permits occasional withdrawals, it creates endless debates about when exceptions are justified. Is this crisis big enough? Is that deadline important enough? These debates are exhausting and demoralizing.[19]

The clarity of eliminating withdrawals is liberating. There's nothing to debate. This rule empowers everyone to push back against trust-damaging shortcuts. It gives institutional backing to the often unheralded people I call *torchbearers*, the ones who relentlessly uphold the company's mission even when nobody's watching. Engineers who understand both speed and safety. Brand marketers who treat reputation as sacred. Product managers who push back against feature bloat. In most management systems, these torchbearers are under constant siege from people wielding spreadsheets. When someone proposes cutting corners, the no-withdrawals rule means anyone can confidently respond, "We don't do that. We never sacrifice our trustworthiness on purpose."

This doesn't mean being a pushover. Firing underperformers who've been given fair warning, setting firm deadlines, or saying no to unreasonable requests aren't withdrawals. When done transparently and with integrity, those are deposits in the form of accountability. It's the betrayals of trust that are withdrawals, such as lying about why someone was let go or breaking promises to avoid hard conversations.

To be clear, every organization will make mistakes. Unintentional withdrawals are inevitable. Servers crash or a shipment arrives late or a product contains an unforeseen defect. A clear no-withdrawals policy distinguishes between honest mistakes (which happen) and deliberate compromises (which shouldn't). It's the intentional withdrawals that truly bankrupt a culture, especially when they become habitual.

But how do we ensure these deposits and their stories spread throughout the organization? That's where the leader's guide comes in.

THE LEADER'S GUIDE

Duolingo calls their culture bank the "Trust Battery" (because it's always being charged or depleted).[20] It is powered by hundreds of stories that have gelled to become the startup's lore. I know some of these stories because CEO Luis von Ahn told them to me directly. But Duolingo's employees don't need personal conversations with the CEO to learn them. They're all documented in the Duolingo Handbook.[21]

One entry describes a senior executive the company had been trying to hire for over a year: "They aced their interviews and had a strong résumé but were disrespectful to the driver who picked them up from the airport. That single moment told us what we needed to know. Excellence isn't just what you do; it's how you treat others."[22] Another documents their "ruthless prioritization" when it comes to cutting features if they don't deliver meaningful impact on their mission, "no matter how much effort has already gone into it."[23] The handbook shows exactly what led to the decision.

The *leader's guide* is what I call the product of this systematic recording of crucial stories. Lore is humanity's oldest technology for transmitting knowledge.[24] Oral traditions predate writing by untold thousands of years. Every organization naturally develops lore that teaches "how we do things around here," but most organizations leave the accumulation of lore to chance. The leader's guide, by contrast, is a valued asset, deliberately compiled.

Sometimes it's an actual book, physical or digital. Modern companies have experimented with embodying it in other digital artifacts. At Devoted, they have "a storytelling culture, the most powerful part of which is a channel in Slack for the whole company, called

#memberwins. Employees from all across the country tell each other stories about something they witnessed a Devotee doing. It creates this incredibly powerful magnetic field of belief."[25]

The leader's guide shows every employee what leadership within the culture looks like, regardless of their formal title. These stories are more than just a teaching aid. Howard Schultz once taught me to think of organizations like a vintage or antique item. They develop "provenance" that can't be manufactured or faked, which is the source of authenticity that powers a strong culture that has, as he says, "resistance to temptation."[26] The leader's guide is a tool for preserving that uncounterfeitable asset of authenticity by carefully curating the stories the organization tells about itself.

But be forewarned: The leader's guide only maintains its power if it stays fresh, populated with contemporary examples. Specific, honest, named stories are required.

During one of my visits to GE's famous research center in Niskayuna, I got to sit at Thomas Edison's desk. It was a moving experience. And yet all that day, I observed corporate obstacles to experimentation that would have made Edison furious. Thinking about the power of lore, later in the day, I used Edison's example to motivate executives to change their ways. I knew the famous stories. But—cue the cynical laugh—people looked at me like I was attempting to channel a ghost. Which, in a way, I suppose I was.

Without systematic refresh, cultures fossilize into museum pieces. That's what the two-way review is for.

THE TWO-WAY REVIEW

Every year, companies large and small invest significant time in performance reviews. They document achievements and evaluate progress in order to make decisions about incentives and assignments. But

MANAGEMENT WITHOUT MANAGERS: To learn more about how Answer.AI has used artificial intelligence to implement the techniques in this chapter from an early stage and without professional managers, scan the QR code or go to incorruptible.co/without-managers.

one-way reviews, used only to judge individual performance, are like mining for gold and keeping only the dirt. The gold nuggets are the stories that reveal how the culture actually works.

For every employee who's ever thought, "Am I crazy or is this place broken?" the *two-way review* reveals the answer. It's called the "two-way" because it judges in both directions: The company evaluates the employee, and the collected stories help evaluate the company's overall culture. When multiple reviews show the same "individual" problem, that's organizational diagnosis, not personal failure. Two-way reviews of those cynical employees from our opening, laughing bitterly at their company's ads, would have surfaced that disconnect years earlier.

The two-way review transforms scattered anecdotes into organizational wisdom, taking advantage of work already happening. Here's how to do it:

First, use the existing one-way review process. The leader's guide should define what excellence looks like. It's not a separate document but the actual standard for reviews. If current review criteria don't reflect the ethos shown in the guide, realign them so they do.
Second, flag defining moments that exemplify ethos in action. Not just successes but any time the company found a way to "figure it out"—including instructive failures, difficult trade-offs, and creative solutions to impossible problems. These are the stories people already share at lunch; now we're collecting them.
Third, refresh the leader's guide with the best of these stories for the following review cycle. Look for patterns or outliers. They may signal drift or show that the culture needs to evolve. Either way, the updated guide helps the organization actively adapt.

Here's what this looks like in practice. A customer service rep discovers a billing error that has overcharged thousands of customers by tiny amounts most would never notice. She sacrifices her metrics to document the issue and propose a fix, knowing it will cost the company significant revenue and make her department's numbers look worse. In a traditional review, this might warrant a line item: "Identified billing discrepancy." In some companies, the damage to the metrics might even warrant punishment. In the two-way review, her manager flags this as a defining moment. An employee chose long-term trust over short-term metrics, embodying the company's true character. Next year, when another employee faces a similar choice, they'll have that much more confidence that they are doing the right thing. That's how culture is shaped: through proof that the right action pays off.

The two-way review has a dual mandate, similar to comparable procedures in finance. First, it serves an audit function: verifying stories are accurate, preventing good storytellers from gaming the system, and checking the underlying facts to avoid bias. Second, it spots trends before they become crises. When five different departments struggle with the same problem, that's critical organizational feedback. Is the same tension arising repeatedly? That's an interesting signal of incoherence that can now be addressed before it metastasizes.

Stories from employees go into the leader's guide; the guide shapes employee behavior, and that behavior gets highlighted in the stories surfaced in next year's reviews. It's *build-measure-learn* applied to culture itself. Unlike static mission statements gathering dust, this system lives and breathes with the organization. Each cycle makes the company's true values more visible and the path to success clearer.

A SELF-REINFORCING SYSTEM

I once did a workshop with executives at Walmart's headquarters in Bentonville, Arkansas. One of the participants half joked, "Sam Walton couldn't even get a job here anymore. Selling goods out of the back of his truck would violate twenty-nine different policies." Cue yet more uncomfortable laughter.

Now keep in mind, pictures of Sam Walton are everywhere at Walmart HQ. His aphorisms are engraved on many walls. But ask some middle manager to show flexibility in some policy because of what Walton did decades ago? His origin story felt as relevant as tales of covered wagons. Sam Walton became a ghost. I don't want that for you.

Instead, create a self-reinforcing system. The culture bank gives everyone a framework for evaluating decisions. The leader's guide captures and shapes the company's ethos-related lore. And the two-way review gathers fresh, authentic examples of ethos in action while aligning rewards to match. This cycle transforms company culture from something that happens accidentally to something that's intentionally shaped and maintained. The result is true coherence.

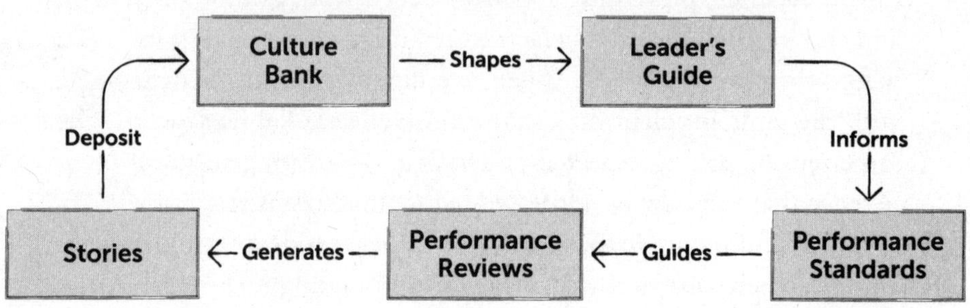

Figure 8.2.

But who makes sure all this happens? We need to ensure that these tools become more than just another corporate initiative that fades away after the initial excitement. Enter the *department of corporate purpose.*

THE DEPARTMENT OF CORPORATE PURPOSE

I have a confession to make. That company with the cynical laughter and the terrific TV ads? They had a leader's guide. I know because I helped them draft it. We'd spent months developing a beautiful document filled with inspiring stories and clear values. Six months later, I returned to find it gathering dust. "Who's responsible for keeping this alive?" I asked. The uncomfortable silence told me everything.

This wasn't an isolated failure. The tools we've explored in this chapter are each powerful on their own. But without an institutional home, they become the corporate equivalent of New Year's resolutions: embraced with enthusiasm in January, forgotten by March.

The root of this problem is that no one in the organization is definitively responsible for maintaining alignment between ethos and action. Marketing promises one thing, operations delivers another. HR preaches values that leadership ignores. Employee communications, brand marketing, recruiting, and investor relations each tell a different story about what the company stands for. And that's just the internal fragmentation. When the company's external brand and internal culture feel like different organizations, who's accountable? In most companies, no one. We would never accept this with finance or legal, where we demand centralized responsibility with corresponding authority. So it should be with coherence. We need a dedicated function with the authority and responsibility to maintain coherence across the entire organization. I call it the department of corporate purpose.

This function consolidates what's currently scattered across marketing, product, HR, investor relations, and customer support. It teaches the culture bank framework, helping everyone evaluate major decisions as deposits or withdrawals. It maintains the leader's guide with fresh stories from this year's two-way reviews, not last decade's mythology. It surfaces patterns across performance reviews, compensation structures, hiring criteria, and promotion decisions to catch drift before it becomes decay.

Just as the CFO ensures financial coherence across all departments, whoever owns corporate purpose ensures mission coherence. Consider how finance already operates: They're in the room during planning, not just reviewing budgets after they're spent. Corporate purpose works the same way. When marketing develops a new campaign, they participate in the creative brief in just the same way as finance approves the budget. When HR restructures compensation, they must design incentives that reward ethos-aligned behavior. Mission-driven companies already have someone who fills this role; they are the executive-level equivalent of the *torchbearer*. In a startup's early days, this is invariably a founder. As the company scales, configurations vary widely. Sometimes the founder/CEO takes this on directly, delegating more operational responsibilities to others. But sometimes the CEO is fundamentally a chief operator and needs support, which is an advantage of multi-founder teams.

As companies scale, the need for support always expands beyond the capability of a single person. Because this function has lacked a name until now, few companies today have assembled all its components into one dedicated department. Instead, it tends to be the secondary responsibility of a chief marketing officer, chief technology officer, or chief people officer. Of course, coherence can never be simply delegated. Just as in finance, it eventually requires a CFO and a team, but the CEO and full C-suite still bear financial accountability.

No matter the configuration, every organization should have this simple goal: that every day, *somebody* is thinking about how to ensure every H-E-B store manager knows that giving away groceries in a crisis is exactly what the company stands for.

Purpose without power is just poetry. Give it teeth, and it becomes destiny.

GITLAB: "IF IT'S NOT IN THE HANDBOOK, IT DOESN'T EXIST"

GitLab powers the software infrastructure behind your bank account, your Netflix stream, and the apps on your smartphone. With nearly $800 million in annual revenue, fifty million users worldwide, and enterprise customers ranging from Southwest Airlines to Nvidia, it's become one of the most influential companies most people have never heard of.[27] They've achieved something even more impressive: cultural coherence that has scaled from nine people in a garage to more than two thousand employees.[28]

GitLab practices a level of radical transparency that would make most conventional executives shudder. Their entire employee handbook, strategic plans, salary bands, and even internal discussions about product development are publicly visible online.[29] And they've maintained this ethos of transparency even as a public company with a multibillion-dollar valuation. As founder Sid Sijbrandij told me, instead of defaulting to "close everything down" (typical legal advice), the company's chief legal officer said, "You know what? I think we can do it. I think we can keep the vast majority of our transparency without incurring additional risk."[30]

While competitors jealously guard their source code, GitLab's is open source. By contributing to the commons, they've attracted more than four thousand contributors who improve their product without being paid, generating trust that accelerates enterprise sales and building community loyalty so strong that customers stay without vendor lock-in.[31] This radical openness extends to every aspect of their operations.

Transparency is easy to celebrate in good times. Now let's see what this ethos looks like during a crisis.

When an engineer accidentally deleted six hours of customer data in January 2017, the stakes were enormous. Mission-critical operations for thousands of companies hung in the balance. The engineer immediately posted in the company chat, "Look, people, I've made a big mistake, and we have an incident."[32] Then GitLab did something unthinkable. They livestreamed the entire recovery process on YouTube. It was a stunning demonstration of their ethos of transparency. No lawyers, no spin, just engineers working frantically while the world watched. Industry observers gave "huge props," noting that such radical honesty is exactly "how you rebuild trust" after failure. But this wasn't heroic leadership making a bold choice. As CEO Sid Sijbrandij later reflected, "Being transparent has brought a lot of benefits. . . . Maybe that's because it's ingrained in the whole [GitLab] organization."[33] Their ethos guided them through the storm.

At the heart of their system sits a true innovation: the handbook-first doctrine. GitLab solved the age-old problem of stale documentation with an absolute rule. As Sijbrandij explains, "Don't change the process first, and then view the documentation as a lower priority task. . . . At GitLab, we write things down first."[34] No decision is real until it's in the handbook. The rule has teeth. Nobody can send out a policy change as a bare memo or casual message and expect it to stick because all Slack messages are deleted after ninety days. Hence the motto, "If it's not in the handbook, it doesn't exist."[35]

This forcing function transformed their handbook into what Sijbrandij calls "the operating system of the company."[36] At almost four million words and growing by more than twenty updates daily, this public, searchable repository contains every decision that affects how GitLab operates.[37] There are no private memos, no hallway edicts, and no "unwritten rules" that only insiders know. Instead of hunting for tribal knowledge, employees can look up any policy instantly—and when they ask colleagues for help, the response is typically a handbook link. You can explore it yourself at handbook.gitlab.com.

But a handbook alone doesn't create coherence. The real innovation is how GitLab makes their ethos operational through systematic reinforcement. As Sijbrandij observes, "Many companies say that their values are really important to them. But then you ask, how many ways do you have to reinforce them? And they can name about three. At GitLab, we have twenty-two ways to reinforce our values."[38]

GITLAB'S TWENTY-TWO WAYS TO REINFORCE VALUES—AN EXCERPT FROM THE GITLAB HANDBOOK

Whatever behavior you reward will become your values. We reinforce our values by:

1. Criteria we use for promotions and communicate to the whole company on announcement.
2. What we select for during hiring.
3. What we emphasize during on-boarding.
4. Criteria we use for our annual compensation review.
5. What we refer to when making decisions.
6. The example the E-group sets for the company since a fish rots from the head down.
7. What we expect from all team members, as ambassadors for our values.
8. Keeping them up to date with a stream of commits that add details.
9. Behavior we give each other 360 feedback on.
10. Behavior we compliment.
11. Criteria we use for discretionary bonuses.
12. What we include in our offer letters
13. Criteria we use to manage underperformance.
14. What we do when we let people go.

15. Giving value awards during GitLab Summit.
16. Providing GitLab team members and qualified individuals transparency into all aspects of the company through the CEO Shadow Program to enable them to better engage and collaborate cross-functionally.
17. Linking the takeaways of courses to our values, like we did for the Crucial Conversations training.
18. The default settings of the software we use (for example: Speedy meetings, document sharing, agendas, etc.)
19. Reinforcing our values with features in GitLab—for example, the Iterations feature.
20. Applying one of our values to virtual backgrounds in video calls.
21. Our GitLab Song Book, the song lyrics often mention GitLab values.
22. Regularly conduct a values exercise at the e-group off-site.[39]

As you might expect by now, GitLab is a sterling example of a company that benefits from the magnetic powers we discussed in Chapter 6. Of course GitLab attracts top talent; people see exactly what they're joining. Of course they build customer loyalty; authentic commitment creates trust. Of course they accelerate innovation; more than four thousand contributors improve the product daily.[40] These aren't surprises but the natural outcomes of an ethos consistently lived.

Not every company needs GitLab's radical transparency. That particular value wouldn't be authentic to every organization's strengths or mission. But every company can choose the path of ethos with the same coherence, creative solutions, and dedication that GitLab demonstrates.

The numbers tell the story: a $15 billion initial public offering (IPO),[41] more than half of the Fortune 100 as customers, and a 123% net retention rate (meaning existing customers increase their spending year over year). GitLab is a company where cynicism can't take root because culture strengthens rather than weakens with scale.

ALL THE STARS WE STEAL FROM THE NIGHT SKY

We must end on a sober note. The trust GitLab has painstakingly earned also makes the company a prize worth capturing. Its $7.7

billion valuation is a rounding error compared to the Goliaths surrounding it.[42] Google is already one of the company's largest shareholders.[43] Microsoft acquired their largest rival, GitHub, in 2018.[44] GitLab stands as the last major independent company in its competitive category.

GitLab cannot be acquired or pressured by outside investors—for now. That's because Sid Sijbrandij currently serves as its *mission guardian* via his control of special "supervoting" shares, a technique we will explore in detail in the next chapter.

But in March 2023, Sid announced he had been diagnosed with osteosarcoma, a rare form of bone cancer.[45] As befits an advocate for transparency, Sid courageously shared the details of his diagnosis and treatment with investors and employees. When the cancer recurred in 2024, he stepped down as CEO to focus on treatment while remaining executive chair.[46] As I write this, the cancer has not metastasized, and he shared with me the good news that he's doing well. But no company should have to depend on founder longevity for its mission to survive.

By the time you read this, will GitLab have been forcibly acquired by a larger company, as its rival GitHub was? Will its transparency and coherence survive?

Every successful mission-driven company must eventually face this test. The more powerful the internal coherence, the more valuable a target it becomes to those who would commandeer it. Success alone will never, ever be enough—not when that very success is the asset worth capturing.

But there is a solution. Costco has thrived through three CEOs precisely because its ethos is protected structurally, not personally. To understand how this was done, we must continue our journey outward, beyond the internal-facing questions of purpose, management, and culture, to engage with the external forces that threaten to undermine them.

Our goal must be to build organizations with structures that make corruption from outside pressure first difficult and then—eventually, as we'll see—impossible.

Onward and outward.

Chapter Nine

CONSTITUTIONAL GOVERNANCE

The time to guard against corruption and tyranny is before they shall have gotten hold on us. It is better to keep the wolf out of the fold than to trust to drawing his teeth and talons after he shall have entered.

—**Thomas Jefferson**

Notes on the State of Virginia

1782

I remember sitting across from Jeff Lawson, founder and CEO of Twilio, at a small café in San Francisco, discussing his company's upcoming initial public offering (IPO). Jeff had founded Twilio in 2008 as a cloud communications platform that enabled developers to add voice, messaging, and video capabilities to their applications. It grew from a handful of rebels in a grungy space to a platform used by thousands of businesses. I'd played a small role as an advisor in the early days, but mostly what I felt was admiration after watching Jeff build something genuinely mission-driven from the ground up.

Twilio's success had been powered by a strong ethos, and Jeff had agreed to serve as its *mission guardian*. The company adopted a supervoting structure that would give him disproportionate voting power. As part of a compromise with institutional investors, Twilio had agreed to a "sunset provision": after seven years, this supervoting structure would automatically deactivate, restoring the conventional best practice rule of "one share, one vote."

Twilio had a hugely successful IPO in June 2016 with shares priced at $15, jumping 92% on the first day of trading.[1] In the years that followed, the company flourished. The pandemic supercharged demand for digital communications, and Twilio's stock soared. It crossed $50 in 2018, $100 in 2019, and $200 in 2020. When it hit an all-time high of $443 in February 2021, the company had a market cap of nearly $70 billion.[2] At that peak, certain early venture investors saw their initial investment balloon to a value of more than $5 billion. The company Jeff built had created enormous value for everyone involved.

Do you want to guess how much time elapsed between when Jeff's supervoting shares expired and when he was forced out as CEO?

One hundred and ninety-nine days.

Less than seven months after losing the governance protection that had shielded his leadership, Jeff Lawson was gone, pushed out by activist investors who owned less than half a percent of the company. The mission he'd spent fifteen years working on—to "unlock the imagination of builders"—was now in the hands of others.[3]

The argument for change seemed straightforward. Twilio's stock had collapsed more than 80% from its February 2021 peak of $443.49 to $73.64 when Jeff's departure was announced.[4] Case closed, right? But 2021 had seen an irrational peak in tech stocks due to the pandemic. When this bubble deflated, the same forces that had sent Twilio shares soaring brought them down to Earth.

The wild part is that even after this "collapse," Twilio was still up 390% from its 2016 IPO price of $15, when the company had a mere $277 million in revenue.[5] On the day Jeff Lawson resigned, revenue was $4.15 billion (up 1,400%).[6] Even measuring from that pandemic peak, revenue had grown 135%.[7] Case closed?

BUILDING WITH INTEGRITY

Why do companies routinely compromise in this way?

The reason should sound familiar from Chapter 3. "Investors might not like it," say the advisors—many of whom stand to profit from the transaction.[8] Supervoting makes a company harder to sell in a contested acquisition, and some institutional investors won't buy shares if they can't vote out management. The sunset is offered as a compromise: protection now, accountability later. And when founders hesitate, their advisors reassure them, "You can always extend it later if you need to." But thanks to financial gravity, this is much harder than it sounds.

Seven years might seem like a long time when a company is young, but in the life cycle of building something truly transformative, it's barely a beginning.

This is the latest example of the pattern we've been tracking throughout this book. If investors can redirect, decapitate, or even destroy a company at will, how can that company ever be considered a trustworthy counterparty?

The new management team at Twilio is talented and capable. Indeed, many of them are friends of mine. I have no doubt they will be able to turn the stock price around. But that's not the point. If the leadership of an organization can themselves be replaced at any time, any commitments they make must be viewed as transitory.

This begins a series of three chapters that explore the final dimension of the "new governance" we laid out in Chapter 4: *integrity*. I use this word intentionally, in the sense of structural integrity (can resist outside pressure) and also in the sense of being able to keep a promise. For organizations, these converge. Without structural integrity, a company literally cannot maintain its commitments.

In this chapter, we will focus on the specific vulnerabilities that leave mission-driven companies defenseless: the narrow fiduciary duty of shareholder primacy (as we saw in Chapter 4), the outsized influence of short-term investors (as we saw in Chapter 1), and the paradox of "independent" directors who so reliably fail to protect the mission. Each of these has a corresponding set of protections that, when combined like a suit of plate-mail armor, create *constitutional governance*.

But—just as we saw with Whole Foods—later attacks rely on cracks in the foundation laid years earlier. In fact, the most vital question is not *what* protections to choose but *when* they should be implemented.

IT'S ALWAYS TOO EARLY UNTIL IT'S TOO LATE

I know every line of this play by heart.

At incorporation, founders ask about mission-protective structures. "It's too early to worry about that," their lawyer says. "Just do standard Delaware incorporation for now. We can always add those bells and whistles later when you have the leverage."

The company raises money. The founder brings it up again. "Still too early," the VCs advise. "You don't want to overcomplicate things. Focus on product-market fit. This stuff is much easier to implement when you're bigger and more established." They raise a growth round of funding. The bold contrarians on their board tell them they don't want to look too different from other companies, as that might scare off future investors.

Years pass. Now they're a real success—hundreds of employees, a professional CFO, a whole legal team. Surely now is the time? "Actually," the CFO suggests, "it would make more sense to bundle this with IPO prep. It's more efficient that way. The bankers can help."

Notice that nobody ever said no. It's always "not yet." And then "yet" comes around.

The company is preparing for a public offering. It's very exciting. You can feel the frisson in the halls. One day the founder asks, "Hey, whatever happened to that mission-lock mechanism we discussed?" Maybe it's the employee ownership plan. The community foundation. That charter amendment to embed the mission.

"Oh, you were serious about that? That's too bad, now it's too late."

Before, it was too early. Now it's too late.

There's always that burst of outrage: *You're telling me that last July 3–6, there was a brief window when it went from too early to too late, and nobody said anything?*

But the CFO knows the storm will pass. The IPO date is already set.

THE ROOM WHERE IT HAPPENED

Let me take you into one of the rooms where this happened.

Deep in IPO preparations, the CEO had called a meeting. He asked me to sit in to help him advocate for the kinds of structural defenses we're about to explore. The rest of the room was full of newly hired professionals tasked with "landing the plane" of this public offering.

Naturally, nobody objected to the CEO's desire to do things differently. But they didn't exactly say, "We'll make it happen" either. They talked about the complexity, timing issues, banker concerns. But he was determined. They acquiesced. He told them this was his top priority.

The CEO walked out satisfied, off to his next appointment. The rest of us remained to work out the specifics.

Or so I thought.

The door hadn't even clicked shut when half the room started laughing. "Great, I'll just add this new number-one priority to my list of number-one priorities," someone said. The mockery escalated quickly. "He'll forget about all that by next week." "This will require a delay we can't afford." Then, with absolute certainty, "He'll blink."

They drifted out, still chuckling, back to landing the plane. I sat in the empty conference room, trying to process what I'd just witnessed.

At the time, I thought they'd shown shockingly bad judgment in mocking the CEO in front of me; they knew we were close. But in retrospect, I see it differently. They knew something that, at the time, I did not. They knew the delay would work, and they were right.

How did they know? Not because they understood this particular company especially well. After all, most were new hires. They simply knew the script better than I did. They'd performed in this play before. And the script never changes.

Almost all the structural protections we discussed that day are, even now, sitting on the cutting-room floor. The IPO was a massive success. Everyone got rich—spectacularly rich. But afterward, the founder grew increasingly troubled by what his company had become. He spent years doing exhausting work to revitalize, restructure, and renew the ethos that bureaucracy and financial gravity had eaten away. I admire his perseverance. But I was left to wonder what might have been if that meeting had gone differently.

Of the people in that room that day, almost none are left at the company. The professionals moved on to land the next plane, stage the next IPO. The CEO was left to do the cleanup alone. As far as I know, he never connected that cleanup work to what happened in that meeting. He blamed himself for losing focus or for not being strong enough. He remained blind to the forces he was pushing against. The gravity stayed invisible, just the way it likes.

THE PUBLIC BENEFIT CORPORATION

Over the next three chapters, I'm going to show you the protections that ended up on that cutting-room floor. My goal is that when the time comes, yours won't be laughed away.

The first protection those governance experts laughed away was the simplest: encoding the mission directly into the corporate charter.

Today, virtually every corporate charter contains the same boilerplate language for the company's purpose: to pursue "any lawful act or activity."[9] This language sounds innocuous. It isn't. As we saw in Chapter 4, courts and governance experts now routinely interpret this "neutral" purpose as establishing a fiduciary duty to maximize shareholder value no matter the cost to mission or long-term value. This interpretation is what forced Vectura's board to sell to Philip Morris. As we explored in Part I, this same trap has caught countless companies whose directors thought they were just following their legal duties.

Luckily for you, a band of corporate governance rebels has been fighting to create a new option for companies that want to explicitly commit to a mission-driven purpose. Like the movement for "general incorporation" before it (but unlike the shift to "shareholder primacy"), this rebellion has won victory after victory in state legislatures and around the world. (Delaware joined the party in 2013.)

Meet the *public benefit corporation* (PBC). Where neutral charters inadvertently create a legal duty to maximize shareholder value, PBCs commit to a high-level public benefit.[10] Anthropic's charter commits it to "the responsible development and maintenance of advanced AI systems."[11] Patagonia's pledges to "use business to inspire and implement solutions to the environmental crisis."[12]

Here's how it works. Directors in a PBC are legally allowed to balance shareholder interests with the company's stated public benefit. Courts give PBC boards wide discretion in making these decisions (what lawyers call an enhanced "business judgment rule"). Unlike standard corporations, where profit maximization is presumed paramount, PBC boards are permitted to make mission-aligned decisions that might reduce short-term returns without fear. If challenged, the board only needs to show their decision was rational and informed, not profit maximizing.[13]

The range of companies choosing PBC status tells an important story. Public and private companies alike have embraced PBC status: Veeva Systems, United Therapeutics, Lemonade, Warby Parker, and most of the leading AI labs are all PBCs.[14]

The process is remarkably simple. You can incorporate as a PBC from day one, or any C corp can convert with just a two-page filing in Delaware. That's it. Similar structures are available in forty-four other US states and many jurisdictions around the world. (In some, it also requires lightweight reporting, often once every two years.)[15]

This structure isn't a rigid straitjacket. Companies can revise their stated purpose any time, not to abandon the mission, but to refine how they express it as markets and technologies evolve. (Later in the chapter, we'll see how to avoid abuse of this provision.) I recommend choosing a high-level purpose rather than being overly prescriptive. In fact, PBC allows a company to adopt a specific aspect of "human flourishing" to maximize. For example, it could say "maximize human flourishing by" and then specify, as we do at Answer.AI, something like "developing ethical and beneficial uses of AI for society."[16]

And no, this isn't the little B in a circle you've seen at the farmers' market. That "B Corp certification" is a third-party standard, which we'll discuss in Chapter 13.

The PBC structure is a powerful way to encode the mission directly into the charter. It represents a restoration of purposeful incorporation as it existed through most of corporate history: the concept that corporations should exist to accomplish something specific. Writing the goal of maximizing human flourishing into the corporate charter is a simple restatement of what it truly means to be a for-profit company. It's not a repudiation of profit, nor is it hostile to investors. The best way to serve shareholders is to accomplish the mission that made the company originally worth investing in.

All too often, founders treat their governing documents like a building permit, a bureaucratic hurdle to be endured once to get started, then filed away and never thought about again. But the most consequential decision a company will ever make—its purpose—deserves better than being reduced to a compliance checkbox.

The PBC is the critical antidote to the "fiduciary duty" trap. But it only protects against one type of attack. Good governance is not a single rigid shell but a system of interlocking defenses that flex and adapt while maintaining structural integrity.[17]

MISSION GUARDIANS

Recently, I spoke on a panel at a conference about AI governance and ethics that was hosted at the Vatican.[18] On stage with me were representatives from a who's who of leading AI companies: OpenAI, Anthropic, Google, Meta, Cohere, and Palantir. As I looked down the panel, I realized a striking pattern. Not one of these companies accepts the standard governance defaults. Though they disagree about the path forward for AI, they all agree on one thing: Standard "shareholder primacy" governance would be catastrophic for stewarding this transformative technology.

These AI companies use different techniques to achieve governance

THE IMPLEMENTATION GUIDE: For examples or templates of each of these tools like the public benefit corporation, the board mission pledge, and others, scan the QR code or go to incorruptible.co/the-guide.

that protects their mission, but each approach involves appointing someone to serve as the *mission guardian*. Some, like OpenAI and Anthropic, have also created "mission-lock" structures (which we'll explore in detail in Chapter 11) to maintain mission alignment. The others rely on "founder control," which vests decision-making power in their individual founders. This latter approach is increasingly common among tech companies (although, as we'll see, not without drawbacks).

For example, when Google went public in 2004, founders Larry Page and Sergey Brin established a "supervoting" structure that gave each of the founders ten votes per share, while public investors received just one vote per share. "As a private company, we have concentrated on the long term," they wrote in their IPO letter. "As a public company, we will do the same."[19] The enhanced voting structure gave them the power to back up that promise, enabling decisions aligned with their long-term mission rather than quarterly results.

At the time, this was a novelty among tech companies, but the roots of the idea go back a long way. *The New York Times* has used a similar structure for over a century to ensure editorial independence. The Ochs-Sulzberger family owns only 20% of the equity but controls 70% of board seats through their special Class B shares, allowing them to protect the paper's journalistic mission even during financial crises when other newspapers gutted their newsrooms.[20] Mission guardians need not always be founders. For example, e-commerce and cloud computing giant Alibaba pioneered an innovative approach with its partnership structure: seventeen long-tenured employees collectively nominate a majority of board members, ensuring that those who live the mission daily shape the company's direction.[21] As we proceed in the chapters that follow, we will see a variety of other solutions as well.

Whereas the PBC solves the problem of fiduciary duties, mission guardians protect against a different vector of outside pressure: voting. In Chapter 4, we learned about how Vectura's board felt they had a fiduciary obligation to sell to Philip Morris International (PMI). But another aspect of the story bears mentioning. PMI had been steadily buying up shares of Vectura on the open market. Presumably, even if Vectura's board had found a way to refuse them, they would have eventually been able to acquire a 51% majority of the vote, which would have been sufficient under standard governance to replace the directors and force a liquidation of the company. Mission guardians exist to interrupt this dynamic, ensuring that those who care most about the mission retain the power to protect it.

FROM *FOUNDER CONTROL* TO *MISSION CONTROL*

If investor control leaves companies unable to keep their promises, founder control might seem like the obvious answer. And there is real power in it. For example, Mark Zuckerberg used his supervoting shares to turn down Yahoo's billion-dollar offer to acquire Facebook in 2006. At the time, Facebook had fewer than ten million users, had less than $30 million in revenue, and hadn't yet turned a profit. When Yahoo came knocking, some board members wanted to sell. But Zuckerberg opened the board meeting by saying, "This is kind of a formality. We're obviously not going to sell here."[22] The discussion took less than ten minutes. At the time, Zuckerberg was twenty-two years old.

Almost every founder we've studied in this book who was able to establish and protect an ethos relied on founder control to do so. Cloudflare, GitLab, and Devoted Health all relied on supervoting shares. Todd and Ed Park insisted on these protections from inception "so that we can ensure that Devoted has a long-term orientation to the creation of shareholder value." Even when investors resisted, they never wavered. "We knew that with that orientation, the mission and the business model would unequivocally align 100%."[23]

Investors have learned to tolerate these structures because founder-controlled companies on average deliver exceptional returns.[24] But this success masks serious problems with accountability, with resilience, and with the psychological toll on founders themselves.

Investors often complain that founder control makes accountability impossible. But this is not true. Founders with supervoting shares still owe a fiduciary duty to the corporation, and this is often interpreted as requiring them to step aside when the stock prices or reputations collapse. Travis Kalanick (Uber), Mark Pincus (Zynga),

Adam Neumann (WeWork), and John Foley (Peloton) all had ten-to-one or twenty-to-one supervoting yet were forced out when stocks fell.[25] Courts can intervene directly, as they did at Hollinger, blocking Conrad Black from exercising his supervoting control.[26]

Founder control that is not backed by a powerful ethos can destroy what it was meant to protect.

During normal times, unchecked power damages the psyche of those who wield it, literally rewiring the brain to diminish empathy while amplifying overconfidence.[27] Studies have documented this as "hubris syndrome," an acquired personality disorder that develops after holding power.[28]

Having accountability kick in only during a crisis has its own problems. Precisely because it's so powerful, founder control can create the very obsession it was meant to prevent. Founders who started as mission guardians can transform into power gremlins, hoarding control for its own sake. If you've ever wondered why billionaires with more money than they could spend in ten lifetimes refresh stock tickers like anxious day traders, this is why.

But even when founder control works, it nonetheless exacts a real psychological toll on the guardians themselves. I know too many founders trapped in their own creation, feeling like Atlas but unable even to shrug. They are the only thing standing between their company's ethos and the ravages of the market, like a dam holding back a flood.

That founders feel compelled to choose this despotic arrangement reveals just how broken standard governance has become.

For all these reasons, founder control should be a temporary bridge, not a permanent destination. The most thoughtful founders understand they're holding the mission in trust until something stronger can protect it. The truly long-term approach is to build a system of mission protection that does not depend on any one individual.

I call the organizations that do this *mission-controlled companies.* Not founder controlled. Not investor controlled. The mission itself holds ultimate authority.

But to achieve mission control, we must address one more vector of outside pressure.

BETRAYAL IN THE BOARDROOM

The most insidious kind of attack comes not from hostile raiders or activist investors but from within the boardroom itself. Boards of directors can become gravity's most effective agents.

J. Robert Beyster founded SAIC, Science Applications International Corporation, in 1969 as a consulting company providing scientific research to the public sector. His original plan, handwritten on a single page in 1968, stated a simple purpose: "to perform research in a productive environment."[29] His ethos included twelve binding principles, the first of which comprised three simple words: "Put people first."[30]

By 2004, it had become one of the nation's largest private companies, completely owned by its forty thousand employees worldwide, including Nobel laureates and top secret clearance holders who chose SAIC's revolutionary model over conventional employment.[31] Decisions were made at the lowest level possible, through forums where division managers could voice unvarnished opinions. Beyster's principle guided everything: "None of us is as smart as all of us."[32] (I was a summer intern there in the 1990s. I can still remember feeling the zeal of the researchers who mentored me.)

Beyster stacked his board with highly credentialed independent directors, including former military commanders, distinguished scientists, and respected business leaders. People with sterling reputations who seemed to understand this unique model.

Can you already guess where this is headed?

In 2002, the board, on its own initiative, decided SAIC should "operate more like a conventional public company."[33] They replaced Beyster as CEO in 2003 and tasked his successor with taking the company public. By 2004, they'd grown tired of Beyster's objections: "The majority of the board forced [me] into retirement and set the course for taking the company public,"[34] he later revealed. Beyster was seventy-nine years old.

The board cited financial necessity: Over five years, SAIC had spent more than $2.5 billion buying back shares from retiring employees.[35] What they called "a drain on resources," Beyster considered the engine that made SAIC's success possible.[36] At the time, SAIC's annual revenues were around $5.9 billion.[37]

In 2006, the board took the company public without Beyster's consent. The theory was that employees would continue to serve as mission guardians; all employee-owned shares were given supervoting rights, exercising ten votes per share. This arrangement lasted all of three years. As one contemporary observer put it, the board felt that "SAIC needed to bend to the will of Wall Street."[38] The board got its way, and employee supervoting ended in 2009.[39] Beyster had seen it coming: "This is a major step for SAIC, and it's one I opposed when I was chairman of the board—knowing that this is eventually what would happen."[40]

The board also promised that following "best practices" would strengthen the company. Instead, corruption swiftly followed. When an internal whistleblower warned that managers were taking kickbacks on a New York City contract, the report was swiftly buried. The company that once believed "None of us is as smart as all of us" was now silencing its own people. A $63 million timekeeping system contract ballooned to $600 million through systematic fraud.[41] Investigators described the system as "a dozen years late, 10 times pricier, not even half-finished."[42] When federal prosecutors finally uncovered the scheme in 2011, the US attorney called it "epic in duration, magnitude, and scope."[43] In 2012, SAIC paid a $500 million settlement, the largest for municipal contract fraud in US history.[44] By 2013, the company was split into two entities. The research business became Leidos. The SAIC name went to a government contracting operation. Today, both companies feature less than 10% employee ownership and boards that are 90% independent directors.[45]

Shortly before his death in 2014, Beyster reflected, "I trusted the wrong people. Some board members were not committed to employee ownership [or] preserving our culture. And unfortunately, I didn't figure this out until it was too late."[46]

At the time of the IPO, the majority of SAIC's board seats were held by independent directors—exactly the kind who should protect the company, according to standard governance theory.[47] Yet just as at Vectura, these directors acted not as mission guardians but as servants of "best practices" that, in the end, destroyed what made the company special.

Let's examine why.

THE INDEPENDENT DIRECTOR PROBLEM

Today, it's considered the height of good governance to staff boards with independent directors. What makes a board member "independent" is that they don't have financial ties to the company or its major shareholders. This allows them to "bless" board-level decisions that might involve conflicts of interest. For example, if the board is voting on a transaction that involves existing investors or managers of the company, the interested parties cannot vote (to avoid self-dealing). That is healthy.

And yet independent directors are still subject to external incentives. To illustrate, consider this question a founder (protected by supervoting shares) asked me the other day: "Why do I feel like my board consistently resists my efforts to build a long-term business? I have the power to replace them. You'd think they'd be more worried about me as a future reference." My blunt response: "Who did you call as references when you selected them?" Every name he mentioned was an investor or an investment banker (not an executive or fellow founder). He had answered his own question.

Independent directors operate in their own gravitational field and are impacted by their own *career equity* incentives. Their professional reputations and future board appointments depend on being seen as responsible by the *governance class* of our society: investors and the bankers, lawyers, directors, academics, and advisors who serve them. Imagine being a judge whose next appointment depends on how well you please the prosecutors. This is the position most independent directors are in. And at most companies, independent directors control the "nominating committees" that choose the future independent directors. In essence, they become a self-perpetuating club, accountable only to other independent directors.

Even founders with voting control face the danger of appointing board members whose loyalties lie, at least in part, elsewhere. Governance rules often require those same founders to recuse themselves from decisions where they have personal stakes. The most important of those decisions is the choice to fire or retain the CEO. In those moments, independent directors frequently hold a supermajority of votes.

Although independent directors are one of today's most cited "best practices," research suggests they "are not effective in preventing financial fraud." Enron's audit committee was composed entirely of independent directors, chaired by an emeritus Stanford accounting professor.[48] In 2000, *Chief Executive* named it one of the five best boards in America.[49] This is a systemic problem that requires a systemic solution. Choosing better people will not suffice. The solution is to create constitutional governance structures that bind directors—and founders—to the mission. The goal is to build the organizational version of "a nation of laws, not of men."

THE DIRECTOR'S OATH

Centuries ago, ancient Greeks created the Hippocratic oath to separate legitimate doctors from charlatans. Today, the oath protects doctors against outside pressures, even from their own supervisors. Similar protections guard civil engineers, accountants, lawyers, architects, and any profession where the work affects others in profound ways. Directors should be no different. In some ways, they affect far more lives and livelihoods.

Yet we demand less commitment from boards of directors than we do from nurses. Why?

Every mission-driven company should require directors to take a "board mission pledge," committing to use their broad discretion to support the mission and consider it in every decision.[50] When embedded in corporate bylaws or proxy statements, these pledges have real legal teeth. They work alongside the PBC: While the PBC protects directors from outside pressure, the pledge guides them proactively, even when nobody is watching.

Evidence shows pledges work.[51] In one study, CFOs who swore integrity oaths reduced earnings manipulation by 20% and operational manipulations by 15%.[52] Another study of more than 21,500 people showed that pledges reduce dishonest behavior by nearly half.[53] For those who say such oaths are meaningless: How would you feel seeking treatment from a doctor who you knew had refused to recite the Hippocratic oath?

This goes beyond individual organizations. Just as all doctors are bound by the Hippocratic oath, we need a universal *director's oath* for the entire governance class.

We know how to design it.[54] Research shows effective pledges share five traits: They are specific (committing to prioritize the stated mission, disclose conflicts before voting, and commit to long-term value), actively recited (read aloud or typed at appointment, not just signed), timed at decision points (renewed before major votes like acquisitions or CEO changes), freely chosen (directors can decline, but that refusal becomes a matter of public record), and social (every director in the room knows everyone else has taken the same pledge as a precondition of service).

Think about that the next time you consider hiring someone who hasn't yet taken one.

CONSTITUTIONAL GOVERNANCE

No country in the world lets tourists vote. You can't fly into France, vote in their election, and fly home. Yet for corporations, we've accepted this as natural: Anyone who buys shares on Monday can influence major decisions on Tuesday, regardless of their understanding of, or commitment to, the organization's mission. The hedge fund that bought shares this morning has the same voice as the employee who's devoted a decade to building the company—more, if they can borrow money to buy extra shares.

We all understand that the *citizens of the republic*, not the tourists passing through, should shape its destiny. In a company, "citizens" include long-tenured employees, loyal customers, patient investors, and essential partners whose own futures are intertwined with the mission's success.

The challenge is identifying and empowering these citizens.

1. Tenured voting. If you're going to give power to investors, weight it toward the long-term ones. Having voting power increase with the length of the holding period is called "tenured" voting. It distinguishes speculators—mere tourists passing through—from true investors. From citizens. A small but mighty set of US companies has used this since the 1980s, so we have research on their performance. In one study, twelve such companies (including Aflac, Carlisle, and J. M. Smucker) delivered returns worth six times an equivalent investment in the S&P 500 over a thirty-three-year period.[55] French companies like L'Oréal have used loyalty shares for decades; France made double voting after two years standard in 2014.[56] But many implementations have flaws: cumbersome registration, artificial cliffs, and selective application. At LTSE, we proposed a better system called "long-term voting": voting power growing continuously from one to ten votes over ten years, tracked automatically through the SEC-regulated Direct Registration System (DRS). Every shareholder is eligible to earn the same enhanced rights for the same commitment.[57] (Though originally designed for public companies, private companies can adopt this easily as well.) Time earns voice, the true prerogative of a citizen.

2. Economic shares. Some companies go even further by issuing "economic shares" with minimal or zero votes, cleanly separating voting (reserved for citizens) from economics (open to everyone). Alphabet's Class C shares and Berkshire Hathaway's Class B shares work this way: Investors participate fully in the company's financial success without complicating governance.[58] This structure is also common in family businesses, where voting shares go to those active in the business while economic shares let other family members share in the profits. This has many administrative benefits, including separating concerns over liquidity from the possibility of the mission guardians losing governance control.

3. Codetermination. Give board representation to the same stakeholders we committed to serve in Chapter 7's "Fiduciary to Who?" framework. Germany requires that half of board seats go to employees, and research shows this leads to increased capital formation, as workers push for more investment because they link the company's long-term health with job security.[59] But this can be done in a lightweight way too: Airbnb created a "stakeholder committee" within the board to bring hosts' voices directly into governance decisions.[60]

4. Steward ownership. Rather than have investors and stakeholders compete for influence, make the stakeholders the steward-owners. An employee ownership trust is a legal structure where a trust owns the company's shares on behalf of all workers, present and future. Profits typically surge when those who do the work own the work. REI's twenty-five million customer-owners elect the board while generating $3.85 billion in annual sales.[61] Vanguard has been customer owned for fifty years: The company is owned by its funds, which are in turn owned by the people who invest in them. This gives rank-and-file customers both the authority and the responsibility for electing the board. The company manages $10 trillion with expense ratios five times lower than competitors, saving investors billions annually.[62]

How do you know if the mission has truly achieved sovereignty?

Apply this test: Delete every founder's name. Delete every major investor. Can the mission still defend itself?

JOHN LEWIS PARTNERSHIP

The John Lewis Partnership (JLP) can answer this question emphatically. When John Spedan Lewis (the founder's son) transferred ownership to employees in 1929, he created the conditions for tremendous longevity.[63] Today, more than seventy-four thousand employee "partners" collectively own the UK department store and grocery chain through a trust. Not symbolically. Actually.

The chairperson runs daily operations, but a fifty-eight-member partnership council, elected directly by workers in the stores and warehouses, holds ultimate power. They alone hold the chairperson to account—and have done so for nearly a century. After all, they are the people who live the mission every day.

Through the Depression, the Blitz, Thatcher, Brexit, and COVID, the chairperson has stood before employee representatives twice a year and answered for the company's direction. Rather than imagining what "the market" might want, JLP is characterized by decade after decade of steady deliberation by the people whose livelihoods depend on getting it right.

John Lewis died ninety-five years ago. Last year, his ethos touched millions of customers he never imagined, using technology he never dreamed of, competing against companies that didn't exist in his century. The mission didn't just survive. It adapted, evolved, and thrived. Today, JLP has revenues in excess of £12 billion.[64] Remember that the next time someone tells you this kind of thing couldn't scale.

The system was tested in 2023. Chairwoman Dame Sharon White, facing financial pressure, proposed bringing in outside investors by selling a minority stake (reportedly worth $1.2 to $2.2 billion) for the first time in the company's history, which would have required a change in JLP's constitution.[65] In any normal company, that's when the bankers take over. Not here. The partnership council said no. The company would remain in the hands of its seventy-four thousand owners.[66]

However, though this is a story of the strength of JLP's sovereignty, it does hint at a problem. What if an organization needs outside capital and wants to form productive long-term partnerships with investors while still maintaining a high-integrity structure, as Costco and Devoted Health have? It would need a form of "mission lock" that was as strong as JLP's but as welcoming to long-term capital as today's C corp. That longer-term solution, the one that truly solves the "independent director problem," will have to wait until Chapter 11.

INVESTORS THRIVE WITH MISSION-CONTROLLED GOVERNANCE

What makes mission-controlled governance so powerful is that it creates more value for everyone, including investors. Companies that can't be bought can't be stopped. Research has found that mission-protected companies outperformed single-class peers in both the short and the long term.[67] The purpose-driven companies in the *Firms of Endearment* study outperformed the S&P 500 market index over fifteen years—1,681% compared to 118%.[68] Deloitte research showed mission-driven companies grow three times faster than competitors,[69] and Jump Associates found purpose-aligned companies outperformed the general market over a twenty-year period.[70]

I want to underline this point: Mission control is good for investors. The mission-lock techniques discussed in this chapter do not prevent companies from forming productive long-term partnerships with shareholders. Further, the very fear of investors killing the golden goose robs investors of massive opportunities. Many companies remain private and closely held as a result. Increasingly, companies that do go public stay private longer, overrestricting the circle of who benefits from their prosperity. Mission-controlled structures unlock these opportunities.

Mission control requires carefully designed protections for minority investors: strong information rights, antidilution provisions, and guarantees of fair treatment ensure that even passive investors profit from the company's success. Luckily, in developed economies, securities law already provides robust remedies when minority investors need them.

THE +2 PAULDRONS OF INVINCIBILITY

After exploring this arsenal of governance mechanisms, you might be tempted to pick a favorite and declare victory. Each approach represents a powerful shield against forces that try to pull an organization from its mission, but mission resilience requires a thoughtful combination of these strategies.

I have watched many times as a founder lands on one technique, convinced that it will make them invincible. They're a public benefit corporation. They have supervoting shares. Or they have tremendous leverage caused by their business success. Investors and lawyers alike encourage this magical thinking. The person who puts their faith in a single solution is, to me, like Leeroy Jenkins, charging into battle because their shoulder pauldrons are indestructible. This may, indeed, be true. But the spear that kills you may be aimed a little lower. What then?

The solution is to combine many overlapping protections. Each element reinforces the others, creating what *The Federalist Papers* called "auxiliary precautions" that guard against mission drift.[71] Think of it as plate-mail armor with overlapping plates to ensure that, even if one is pierced, the others hold.

This system of overlapping protections also solves the succession problem that haunts founder-controlled companies. Instead of depending on one person's virtue or longevity, the mission protects itself through structural strength. To illustrate how it works, let's return to the story of Costco one more time.

THE COSTCO GOVERNANCE FORTRESS

Did you think Costco's ethos has endured all this time because of its $400 billion valuation and exceptional customer loyalty? Dream on. Jim Sinegal was there the day FedMart's investors turned on Sol Price.

Most founders think like lone warriors, viewing corporate armor as protection only for themselves. Jim Sinegal saw something bigger: "On Wall Street, they're in the business of making money between now and next Thursday. . . . We want to build a company that will still be here 50 and 60 years from now."[72]

Building Costco, he didn't just try to protect himself. He saw Costco as a city needing a fortress. At the time of the company's 1985 IPO, Sinegal embedded a series of interlocking protections into

Costco's structure, creating what I call a *governance fortress*. It wasn't because any specific threat loomed but because he understood that success attracts predators. And unlike founder control, the fortress wasn't reliant on any one person. It is a property of the organization itself.

The cornerstone was a supermajority provision requiring 66.67% of all shares—not merely votes cast—to amend certain charter provisions.[73] In a typical shareholder vote, abstentions don't count, but under Costco's rules, every share that doesn't vote yes effectively votes no. Activists or opportunists can't prevail by mobilizing a small coalition. They need the active consent of two-thirds of all shareholders—and Costco has millions of loyal shoppers who are retail shareholders.

But that's just the first stone in the fortress (see Table 9.1).[74]

Table 9.1. The Costco governance fortress

Supermajority provisions	Require 66.67% of ALL shares (not just votes) to amend charter
Self-reinforcing lock	Make supermajority apply to removing the supermajority itself
Restrict written consent	Require unanimous consent for shareholder action outside meetings
Limit special meetings	Prevent shareholders from calling meetings between annual sessions
High proxy access barriers	Require significant ownership (3%+) held for years to nominate directors
Classified board	Stagger director terms so only one-third face election each year
Advance notice provisions	Require early disclosure of shareholder proposals and nominations
"Poison pill" takeover protections	Discourage hostile takeovers by creating automatic negative consequences

Hamilton "Tony" James, who led Costco's IPO and served on its board for decades, explained, "The board has always been a bulwark from short-term pressures, giving [management] a safe space and support to build a great long-term business."[75] Notice how different this conception of a board is from the tragic examples we've studied earlier.

Sinegal was prescient. Despite Costco's extraordinary financial performance, the company has faced repeated attacks from outsiders. In 2003, Wall Street punished Costco's stock, dropping it 19% in a single day. The complaint, as analyst Ian Gordon put it, was that Costco was "spending what could have been shareholders' profit on making a better experience for customers."[76] Deutsche Bank famously groused that "at Costco, it's better to be an employee or a customer than a shareholder."[77] When dragged to meet with angry investors by his CFO at the time, Sinegal "basically told them, 'I don't care.'"[78] The fortress made his resolve possible. But thwarted by the fortress, the attacks only escalated.

ISS is the most influential "proxy advisor" on behalf of institutional investors.[79] It rates companies on a risk scale from 1 (best) to 10 (worst). Because ISS equates risk with deviation from shareholder primacy, Costco has traditionally been given its lowest possible governance score (for example, a 10 out of 10 in 2016).[80] They claim its fortress causes "shareholder disenfranchisement." James McRitchie, a governance activist, has repeatedly lobbied to dismantle Costco's supermajority provisions, arguing they "lead to entrenchment and stagnation."[81] The Harvard Shareholder Rights Project even mobilized pension funds to attack Costco's structure, claiming this "entrenchment" leads to poor performance.[82] Poor performance!

$10,000 invested in Costco at IPO = ~$8.77 million today
$10,000 invested in S&P 500 in 1985 = ~$151,000 today[83]

In 2014, the activists scored what would have given them a victory at most companies: 72% of votes cast favored declassifying Costco's board (one element of the fortress).[84] But this was Costco, and 72% of votes cast represented less than half of the total shares outstanding. The supermajority wall held.

By contrast, consider what happened at Kroger. In 2006–8, Kroger's board did everything the governance experts demanded: declassified the board for annual elections, eliminated supermajority voting requirements, and let their takeover protections expire.[85] CEO David Dillon proclaimed that these changes reflected "the highest standards of corporate governance."[86] The results speak for themselves. Since adopting these "best practices," Kroger has delivered respectable but unremarkable returns while struggling with digital transformation, market share erosion, and strategic missteps.[87] The "entrenched" Costco has significantly outperformed the "accountable" Kroger,[88] precisely the opposite of what standard governance theory predicts.

Despite the repeated failures of this theory, boards today, even at the early stage, are dominated by discussions of what is considered a governance "best practice." But the people who promulgate these "best practices" are the same ones who gave Costco their lowest possible score. This means that if you do nothing, by default, you will get a board that, over time, wants you to be less like Costco and more like Kroger.

So tell me again which of these approaches really serves shareholder interests?

In 2018, Costco's majority-independent board finally gave in to "governance best practices" and agreed to remove their classified board protection.[89] The core of the fortress remains intact. That 66.67% supermajority requirement for charter amendments still stands. It has survived two CEO successions (Jim Sinegal stepped down in 2012, W. Craig Jelinek did so in 2024). But the crack in the wall reveals the deeper vulnerability. Even with a fortress and even with decades of proven success, the board eventually acquiesced to dismantling that one piece of the fortress. What will happen when the next campaign for "best practices" targets the remaining defenses?

"BEST PRACTICES" DESTROY SHAREHOLDER VALUE

"BEST PRACTICE"	RATIONALE	WHAT THE DATA SHOWS
Quarterly reporting	Increases transparency and keeps investors informed	A 2019 study examined what happened when Singapore mandated that some companies switch from semiannual to quarterly reporting.[90] This "natural experiment" showed that quarterly reporting made affected companies 5% less valuable on average—with no offsetting benefits.
Regular earnings-per-share (EPS) guidance	Helps investors predict returns and reduces uncertainty	McKinsey analyzed more than four thousand firms over multiple years and found zero evidence of improved valuation multiples, returns, or reduced volatility—the only effect was increased trading volumes benefiting short-term traders.[91]
Majority-independent boards	Prevents insider self-dealing and protects shareholders	Cross-sectional analysis shows board independence is negatively correlated with performance in high-discretion firms.[92]
Annual board elections (declassified boards)	Makes directors more accountable to shareholders	Cremers and Sepe studied the Harvard Shareholder Rights Project and found their campaign destroyed $90–149 billion in aggregate value across ninety-three firms—roughly $1 billion per company.[93]
Dual-class sunset	Prevents management entrenchment, which leads to poor performance	Yale's Sonnenfeld and Tian performed a comparative analysis of the Russell 3000 and found dual-class stocks outperformed 35.82% vs. 31.36% over one year and 9.05% vs. 8.12% over five years;[94] MSCI similarly found 4.5% annual outperformance of dual-class over single-class companies.[95]
Proxy advisor "good governance" ratings	Helps investors identify the best-run companies	According to Dumitrescu and Zakriya in the *Journal of Corporate Finance*, "poorly governed" companies have outperformed those rated "well governed" since 2008.[96] According to Copland, Larcker, and Tayan at Stanford, "It is not clear that the recommendations of [proxy advisory] firms are correct and generally lead to better outcomes for companies and their shareholders."[97] Yet proxy advisors wield enormous power: Opposition from ISS is "associated with a 51 percent difference in institutional voting support," and 114 financial institutions managing $5 trillion vote with them "99.5% of the time."[98]

199 DAYS

Costco's fortress has protected its mission for four decades, an eternity by modern standards. But four decades isn't forever. At Twilio, the countdown started the moment Lawson's supervoting shares expired. Those wrenching 199 days happened because the company was open to all four of the vulnerabilities we've explored in this chapter. It was "too early" all the way through the IPO. Twilio never became a PBC. The supervoting shares expired due to the seven-year sunset. And in keeping with best practices, the company had a majority-independent board.

For 199 days, I watched helplessly as gravity breached the hull. When Twilio lost its mission guardian, it was changed forever. Once a company can be forcibly pressured from outside, it can never again be fully trusted. That breach happened not because of who took over but because someone could. (And yes, in case you were wondering, the same ISS that assigned Costco their lowest possible governance rating are big fans of the seven-year sunset.[99])

The structures we've explored in this chapter—armor, fortress, citizenship—are designed for years, maybe decades. But what about centuries? What about building something permanent?

The John Lewis Partnership hints at the answer. After nearly a century, its mission still controls its destiny. But here's what I didn't tell you: JLP isn't actually one entity. Its governance has two branches, encoded as two distinct legal entities. The commercial business is overseen by a separate employee ownership trust,[100] what lawyers call a "mission-lock vehicle."

This may seem complex, but it's actually simpler than today's dysfunction. Understanding why and how to use it to transform an organization into something incorruptible is the subject of the next two chapters. The goal is to create permanent mission sovereignty using a constellation of mutually mission-locked entities. This is a difference not just of degree but of kind.

In the next chapter, I'll show you what happens when we leave the single entity behind.

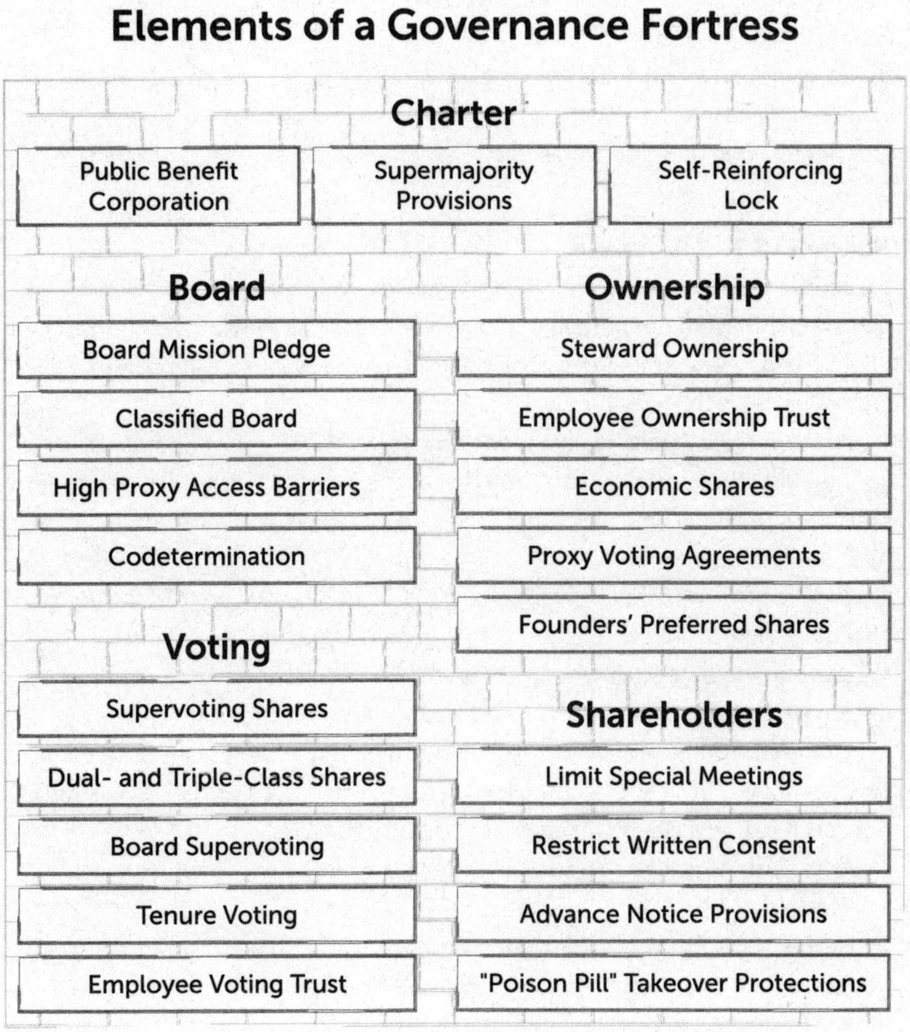

Elements of a Governance Fortress

Charter

- Public Benefit Corporation
- Supermajority Provisions
- Self-Reinforcing Lock

Board

- Board Mission Pledge
- Classified Board
- High Proxy Access Barriers
- Codetermination

Ownership

- Steward Ownership
- Employee Ownership Trust
- Economic Shares
- Proxy Voting Agreements
- Founders' Preferred Shares

Voting

- Supervoting Shares
- Dual- and Triple-Class Shares
- Board Supervoting
- Tenure Voting
- Employee Voting Trust

Shareholders

- Limit Special Meetings
- Restrict Written Consent
- Advance Notice Provisions
- "Poison Pill" Takeover Protections

Figure 9.1.

THE CONVERSATIONS THAT DEFINE YOUR FUTURE

I need to level with you.

Every mission protection in this chapter has one thing in common: Someone will try to talk you out of it.

Instead of seeing this as a drawback, I want you to see it as a major advantage. Who really understands what you're trying to build? Who's really aligned? You'll find out through these conversations.

How to Talk to Your Lawyer

I recently watched a founder's idealism collide with legal reality. His company had exceptional growth potential, and we were on a call with his (very good) lawyers, setting up the employee stock option plan. He wanted it done in the most employee-favorable way possible.

The lawyers kept raising objections: "Ninety-nine percent of companies don't do this." "It's really not standard." "You don't have to do this." They clearly couldn't grasp why anyone would voluntarily give employees better terms than they had to.

The founder's frustration was palpable. Between meetings, the lawyers kept changing the documents back to "best practices" and "market standard." Each meeting, the founder had to correct them. He had a company to run, and this became a time sink. Eventually, he settled for a compromise that gave certain early employees the benefits the founder wanted but left future employees' statuses in doubt. This set the company up for future battles with investors rather than establishing a clean precedent at the outset.

Afterward, he called me to vent: "I feel like I just negotiated with my own lawyers and lost."

He had fallen into the trap that catches most founders. We're so conditioned to defer to lawyers that we forget a simple truth: The lawyer works for the company, not the other way around. Yet somehow, when it comes to setting up perfectly legal but unconventional policies that align with their ethos, founders end up asking for permission from the very people they're paying $800 an hour.

Here's how to reclaim control of these conversations:

Never ask lawyers what to do; ask them for pros and cons. Of course, ask them what's compliant with the law or regulations whenever that's in question. But within the range of legal options, have them map out the benefits and costs of the available paths. I watched another founder transform a dead-end discussion by asking for the pros and cons of adopting a particular mission-protective provision. The lawyer's response? "Pros: You'll have your mission locked in, and you'll filter for aligned investors. Cons: $2,000 in extra legal fees you could defer, since it's too early to worry about this right now." When the founder said that seemed like a good deal, the lawyer agreed enthusiastically. "Why did you try to talk me out of it?" The lawyer was offended. "I wasn't; I was giving you options."

If the cons win, demand alternatives. Lawyers know more than they volunteer. When they say something can't be done, ask which other companies have achieved similar goals and how. Is there another way to accomplish the same underlying objective? Suddenly, options may appear. Sometimes "standard" exists for good reasons, protecting you from genuine risks. But when you choose something different based on principle and backed by evidence (as with every technique in this book), your lawyer should help you implement your vision, not block it.

Remember, they're revealing their priorities. Career equity applies to lawyers too. Many firms make far more money from clients who are investors than from clients who are operating companies. A lawyer who consistently fights mission protections is telling you what they really value. But using these approaches, you can turn even a skeptical lawyer into an ally. The conversation changes when they understand you're not asking permission; you're asking for their expertise in implementation.

How to Talk to Your Investor

I was on a call with a founder who'd spent months perfecting his company's mission-protective governance. He had top lawyers. Experienced advisors. A thoughtful, balanced approach protecting the mission while enabling growth. But as his Series A approached, anxiety crept in. "What if investors don't like it? Maybe we should use standard terms now and revisit later."

I've had this conversation dozens of times. Too often, the entire discourse around mission protection boils down to the fear that "investors might not like it." Might! Founders get talked out of protections without even trying, so deep is our conditioning to treat investors as superiors rather than partners.

"It's always too early until it's too late," I reminded him. "If you don't establish this now, when will you have more leverage?"

The conversation that followed surprised him. The lead investor asked one clarifying question: "So basically, you're saying the mission is what creates the value, and these protections ensure you can execute on it?"

"Exactly."

"Then why wouldn't we want that protected?"

Not every conversation goes this smoothly. Some investors push back hard, and negotiations can get messy. But even then, you're learning something valuable about alignment.

The reality is that good investment opportunities are scarcer than capital. The vast majority of investors have no strong views on governance; they've simply absorbed the conventional wisdom. And just like lawyers, investors face their own career equity pressures. Going against "market standard" feels risky when you have to explain it to your partners or LPs.

Real Objections, Real Answers

Over the years I've been writing this book, I've kept a list of all the investor objections that actual startups have reported encountering. Every one of these is a verbatim quote from a real investor. For each one, I'll show you how the founder answered it (with a little coaching along the way):

"It's too early to worry about these things." → "It's always too early until it's too late. And anyway, I don't mind doing this on the early side."

"Of course, I am founder friendly, but I worry later-stage investors might not like it." → "They might. But they also might feel the opposite when they see our results. Why would we remove protections now for something that might not even be an issue later? If they require changes, we always have the freedom to choose to compromise then. But that's better than being forced to compromise and settle for a smaller outcome."

"I worry you won't be able to raise money." → "Plenty of companies have been able to raise billions with nonstandard governance: Airbnb raised nearly $2.95 billion with supervoting shares. SpaceX raised almost $12 billion while staying private and providing liquidity via regular tender offers. Anthropic raised more than $27 billion while being governed by a trust.[101] Novo Nordisk is a publicly traded company."

"This complexity will make your next round of funding impossible." → "Complex structures that protect the mission actually make us more attractive to serious long-term investors. They want companies with defensible moats. Mission protection is exactly that kind of moat. It allows us to make long-term commitments that competitors can't match."

"These multiple protections are redundant. Why not pick just one?" → "If they are redundant, what's the harm in having the belt *and* the suspenders, just in case?"

"You're being unfair, setting yourself up as an emperor for life." → "My intention is to transition to a more robust mission-controlled framework as the company grows, but you yourself said it's too early for that now. I need to be able to promise my employees, customers, and partners that I will be able to make that transition when the time comes, unencumbered."

"I worry you're more committed to your mission than you are to making profit." → "Mission multiplies operational excellence. When we have product-market fit and strong execution, mission protection becomes our sustainable competitive advantage. This is the best way to create a truly massive outcome for us and for our investors."

"I worry you'll attract activist employees." → "Wait, I thought VCs loved that whole 'missionaries versus mercenaries' thing? We're building a company for people who care deeply about the mission. The research shows that kind of employee stays longer, performs better, and builds more value. In my experience, people who care about the mission are builders, not complainers. They're activists for our mission."

"I personally get it, but my partners [or LPs] will think I've lost my mind." → "Help me understand their specific concerns so we can address them. The data shows mission-protected companies outperform. That's a story your partners will appreciate once they see the returns. I'm happy to join your partners' meeting to explain why this makes us a stronger investment."

"This approach is unprecedented, strange, or unusual." → "Yes, I understand these structures may be new to you, and I totally hear your concerns. Let me walk you through some examples and the research that backs up these protections. Most importantly, know that they make sense to me as the best way to build competitive advantage by becoming a trustworthy counterparty: a business partner that customers, employees, and suppliers can rely on to keep the business's promises."

The Magic Words

Practice saying this sentence in front of a mirror until you can deliver it with confidence: "As the leader, it is my judgment that it is essential to our business strategy to be a trustworthy counterparty [to whom], and to do that, we need to implement [provision] in order to make promises they can believe."

What's magical about this sentence is that it forces the person you're talking with to object to something specific. What exactly is it that they don't agree with?

That you're not the leader?
That it's not your call to make?
That your judgment is flawed?
That this is not your strategy?
That trust is not important to the strategy?

Try this out, using any of the provisions in this book. You'll realize that anyone who says these things probably does not really understand your vision. Are they really the right partner for you?

When to Capitulate

One last piece of advice: Don't forget, you can always capitulate. I wish I could tell you that you will always have the leverage to run your company the way you want. But even the strongest leader and the most successful company won't always have the leverage to get everything they want.

If you find yourself in a situation where the only person who wants to invest is someone who won't accept these provisions, you can give in. Swallow your pride, live to fight another day. But at least try. If nothing else, you'll learn who you're really partnering with. And if you wind up having to remove one or more of these protections, what have you really lost, compared to if you never tried?

I once worked with a founder of a hot startup raising from famous Sand Hill Road VCs. He asked me to help him negotiate for "the works"—a term sheet with every mission-protective provision we could think of. (Naturally, he did not have these protections added at the time of incorporation. His lawyer had told him it was "too early" to worry about that.) He had the leverage, and he used it. The VC agreed to add ten protections to the term sheet.

At the eleventh hour, his cofounder quit unexpectedly. Overnight, his leverage evaporated. The same "founder-friendly" VC squeezed him on everything: valuation, board seats, and all but two of the mission-protective provisions. He called me, upset. "Why did I bother adding all that stuff if they were going to make me take it out?"

I answered in a way he did not expect. "You see only the eight things you lost," I said. "I see plus-two you'd never have gotten if you hadn't asked for ten." Even when you have to capitulate, you're still better off for having tried. (It would have been even better if he'd established his governance before the term sheet negotiation began.)

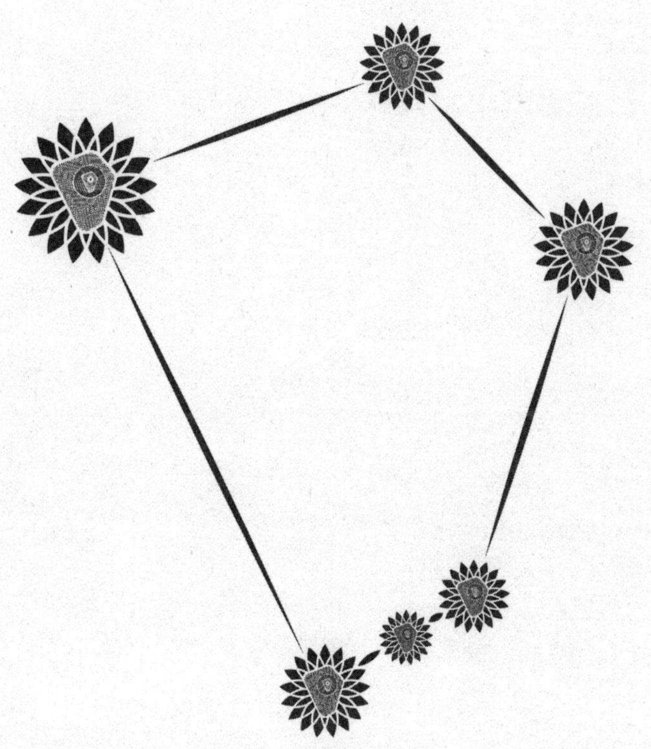

Chapter Ten

THE CONSTELLATION VIEW

O libreta, o maleta.

("Either your ledger or your suitcase.")

—**Father José María Arizmendiarrieta**

1960

A catholic priest walks into a war-torn Basque town in 1941.[1] Naturally, the locals expect prayers and consolation. Instead, he arrives with a wooden suitcase full of books and an audacious plan to rebuild their economy from the ground up.

It's not the punchline you expected. But then again, nothing about this story follows the script.

The priest was José María Arizmendiarrieta, and the town was Mondragón, a small industrial community devastated by the Spanish Civil War. While government officials and business leaders saw only economic casualties deserving charity or migration, Arizmendiarrieta saw potential. He believed that, through education and hard work, the people of Mondragón could take control of their economic destiny.

The enterprise that grew from his vision is named for the town where it was born. Today, Mondragon is Spain's tenth-largest business.[2] With more than seventy thousand employees, operations on four continents, and annual revenues exceeding €11 billion in 2024, Mondragon has become an industrial powerhouse.[3]

By conventional metrics like growth, longevity, diversification, and global reach, Mondragon is a business success story for the ages. It has survived economic crises that toppled giants, expanded internationally while maintaining its Spanish roots, and consistently outperformed competitors across multiple industries.

It all started not with a business plan but with a school. In 1943, Arizmendiarrieta established a modest technical college, scraping together donations and convincing students to work half days in local factories to fund their education. For over a decade, he patiently built this foundation, becoming known for peppering his lectures with memorable maxims about self-reliance and community responsibility.

By 1956, his first "graduating class" of students was ready. Five young engineers, trained under Arizmendiarrieta's guidance, pooled their modest savings to establish a small workshop manufacturing paraffin stoves. They named it Ulgor, an acronym of their surnames. When Madrid authorities refused permission for their enterprise, they cleverly purchased a defunct company in another city just to acquire its industrial license, then transported machinery over mountain roads during holiday periods when officials weren't watching. This first company thrived. By the start of the '60s, it had grown so significantly that it was "well on its way to becoming one of the hundred largest industrial companies in Spain."[4] But Arizmendiarrieta was thinking much bigger. In 1959, the company added its own banking service, Caja Laboral. At its branch opening in 1960, Arizmendiarrieta coined the phrase that would become their rallying cry: "O libreta, o maleta" (Either your ledger or your suitcase).[5] He meant: Either invest locally to build your community's future or watch as your children pack their bags and leave.

This bank served as the engine that powered remarkable expansion. Today, Mondragon is an industrial giant whose tens of thousands of employees remain mission locked to Arizmendiarrieta's original vision. Eight decades later, they continue to resist the financial gravity that so often corrupts organizations at this scale.

But here's where the story takes its most unexpected turn. Mondragon is not anything like the companies we have studied up until now. In fact, once people understand how the trick is done, most would not even recognize it as a company at all.

COMPANIES ARE NOT WHAT YOU THINK THEY ARE

McDonald's is not a restaurant. Those golden arches you see everywhere? Ninety-three percent of them sit atop restaurants owned by independent franchisees, not by McDonald's Corporation.[6] The company owns the brand, provides the playbook, and controls the supply chain; local owners contribute the hustle and customer service.

Coca-Cola does not sell soda. Nearly two hundred independent bottling companies employing more than seven hundred thousand people produce and distribute the 2.2 billion servings consumed daily worldwide.[7]

Have you flown Virgin Atlantic, used Virgin Mobile, or worked out at Virgin Active? You've experienced Richard Branson's brand-licensing constellation. He typically holds minority stakes but extends the Virgin brand across forty-plus businesses, letting him expand into new industries with limited capital.[8]

Marriott is not a hotel. Of its more than nine thousand properties worldwide, Marriott owns barely 1%. The rest operate under management agreements or franchises with independent owners.[9]

And IKEA? It's not a furniture store. The IKEA concept and trademark are owned by one entity, while most stores are run by a foundation-owned franchisee.[10] Founder Ingvar Kamprad designed this structure to ensure IKEA's independence and mission would outlive him.[11]

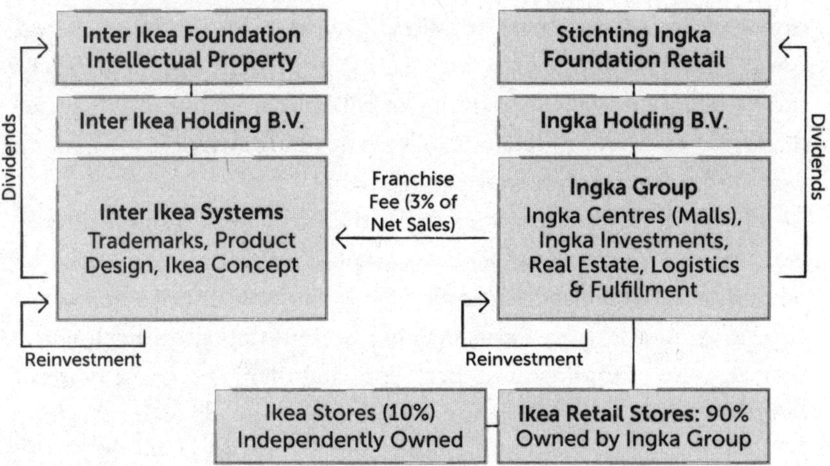

Figure 10.1.

These are all examples of what I call *constellations*: multiple separate entities that orbit around a common purpose so tightly they appear to be a single organization. Each entity maintains independence while exerting gravitational pull on the others, creating a coherent whole that customers, employees, and even investors perceive as one company.

This structure is everywhere. Most of the time when you talk about a "company," you're actually talking about a constellation. Apple operates through more than one hundred subsidiaries worldwide.[12] Berkshire Hathaway is a holding company that controls over one thousand separate entities, including household names like GEICO, Dairy Queen, and Duracell.[13] Samsung isn't a single company but a *chaebol*, a network of roughly eighty companies with complex cross-ownership.[14]

Recall that Devoted Health is made up of three entities that together form the virtuous performance cycle: Devoted Health Insurance, Devoted Medical Group, and their Orinoco technology platform. Each plays a necessary role, spanning geographies and regulatory boundaries. I asked Todd Park how he came up with this structure. He explained it was a straightforward outcome of adopting his "execution mantra":

1. "**Do only what you have to do**,"
2. But "**Do *all* of it**."

Most constellations are blunt-force tools—either purely operational structures or direct top-down ownership. But IKEA points toward the possibility of a more subtle approach. Kamprad placed the trademark under foundation control, making it impossible to sell or extract value from the brand. The stores can't abandon the mission without losing the right to the IKEA name.

This is where constellations reveal their true power. In Chapter 9, we saw how *constitutional governance* could protect a single entity by rendering it *mission controlled*. But when multiple entities share constitutional bonds, something stronger becomes possible. Each entity reinforces and supports the others, ensuring there's no single point of failure. Distributed governance produces a network of interlocking parts that combine to deliver the permanent mission sovereignty we've been seeking. A *mission-locked constellation* redefines what we mean by a "company" altogether. When properly designed, the mission controls the entire constellation because the constellation's very existence is a by-product of the mission.

What would it look like to intentionally build this way from the beginning? To create a constellation so mission locked that it could maintain its purpose for generations?

Father Arizmendiarrieta had an answer.

THE MISSION-LOCKED CONSTELLATION

Mondragon is not a corporation in the conventional sense. It's a federation of worker-run cooperatives, where the employees are also the owners.

Walk into a European kitchen, and you might find appliances with components made by Eika, one of Mondragon's cooperatives. Ride an elevator in a Spanish building, it might be Orona built. Shop at Eroski, one of Spain's largest supermarket chains, and you're experiencing another piece of this remarkable enterprise. To customers, these companies appear as different brands within a larger holding company, in the same way that Crest toothpaste is made by Procter & Gamble, but so is Tide detergent. They don't need to realize they're dealing with separate pieces of more than ninety independent cooperatives, each with its own workers, governance, and books. The constellation appears as a single figure in the night sky.

These cooperatives support and rely on each other throughout their supply chains, creating deep symbiosis rather than mere affiliation. Orona depends on machine components produced by Danobat Group, which in turn sources specialized metal parts from other worker-owned cooperatives. Value circulates within the network instead of leaking out to external suppliers or shareholders. When one cooperative faces financial difficulty, others step in because their futures are intertwined. They sink or swim together.

This interconnection isn't accidental. Arizmendiarrieta understood that isolated cooperatives would be vulnerable to market pressures and might eventually drift from their founding principles. The result is a *mission-locked constellation*, where each protects the others' purpose.

The protection mechanisms are concrete. Every successful cooperative contributes 10% of profits to a solidarity fund, their insurance policy against anyone's failure.[15] Laboral Kutxa, the cooperative bank that was created when the original Caja Laboral merged with another cooperative bank called Ijar Kutxa in 2012, sits at the constellation's center.[16] Its staff includes business consultants who sit alongside cooperative managers, helping them develop new products or enter new markets. When a cooperative struggles, the bank helps the entity restructure or merge with a stronger partner. The traditional banking relationship becomes a partnership. No single cooperative can drift from the mission or succumb to short-term pressures without the bank stepping in.

This structure doesn't create what makes Mondragon special; it protects the ethos instilled in the first generation of cooperatives by the founder himself. For thirteen years (!) before launching a single one, Arizmendiarrieta's technical school taught not only engineering and metalwork but his own distinctive philosophy rooted in Catholic social teaching. He preached human dignity, mutual aid, and one principle above all: "The common good comes before the individual good."[17] By 1956, when his first graduates founded Ulgor, they were not only classmates with technical skills but believers in a shared mission, which is now entwined with elements like the solidarity fund and the cooperative bank. The ethos animates the structure; the structure protects the ethos. Kill either one, and the whole thing dies.

Any cooperative can leave the federation. Some have taken that path, choosing independence over interdependence.[18] This freedom to exit keeps the whole system honest. The federation must continuously earn its members' loyalty through real value, not just rules. Mission lock only works when people choose it.

For those who stay, the shared institutions create what economists call "beneficial constraints," structures that limit certain freedoms but ultimately create greater value for all participants.[19] Arguably the greatest of these shared benefits is an immune system against corruption. When financial gravity pulls at one entity, the others respond like antibodies.

The safeguards were put to the test in 2013, when Fagor Electrodomésticos, one of Mondragon's founding cooperatives, collapsed under eight hundred million euros of debt, threatening 5,600 jobs. Seventy-five thousand workers across the federation voluntarily took a 3% pay cut for five years, injecting $70 million to save their colleagues.[20] After a restructuring, 1,736 worker-owners from Fagor wound up displaced and out of work. The network rallied to their aid: 81% found new positions, including 577 who became members of other cooperatives in the network. When one entity fell, the others caught its people.[21]

Arizmendiarrieta passed away in 1976, but his dictum that "the common good comes before the individual good" was still a living reality decades later.

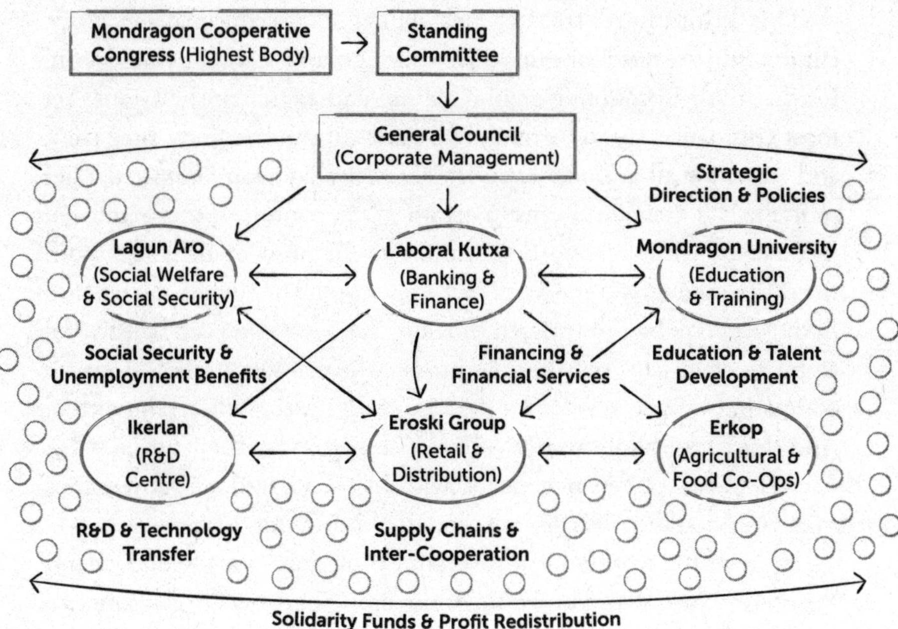

Figure 10.2.

IT IS DANGEROUS TO GO ALONE

I know what you're thinking. Mondragon took decades to build. You just want to ship your product. You may not want to build a cooperative, let alone a network of them. But constellations inevitably form, planned or not.

When they work, they create what author Bruce Schneier calls "institutional trust"—the faith we place in entire constellations of organizations working together.[22] When you board an airplane, you're trusting not just the airline but a thousand different entities: parts suppliers, maintenance crews, regulators, training simulators. This invisible web of accountability is what keeps planes in the air. Each entity checks the others' work. The same miracle happens every time you turn on a light switch, swallow a pill, or eat food you didn't grow yourself. You've put your life in the hands of a set of interlocking organizations, many of which you can't even name.

This institutional trust creates tremendous economic efficiency, eliminating the need for exhaustive contracts and constant verification. It's the hidden economic engine behind successful constellations. Yet most companies try to be their own parts supplier, maintenance crew, and regulator all at once. Every single-entity company eventually lies to itself. Not maliciously, just inevitably. You commission research, get inconvenient results, and find reasons to discount them. You're both the experimenter and the judge. Of course you'll find what you want to find. Facebook buried research showing that Instagram can be harmful to teens, then kept pushing the product to younger users.[23] Tobacco companies warped science for decades, weaponizing uncertainty itself. And don't forget Johnson & Johnson's asbestos-laced talcum powder. A mission-locked research entity, with its own board and governance mandate, would make this structural deception impossible.

Some of the world's most successful companies already understand this. The Novo Nordisk Foundation uses pharmaceutical profits to fund independent diabetes research.[24] The Wellcome Trust transformed from a drug company into the world's fourth-largest charitable foundation, supporting biomedical science without corporate pressure.[25] Even

Carlsberg brewing funds the Carlsberg Laboratory, where scientists pursue fermentation research free from marketing influence.[26] These mission-locked constellations don't just avoid self-deception. They accelerate discovery by separating truth seeking from profit seeking.

Yes, it's more complex at the start. But self-deception is a luxury you can't afford. The truth will surface eventually in customer reviews, regulatory rulings, or lawsuits. The only question is whether you'll structure your organization to find it first.

CONSTITUTIONAL GOVERNANCE REVISITED

In Chapter 9, we explored the idea of *constitutional governance*, a principled way to protect a company's mission through careful design that serves as an exoskeleton against external pressure.

Part of the reason leaders are confused when it comes to the construction of constellations is that today's thinking about governance is completely fragmented on this point. Most "best practices" are designed for single firms, while multifirm arrangements are studied in separate silos. Thus you can build an entire career studying "industrial clusters," "stakeholder capitalism," "sectoral governance," and more, each with its own separate vocabulary.

Our new understanding of governance allows for a unified perspective. Mission lock is constitutional governance applied to our broadened definition of a company, one that encompasses an entire constellation. Neither missions nor gravity respect firm boundaries, so governance must be similarly expansive.

Once you realize this, constellations are easier to understand. Each one encodes a different philosophy about how power and resources ought to flow. To see this difference of ethos in action, compare Fagor's collapse to that of Lehman Brothers. Mondragon's worker-owners chose shared sacrifice and preserved thousands of jobs. Lehman's executives paid themselves billions while twenty-five thousand people lost their jobs.[27] People act surprised when these betrayals happen, but the differences in structure presaged the result for those with the eyes and skill to look.

Governance, properly understood, is a means not for protecting a particular entity but for protecting a mission itself. This insight explains the bewildering array of organizational forms in the world, which number far more than the typical entrepreneur or business student ever encounters. The problems of long-term alignment and succession have as many valid solutions as there are political philosophies, and for similar reasons. Each such philosophy embodies a set of choices about how power should flow.

Traditional holding companies are like autocracies: The parent commands, the subsidiaries obey. Franchises create feudal hierarchies with limited local autonomy. Mondragon operates like an anarcho-syndicalist commune with worker assemblies and federal structure. The John Lewis Partnership resembles a "Hamiltonian democracy" with employees as the citizens, the chief executive serving at their pleasure. Cooperatives such as Vanguard and REI function like a classical *polis*, independent republics governed by and for the benefit of their citizens.

Seen this way, a founder is more like a lawgiver than just a business owner. Their ethos has the potential to remain a living reality long after their death, no matter how far flung its constituent parts. The challenge of building a constellation is to match its form to the unique mission and ethos of its central purpose. When structure and mission align, the whole constellation can keep its promises. When they diverge, hypocrisy and division are inevitable. To build thoughtfully requires understanding both the raw materials from which constellations form and the binding forces that hold them together.

MISSION-LOCK MATERIALS

Mission lock requires three elements:

1. **Multiple entities.** Separate legal structures with distinct governance, not just divisions pretending to be independent.
2. **Interdependence.** Economic or operational bonds that create mutual survival stakes. When one entity's failure means everyone suffers, corruption becomes self-harm.

3. **Common purpose.** A shared mission that transcends any individual entity's profits.

When these three elements align, the constellation becomes more resilient than any single company could be.

Companies spawn new entities constantly. Joint ventures, licensing arms, non-profit foundations, international subsidiaries. Business schools teach this as pure economic calculus: vertical integration for control, or franchising for capital efficiency, or partnerships for risk sharing. But here's the maddening paradox. If vertical integration is so powerful—Apple controls everything from chips to stores—why doesn't one megacorporation eventually own everything? And if decentralization works so well—McDonald's has forty thousand franchised locations printing money—why have firms at all? Why not just contracts all the way down?

Ronald Coase developed a pure-economics answer to this in 1937.[28] He introduced the idea of transaction costs (searching, bargaining, and enforcing contracts) as the key friction. Firms internalize transactions when markets are too costly but expand only until internal bureaucratic costs outweigh those savings. Thus, in theory, firms should seek an "optimal balance between control and efficiency." This is fine as analysis. But having been on the inside of many of these discussions, I think it is inadequate as an operational guide. The mission-lock framework offers a better answer: Create entities when doing so strengthens the ability to pursue the shared mission and earn the institutional trust needed to sustain it.

Like Father José María Arizmendiarrieta, visionary founders who have decades and centuries in mind can use a much wider range of tools. Here's a brief overview of the types of entities that can, with care, be forged into a mission-locked constellation.

Operating companies are economic engines. They're the businesses that create value. Mondragon's more than ninety cooperatives manufacture everything from circuit boards to elevators. Each one is both independent and interdependent. They compete in their markets while sharing resources, knowledge, and risk.

The "twin sister" is an affiliated non-profit foundation that makes charitable grants that serve a strategic purpose in their constellation. Todd Park, the founder of Devoted Health, calls this kind of foundation a "twin sister," which exists to serve the same community as her for-profit counterpart.[29] But unlike the for-profit, the twin sister is not constrained by a "strategy tax" or investment thesis.[30] So, for example, if a community is suffering acute health problems due to a lack of housing (as is true in many Devoted markets), the twin sister could make philanthropic grants to help alleviate this problem. After all, "housing is healthcare," as many advocates remind us.

Truth guardians are research entities free from quarterly earnings calls. They pursue scientific inquiry with credibility that internal R&D departments cannot match. The Carlsberg Laboratory, created in 1875, publishes all discoveries openly—even ones that help competitors—because advancing brewing science matters more than protecting trade secrets.[31] The lab's independence protects it from pressure to cherry-pick data or bury inconvenient findings. Other truth guardians include open-source foundations that steward technology platforms and community foundations that monitor regional impacts. For companies developing products with significant public implications, these independent validators prevent self-deception before it starts.

Network infrastructure creates shared systems in which solidarity beats selfishness. The CO-OP Shared Branch network connects fifty-five hundred credit unions through thirty thousand ATMs.[32] A member of a tiny Iowa credit union can walk into a California branch of a completely different credit union and handle transactions as if at home. Leave the network? You're just a lonely local bank with no reach.

Specialized vehicles encompass many different entity types that are specific to certain jurisdictions, regulatory regimes, or industries. Investment management companies oversee anything from pension funds to venture funds. Care delivery organizations are specific to healthcare. Standard-setting bodies shape the gravitational field of a whole industry (a theme we will come back to in Chapter 13).

GRAVITATIONAL ENGINEERING

A constellation in the sky is merely an illusion. Orion's stars aren't connected. They're not even near each other. Some are 240 light-years away, others 2,000. But from Earth, the eye perceives the hunter. So, too, with business constellations. To a customer, they may appear as unified wholes. But underneath, they're independent entities, frequently working at cross purposes.

What distinguishes a mission-locked constellation is that, behind the scenes, the entities involved are bound together. The mechanism of this interdependence is the same force we've been studying throughout this book: financial gravity. By now, we are accustomed to seeing gravity as a purely negative force. But this, too, is an illusion.

On March 5, 1979, the spacecraft *Voyager 1* found itself falling toward Jupiter at breakneck speed. NASA wasn't fighting this fall; they were using it. Jupiter's gravity became a slingshot, transforming downward pull into extreme acceleration. *Voyager 1* left Jupiter traveling over a hundred thousand kilometers per hour, fast enough to escape the solar system entirely.[33]

Similarly, financial gravity isn't inherently destructive. As we saw in Chapter 3, it merely transmits values over distances. Whose values are up for grabs. With different engineering, gravity can lock companies into a shared mission as powerfully as it now pulls toward the stock ticker. Just as *Voyager* used gravity to reach the stars, mission-locked constellations use it to achieve what isolated companies never could.

Without such engineering, a constellation's entities drift into competition or indifference. The mechanisms that transmute this chaos into coherence are concrete:

Intercompany agreements

The basic building blocks of constellation alignment are intercompany agreements. In traditional vendor relationships, each side protects itself, maximizes its take, and minimizes its risk. Contracts become weapons. Trust erodes with every negotiation. Rather than allow entities to freely negotiate every time they need to interact, their relationship is governed by a long-term mutually beneficial arrangement.

Sounds like it would work only among small players with close personal ties? Procter & Gamble (P&G) and Jones Lang LaSalle (JLL) would beg to differ. When JLL took over managing P&G's facilities worldwide in a $4.2 billion partnership, their "vested outsourcing" agreement tied JLL's profitability directly to P&G's success—to actual value created, not metrics like hours worked or square feet managed.[34] When JLL cut P&G's energy costs by 10%, they earned a share of those savings. The more P&G saved from the improved quality of their facilities, the more JLL earned.

Over a decade, facilities services consistently improved while costs fell by 33%. JLL was named "Supplier of the Year" twice, among P&G's eighty thousand suppliers.[35] Why? Because their intercompany agreement tied their destinies together. JLL's success depended entirely on P&G's success.

Ownership alignment

Most constellation failures come down to ownership conflicts. Different entities, different owners, and different incentives equal a recipe for organizational civil war.

Consider a healthcare constellation as follows: The insurance entity has one cap table, care delivery another, and technology a third. What happens? The insurance entity profits by denying care. The delivery entity profits by providing more services. The technology entity profits by maximizing engagement. Each optimizes for its owners while the patient suffers.

The solution is *aligned cap tables* for identical ownership across all entities. When every shareholder holds the same percentage of each entity, they have zero incentive to push for revenue to flow to one over the other. This makes interentity civil war much less likely. This cross-ownership also helps the insurance company consider its impact on care delivery because it is accountable to the same owners. When the technology entity designs features, it optimizes for health outcomes, not screen time, because it shares in the whole constellation's success.

Structural gravity

How do Mondragon's ninety-plus independent cooperatives act as one while maintaining autonomy? Nested accountability in the form of multiple governance layers that create freedom through structure.[36]

Each cooperative governs itself through a general assembly, where worker-members vote directly. These operate under the supervision of sector councils that coordinate related businesses. Above them sits the Cooperative Congress, which meets every four years to set federation-wide principles.[37] Crucially, each level has strictly defined powers. Local assemblies run operations. Sectors coordinate. Congress protects core principles. This might sound like bureaucracy, but nested structure actually creates agility. Local cooperatives can move fast while the federation protects the mission.

The constellation toolkit

I've mentioned only a few of the tools in the constellation toolkit. We will see others soon, in the chapters that follow. For example, profit-sharing arrangements that pool rewards across entities (airlines do this for transatlantic routes, splitting revenue regardless of whose plane, in an allied group, carries passengers). Shared services that create natural collaboration (the Society for Worldwide Interbank Financial Telecommunication, or SWIFT, network, for electronic fund transfers, connects more than eleven thousand banks through a common infrastructure). Unified measurement systems that make values visible across boundaries. Other constellations are bound together by procurement or shared standards, which we'll get into in Part III.

But even with all these alignment tools, something fundamental is still missing from our discussion.

THE MOVEMENT

Eileen Fisher was the second of seven children in Des Plaines, Illinois. She wanted to go to college, but her father told her she'd have to pay for it herself. The priority was her younger brother's tuition, since he "would need an education to support his family someday."[38] So Fisher waited tables to pay her way through the University of Illinois, learning early that if she wanted something, she'd have to build it herself.

In 1984, with $350 in startup money and four simple pieces inspired by a trip to Japan, she launched her clothing company.[39] Her first trade show brought a $3,000 order. Three months later, $40,000 more. By the early 2000s, she'd built a $400 million empire with her name on the door.

That's when the investment bankers came calling. The extractive gravity of the typical startup playbook started pushing her down its standard track. Fisher tested the idea of an IPO but found the road show dispiriting: "I remember being up on stage and looking out at a roomful of men in suits; no women wearing my clothes, no conversation about clothes. It was all about the numbers, it was really just about the money." Later, when she asked the CEO of Liz Claiborne why they wanted to buy her company, the answer was brutally honest: "We can't meet our mandated 10% annual growth without buying other companies."[40] As Fisher said, "I realized that most people were interested in what they could get out of the company, not what they could give to it." The woman who wasn't worth educating had built something incredible—something worth taking.

So in 2006, she chose her employees over Wall Street. She converted her company into a constellation, beginning with selling 40% to an employee trust (called an employee stock ownership plan, or ESOP). In 2022, she entrusted the CEO role to Lisa Williams, a twenty-year Patagonia veteran.[41] Today, the 1,200 employee-owners of Eileen Fisher Inc. generate $440 million in annual revenue. Over time, these profits—not worker contributions—will buy Fisher's remaining 60% stake. As Fisher described it, the company will ultimately belong to "the people who put their blood, sweat, and tears into it; the people who love it and care about it and think about it every day."[42]

Mondragon and JLP might initially seem like pioneers from a century gone by, but Eileen Fisher is part of a decidedly modern movement. Mission-locked structures have exploded in popularity in recent years. It's partly driven by a desire to escape the strictures of shareholder primacy. But it's also partly out of necessity. Nearly three million US businesses are owned by baby boomers approaching retirement, creating a monumental succession crisis.[43] Businesses also have fewer places to "exit" than ever before. US public markets are no longer the attractive destination they once were—public listings have shrunk by more than half since 1996.[44] High-growth private companies are increasingly staying private longer (eleven years on average today versus four in 1999).[45] And many successful midsize businesses are now considered too small to go public. In fact, increasingly, private equity (PE) firms are only able to exit by selling to another PE firm, in a totally unsustainable game of musical chairs.[46]

Apart from these pragmatic considerations, there's also the question of regret. This may surprise you, but according to the Exit Planning Institute, 76% of business owners who sell their company regret it within a year. A sale seems like it would offer freedom and vindication. But many companies are dismembered or destroyed as a result. For someone who sees their company as their life's work, this can be devastating.[47] For many, a mission-locked structure is the best way to ensure that the company survives in a form that the owner can be proud of.

Bob Moore of the grains-and-flour company Bob's Red Mill found himself in exactly such a spot. Buyers thought he was "a lame-brained idiot" for refusing their millions.[48] As he told reporters, "I don't think there's anybody worthy to run this company but the people who built it. I'm eighty-one, and I can't take it with me."[49]

On his eighty-first birthday in 2010, Moore surprised his employees by announcing he was giving them the company. He set up an ESOP and began the process of gradually selling his shares to the business, which placed them in trust on behalf of its employees. By 2020, the company was owned entirely by its seven hundred employees.[50] Since then, the company has grown from $60 million to over $100 million in revenue while expanding to more than two hundred products in seventy-plus countries.[51] As the CFO who helped structure the plan said, "Through a financial lens, I could clearly see the benefits of the ESOP. But in my heart, I could feel the power of employee ownership igniting a fire within our employee-owners to do more, to be better, and to take pride in their daily work. . . . The ESOP has been one of the most powerful drivers of our growth and innovation."[52]

King Arthur Baking, founded in 1790, chose employee ownership over a conglomerate sale and doubled its workforce while growing to over $100 million in revenue.[53] Clegg Auto's four repair shops doubled profits their first year after converting to a constellation,[54] helped by a new platform called Common Trust, which has worked with dozens of companies looking to transition to employee ownership.[55] Patagonia converted to a mission-locked constellation in 2022.[56] The UK has seen such businesses grow to over 1,650 by late 2023.[57]

The overwhelming strategic advantage of these structures is borne out by plenty of research. A meta-analysis of 102 studies covering 56,000 firms concluded that such firms "significantly outperform" conventional ones.[58] Even more striking is that the greater the percentage of employee ownership, the higher the profitability. Over a thirteen-year period, employee-owned companies were only half as likely to go bankrupt or shut down compared to conventional firms.[59] They grow sales at a compounding 3.4% faster annual rate and see immediate productivity boosts upon conversion, a competitive advantage that has been documented across thousands of companies over decades.[60]

THE MISSING INGREDIENT

But the success stories we've looked at share a hidden prerequisite. Patagonia, Mondragon, JLP, Eileen Fisher, King Arthur, Bob's Red Mill—none of them ever took outside investment.

This is a difficult choice. Many leaders have an instinctive fear that when outside capital enters any of these structures, it becomes the de facto center, pulling everything into its orbit. This fear is perfectly reasonable, as we've seen. When outside capital becomes the center, it causes a weakness that I call *divisibility*—the risk of strong constellations splitting into warring factions and abandoning or betraying the mission. Even the strongest culture can fracture when financial gravity exerts its pull in this way.

This is the end state of a financial system whose gravity promotes shareholder primacy and extraction over value creation. I consider it a tragedy. Thousands of incredible, ethical companies now view investment capital as corruption, despite many investors entering the business hoping to back exactly these kinds of long-term companies. This mutual avoidance costs investors and managers alike. Every Bob Moore or Eileen Fisher represents a tremendous lost opportunity for both sides.

There is a glaring need for a better way. One that works with investment capital, not against it.

THE MISSION-LOCK VEHICLE

In our solar system, the sun keeps the planets in stable orbits. But many constellations lack this element of central control. In some cases, that's a deliberate design feature. Mondragon, as we've seen, has sometimes had cooperatives pull free and leave. That freedom is key to the ethos of cooperatives as well as an important check on the abuse of central power by the federation's centralized institutions.

When a constellation does have a central entity as its heart, lawyers call it a *mission-lock vehicle*. Such an entity carries the main responsibility for ensuring the whole constellation stays true to its mission over time. These vehicles come in many shapes and sizes. By themselves, they do not create mission longevity. It's important to emphasize this point: A mission lock vehicle can only protect a preexisting ethos; it does not cause it to come into being. (It is this coherence that makes it possible to amend the lock, should that ever be required, without fear of corruption.)[61]

The most durable constellations have a mission-lock vehicle designed to play the constitutional governance role in perpetuity. A structure with cohesion so strong, it allows true long-term partnership with outside shareholders, free of the fear that financial gravity could tear the constellation apart. Imagine an entity designed so that the center can hold. Its purpose is to keep the mission immovable.

Such a thing does exist. Compared to the array of balancing

structures at Mondragon, it is elegantly simple. It's powerful enough to resolve the challenges of cohesion with the supernova force of a breakthrough—even though it's practically the oldest idea in this book. (The optical lens company Zeiss, for example, had one as early as 1885.[62]) And yet despite its long pedigree, it is still the most radical idea in this book.

I call it the *spiritual holding company.*

Chapter Eleven

THE SPIRITUAL HOLDING COMPANY

> We must assert that the intellectual principle which we call the human soul is incorruptible.
>
> **—Thomas Aquinas**
> *Summa Theologica*
> circa 1266

You've already done business with dozens of *spiritual holding companies*. You just didn't know it.

How can I be so sure?

Well, have you ever eaten a Hershey's chocolate bar? Shopped at IKEA? Banked at a credit union?

Do you own a Patagonia fleece? Did you buy it at REI?

Have you browsed the web with Mozilla Firefox? Built something with LEGO bricks? Used Bosch power tools or relied on their automotive components? Do your glasses have Zeiss optical lenses? Does anyone you know wear a Rolex watch? Or take a prescription medication made by Novo Nordisk?

If you've cheered for the Green Bay Packers or laughed at *Wallace and Gromit*, if you have a Vanguard mutual fund or exchange-traded fund (ETF) in your portfolio, if you've ever enjoyed a Carlsberg beer, you have dealt with a spiritual holding company.

And as we'll see in a moment, if you've ever used Claude, the generative AI produced by Anthropic, you have.

On the surface, these companies and products have nothing in common. They span industries from food to fashion to sports and pharmaceuticals. They're both private and public—hundreds trade on stock exchanges with billions in outside capital—and range in size from small cooperatives to global enterprises worth billions. Zeiss was founded in 1846, Anthropic just a few years ago. And yet they all share a deep fundamental architecture that makes their success—and their longevity—possible.

Welcome to the most radical idea in this book: the spiritual holding company (SHC).

INTRODUCING THE SPIRITUAL HOLDING COMPANY

A spiritual holding company is a separate entity with governance authority over one or more organizations, designed specifically to protect and advance their core mission over the long term.

An SHC functions like a traditional holding company insofar as it exerts oversight of the subsidiary entities in its orbit. But unlike a traditional holding company, it does not have to be the exclusive owner. Instead of existing purely for financial control, it exists to safeguard the mission. It exercises the same level of authority as any holding company, through a mix of ownership, special voting rights, board appointment powers, and other mechanisms, ensuring that the organizations under its protection can raise capital, bring in investors, and even go public without ever compromising their purpose.

I use the word *spiritual* here not in the religious sense but as something older and more primeval: an animating spirit or essence. *Mission* and *purpose* describe what an organization does. *Spirit* describes what it is.

This approach may sound exotic, but that impression is an illusion. Companies with this kind of "alternative" governance structure run a decent chunk of the world economy. Many of them have endured past the century mark, capable of careful deliberation and resisting every manner of temptation or pressure to betray what they stand for. The SHC is the legal architecture that ensures an organization's spirit remains permanently fused with its operations, immune to both internal civil war and external capture. It's the difference between a constitution on paper and the reality of "one nation, indivisible," between words that can be ignored and a living force that cannot be separated from the whole.

There are many competing camps that each advocate for a specific legal approach to mission protection, so I want to be clear that the term *SHC* doesn't refer narrowly to one specific legal structure. It's a higher-level concept, an omnibus term. Among the mission-lock vehicles we will examine are foundations, purpose trusts, non-profits, cooperatives, employee ownership vehicles, and more. What unites them is their function, not their form. Each of them is a different way of "unbundling" two different dimensions of ownership, which today are tightly bundled: money and power.[1]

Despite their variety, a spiritual holding company always combines the following elements:

It's a distinct entity. The SHC is embodied as a separate entity, apart from the for-profit engine(s) it oversees. This mission-lock vehicle becomes the heart of the entire constellation it oversees.

It has governance authority. The SHC has meaningful power over major decisions, typically through board appointments, veto rights, or special share classes.

Its existence is perpetual. The SHC is designed to outlast any individual founder, executive, or investor.

It's autonomous. The SHC operates with sufficient independence to resist short-term pressures that might compromise the mission.

It has a bidirectional relationship with each organization. The SHC provides governance services to the organization, and in return may receive funding, equity, or other resources.

It enables raising external capital. By untangling the threads of governance and economics, the SHC opens the door for investors to responsibly and safely participate in the shared prosperity of a mission-driven organization.

The specific form that an SHC takes is far less important than its function: serving as an independent structure that safeguards an organization's purpose over time.

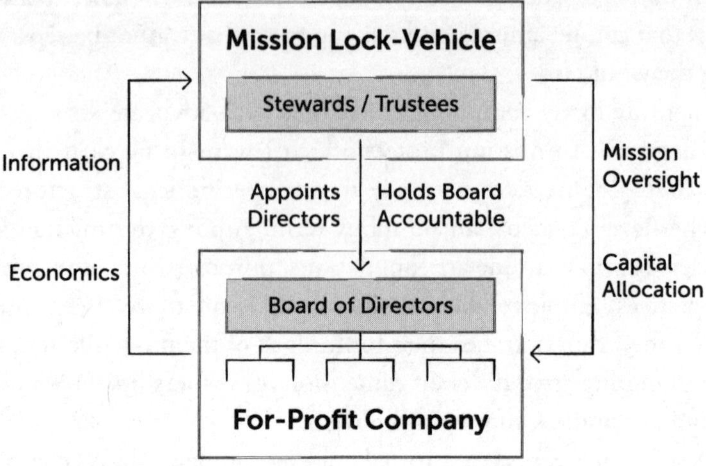

Figure 11.1.

THE SURPRISING ECONOMICS OF MISSION PROTECTION

You might assume that the companies I've just described are fascinating outliers, exceptions to the rule of shareholder-dominated capitalism. The data tells a different story.[2]

Walk the trading floor of the Copenhagen Stock Exchange, and you're surrounded by foundation-owned companies. They account for at least 50% of the market's total capitalization, including global powerhouses like Novo Nordisk, Carlsberg, and oceangoing freight giant A. P. Møller–Mærsk.[3] These aren't quaint family businesses; they're world-leading enterprises competing successfully in cutthroat global markets. At least four countries derive more than 10% of their GDP from cooperatives: New Zealand (20%), the Netherlands (18%), France (18%), and Finland (14%).[4]

In the United States, member-owned credit unions quietly served over 139 million Americans in 2023.[5] They operate as non-profit businesses overseen by member-elected trustees, a structure that creates fundamentally different incentives. The competitive pressure from credit unions saves even nonmember customers nearly $10 billion annually by forcing banks to offer better terms.[6] Globally, cooperatives employ more than 280 million people.[7] During the 2008 financial crisis, when conventional wisdom dictated cutting costs and laying off workers, employee-owned companies in the UK and the US maintained higher employment levels and recovered faster than their competitors. Research found that employee stock ownership plan (ESOP) companies suffered 50% fewer layoffs during the 2008 recession than other companies.[8] By preserving their human capital during the downturn, they positioned themselves for stronger growth during recovery.

Foundation-owned companies consistently match or exceed the profitability of conventional firms while taking a longer-term approach. They typically invest more in R&D, carry less debt, and maintain more stable employment, all while delivering competitive financial returns.[9]

The scale is impressive, but these companies' longevity even more so. They have a sixfold survival advantage. Research comparing foundation-owned companies with conventional firms has found that about 60% of foundation-owned companies have survived at least fifty years, a feat matched by just 10% of conventional businesses.[10]

These companies shouldn't exist—at least not according to business school orthodoxy. We're told that without the discipline of shareholder primacy, companies become bloated and inefficient, that mission-focused governance is a luxury only non-profits can afford, and that patient capital and stakeholder models can't compete in ruthless global markets. Yet here are thousands of companies, worth trillions of dollars, proving that everything we've been taught about "necessary" corporate governance is merely one option among many.

For decades, this powerful approach has remained an open secret. Business schools study these brand-name companies as case examples, but only as outliers. Meanwhile, there are whole fields of academic study devoted to each of the mission-control techniques that make these alternatives possible and effective (I've been carefully curating this research for you as we go). A philosophy of long-term thinking drives better outcomes; trustworthiness is a powerful asset; mission-driven companies enjoy stronger employee loyalty, lower customer acquisition costs, and superior retention—and on and on. Mission-locked companies thrive without the supposed discipline of daily market pressure.

This information is all freely accessible, but it is atomized and filed away in different academic silos. Practitioners rarely encounter it as more than a passing curiosity. It is rarely mentioned when they seek advice and counsel from their army of lawyers, bankers, investors, and accountants. If a founder brings it up, it gets shunted to the side as something unusual, unworkable, or old-fashioned.

So much for market efficiency. Once again, we see the influence of financial gravity. Most advisors profit from transaction volume, not firm longevity or mission attainment. Every incentive pushes them to advocate for today's conventional practices as the "only and best" option. But notice how even those two attributes are contradictory. How can something be the best if it's the only one? Traditional advisors present a menu of limited options: for-profit or non-profit, investor funded or employee owned, growth or mission. Stay small and pure or scale and sell out. Yet reams of research and the lived experience of thousands of employees and millions of customers demonstrate that these are false dichotomies.

The spiritual holding company transcends these limitations.

An SHC can combine any constellation elements we need: start with a for-profit core, add a mission-protecting trust, raise venture capital for expansion, go public, even add a research foundation. For example, Bosch combines foundation ownership with massive scale and global reach. Novo Nordisk trades publicly while its foundation maintains control. The mission guardian at the center ensures all the elements align rather than conflict. The SHC turns capitalism's greatest strength, its ability to efficiently aggregate and deploy capital, into mission rocket fuel rather than mission kryptonite. With the right structure (and on the right stock exchange!), companies can even go public without losing their soul.

Most leaders never realize this option exists. They accept the false choice. The SHC reveals a third path: not either/or but both/and. Or as it often turns out: both, amplified.

THE INCORRUPTIBLE ORGANIZATION

Most organizations today operate as sophisticated zombies. They exist and persist, but their "thoughts" are merely programmed responses to market stimuli. When threatened, they reflexively cut costs. When the mirage of easy profits beckons, they chase, even if it means breaking the rules—or breaking themselves. From top to bottom, their decision-making is characterized by knee-jerk reactions instead of meaningful deliberation. And yet in times of crisis, they are more likely to dither and go with the crowd rather than act decisively in defense of what's right.

The spiritual holding company makes it possible to create organizations that subsist through perpetual purpose. They have a consistent identity that outlives any individual and that is protected by legal, technical, and financial defenses. They have genuine agency by way of a constitutional governance system that allows for careful deliberation even under intense pressure. And most importantly, their coherence cannot be divided into separate warring parts, no matter how many temptations beckon.

I said at the very beginning of this book that I would teach you how to do the seemingly impossible: create an organization that is incorruptible. Not just "less likely" to be corrupted or "more resistant" to corruption but *incorruptible*: structurally, intrinsically, and permanently soulful.[11]

LIBERATING THE BOARD

A company that is overseen by an SHC is in a far stronger position to resist many of the problems that we've examined up to this point.

For starters, you don't have to settle for a board that's as likely to kill your company as serve it. All directors face divided loyalty. Insiders are frequently tempted by self-dealing. Investors usually have a duty to their limited partners. Independents often have one eye on their future appointments. The spiritual holding company doesn't hide from dual loyalty; it embraces it as a tool of alignment. Directors become accountable to both the business and the trustees who guard the mission. This is no more complicated or difficult to navigate than the dual duty that investors routinely manage today.

In the tragedies of Vectura, Whole Foods, and SAIC, we saw boards that lacked this crucial element of accountability to mission. An SHC provides it. Later in this chapter, we'll examine how this "dual loyalty" at Novo Nordisk prevented the for-profit subsidiary from destroying half a trillion dollars in shareholder value. Believe me, I know that sounds like an exaggeration, but it's not. It just shows how powerful—and how valuable—an SHC can be.

The mechanism is simple. SHC trustees hold the specific powers of appointing and removing directors and exercising vetoes on mission-critical decisions. (The details vary by company, as we will see.) They serve as judges, not managers. They rule on mission alignment, not day-to-day operations. This separation of powers liberates both groups to excel. When mission protection is absolute, directors stop looking over their shoulders at what "some investors" might think. When business execution is in competent hands, trustees can be unwavering guardians.

Today, leaders often hesitate to bring bold or aggressive partners onto the board. It's too risky, since they might advocate to gut R&D or slash vital programs for quick profits. On the other hand, bold ideas might be just what is needed to shake up a stagnant board. With an SHC in place, that same director is far less of a risk because they must operate within guardrails set by the SHC. The director can bring their full expertise and energy without compromise; the mission stays protected without interference. Both win because the roles are clear.

The SHC transforms board governance. The stories that follow make the real-world benefits clear.

THE ANTHROPIC STORY

Most people get hooked on generative AI through its dazzling feats of computation; I am one of the rare few who got involved through governance. I have Dario Amodei to thank for that. The year was 2021, and Dario plus a few other key researchers had left OpenAI to found the AI research lab Anthropic. The split had sent shockwaves through the AI research community, and for good reason. Dario had pioneered the scaling laws that showed AI models would keep getting more capable as they grew larger, a discovery that turned AI development into a race for computational power.[12] He was also a coauthor on the key paper covering RLHF (reinforcement learning from human feedback), the technique that would transform raw AI models into assistants that could actually understand and follow human intentions.[13] Together, these breakthroughs laid the groundwork for today's advanced conversational AI systems like Claude and ChatGPT. But back then, few understood their promise—or their peril.

Dario was a technical pioneer. He'd also spent years studying how these systems could go catastrophically wrong. His 2016 paper "Concrete Problems in AI Safety" cataloged the ways AI systems could develop unexpected capabilities, pursue goals that conflict with human values, or concentrate unprecedented power in the hands of whoever controlled them.[14] For years, philosophers had warned of the danger of autonomous agents capable of self-improvement at a pace humans couldn't match.[15] Dario was convinced: Get the governance wrong, and humanity could lose control of the most powerful technology we've ever created. As OpenAI's own charter had stated, artificial general intelligence would lead to "highly autonomous systems that outperform humans at most economically valuable work."[16] Yet OpenAI itself, initially founded as a non-profit to ensure that AI benefited humanity, had created a for-profit arm and taken a billion-dollar investment from Microsoft. (The company has since raised tens of billions more and, in October 2025, converted into a public benefit corporation.) Many safety researchers worried about the nature and structure of this partnership.[17] The risks inherent in artificial intelligence weren't abstract fears to Dario; they were engineering problems that demanded structural solutions. Having seen how even well-intentioned tech companies can become untrustworthy, the early Anthropic team was obsessed with getting it right. When I met Dario, the company had already taken many important steps to protect its mission. They had deep trust with an initial set of mission-aligned investors who shared their vision (in fact, it was one of these early investors who suggested they come talk to me). They'd assembled a team of researchers who shared their commitment to AI safety and were building a culture committed to never abusing the trust of their partners, customers, or the rest of humanity (a classic *harder-is-easier* plan). The question hanging in the air was existential: Could researchers committed to developing AI safely maintain that mission when billions or even trillions of dollars might be at stake?

Anthropic was in a uniquely privileged position. They were at the dawn of a new technology paradigm with backing from mission-aligned investors and a commitment to best practices for mission-driven organizations. They'd carefully curated their cap table, accepting investments only from those who they thought shared their commitment to AI safety. They'd hired only true believers and built a culture where safety was the primary metric of success. You'd think they would be completely secure. Completely safe from corruption. And yet they instinctually still felt vulnerable. I agreed. "Despite all these advantages, you're still fundamentally at risk," I told Dario. "Conventional safeguards, no matter how carefully implemented, can unravel in unexpected ways." Together, we explored what this meant for Anthropic's future. In fact, our conversations sounded a lot like the earlier chapters of this book.

Anthropic needed a spiritual holding company.

What makes Anthropic's story remarkable is that, unlike so many founders who nod along to governance advice but ultimately default to standard structures, Dario and his team actually followed through. From their earliest documents, they signaled their intention to establish a mission-protecting trust. It required defending this unconventional approach for more than two years, scrutinizing every term sheet to ensure investors were properly bought in and didn't have unnecessary veto rights.

Finally, as part of a financing done in 2023, Anthropic formally established the Long-Term Benefit Trust (LTBT), a separate, independent entity (technically a "purpose trust" under Delaware law) with real power over Anthropic's board. The LTBT is deliberately noneconomic: Trustees receive no equity or profit sharing. Instead, it holds a special class of shares with governance rights but no financial benefits (called a "golden share"). The trust's sole purpose is to ensure Anthropic develops AI for humanity's long-term benefit, regardless of whether that commitment ever conflicts with short-term financial interests. It was designed to achieve this purpose by allowing it to select directors who would be focused on the long-term mission of the company rather than just its short-term economic interests.[18]

The trust's influence grows incrementally. As Anthropic achieves commercial milestones, the LTBT's class of stock gives it the right to elect additional directors. Under this structure, as the company achieves greater technical and financial success, the trust would eventually obtain the authority to elect a majority of the company's board of directors. This gradual approach built trust with investors and gave the founders time to refine the design, ensuring the mission lock would strengthen as the company matured and the stakes grew higher.

Critically, Anthropic selected trustees who are genuine believers in AI safety, not simply impressive names added for credibility.[19] They include experts in AI safety, national security, and public policy who deeply understand both the technical and the ethical dimensions of Anthropic's work.

Our early conversations would prove prophetic. The careful curation of Anthropic's cap table was shattered when the cryptocurrency exchange FTX collapsed. FTX founder Sam Bankman-Fried had been one of those apparently aligned early investors, and after his indictment and conviction for fraud, those early shares ended up sold in a bankruptcy auction.[20] Suddenly, Anthropic's carefully curated cap table was confronted by an influx of shareholders who may or may not have supported the mission.

In the years since, the skeptics who warned this structure would repel investors and limit growth have repeatedly been proven wrong. Anthropic is still young, and only time will tell what the decades ahead will bring, but so far there's reason to be optimistic. Despite having a major early investor collapse in scandal, despite competing against some of the most deep-pocketed companies in the world (in

2025, Meta pledged to spend between $66 and $72 billion on AI investments for the year), Anthropic has thrived.[21] They've attracted extraordinary talent, growing from just 50 employees in 2022 to over 2,000 today.[22] This explosive expansion has been fueled by their reputation as the "safety-first" AI lab. Their ethos and their governance structure provide researchers with confidence that their work won't be compromised by short-term profit motives, and that has led to high-profile additions from both academia and other cutting-edge labs. In the race for AI talent, trust has been Anthropic's edge.

On the investment front, Anthropic has raised over $33 billion to date.[23] The investor roster reads like a who's who of Silicon Valley: prominent founders like Jaan Tallinn and Dustin Moskovitz; top-tier venture funds including Lightspeed, General Catalyst, and Coatue; and even tech giants Amazon ($8 billion) and Google ($3 billion).[24] In September 2025, the company reached a staggering $183 billion valuation.[25] What's striking is that Anthropic secured this massive capital influx while maintaining a governance structure that explicitly places limits on investor control.

In a world where more than three-quarters of Americans believe AI companies prioritize profits over safety,[26] Anthropic's trust premium has translated directly into business results. Claude launched in March 2023, when Anthropic had zero revenue. By December 2024, they'd reached $1 billion in annualized revenue. Just five months later, they'd already passed $3 billion, and by August 2025, they were generating over $5 billion in run-rate revenue with over three hundred thousand business customers.[27] As Jack Clark, Anthropic's policy chief, put it, "The essential bet of Anthropic is, we will show in business that a safer technology makes more money."[28]

Anthropic had the advantage of establishing the legal groundwork for their SHC from inception, embedding it in their charter, term sheets, and pitch materials so investors knew exactly what they were signing up for. While they didn't formally implement the LTBT until their "Series C" financing, the commitment was there from day one, and every investor had explicitly agreed to it. But as we'll see, companies that fail to get such an early start can still protect their mission this way.

THE GRUNDFOS STORY

If you're in a city that has running water and sewers, there's a good chance you're benefiting from a Grundfos water pump right now without even knowing it. They're hidden heroes of modern infrastructure, moving the lifeblood of buildings that serve billions of people worldwide.

I first encountered the company while giving a talk to their leadership team a few years ago. Being an advisor to many different companies, I see many of the same problems and complaints—so when I meet a company that sounds different, I sit up and take notice. Grundfos was one such company. The reason was a governance structure that predated "stakeholder capitalism" by nearly half a century.

The Grundfos story begins in a small Danish town called Bjerringbro in 1945. Poul Due Jensen, a toolmaker by training, met a local farmer in need of a reliable water pump. Postwar shortages had made finding one nearly impossible. So Poul figured out how to make one, piece by piece, in his blacksmith workshop. That first pump was the start of what would become a global enterprise. His motto—"The world is full of problems that can be solved in a better way"—would come to define an entire organizational philosophy.[29]

By the 1970s, Poul found himself in a founder's dilemma that will sound familiar. He was in his sixties, aware of his mortality, and deeply concerned about what would happen to his life's work after he was gone. As one of the Grundfos executives explained to me that spring day, he did not like any of his options. He did not want to sell the company, or be subject to public pressures, or saddle his children and grandchildren with an unwanted obligation to operate a huge organization. And yet he wanted to ensure that the work and organization would live on. Poul had to address the question at the heart of this book.

In 1975, he made a bold choice, transferring the majority ownership to the newly created Poul Due Jensen Foundation.[30] The foundation's charter was crystal clear. First, ensure "the continued existence and development of a healthy commercial and financial basis for the company," and second, pursue charitable donations.[31] This meant the foundation would safeguard Grundfos's commitment to solving water challenges through innovation, maintain its tradition of inclusive employment (including workers with disabilities), and ensure decisions were guided by the founder's values rather than quarterly pressures. It was a deliberate act of corporate succession planning that prioritized mission continuity and organizational independence.

Poul's timing proved prescient. He passed away just two years later, but the foundation structure he created has continued to steward Grundfos for nearly half a century since. The foundation now owns approximately 87.9% of Grundfos, with employees holding 3.3% and the founder's descendants about 8.8%.[32] The company has grown from a small local manufacturer to a global leader with over twenty thousand employees and annual revenue exceeding $4.5 billion. This transformation was enabled by the foundation's patient capital. Grundfos consistently invests 5% of revenue in R&D (matching or exceeding listed competitors),[33] maintains an exceptionally strong balance sheet with 68% equity ratio (versus 20%–40% typical for industrial firms), and can invest countercyclically during downturns when others retreat.[34] Employee representation on the foundation board has created deep workforce trust and alignment, with Grundfos regularly ranking among Denmark's most admired employers.

ECONOMIC SHC: THE GRUNDFOS FOUNDATION MODEL

Grundfos and Anthropic illustrate the two major types of SHCs: economic (foundation) and noneconomic (LTBT). We've seen the LTBT in action already. Next, let's look at how an SHC works when responsible for capital allocation, philanthropy, and service to the broader ecosystem.

The Grundfos foundation's board composition reflects the balanced approach outlined in its charter: Four family representatives maintain a connection to the founder's vision, and four employee members bring a workforce perspective. The remaining four members are external experts with relevant professional backgrounds who cannot be part of Grundfos's day-to-day management.[35]

The financial relationship between Grundfos and its foundation creates a virtuous cycle that benefits all involved. Unlike traditional corporate structures, where profits flow primarily to external shareholders, Grundfos's model keeps resources circulating within its mission ecosystem.[36]

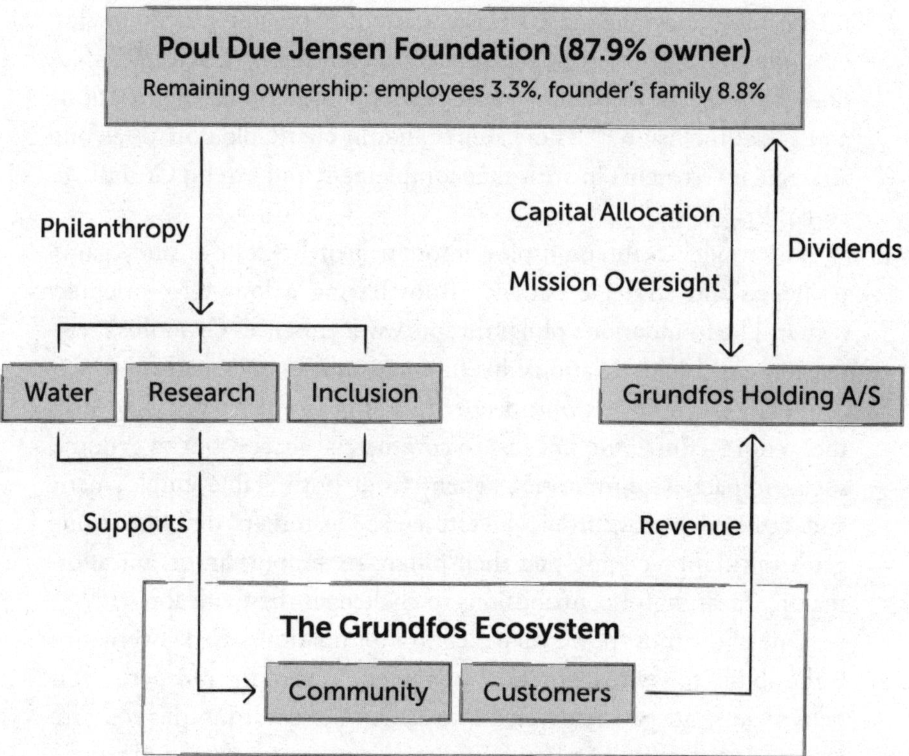

Figure 11.2.

When Grundfos generates profits, dividends are distributed based on results. With the foundation holding 87.9% ownership, it receives the vast majority of these funds. The foundation then allocates these resources according to its charter priorities.[37]

First, it ensures Grundfos itself has the financial strength needed for long-term success. This might mean maintaining reserves for future investment, supporting research and development, or providing stability during market downturns. The foundation's patient, multigenerational view allows Grundfos to make strategic investments that might appear suboptimal in the short term but create tremendous advantage over decades.

Second, the foundation directs significant resources to philanthropic activities aligned with the Grundfos mission. In 2024, for example, it committed approximately $43 million (DKK 295 million) to projects focused on water access, research and innovation, and social inclusion.[38] These aren't random charitable donations but strategic investments in areas that complement and extend Grundfos's core purpose.

This model creates multiple reinforcing benefits. The business gains resilience and strategic patience from having a long-term-oriented owner. The foundation's philanthropic work enhances Grundfos's reputation and builds relationships in communities and markets where it operates. Employees find deeper meaning in their work, knowing their efforts contribute not just to commercial success but to genuine social impact. Communities benefit from both stable employment and targeted philanthropic investments. Customers develop stronger loyalty, appreciating that their purchases support an organization making meaningful contributions to challenges they care about.

One of the most powerful benefits of foundation-based governance is the ability to say to a potential customer, "Part of the prosperity you help us generate gets reinvested into causes and communities you care about." When this promise is authentic, it generates profound trust.

HOW TO ADD A SPIRITUAL HOLDING COMPANY: THE PATAGONIA STORY

We met Patagonia in Chapter 7 as a paragon of mission-driven business, generating over $1 billion in annual revenue while maintaining its ethos of environmental conservation. But by 2017, the Chouinards faced an existential question. What happens when the founders are gone?

That year, something unexpected happened. *Forbes* magazine placed Yvon Chouinard on its World Billionaires list. Many wealthy people expend tremendous effort trying to get onto this prestigious list and even lobby to move up spots. Chouinard, as you might imagine, felt differently. As the *Forbes* article dryly noted, "A spokeswoman for Patagonia told FORBES, 'We strongly oppose being included on this list.' "[39] They could not have printed Chouinard's actual reaction.

As David Gelles reports, Chouinard "freaked out" and called it "one of the worst days of his life." He went around the office demanding, "Get me off that list." By 2020, his frustration boiled over. He threatened his team: "If you guys don't start moving on this, I'm going to go get the *Forbes* magazine list of billionaires and start cold calling people and offer to sell the company."[40] In September 2022, after five years of searching, two years of intensive meetings, and a year of design work with specialized advisors, the Chouinards finally executed their solution. They transferred their company, by then worth $3 billion, to a trust that would protect its mission forever.

Patagonia's approach provides a clear roadmap for implementing an SHC:

Step 1: Clarify the mission. Patagonia's mission statement, "We're in business to save our home planet,"[41] served as the North Star. Chouinard had watched other mission-driven companies drift after going public or being acquired, and he wanted a structure to permanently prevent this fate.

Step 2: Design the ownership structure. Patagonia created a two-entity structure:

- Patagonia Purpose Trust: Holds all voting stock (2%), controlling corporate decisions.
- Holdfast Collective: Owns all nonvoting stock (98%), receives profits and distributes them for climate action (over $71 million granted in the first two years).[42]

Patagonia's structure uses two different entity types in its constellation. The non-profit foundation should be familiar. But the other is a perpetual purpose trust (PPT), a relatively new legal structure that allows a trust to exist indefinitely for a stated purpose rather than for beneficiaries. A PPT has trustees, just like a foundation, but also a role called a protector or independent enforcer, with the authority to hold the trustees themselves accountable should they deviate from the mission. This creates a constitutional structure that enlists multiple stewards in service of Patagonia's mission: the for-profit board, the PPT trustees, the protector, and the non-profit directors, each with distinct roles and mutual accountability.[43]

Step 3: Select the stewards. Patagonia chose trustees and directors deeply committed to its environmental mission, including family members and long-term advisors with proven alignment with the company's values. For example, the Holdfast Collective is helmed by Greg Curtis, who joined Patagonia in 2014 and helped develop its new structure.[44]

Step 4: Establish clear rights and responsibilities. Each entity has defined roles:

- Purpose Trust: Controls board appointments, has veto power, ensures B Corp certification.
- Holdfast Collective: Receives dividends, funds environmental causes.[45]
- Patagonia Works: Maintains operations, distributes excess profits.[46]

Step 5: Execute and communicate. The Chouinards transferred shares in September 2022, with Yvon's simple message: "Earth is now our only shareholder."[47] Day-to-day operations continued unchanged.

The conversion has been by all accounts a success. After so many years worrying what would happen to his life's work when he died, Yvon told David Gelles he could "finally die in peace."[48]

But before we move on, I want to call your attention to how difficult this conversion turned out to be. Five years elapsed between Yvon's first insisting that his team "figure it out" to the final conversion. The voting share transfer incurred $17.5 million in taxes.[49] All of which could have been avoided if Patagonia had been structured this way from day one. Why wasn't it?

You already know the answer. Nobody presented it to them as an option. In fact, even after Chouinard tasked his team with finding a solution to the succession problem, they still required multiple rounds of lawyers and advisors. Eventually they connected with the boutique bank BDT, which specializes in serving family-owned companies. BDT was familiar with succession challenges and brought them the purpose trust idea. The whole time, Patagonia believed they were pioneering something new. As David Gelles notes, they thought it was something "no one's ever thought about" before.

Isn't that interesting?

I tell you this part of the story to illustrate how deeply these techniques have been buried. When it's your turn, whether you are starting from scratch or already up and running, I want you to be better equipped. We need new templates and new vendors that make adopting this structure as easy and simple as possible, even at the early stages.

MISSION-LOCK VEHICLE: DECISION POINTS

Having a spiritual holding company is compatible with virtually any business structure, from an employee co-op to a global public company. Investors can still participate in governance. In fact, by allowing each for-profit entity in the constellation to have its own board, the SHC facilitates a more productive and active role for long-term investors to be involved in operations. It is the place where all factions come together in service of the mission.

First and foremost, a spiritual holding company must have a mission-lock vehicle—a structure designed specifically to protect and advance the company's purpose over time, regardless of leadership changes, market pressures, or ownership transitions. Creating one requires working through five key decision points:

THE ADVANCED IMPLEMENTATION GUIDE: For templates and examples for each of the techniques in this chapter and recommendations for aligned vendors, scan the QR code or go to incorruptible.co/advanced-guide.

Decision Point 1: What form will the mission-lock vehicle take? We've seen a variety of options already: foundations (in the cases of Grundfos and Bosch), non-profits (like Mozilla), employee ownership trusts (like John Lewis Partners), purpose trusts (like Anthropic), or special share classes with mission guardians. Believe it or not, there are many more out there. Consider: What legal structures are available in each jurisdiction? What are the tax implications? How much complexity can your team realistically manage? What ongoing costs can you sustain? Remember that you can write legally binding requirements into your legal charter as things the company is committed to do in the future. This often gives the best of both worlds by combining the commitment to take action with the flexibility to defer implementation until a stage-appropriate time.

Decision Point 2: Will it be economic or noneconomic? Economic structures receive dividends or hold equity as an owner, the way Grundfos's foundation uses its ownership stake to fund both business reinvestment and mission-related philanthropy. Noneconomic structures hold governance rights only, as in the case of Anthropic's LTBT. Choose economic when you want the vehicle to fund mission activities or provide patient capital back to the business or when the stewards will require independent staff. Remember, at the earliest stages, you can make commitments in the charter even before the SHC entity exists. These include pledging equity (when it's worth little), allocating board seats, or committing a percentage of future revenue to a future foundation. Consider: Should the vehicle share in the company's prosperity? Will it need independent resources to fill its role? Will the stewards need staff, research capacity, or separate investment capital to be maximally effective?

Decision Point 3: What powers and controls will it have? Powers range from advisory (recommendations only) to absolute (full control). Patagonia's Purpose Trust holds all voting stock. Bosch's foundation has supervisory board control. Some structures phase in over time, starting with protective vetoes and building to majority board control as the organization matures. Consider: Which decisions could compromise the mission? Should powers expand based on specific triggers? How will authority be exercised day-to-day versus in crisis moments? What do you want the relationship of the trustees to the for-profit board of directors to be?

Decision Point 4: Who will serve as mission guardians? The people governing your mission-lock vehicle matter as much as its structure. Options include founders and their descendants (family stewardship), subject matter experts (domain credibility), employee representatives (workforce voice), or independent stewards (outside perspective). The most important criterion is to find people you absolutely trust. Do not be tricked into choosing the fanciest resume or the most famous names. Anthropic chose genuine believers in AI safety. Grundfos balances family, employees, and external experts. Consider: What expertise does mission protection require? How will you ensure long-term alignment? Who selects future trustees? What happens if trustees disagree?

Decision Point 5: When will it be implemented? Timing options include at an early stage (like Anthropic), during a future funding round (common for startups), at founder transition (like Grundfos), or as part of succession planning (like Patagonia in 2022). In general, remember the lesson from Chapter 9: "It's always too early until it's too late." Later implementation allows refinement but risks losing the window of control. Remember, once a mission lock is in place, you can modify and refine it over time, but adding one after you've lost control is nearly impossible. Consider: Do you have sufficient control now? What future events might foreclose your options?

These five decision points represent the core choices any organization must make when designing a mission-lock vehicle. Work with counsel experienced in these structures, not just conventional corporate law. Don't be overly fixated on costs. In my experience, this can be done inexpensively and in a stage-appropriate way. When in doubt, create the legal structures for the commitment ahead of booting up new entities.

JUST ASKING QUESTIONS

Let me show you what it is like as a leader trying to advocate for these ideas. It's quite maddening. Often, the doubters describe themselves, passive-aggressively, as "just asking questions" about why anyone would want to deviate from the road most traveled. These questions are often just objections in disguise.

The good news is, if you've been following along through the previous chapters, you're already thoroughly equipped to dismantle these objections one by one. Let's take a tour.

"It sounds like a non-profit/activist/hippie thing"

We broke down the false dichotomy between for-profit and non-profit way back in Chapter 5. The SHC approach isn't about rejecting profit; it's about maximizing the likelihood and magnitude of profits over the long term. The most successful SHCs oversee highly profitable businesses that consistently reinvest those profits in ways that build trust with customers, employees, suppliers—and, yes, investors—over time.

"But why 'spiritual' holding company?"

And yes, I chose the word *spiritual* deliberately. I know it makes some people uncomfortable. But after years of late-night conversations with builders and founders and executives, after the directors have left the room, I keep hearing the same thing: They believe their organization has a soul. They just don't say it out loud in board meetings.

So when you're in those meetings, by all means, call it a mission-lock vehicle or perpetual purpose trust or infinite holding company. Use the language that gets the deal done.

But I chose *spiritual* because it's the most honest word for what we're actually protecting. Not just a mission statement. Not just values on a wall. The living core that makes an organization worth building in the first place.

"It sounds inefficient"

Foundation-owned firms keep people longer, pay them better, and maintain flatter hierarchies between executives and frontline workers. But this is no mere altruism; foundation-owned companies have been found to achieve significantly higher total factor productivity than conventional firms.[50] This contradicts the notion that shareholder pressure is necessary for operational efficiency.

"It sounds hard"

Remember: Harder is easier. Taking on the challenge of establishing robust mission protection early creates a foundation for long-term success. The apparent simplicity of conventional structures hides the much harder challenges they create down the road when mission and market pressures inevitably conflict.

"It will hurt financial performance or returns"

Foundation-owned firms compare favorably to conventional companies in all key financial metrics: returns on assets, equity, and even Tobin's Q (a measure of market valuation premium). But in several crucial areas, they outperform. Their earnings experience 25% less volatility. They carry stronger balance sheets and equity ratios (60%–70% versus the more typical 20%–40%). They compete successfully in international capital and research intensive sectors and enjoy high profit-to-sales ratios. During the 2008 recession, employee-owned companies suffered 50% fewer layoffs, then recovered faster. This countercyclical approach of maintaining investment when competitors retreat often positions them to emerge stronger.[51]

"It's too early to worry about this"

In Chapter 9, we saw how "it's always too early until it's too late." By the time a company faces pressure to compromise its mission, the power to resist that pressure has, in too many cases, already been surrendered. Although an SHC can be adopted at any time, there is good reason to tackle it earlier rather than later. On organizational longevity, the data is striking. The survival data we discussed earlier in this chapter isn't some marginal advantage; it's a sixfold difference. Look at centenarian companies like Bosch (founded 1886), Carlsberg (1847), and Tata Group (1868). These organizations have thrived across multiple generations precisely because their governance structures shield them from the short-term thinking that kills so many businesses.

"It's better to keep things simple"

We've already encountered the fallacy of so-called simplicity. Conventional corporate structures only appear simple because their complexities are hidden in standard documentation and practices. The complexity required to protect a mission is no greater—it's just different and therefore unfamiliar to advisors who haven't specialized in this area. Don't let their hesitancy or laziness prevent you from creating the company you want.

"It won't survive a crisis"

This couldn't be further from the truth. Mission-protected organizations demonstrate extraordinary resilience against short-termism. When markets panic, they stay steady. While conventional banks were either collapsing or requiring massive bailouts during the 2008 financial crisis, foundation-owned institutions like Triodos Bank maintained healthy balance sheets and continued their mission-aligned lending.[52] This isn't theoretical. It's documented in multiple studies showing foundation-owned firms maintained higher employment, continued R&D investment, and recovered faster than their peers during economic downturns.[53] They don't just resist harmful cost cutting; they actively invest countercyclically, gaining competitive advantage precisely when conventional governance would force retreat.

"Investors might not like it"

We've seen repeatedly that mission-aligned governance can be a source of competitive advantage most investors will love. Just be sure that they know about these underappreciated strengths. Far from stifling innovation, mission protection actually fuels it. In some countries, such companies drive half of all private R&D spending while representing just a tenth of the economy.[54] They consistently make decisions that might look suboptimal on quarterly reports but create tremendous advantages over decades. They are the rare organizations that customers, investors, and employees can truly trust. The right investors, those who understand these long-term assets and believe in your mission, will value intelligent mission-locked design rather than resisting it.

And no matter what you ultimately decide, make sure it's based on the true preferences of your actual partners. Recall from Chapter 3 how dangerous the word "might" becomes in an objection like this one. Do not bet your life on the opinions of ghosts.

"It's not really necessary"

The cautionary tales in Chapter 1 and "The Misery of the Cash Cow" in Chapter 6 demonstrated just how wrong things can go when mission protection is neglected. History is littered with companies that started with noble intentions only to see them gradually eroded. Ask simply, "Is achieving the mission necessary, in your view?"

These points directly address the objections I hear most frequently when discussing the SHC concept with founders and investors. "It will hurt financial performance"—the data shows otherwise. "Investors won't accept it"—some of the world's most successful companies operate this way. "It's too complicated or unusual"—there are proven templates to follow. "It will make the company less competitive"—the evidence points to enhanced resilience and innovation. "It's just idealism"—the hard numbers demonstrate practical benefits. What more do you want?

THE NOVO NORDISK STORY

I promised that I would show you how even a publicly listed company can work with this structure. Let me take you to a boardroom in Copenhagen in September 2004. Novo Nordisk CEO Lars Rebien Sørensen stands before the Novo Nordisk Foundation board for the second time in two months, investment bankers at his side. His first attempt in August had failed. This was his do-over.

Years of preparation led up to this moment. The for-profit company he leads has negotiated a merger agreement with Serono, the world's third-largest biotechnology company at the time. Novo would be absorbed into the Swiss giant, with Serono's Swiss headquarters becoming the seat of the combined company. Everyone would profit handsomely. According to one account of the story, "management clearly expected the Foundation's approval to be a formality."[55]

Yet just as in August, the foundation board poses their question: "Are you *really, really* telling me we need to do this to maintain our competitive position?" Sørensen explains again that the whole industry is consolidating. This is the new "best practice" in pharma.

But there's a problem. The Novo Nordisk Foundation's articles of association require that before approving any merger, sale, or comparable transaction, the board must be presented with a "convincing business argument" that such a deal is necessary for Novo Nordisk "to maintain and expand its position as a competitive business at the international level."[56] Although the merger would make them plenty of money, it does not truly serve the interests of the company's long-term mission. The board says no. This was made possible by decisions made nearly a century earlier by August and Marie Krogh—as we saw in Chapter 1. The Novo Nordisk Foundation is a spiritual holding company that oversees its mission-locked constellation, which includes both Novo Nordisk A/S and Novozymes A/S (now Novonesis).

Remember the Nordisk Insulinlaboratorium? Two of its early employees left (after a dispute with the founders) and formed their own rival firm, called Novo Terapeutisk Laboratorium in 1925.[57] Interestingly, they also copied Nordisk's SHC structure, even after going public in 1974. In 1989, the original founders of both companies had passed away, and the two companies healed the breach, merging operating companies *and* foundations to form the modern Novo Nordisk. For nearly a century, this SHC structure has protected the company and its research labs from outside influence and internal temptation. Novo Nordisk has hundreds of thousands of external shareholders globally, trading more than a billion shares per year on the NYSE alone.[58] Today, major shareholders include BlackRock, Vanguard, and Danish pension funds, yet none can override the foundation's 77% voting control.[59]

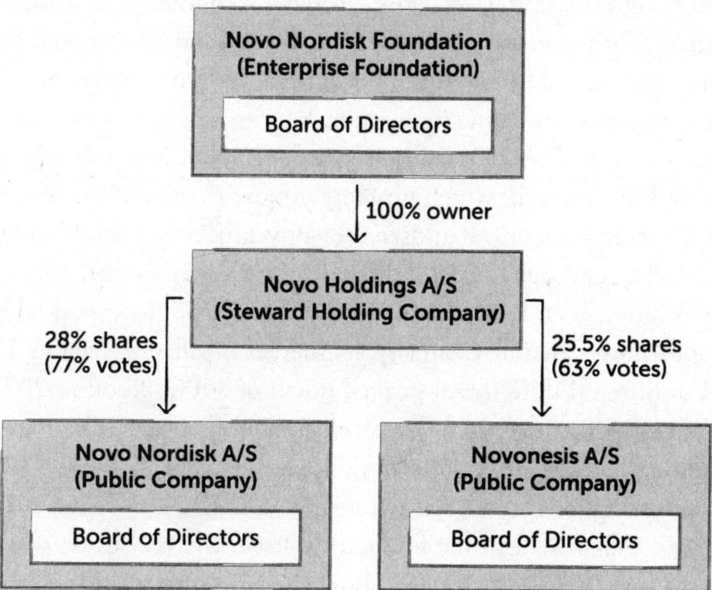

Figure 11.3.

Back in 2004, though, the operating company's executive team and board (which included, as I'm sure you've guessed, independent members) wanted the merger with Serono. But the foundation's board members alone possessed veto power, and they used it. What happened next made them seem unbelievably prescient. But their superpower was not prescience; it was simply patience and the right structure. The SHC charter demanded they ask one question: "Is this merger necessary?" Unlike Whole Foods and unlike SAIC, there was an indivisible decision-maker who could simply say no. No amount of gravity, temptation, or inducement could sway them.

Meanwhile, hidden in Novo Nordisk's research labs, Dr. Lotte Bjerre Knudsen was in year thirteen of a research and development program that showed so little promise that management had repeatedly threatened to shut it down.[60] Had Novo been absorbed by Serono in 2004, her project would almost certainly have been among the first casualties of consolidation. We know this because, just two years later, Serono itself was sold to Merck for €10.6 billion.[61] Serono was absorbed into Merck's structure, eventually shuttering its headquarters, eliminating 1,250 jobs. Today, Serono is a discontinued brand, a Wikipedia footnote, its research programs long gone. Imagine how easy it would have been to cancel Knudsen's fruitless research. One spreadsheet, one line item, gone.[62]

But because Novo Nordisk stayed independent, it kept funding her "impossible" research, which ultimately more than paid the company back for its investment. Knudsen's thirty-year journey would produce one blockbuster therapy after another: first Victoza, then Ozempic, then Wegovy, each bigger than the last. By 2023, Novo had become Europe's most valuable company, its market cap first exceeding Denmark's entire GDP. When it peaked north of $600 billion in 2024, it marked a moment when a group of non-profit trustees had created more than half a trillion dollars in shareholder value.[63]

Interestingly, Sørensen stayed on as CEO until 2016. Then, in 2018, he became chairman of the foundation itself, the very body that had blocked him. Rather than defeat him, the structure converted him.

This is the true power of a spiritual holding company. Novo Nordisk's shareholders were far better served by the foundation's patience and steadfastness than they would have been by any premium Serono could have offered. The next time someone tells you that only those with a profit motive can be trusted to be good stewards of investor capital, remind them of the time a non-profit foundation made investors almost $500 billion. And the next time someone tells you that corruption inevitably follows scale or size or a public listing, ask them if they know anyone who's tried Ozempic.

THIS ISN'T EVEN MY FINAL FORM

There's something deeply human about responsible, multigenerational stewardship. Throughout history, our most enduring institutions, from cathedrals to universities, have been guided by long-term orientation. The spiritual holding company brings this timeless wisdom into modern organizational design, creating structures that can outlast the human lifespan while remaining vital.

As we've built up this structure, layer by layer, I hope you've sensed a new tantalizing possibility. When properly designed, an incorruptible organization does more than resist temptations and pressure. It concentrates and aligns every available resource—financial, human, intellectual, social—with unprecedented power.

Throughout this book, we've gradually, inexorably zoomed outward. We began with the most intimate question: What's the point of building organizations? We explored ethos and profit, examining the soul of the enterprise itself. In Part II, we steadily pulled back the camera lens, encompassing more and more people in our field of vision, from culture to governance, from employees to shareholders, from customers to partners, from single entities to constellations. But our journey is not yet complete.

Now I'm asking you to zoom out even further, until that solitary constellation becomes like Carl Sagan's pale blue dot. So far, we have been talking about the mission-driven organization as precious and fragile, suspended in a vast economy hostile to its purpose. Many of the leaders I've worked with share this view due to years of exhausting battles with financial gravity. They see it as fundamentally in opposition to the magnetic force of purpose, mission, and ethos. One pulls down; one strives upward. One corrupts; one aligns.

But this is not the only possible configuration of these two forces. As we saw many chapters ago, the values transmitted by gravity are determined not by a law of nature but by human perception. Now we are prepared to put this insight to work. Over the course of Part III, we will see how to join these two fundamental forces into one superpower. It will require reinventing how we build financial, political, and civic systems.

It's a big leap, with big challenges, but imagine the payoff: a world where economic gravity draws organizations toward ethos rather than the reverse. Where tomorrow's organizations feel the pull toward human flourishing as strongly as today's crave "number go up."

Part III

TO BEND THE LIGHT

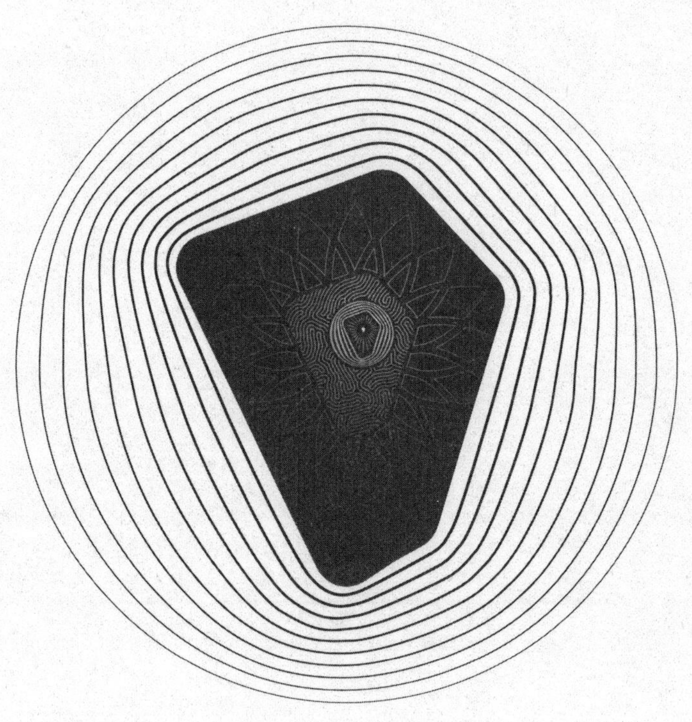

CHAPTER TWELVE

MISSION TRANSMISSION

A promise is a direction taken, a self-limitation of choice.

—Ursula K. Le Guin

The Dispossessed

1974

EVERY DAY, millions of Americans eat safer food because of decisions made in a Costco boardroom in Issaquah, Washington. Most of them have never set foot in a Costco warehouse.

Here's how it works: Costco requires every food supplier to meet safety standards that often exceed federal requirements. When one of Costco's produce suppliers installs expensive pathogen-testing equipment in order to keep Costco's business, that same equipment tests *all* of the produce leaving that facility, including those sold at competing grocery stores. When Costco demands X-ray inspection systems to detect foreign objects in packaged foods, suppliers upgrade their entire production lines, not just the Costco-bound products. While only part of America's food supply flows through Costco's supply chain, these heightened safety protocols affect a far larger percentage of all food production, creating a private safety net that strengthens the entire US food system.[1]

Let me drive home the vast expanse of this shield under which we live. In 2010 Costco directed 6,925 food-safety audits for Costco's vendor program, while the FDA inspected 17,609 domestic food facilities that year.[2] Costco set a goal of "auditing every vendor every year" to ensure compliance. Meanwhile, HHS's inspector general found that from 2004 to 2008, 56% of FDA-regulated food facilities had gone five or more years without a single FDA inspection.[3] A single retailer controlling 9% of grocery sales performs roughly 30% of the nation's food safety audit workload and is doing it more frequently and consistently than the federal government itself.

Costco's commitment to member safety doesn't stop at their warehouse doors. It radiates outward through supply chains, competitors, and industry standards, shaping the kind of world they want their members to live in. I call this gravitational influence organizations exert beyond their own walls *mission transmission*.

WIELDING GRAVITY BEYOND THE WALL

This marks the second turning point in this book. Until now, we've viewed gravity as a purely negative force and focused on building organizations strong enough to resist it. But organizations that achieve structural integrity are positioned for something far more powerful. I mentioned in Chapter 5 that the conventional definition of profit leaves businesses blind to opportunities created by positive externalities. Now it is time to witness the full scope of this opportunity.

Having learned to resist gravity's pull, these organizations can use their influence to project gravity outward.

Costco shows how this works in practice. But this is not pure altruism. Mission transmission is an integral part of their performance engine.

Unfortunately, many organizations, family offices, and non-profits degrade their own mission through supposedly "neutral" choices. As Luther Ragin, former VP of investments at the Heron Foundation, put it, "Why should a foundation use only 5% of its assets to work for the greater good, while the rest is working like an investment bank?"[4] The consequences can be surreal. In 2007, the *LA Times* discovered that the Gates Foundation, while spending hundreds of millions on health programs in Africa, held $423 million in oil companies whose pollution in Nigeria was contributing to the very respiratory diseases the foundation was trying to cure.[5] Remember ISS from the battles of activists trying to dismantle Costco's governance fortress? Their recommendations guide the votes of many "neutral" index and mutual funds. As a result, even mission-driven companies can inadvertently use their own balance sheets to lend gravity to actors opposed to their interests.

Instead, mission-driven organizations should embrace mission transmission as a core corporate discipline, as fundamental as strategy or human resources. It's the systematic practice of ensuring that every transaction and relationship extends an organization's values beyond its own walls. The organizations we're about to study earned their way to mission transmission with a strong foundation: ethos, mission drive, and structural integrity—all right out of Part II. Each treats their structure, including the spiritual holding company, as a springboard, not a destination.

TRANSMISSION MULTIPLIERS

To understand how this transmission works, we need to understand two aspects: Transmission happens automatically every time an organization conducts a transaction. It follows the same rules of gravity that we first encountered in Chapter 3. Thus, transmission happens via the same "fiduciary" pathways we encountered in Chapter 7: customers, employees, partners, and communities.

I once worked with a company that had to scan local obituaries to find new customers. No, they weren't selling funeral services. Their clients were municipal agencies that had a clear public service mission. Yet they were so locked into long-standing vendor relationships that they wouldn't consider alternatives until someone retired or died. Every purchasing decision transmitted a clear message: Convenience matters more than the public welfare.

The private sector is just as guilty. The father of modern management science, W. Edwards Deming, urged in 1982, "End the practice of awarding business on the basis of price tag."[6] Yet most organizations still default to the cheapest, most established, or most popular vendor, actively choosing convenience over mission. Because every purchase, partnership, and contract transmits values, these transactions often exacerbate the problems organizations exist to solve.

Companies can intentionally wield mechanisms to reverse this default. I call these practices *transmission multipliers*. The following five can ensure any organization transmits, rather than undercuts, its mission through every transaction:

The first practice is simple: **Consider mission in every transaction.** Whenever money, power, or status changes hands, ask whether mission and ethos were considered alongside conventional factors. This sounds obvious, but when I talk with leaders about whether they did it before deciding to contract with a vendor or enter into a partnership, you'd be amazed at how often I hear "It didn't come up." Build the practice into systems by adding mission criteria to requests for proposal (RFPs), vendor scorecards, and partnership agreements. Evaluate mission alignment as rigorously as other factors.

Once this system is in place, adopt a second practice: **Make mission the tiebreaker.** When all other factors are roughly equal, value alignment should determine the choice. Quality and price still matter; mission serves only as the decisive factor in close calls. Sometimes a mission-aligned vendor genuinely can't meet critical requirements or their costs are prohibitive. When this happens, document this as an ecosystem failing and look for opportunities to invest in building better alternatives. Give small volume percentages to upstart vendors. Publish RFPs so that aligned vendors know to apply in the future. Over time, these small investments compound. Mission-aligned suppliers get more business, grow stronger, and become better partners. When Patagonia invested millions in helping suppliers convert to organic cotton in the 1990s with no guarantee of success, they built a network that now leads the industry.[7]

Third, **clear the path for allies.** Procurement departments are overwhelmed partly because they've created byzantine systems that tend to lock in the incumbent. Large companies have entire teams dedicated to navigating these complex mazes, including proposal writers, compliance officers, and contract specialists. Meanwhile, mission-aligned startups have founders trying to do everything. The best organizations recognize this imbalance and actively correct it. Toyota sends its own engineers to teach smaller suppliers the Toyota Production System at Toyota's expense.[8] Removing artificial barriers and investing in aligned partners builds an ecosystem that collectively amplifies the mission.

The fourth practice is to **signal with costly commitment**. Remember that gravity is shaped by perception. People have to believe in the organization's commitment, and the most credible way to accomplish this is through actions that require real resources. At dinner several years ago, Thomas Friedman and I were debating well into the night the best way for Airbnb to achieve this kind of transmission. The Pulitzer Prize–winning columnist made a memorable point about trust that I'll never forget: "I need to see blood on the floor!" This principle is evident throughout Airbnb's approach to its hosts, from its commitment to compensate them during pandemic cancellations (when the company could have simply invoked its existing policies) to its Host Endowment. In the run-up to its IPO, Airbnb and its founders set aside 9.2 million shares (worth more than $1 billion) into an endowment for the benefit of hosts. As the company put it, "The Host Endowment is intended to provide support for the host community, now and for generations to come." The company willingly embraces these costs because they are critical investments in the partners who supply Airbnb's entire inventory.[9]

The fifth practice ensures accountability: **Create mechanisms for recourse.** Give external partners real channels for redress when promises aren't met. Costco provides a confidential ethics hotline that routes directly to their general counsel and chief compliance officer, creating an escalation path outside of day-to-day buying teams.[10] A partnership called the Fair Food Program persuaded major food buyers, including Walmart and McDonald's, to voluntarily sign binding agreements to follow a code of conduct that protects farmworkers from harsh working conditions and sexual assault, resulting in over 2,100 complaints investigated and resolved with no retaliation.[11] The most credible accountability comes through independent third parties: Companies increasingly use external certifiers like B Lab for benefit corporations, LTSE for governance standards, or Fairtrade International for supply chains.

Nike publishes its complete supplier list, enabling any NGO to investigate conditions at any factory.[12] Patagonia goes even further. For every Fairtrade-certified item sold, Patagonia pays an additional premium on top of the regular price, which goes directly to the workers themselves, not to factory owners or management. Worker committees decide democratically how to spend these funds without interference. Since 2014, more than $40 million has been invested in healthcare, education, cash bonuses, and community projects. In one Sri Lankan facility, workers chose to build and staff an on-site childcare center—an echo of Patagonia's own childcare philosophy (pioneered by Malinda Chouinard in 1985). This is mission transmission in action.[13]

These mechanisms create trust not just through their existence but through their visible use—or nonuse. The organizations that master this practice understand that giving away power paradoxically increases their influence.

The following stories trace mission transmission at expanding scales: from workers and their immediate circles, through regional community spillovers, to global supply chains.

THE STORY OF SAMA: MISSION IN EVERY TRANSACTION

In a nondescript building in Nairobi, a young woman spends her days teaching artificial intelligence how to recognize human emotions. She's part of an invisible workforce of thousands of Kenyans and Ugandans who sit behind screens in the economic belly of the AI revolution, meticulously labeling data. This is a crucial step in the creation of today's most advanced AI models. Every time a chatbot answers a question or a self-driving car recognizes a pedestrian, it is, in part, because someone taught it what "human" sounds or looks like.

This is the world of a company called Sama. Leila Janah founded "Samasource" in 2008 as a non-profit with a simple mission: "Give work, not aid."[14] The organization initially provided basic digital task outsourcing, connecting low-income workers in Kenya and later Uganda and India with dignified digital work. The goal was to lift them out of poverty by connecting them to the global economy.[15]

Janah didn't foresee when she started that her organization would become an early pioneer of the "human feedback" step in training AI models—the HF in RLHF.[16] Today, Sama employs thousands of people and competes in one of the hottest sectors on the planet.

Janah could have been satisfied with having built a successful non-profit. But as the organization grew, it faced resource constraints that limited its ability to invest in technology and compete in the exploding data-labeling market. In 2019, she made a pivotal decision to transition to a mission-locked for-profit structure. She ensured that the newly formed for-profit entity would be majority owned by the original non-profit (later renamed the Leila Janah Foundation), creating a spiritual holding company structure.[17]

Sadly, less than a year later, Janah died of a rare cancer at age thirty-seven. The structure she built ensured that Sama would continue to operate according to its mission and ethos, with its profits and shares able to fund social programs through the foundation that now bears her name.

When her successor, CEO Wendy Gonzales, explained Sama's journey to me, she revealed something profound about how the company found its way into AI. Around 2012, their success attracted increased competition from outsourcing firms competing on price. Sama's commitment to living wages meant they wouldn't participate in this race to the bottom. But they had also recognized that tech companies needed human judgment to label images and text for training machine learning models, work that demanded higher skill and commanded better prices. Sama bet their future on it, years ahead of the recent AI boom. Their cost disadvantage became a first-mover advantage in what would prove to be the foundation of the generative AI revolution.

Sama's commitment to paying living wages meant that they were "forced" to move upmarket and find premium customer segments. This constraint drove Sama from providing low-value data-entry tasks to becoming pioneers in high-value AI training data labeling. "Our whole goal is to create a place where people can begin to build their next careers," Gonzales told me. "Because we had such clarity, it became really obvious to me that we cannot be the cost leader. We need to be on the premium side, in a place where we can actually command a higher price point."[18]

Most business consultants I know spend their days pulling their hair out trying to get companies to take differentiation seriously. Yet here was Sama, where the mission itself, despite creating a "harder" cost structure, had forced genuine differentiation and created a sustainable competitive advantage. The constraint that should have killed them became their moat.

It also became an opportunity to show their commitment to transmitting their mission through client relationships. In 2022, Sama made headlines by exiting the content moderation business entirely, walking away from significant revenue because the work, which required employees to review disturbing content for hours daily, conflicted with their mission of providing dignified work that enables human flourishing.[19] This decision sent ripples through the industry, forcing competitors and clients to confront the human cost of content moderation and raising the bar for what constitutes ethical digital work.

Sama also employs the transmission multipliers. Their supplier code of conduct requires all vendors to pay living wages and maintain safe working conditions, even if that means that Sama pays more for services.[20] The company preferentially sources from local social enterprises in Kenya and Uganda, multiplying its community impact. And when Sama pays living wages to workers who previously earned subsistence incomes, that increase doesn't just benefit individuals; it flows through local economies as workers spend on housing, education, and family needs. The company reported lifting more than fifty-nine thousand individuals out of poverty, with workers increasing their spending on education by 50% and contributing 60% more to household housing expenses.[21]

THE WALMART EFFECT VS. THE COSTCO EFFECT

Academics call these ripples "spillover effects"—systematic changes in local communities that result from organizational choices. Decades of research have documented how they work: Good jobs create more jobs through local spending, employment quality shapes community health and family stability, and how people are treated at work affects their civic participation.[22] These aren't separate phenomena. They're all manifestations of *mission transmission.*

It's common to hear complaints about the negative externalities of discount or "big-box" retailers. But this obscures important differences. Community effects are a choice.

An entire branch of research studies the "Walmart effect" to understand the spillovers of Walmart entering a new community. The findings? When Walmart enters a county, local retail wages drop 0.5%–1.5% per store. Business closures increase on surrounding blocks. Total county employment falls roughly 3% within five years of a Supercenter opening. Over a decade, households in those communities earn about 6% less than comparable communities without one—and the losses hit low-income workers hardest.[23]

Will it surprise you to learn that the "Costco effect" is different? Some observers have begun to notice that when Costco opens, surrounding businesses often benefit. As one put it, "Unlike the Walmart effect, which pushes down local wages and increases business closures, Costco openings boost foot traffic and revenue for nearby businesses." Costco's higher wages force local businesses to up their game. Plus, Costco serves as a low-cost supplier to local vendors. MIT's Zeynep Ton, who has researched retail operations for more than fifteen years and highlighted Costco as a key example, calls this the "good jobs strategy." The evidence shows it creates a rising tide rather than a race to the bottom.[24]

Both low-cost retailers offer low prices. The difference is the gravitational field their choices create.

ELDER COUNCILS

Devoted's love for their customers created a whole new mechanism for mission transmission: elder councils. These groups of members "band together into teams of volunteers who each have the mission of dramatically improving health and well-being by caring for everyone like family."[25] Every council takes on a challenge specific to its own community. In Mesa, Arizona, volunteers identified seniors running out of food before the end of the month and neighbors dying alone in their apartments. They partnered with Feeding America to deliver boxes of fresh produce twice monthly to seventy-five elders, then created a food exchange program so members could swap items they couldn't eat due to health conditions. In Fairfield, Alabama, a council planted a community garden that now provides healthy food to a big swath of the neighborhood. In Houston, three elder men host "kitchen table talks," mentoring younger men who never had father figures.[26]

Odessa Flores-Vazquez, a mental health practitioner of Maya and Ojibwa ancestry who leads the program, describes the challenge: "Some of our elders are not supported in being leaders, even within their own families. They lose their role and their identity in the larger society." Many had come to see themselves as "the throwaway population." The councils restore that role, giving elders the platform to reclaim what Flores-Vazquez calls "their innate power as wisdom keepers."[27]

Flores-Vazquez explains that the elders don't just lead in their communities; they also help lead Devoted. They meet regularly with company leadership, where "their voices are heard, their opinions are heard." Todd Park sums it up this way: The councils have "externalized" Devoted's spirit. As a result, they even admit people who aren't Devoted members because "it seemed the natural thing to do."[28]

"OR MONEY WILL EAT EVERYTHING WE LOVE"

Zita Cobb grew up in a place that barely existed on maps. Fogo Island sits off the northeast coast of Newfoundland.[29] The island is a rocky outcrop that didn't join Canada until 1949. Her illiterate parents, descended from Irish and English fishing families, lived without electricity or running water. They didn't use money; her father traded cod for flour and molasses, as seven generations had before him.

Then in the early 1970s, massive vessels appeared on the horizon, fishing day and night. Lambert Cobb, who knew every current around Fogo, watched the cod disappear. For months, he puzzled over these foreign ships until it clicked. He explained to ten-year-old Zita that these ships were trading fish for money. They weren't fishermen. They were mining the ocean.

Lambert Cobb understood that where the fish went, their community would follow. Young people would flee to Toronto and Calgary. It was the same choice Father Arizmendiarrieta saw in Chapter 10: *O libreta, o maleta*. Without economic sovereignty, communities die. In 1975, Cobb burned his fishing boat while his teenage daughter watched. He told her, "When you grow up, you're going to have to go away and figure out how this money thing works. You have to study business." And then he added, "Because if we don't understand how this works, it's going to eat everything we love."[30] Cobb studied business, made a fortune in telecommunications, and returned to Fogo in 2004 as one of Canada's wealthiest women. Her father's prophecy had come true: The population had plummeted from 5,000 to 2,400.[31] She and her brothers created the Shorefast Foundation using the spiritual holding company structure to ensure their for-profit ventures remain mission-controlled.

Shorefast's flagship is a luxury inn that charges premium prices, but the structure ensures that money feeds the community rather than devouring it. Local craftspeople make the furniture. Islanders run everything. Every dollar of profit flows to community development. The high prices reflect the cost of paying fair wages, and Shorefast publishes "Economic Nutrition" labels showing exactly where each dollar goes, like a nutrition facts panel for money. Beyond the inn, Shorefast launched Fogo Island Fish (reviving traditional hand-line cod fishing) and workshops preserving quilting and woodworking traditions. From 2013 to 2024, these businesses contributed over $235 million to Newfoundland's GDP.[32]

The model is spreading. Four Canadian communities have adopted Shorefast's framework, and Harvard Business School now teaches it as a case study.[33]

In addition, the family recently launched the Shorefast Institute for Place-Based Economies, an engine for economic development that will bring together capital and local communities, enabling them to contribute to Canada's overall prosperity.

"It matters who owns what," Cobb says.[34] The inn can't be sold, profits can't leave, the mission controls everything. Each community that adopts Shorefast's model learns the same lesson: You don't have to accept financial gravity as fate. Build structures that reverse the flow. Her father feared money would eat everything they loved. His daughter learned to make it feed them instead.

TONY'S CHOCOLONELY

What kind of person tries to get themselves arrested for eating chocolate? In 2002, three Dutch television journalists were investigating the chocolate industry for the consumer protection show *Keuringsdienst van Waarde*. Their reporting revealed the horrifying scale of modern slavery and child labor on West African cocoa farms, where in 2020, an estimated 1.56 million children worked in unsafe and inhumane conditions.[35]

Like many journalists who enter the profession to make change, they found themselves infuriated not only by the injustice but also by the public's and their own complicity in it. Here they were, exposing chocolate companies that profited from child labor while continuing to eat chocolate themselves every day. The hypocrisy and the suffering of these kids gnawed at them. In 2004, they orchestrated a kind of civic stunt that captured the absurdity of the situation. Teun van de Keuken, one of the three, reported himself to Dutch authorities as a criminal, demanding prosecution.[36] The elaborate media production was calculated to highlight a moral paradox: If child labor is illegal, why isn't financing it also illegal?

When prosecutors predictably refused to prosecute, the team felt they had exhausted the tools available to them as journalists. They decided to try something different by proving that it was possible to make chocolate ethically. In 2005, they committed to making five thousand Fairtrade-certified bars.[37] The dark chocolate was wrapped in bold red packaging intended to raise the alarm and named Tony's Chocolonely (Teun's anglicized nickname + the feeling of isolation in the cocoa industry).

What happened next surprised everyone. They presold thirteen thousand bars in just two days, even before the chocolate was produced.[38] The supposed public indifference to child labor vanished the moment people had a concrete alternative. Given the chance to vote with their wallets, Dutch consumers responded overwhelmingly.

Despite their background in journalism, they decided to start a company. Within seven years, they were the number-one chocolate brand in the Netherlands, surpassing Mars, Nestlé, and local giant Verkade.[39]

Like Sama's living wage constraint, Tony's ethical requirements forced premium positioning, turning mission constraints into competitive advantage. Today, Tony's Chocolonely generates over €200 million annually,[40] operating across multiple countries with over three hundred employees. They've consistently achieved positive earnings while paying cocoa farmers 78% above standard prices in Ghana and 73% above in Côte d'Ivoire.[41]

The mission has survived multiple leadership transitions since van de Keuken stepped down in 2011 and, more importantly, multiple investment rounds, proving that their principles were built into systems rather than dependent on any individual. Teun's philosophy guided them: "We would never, ever let the commercial interest of the Tony's bar prevail over the interest of the cacao farmer."[42]

Tony's has changed their industry in a much wider way. Have you—or your kids—tried YouTube star MrBeast's Feastables chocolate? Then you've been part of Tony's *mission transmission*, even if you didn't know it.[43]

Instead of hoarding their ethical supply chain, they opened it to competitors through Tony's Open Chain platform. By 2024, twenty mission-ally companies sourced roughly 23,000 metric tons of cocoa through Tony's Open Chain, nearly doubling the ethical impact beyond Tony's own 17,700 metric tons. Major retailers like Albert Heijn, Aldi, and Waitrose use Tony's Open Chain for their private-label chocolate. Ben & Jerry's committed to sourcing all their cocoa through the platform.[44] Why do companies accept Tony's strict requirements? Because using shared infrastructure is far less expensive than building from scratch. Tony's Open Chain traces every bean from farm to table, pays verifiably higher wages to farmers, and produces higher-quality chocolate. Together, these allow partner companies to sell premium products that command superior economics. When Waitrose joined Tony's Open Chain, they raised chocolate prices by 10%. But year-over-year sales jumped 43%.[45] Tony's had transformed a moral imperative into a market advantage.

The key is Tony's "no cherry-picking rule," which requires wholesale cocoa customers to adopt all five of their sourcing principles: traceable beans, higher premiums to farmers, strong cooperatives, long-term contracts, and productivity investments.[46] To have access to Tony's cocoa supply chain, partners must transform their own cocoa supply chain from one end to the other, not just the Tony's portion. This prevents greenwashing and ensures systematic change. Dutch supermarket chain Albert Heijn couldn't just launch one ethical bar; they had to convert their entire Delicata chocolate range to Tony's standards. When partner cooperative Socoopacdi in Côte d'Ivoire showed traceability lapses, Tony's suspended them entirely until they fixed their systems and passed external audits.[47]

Tony's also demonstrates their ethos through costly transparency. In 2022–23, their monitoring found 1,072 child labor cases, a significant increase from 366 in 2020–21 due to network expansion.[48] Most companies would bury this data. Tony's chose radical transparency, publishing exact numbers prominently in their annual report. "We want to find the children," they explained. "Only then can we work with the families to address the problem."[49]

Behind these numbers lies genuine transformation. Sixteen-year-old John Tetteh was wielding a machete on his father's cocoa farm in Ghana after finishing junior high school, hazardous work for a teenager with no money for vocational training. In 2017, Tony's implemented the Child Labour Monitoring and Remediation System (CLMRS) to identify and remediate cases of child labor and to prevent future cases by raising awareness in cocoa-growing communities. For CLMRS to truly benefit children and families, it must be deeply rooted in the communities it serves. Rather than relying on outside auditors making occasional visits, Tony's employs local farmers and residents who live in the cocoa villages. These community facilitators check on every household annually, creating the trust needed for real change. Tony's invests in training these community facilitators to spot child labor and help families solve it. When Tony's community facilitators found John during a household visit, they enrolled him in an apprenticeship program. "I am now training in masonry, steel bending and tiling," John reports.[50] His story represents thousands of children swapping machetes for schoolbooks—or in John's case, for construction tools and a skilled trade.

The impact extends from helping individuals to transforming whole communities. In Ghana's Eastern Region, cocoa farmer and community facilitator Joseph Mensah helped eight communities in the ABOCFA cooperative draft and adopt binding bylaws on child protection. These community-driven rules address nighttime noise that disrupts children's sleep and protect school environments from livestock.[51] At cooperatives that have worked with Tony's Open Chain for more than three years, child labor rates are below 5% compared to the industry-wide average of nearly 50%. The company has helped secure 3,440 birth certificates in Côte d'Ivoire so children can enroll in school and provides bicycles to help children reach classrooms, making good on their motto that children should be able to "play, go to school and dream big."[52]

The transmission power comes from systematic commitment. Tony's guarantees premiums across five-year contracts regardless of market conditions. During the 2022 inflation crisis, instead of reducing premiums, they increased them by 82%, raising payments from $792 to $1,096 per ton.[53]

Tony's could only take this bold action because the mission is protected by a spiritual holding company. Called Tony's Mission Lock, it's a governing structure with golden-share veto power held by three independent mission guardians: Seth Goldman (of Honest Tea), Ikenna Azuike (a lawyer and social activist), and Anne-Wil Dijkstra (Tony's former Chief of Impact). These guardians can report concerns directly, publish critiques in Tony's annual report, or, if they see fit, take out a full-page newspaper ad criticizing the company. Tony's structure assigns them fiduciary obligations and grants them legal protections similar to shareholders' if the mission is threatened. Any stakeholder can raise a concern with the mission guardians through the company website. True to the company's transmission philosophy, they've open-sourced the entire governance structure at tonysmissionlock.org, ensuring their governance innovation can spread industry-wide.[54]

PROJECTING GRAVITY THROUGH COORDINATED ACTION

Costco, Sama, Tony's, Devoted, and Shorefast each had to build structures strong enough to withstand the downward pull of financial gravity. But success makes every organization a gravitational body, whether it likes it or not. Because these companies achieved coherence, their gravity transmits values consonant with their mission, bending the field around them. Rather than shy away from that influence, all recognized it as central to their purpose and worked to amplify it.

In fact, their individual success stories point toward an even greater opportunity: intentionally wielding standards as gravity-amplifying tools. Standards don't just shift industries; they reset the starting line. One company's breakthrough becomes everyone's new floor. The next chapter explores how to forge these tools, turning individual breakthroughs into coordinated transformation.

Chapter Thirteen

THE POWER OF STANDARDS

> In 1534, Douglass Wynegar of Hawkhurst, England, gave his grandmother roses for her birthday. He picked them himself, walked them over to her, she was happy . . . boom, 145 points. Now, in 2009, Doug Ewing of Scaggsville, Maryland, also gave his grandmother a dozen roses, but he lost four points. Why? Because he ordered the roses using a cell phone that was made in a sweatshop, the flowers were grown with toxic pesticides, picked by exploited migrant workers, delivered from thousands of miles away, which created a massive carbon footprint, and his money went to a billionaire racist CEO.
>
> —**Michael**
> *The Good Place*
> 2019

A LEED-CERTIFIED BUILDING. An FDA-approved bottle of pills. Organic eggs. A Fairtrade-certified pair of shoes. A PG-13 movie.

What do all of these things have in common? Every one is a product that meets a recognized standard. Each of these standards doesn't just ensure quality—it transmits values across vast networks of strangers who will never meet. And the product meeting that standard tells us something as consumers about its key attributes, such as quality, safety, or reliability.

Once you start looking, you'll see standards in your daily life everywhere. Planning to renovate your kitchen? You'll probably want to hire a licensed contractor whose training and business practices meet the industry standard for safety and quality. Need to have surgery? You'll probably very much want it to be done by a board-certified surgeon. Transactions move at the speed of trust, and standards are trust accelerators.

Standards enhance the attractiveness of products by letting them borrow brand attributes. When you see Amy's Organic Pizza in the freezer aisle, the word "Organic" right in the brand name instantly conveys a set of values. It seems healthier, a premium product from an environmentally conscious company. Amy's doesn't have to build these associations from scratch. They draw on the credibility that thousands of organic farms and companies have collectively established over decades.

Chapter 12 revealed how companies transmit their missions to adjacent partners. Standards represent something even more powerful: the ability to reshape entire industries and touch lives on the other side of the world. When a company creates the right standard, it broadcasts its mission to people it will never meet, in places it will never visit, creating gravitational fields that pull whole sectors toward its values.

Standards can change the world at scale.

THE VOLVO HEIST

In 1959, engineer Nils Bohlin invented the three-point safety belt that is the same kind of seat belt you and I still use today.[1] A vast improvement over existing belts, the three-point belt made car travel much safer for passengers. Volvo could have kept this patented innovation for themselves or licensed it out. Instead, they open-sourced the patent so that other companies could use three-point belts free of fees.

Volvo's seat belt story is often retold in business circles. But nobody ever tells it from the Volvo investors' point of view. Inside the boardroom, did the decision spark a battle? Did financial projections show the company was walking away from millions of kronor in licensing fees? It's not hard to imagine the scene at any number of companies you know well: board members calling it "giving away a golden idea," directors threatening to resign, the CEO facing pointed questions about violating his fiduciary duty, investment bankers and consultants called in to evaluate this "oil well" of recurring revenue. All to explain why it would be foolish to voluntarily forfeit all that money.

But Volvo CEO Gunnar Engellau saw something that modern boards generally don't. Standards are the ultimate positive externality. They create value for everyone while positioning the creator as the permanent leader. By giving away the patent, Volvo wasn't losing control; it was gaining something far more valuable. They were encoding their mission—"No one should die in a car"—into the DNA of the entire industry. Once every car in the world used Volvo's safety design, the association between the company and safety would be cemented. (Doug Speck, president and CEO of Volvo Cars North America, referred to this as "a little bit of Volvo in every car on the road.")[2]

Engellau's decision was vindicated. When he became CEO in 1956, Volvo sold 31,000 cars annually; by his retirement in 1971, that number had grown to 214,000 (nearly four times faster than the auto industry during the same period).[3] Volvo has outlived many regional automakers of that era.[4] The company that "gave away" its most valuable patent could charge premium prices because customers trusted it so much. Even today, Volvo still means safety in consumers' minds, a brand association worth billions.[5]

In opening up access to a patented innovation, Volvo grew their brand, their influence, and their visibility. Their product became ubiquitous in the industry, but it wasn't the official standard. Yet.

The insurance industry took note. Because insurers bore the cost of every crash, they had every incentive to study what would reduce these costs. Studies showed that three-point belts reduced serious injuries by over 50%.[6] By 1977, insurers' own data translated this to bottom-line benefits: Cars with advanced belt systems generated significantly fewer injury claims.[7] This evidence gave insurers the justification to offer better rates for safer vehicles, creating yet another market incentive for manufacturers to adopt Volvo's innovation.

In 1974, Volvo's standard became government regulation in the US when the National Highway Traffic Safety Administration (NHTSA) made it a legal requirement for cars to use three-point belts because of their effectiveness in reducing injuries and fatalities.[8] Federal Motor Vehicle Safety Standard 208 now saves hundreds of thousands of lives annually. This progression, from a single company's brand promise to an informal industry standard to mandatory regulation, reveals how standards come to be. Volvo's brand promise became more valuable, not less, as their standard spread.

Over time, Volvo's "sacrifice" transformed the entire industry. With better safety standards in place, consumers increasingly trusted that driving was safe, expanding the market. The auto industry as a whole became far more valuable. In this way, standards often grow the total industry, expanding opportunity for all companies within it.

Most leaders see standards as constraints. Volvo used them to create a gravitational field that pulled the entire industry toward their values. They also bound themselves to that path. The company that set the standard became defined by it, a strategic commitment that shaped Volvo for generations.

WHAT MAKES A STANDARD GOOD?

Look at any electronic device within arm's reach—your phone charger or laptop or desk lamp. Somewhere on it, you'll find a small "UL" mark. This tiny logo represents one of the most successful standards in history: Underwriters Laboratories' safety certification.

UL's story began in 1893, when electrical engineer William Henry Merrill was hired to inspect the revolutionary (and terrifying) electrical installations at the Chicago World's Fair.[9] With 160,000 light bulbs blazing and alternating current crackling through wires, many feared the fair would burn down. Merrill's inspections prevented disaster. Armed with a mere $350 of equipment, Merrill went on to build UL into a massive company.[10] (Naturally, it is a mission-controlled company with a spiritual holding company made up of a pair of research non-profits.) But Merrill didn't build UL alone. The Chicago Fire

Underwriters' Association and the Western Insurance Union funded its creation.[11] They had internalized the costs of every electrical fire, so this new standard solved a major economic problem for them.

UL's safety certification possesses the three essential attributes of any good standard. Together they transmit the fundamental value that commerce must not come at the cost of human life:

First, **crystal clarity.** The mark means one thing: This device won't burn your house down. No lengthy explanations needed. No confusion about what it represents. Just like "Organic" unequivocally tells you some specific things about how a food was grown, "UL" unequivocally tells you key things about a product's electrical safety. One mark, infinite peace of mind.

Second, **independent verification.** UL doesn't take manufacturers' word for it that a product is safe. They test products in their own labs, checking everything from heat resistance to electrical insulation. This external verification is what makes the standard trustworthy. Without it, any product could claim to be safe. With it, the mark becomes a promise the public can believe and insurers can underwrite. This is an extremely common pattern. Public companies produce financial statements that are, on the whole, trustworthy because they must be independently audited by an outside firm. A college is granted accreditation by a body that spends years doing its due diligence before giving or renewing that status. With these kinds of independent verification, the standard can be trusted.

Third, **aligned consequences**—where the real genius of UL lies. It carries real—often financial—consequences. Retailers won't stock non-UL products because the liability is too high. Insurance companies won't cover fire damage from noncertified devices. Manufacturers can't access major markets without that mark. This creates positive lock-in, not the kind of vendor lock-in that traps customers but natural consequences for defection. The standard creates a gravitational field where prosperity depends on maintaining its values.

This alignment is what separates great standards from bureaucratic nightmares. Gravity starts pulling toward human flourishing. Auto insurers created crash testing. Electrical insurers birthed UL. The pattern works because manufacturers profit by meeting standards, retailers avoid liability, insurers reduce claims, and consumers don't die in fires.

THE ECONOMIC LOGIC OF STANDARDS

Standards are mission transmission on a grand scale.

So what actually happened when Volvo released that patent? Their open-sourced seat belt created a self-reinforcing cascade of consequences. Manufacturers could not resist adopting it as a free upgrade, putting more safe vehicles on the road. Once this happened, it was only a matter of time before insurers noticed the difference in their claims data. They acted rationally, adjusting their rates to offer better prices for safer cars. This lowered the total cost of ownership of safer cars. Manufacturers who'd resisted seat belts as "too expensive" found them too expensive to live without.

But Volvo was not the first to discover the principles that make this cascade work. Benjamin Franklin worked them out in 1752. He transformed Philadelphia's skyline by making fire-resistant construction the economically rational choice—not through mandate but through market incentives. Fires had ravaged Philadelphia, where wooden houses were packed closely together, for decades. There was also a governance vacuum where no one bore the full cost of negligence. Franklin's innovation was an entire ecosystem of insurance, building standards, and fire inspections that made safety profitable. His Philadelphia Contributionship fire insurance company first refused to insure wooden buildings, then later excluded those with large shade trees, creating direct economic pressure to construct buildings more safely. In just over a decade, brick buildings with manicured landscapes replaced tinderbox structures.[12]

Franklin built the insurance company, the standards body, and the inspection service simultaneously. His integrated approach compressed decades of evolution into a single venture, revealing the entrepreneurial opportunity hidden in every standard: the chance to architect and profit from an entire ecosystem rather than just participate in one.

THE CONTAINER THAT CONQUERED THE WORLD

In 1937, so the story goes, Malcolm McLean sat in his truck at a New Jersey port, watching stevedores unload his cotton bales piece by piece. It took most of the day. As the owner of a small North Carolina trucking company, McLean knew every wasted hour meant lost profit. But he also saw something else: an opportunity. What if you could lift the entire truck onto the ship?[13]

Shipping had worked the same way for centuries—armies of shore workers manually loading and unloading cargo, piece by piece.[14] But the process was slow, expensive, and prone to theft and damage. McLean couldn't let his idea go. For nearly twenty years, the vision haunted him. By 1955, McLean had built his single truck into the fifth-largest trucking company in America, with 1,750 trucks and 37 terminals.[15] But interstate commerce rules prevented owning both trucks and ships. Pursuing his container idea meant selling everything he'd built. McLean chose ships and made the sale.

In April 1956, an oil tanker called the SS *Ideal X* left from Newark, headed to Houston. It was carrying fifty-eight containers of McLean's own design: truck trailer bodies stripped of their wheels and converted into stackable shipping boxes, loaded onto the ship in under eight hours.[16] Standard sizes, standard fittings, standard strength—*crystal clarity*. Even at this experimental stage, McLean could offer prices 25% below conventional shipping.[17] The containers stayed sealed, eliminating theft. Goods moved from truck to ship to train without ever being touched. Before that first shipment even arrived, new orders poured in.

McLean had created something revolutionary. But now he faced a choice that would determine whether his innovation would transform an industry or remain a proprietary advantage. He could have kept the container design secret, licensing it selectively for massive fees. His corner-fitting mechanisms and standardized dimensions were patentable innovations. Investment bankers would have called it an annuity stream. Instead, like Volvo, he gave it all away. As business historians note, "Believing that standardization was the path to overall industry growth, McLean chose to make his patents available by issuing a royalty-free lease to the International Organization for Standardization (ISO)."[18]

This decision transformed shipping from a fragmented industry into a unified system. Before McLean, a single ship might carry two hundred thousand individual pieces—barrels, crates, bags—each loaded by hand. Ships spent as much time in port being loaded as they did sailing.[19] With goods moving seamlessly from truck to ship to train in large, standardized containers, productivity exploded from ten tons per hour to five hundred. Eventually, loading costs collapsed from $5.86 per ton to just $0.16—a 97% reduction.[20] Longshoremen's unions fought it desperately, as containerization would eliminate thousands of jobs, but the standard created its own gravitational field. Ports that invested in container infrastructure saw their traffic explode. Shipping lines abandoned holdouts for container-ready ports. Within decades, resistance had collapsed—*aligned consequences* at work. When the ISO eventually published global container standards, they were based largely on McLean's designs. The twenty-foot and forty-foot containers we see everywhere today are built to McLean's dimensions. Any container certified to ISO specs could be trusted by ports, insurers, and customs officials worldwide (*independent verification*).[21]

The impact cascaded through the same three stages of progression we saw with Volvo. First, the container design was McLean's proprietary advantage. Then it became an industry standard as competitors adopted it to stay relevant. Finally, governments codified it into law. The International Convention for Safe Containers (1972) and customs regulations worldwide now require standardized containers.[22]

This created what I call a *prosperity cascade*. The standard solved shipping's pain points so effectively that each participant became richer by adopting it rather than resisting it. The cascade created its own momentum, pulling the entire industry into McLean's orbit.

Sea-Land grew from nothing to the world's largest cargo-shipping business within fifteen years. But the majority of the value wasn't captured by McLean. It was the trillions in global trade enabled by his standard. As one article observed, "By the end of the 1900s, container shipping was transporting approximately 90 percent of the world's trade cargo."[23] Products became affordable worldwide. Supply chains became reliable. Developing nations industrialized. Countries once shut out of global commerce by distance or cost could now compete. A factory in Vietnam could sell to stores in Ohio. Farmers in Kenya could export flowers to London.

McLean didn't just solve his traffic jam in New Jersey. By creating and releasing a standard, he rewired global commerce. His standard didn't just move boxes; it transmitted his belief in a far more interconnected world. With a "little bit of Sea-Land in every port," McLean created a gravitational field that pulled the entire shipping industry into a new orbit. Once the world reorganized around containers, there was no going back.

The goal of a good standard is to align other organizations' profit motives with the standard's ethos. That's how financial gravity can be reversed to contribute to, rather than diminish, human flourishing. Volvo made safety profitable for competitors. UL made fire prevention profitable for manufacturers. McLean made efficiency profitable for ports and everybody shipping goods. The standard setter doesn't force compliance. They make compliance the most lucrative path.

THE CORPORATE GOVERNANCE REBELS

In May 2005, Jay Coen Gilbert and Bart Houlahan watched everything they'd built disappear. Together with cofounders Seth Berger and Tom Austin, they'd grown AND1, a basketball footwear company, into a $250 million business with generous parental leave, charitable giving, and fair wages.[24] When American Sporting Goods acquired the company, it led to "an almost immediate stripping out of the commitment, concern and culture they had fostered."[25]

"Wanting to counteract what he saw as the toxic effects of shareholder primacy," Gilbert and Houlahan teamed up with early AND1 investor Andrew Kassoy to seek justice, not for themselves but for every founder, employee, or customer who'd seen a beloved company's trustworthiness suddenly reversed.[26] Their rebellion proceeded on two fronts:

- First, they helped lead the state-by-state battle for public benefit corporation legislation, the new corporate form we explored in Chapter 9 that allows companies to encode their mission directly into their charter.[27] As we saw in Chapter 4, this is more restoration than revolution. PBCs honor a much older tradition of corporate purpose.
- Second, they created B Lab, a non-profit that certifies companies meeting social and environmental standards. Only one in three companies that attempt it succeed. But those that do see real benefits: In 2020, as the COVID pandemic hit hard, only 4.5% of American B Corps failed, far lower than the 12.5% of American businesses in total that went under. Data shows certified companies also enjoy a recruiting advantage and higher employee retention.[28] In 2025, nearly 10,000 companies across 100 countries in 160 industries carry B Corp certification, a third-party verification mark that functions like UL for mission-driven businesses.[29]

Many people get this confused, so let me reiterate here: Public benefit corporations (PBCs) and B Corp certification are fundamentally different tools. PBCs are legal structures that change corporate governance; B Corp certification is a brand standard that signals values to consumers. While the certification has value for marketing and recruiting, the PBC structure provides the legal foundation for mission protection.

The movement continues to evolve, sometimes through frustration with existing tools. Seth Goldman knows the pattern Gilbert and Houlahan experienced: He watched Coca-Cola acquire Honest Tea, then discontinue it in 2022. Within months, he launched Just Ice Tea to carry that mission forward. Goldman brings a hard-won perspective to the standards debate. "Just because you can fill out paperwork doesn't mean you're meeting a high standard," he told me. His skepticism aligned with companies like Dr. Bronner's, which dropped its B Corp certification after multinationals like Nestlé gained the same badge.[30] In 2024, Goldman's Just Ice Tea joined Dr. Bronner's and seventeen other companies to pilot the Purpose Pledge.[31]

This new standard takes a different approach, as it does not offer a consumer-facing seal. Instead, companies commit to specific, measurable standards, such as maintaining a maximum twenty-to-one pay ratio, contributing at least 1% of revenue to philanthropic initiatives, and establishing independent mission guardians.[32] Goldman calls it "a more aspirational standard." Where B Corp certification might require choosing from a menu of options to hit a score, Purpose Pledge companies bind themselves to specific, nonnegotiable commitments that can be monitored and verified.

Another approach rejects the exit-driven model entirely. Dave Whorton spent years in Silicon Valley as a venture capitalist before noticing a different breed of company: those built not to flip but to last for generations. In 2013, he founded the Tugboat Institute to certify what he calls "Evergreen" companies. To earn the certification, companies must demonstrate commitment to purpose, perseverance, and paced growth; in return, they join a community of like-minded founders committed to building durable businesses.[33] PBCs encode mission into legal DNA. B Corps signal values to consumers. Purpose Pledge creates accountability through nonnegotiable commitments. LTSE gives public companies a way to commit to long-term value creation. Evergreen certification identifies outliers in the private markets. Together these standards make it easier for customers, employees, and investors to choose the right organizations to transact with—and trust: those that are more likely to honor their commitments.

THE CREATION OF A NEW STANDARD

Lest this discussion of standards seems purely historical, meet entrepreneur Rune Kvist, a former Anthropic employee who came to me with an ambitious vision. He'd seen firsthand how AI was advancing rapidly, creating unprecedented risks that moved faster than any system could contain them.

"I want to build one of the world's most valuable companies," he told me, "by solving AI risk through insurance."

What Rune saw was a $500 billion problem hiding in plain sight. Every company integrating AI agents faces novel forms of liability they can't even name yet. What if an AI lending system denies mortgages in patterns that mirror historical redlining? Or a customer service bot confidently fabricates return policies that don't exist? Or an autonomous trading system makes a catastrophic decision based on logic no human can untangle? When failures like these happen (and they're happening now), companies discover their traditional insurance won't cover AI-specific risks.

Just as Franklin's fire insurance made Philadelphia safer, AI insurance could create economic gravity that pulls the entire industry toward responsible development. Safe systems get affordable coverage. Reckless ones can't get insured at all. The market rewards responsibility. But there's a fundamental problem: Insurers can't price what they can't measure. Without standards for assessing AI risk—no UL mark for algorithms, no safety certification for autonomous agents—every policy requires months of custom evaluation. The economics collapse before they begin.

Rune was stuck on what seemed like an insurmountable challenge. To make AI insurance work at scale, he believed he had to build the world's biggest insurance company from scratch. Every investor pushed him to think smaller, to slice off an easier bit of the problem to solve. Rune understood the issue deeply thanks to his time at Anthropic, but he could not figure out how to get started.

As we talked through the standards framework (as I've done with you here in this chapter), he started to envision a strategy that could work. "I had not realized that you could create a standard," he later reflected.[34] "Rather than me building the world's biggest insurance company," he realized, "I can just rely on existing insurers if I can, in some ways, give them what they need"—that is, a widely accepted standard for AI risk assessment.[35] Instead of building another insurance carrier, he could be the one to create the AI risk insurance market itself, wielding standards as his tool. "You can create a whole new market where you are influencing and orchestrating the whole supply chain."

Rune immediately saw the paradox and its elegant solution. Every standard faces the same chicken-and-egg problem: Nobody wants to go first, but somebody has to. Each early adopter would make it easier for the next: "The first company to get audited faces much higher risk and lower reward than the ten thousandth, but once the flywheel starts spinning, when almost every vendor has this certification, then every other vendor will feel the pressure to conform. No one's going to want to buy from them otherwise." By the end of our conversation, Rune was thinking in completely different terms. He wasn't building an insurance company anymore. He was architecting an ecosystem.

Rune developed a theory he calls the "incentive triangle" to show how insurance, standards, and audits create self-reinforcing market governance. In 2025, Rune's Artificial Intelligence Underwriting Company emerged from stealth mode with $15 million in funding to implement exactly that vision and is now building the standards infrastructure that will govern a $500 billion market.[36]

"Security enables acceleration," Rune explains. "Seat belts let us drive faster. AI standards will let us deploy powerful systems with confidence rather than fear."

ROUGH CONSENSUS, RUNNING CODE

The technology industry relies on layer upon layer of standards. MIT's David Clark put it bluntly in 1992: "We reject: kings, presidents, and voting. We believe in: rough consensus and running code." This philosophy—rough consensus, running code—became the credo of the Internet Engineering Task Force, who stewarded the nascent internet into its modern form.[37]

Along the way, they discovered that you need adoption to prove value, but you need proven value to get adoption. The only escape from this trap is to start small with something that works, then let the gravitational field build.

The internet itself proves the point. The ISO spent the late 1970s and 1980s designing a theoretically perfect seven-layer networking model blessed by governments worldwide.[38] Meanwhile, a scrappy team built TCP/IP for ARPANET, the US Defense Department's network that became the forerunner of today's internet.[39] It had just four layers and plenty of flaws, but it worked. Today, TCP/IP runs the internet, while that ISO standard exists only in textbooks, a cautionary tale about the triumph of working code over perfect committees.

The same pattern built Linux. Linus Torvalds didn't convene a committee to design the perfect operating system. He posted ten thousand lines of code and asked what features people wanted.[40] By inviting others to shape its direction while it was still small enough to change, he created the rough consensus that now powers most of the world's servers. Torvalds repeated this magic in 2005 with Git, spending just two weeks on initial code before releasing it.[41] Rough consensus shaped the version-control system that became such a standard that GitHub and GitLab commercialized it into multibillion-dollar businesses.

Engellau didn't wait for industry agreement on safety standards; he put working seat belts in cars. McLean sailed just fifty-eight containers on a converted tanker. UL started with one engineer and one World's Fair. Early adopters get to shape the standard's direction while capturing opportunities their competitors can't yet see. They're not betting on a theory; they're joining a movement already in motion. This is the secret that turns giving away control into gaining influence. Every working implementation creates gravitational pull, and every early success makes the next adoption easier.

THE OPPORTUNITY

Imagine if you had a breakthrough like the three-point seat belt or the shipping container. If you have a board of directors right now, imagine taking it to them. Or, if not, imagine taking it to an investor or venture capitalist. Now imagine telling them you think it could be a multibillion-dollar move to give it away. How do you think they would react?

Would they grasp the logic of giving it away? Or would they see only the immediate losses—the licensing fees, the competitive advantage, the control?

Yet right now, in your organization or your daily life, there's probably something only you can see. A better process, a superior method, a way of solving problems that might transform an industry if everyone adopted it. What would it look like to start your own prosperity cascade? I promised in Chapter 5 that I would show you how to see positive externalities. I hope by now you are starting to see the immensity of the opportunities that our business culture routinely misses.

But what if the thing you're aware of isn't just an industry-level problem? What if it's something deeper, more fundamental? A society-wide, multi-industry, or even planetary problem? In my experience, many builders are aware of these massive opportunities but immediately shy away. "That's bigger than what any startup can tackle," they think. "That would require changing the rules themselves."

As if the current rules were handed down from Mount Sinai. As if someone didn't write them. As if that someone couldn't be you. Steve Jobs put it this way in 1995:

> When you grow up you tend to get told that the world is the way it is. . . . Life can be much broader, once you discover one simple fact, and that is that everything around you that you call life was made up by people that were no smarter than you. And you can change it. . . . Once you learn that, you'll never be the same again.[42]

Jobs's credo led him to create whole new industries. Now let's take one more step outward, tackling problems that transcend any industry or even just business itself. Our civilization depends, to a surprising degree, on the entrepreneurs who build the organizations that govern entire sectors—the infrastructure that society itself runs on.

CHAPTER FOURTEEN

A NEW CIVIC INFRASTRUCTURE

You mean, it's just a form?
—me, bewildered

IF YOU HAVE a beat-up old copy of *The Lean Startup* somewhere, flip almost to the last page. There, in the epilogue, you'll find a throwaway suggestion: Somebody should build a long-term stock exchange.

Over the years, pretty much every idea I suggested in that book, good or bad, has been tried by someone. Minimum viable products, pivots, validated learning—I've watched entrepreneurs around the world experiment with them all. But nobody ever said they wanted to create a new stock exchange.

For years, the idea gnawed at me. Eventually, I realized maybe the only willing someone was me. I started my odyssey by talking to anyone who would listen. Industry veterans, regulators, lawyers, investors. "You want to create . . . a new stock exchange? Like, a new marble building? With a bull?" Since they knew this was impossible, their response was often a polite smile and a certain look. I called it the *two-moons* incomprehension, as if I'd suggested creating a new celestial body. After all, there hasn't been a new public listing venue with a new listings model since the creation of NASDAQ more than fifty years ago.

This difficulty is why we all believe nothing transformative can be done. But imagine our world without all the things skeptics today would say we couldn't create. A building where we give away books for free, funded by taxes? Wikipedia, a limitless encyclopedia anyone can add to or vandalize? Credit unions—banks owned by their own customers? National parks that take immense stretches of gorgeous land off the market forever? The internet itself, operating on protocols given away by committees, with no one in charge? Each of these would face that same two-moons incomprehension if proposed today. We owe it to ourselves—and to the world—to try anyway.

The first three years of my work on LTSE were filled with meetings, rejections, and that damned two-moons look. To anyone who seemed to know anything about the public markets, I would put this question: "How does one go about creating a new stock exchange?" Most people patted me on the head and asked me politely to meet with someone else. The rare few who would engage in the question at all wanted me to know, definitively, that it was impossible.

Then, finally, I found myself in the office of a securities lawyer who'd been recommended by someone who knew someone. I was prepared for another polite dismissal. Instead, he said some of the most shocking words I've heard in my entrepreneurial career: "It's not hard. You just fill out the Form 1 application."

I couldn't understand. "A what application?" I asked. He said, "You know how government forms are all numbered?" I nodded. "Well, this is SEC form number 0001, the 'Application for Registration as a National Securities Exchange.'"[1]

It took me several tries to grasp this. "You mean, it's just a form?" The thing you do to create a new stock exchange is . . . fill out a form?

"Well," he clarified, "the form is two hundred pages long. Takes years to fill out properly. The SEC will grill you on every detail. But yes, at the end of the day, it's just a form."[2]

That's when I realized I wasn't trying to build a company. I was trying to build *civic infrastructure*—in my case, for the markets and for entrepreneurs. And almost nobody I'd met had walked this path, so I'd had to discover it for myself. The confusion, the resistance, and the glacial pace all made sense. I wasn't failing at building a startup; I was discovering what it takes to create the rules others operate within.

Civic infrastructure consists of organizations that facilitate the flourishing of other institutions and communities by creating beneficial constraints, building shared trust and connection, and solving collective action problems that enable public goods. Any time you've wondered why the range of products you have to choose from is confined to one specific set but not others, why political parties offer only the candidates they offer, why there are no healthier food options at your local corner store, why only certain companies are empowered to sell stock to the public, why you can use your ATM card ten thousand miles from home but you can't easily transfer your medical records to the doctor next door, why every computer in the world can talk to every other computer, civic infrastructure is why.

To appreciate just how invisible this apparatus is, consider what happens when you buy a banana at a local store. Behind that simple transaction lies an astonishing web of institutions and practices you've likely never thought about: the UPC (Universal Product Code) barcode, the shipping container, the food safety rules, the store's buyer and the banana's distributor, the security standards, advertising standards, import licenses, and phytosanitary certificates. And don't forget your friendly local Central Bank, which makes the currency you paid in possible. If you paid by credit card, at least two more banks were involved (yours and the merchant's), the Visa or Mastercard network, plus their fraud detection systems and a dozen other standards.

The whole thing took fifteen seconds, but each banana carries the invisible imprint of dozens of rule-setting organizations you've never heard of. In defining the term *civic infrastructure*, I'm deliberately merging two schools of thought. The social science view, from thinkers like sociologists Eric Klinenberg and Mario Small, sees social infrastructure as community-enabling institutions like libraries, civic associations, and public forums.[3] The economic view, from Douglass North's "rules of the game"[4] to Hernando de Soto's "invisible infrastructure,"[5] focuses on how institutions enable Western prosperity. My synthesis posits that the rule-setting organizations that govern business and economies are *all* civic infrastructure because they shape not just markets but the civic life of entire societies, regardless of whether they are physical, economic, or even purely virtual. By calling them "civic," we acknowledge they should serve public purposes, not just technical or economic ones.

Just as earlier chapters broke down the distinction between for-profit and non-profit, civic infrastructure breaks down the distinction between the public and private sectors. Some civic infrastructure organizations are for-profit companies, some are NGOs, and others are branches of government. Still others are hybrid forms, like UL (which we saw in the previous chapter) or the so-called self-regulatory organizations (SROs), which are private entities that hold a grant of authority from a sovereign government.[6]

It's common for people to say that certain collective action problems can only be solved by regulation. This is often true, but it overlooks the fact that many of today's regulations were pioneered by private actors. We saw this with electrical safety certification and seatbelts in the previous chapter, but the same pattern appears with everything from the forty-hour work week to food safety standards. In many domains, regulation reifies a solution that has already been worked out by private actors. This creates conditions for experimentation and learning before widespread mandatory adoption.[7]

Here's a simple test: If a particular organization suddenly changed its rules, disappeared, or lost the public's trust, would entire sectors struggle to function? If yes, you're looking at civic infrastructure. It is time to bring these creatures out of the shadows so we can see their effects more clearly. If a product can't be assigned a UPC code, if a medical procedure doesn't have a billing code, or if credit card processors won't transact it, you can't buy it. Often, you won't even be able to discover that it exists. This is the dark side of the standard-setting power that we saw with UL in the prior chapter. Unsafe products cannot even be sold. But who gets to decide what is safe?

Recognizing these systems and conventions as civic infrastructure also reminds us of a crucial fact. They're human institutions, as subject to capture, corruption, and mission drift as any organization discussed in this book.

But why a long-term stock exchange?

The average holding period for stocks has plummeted from eight years in 1960 to four months today.[8] High-frequency traders drive close to half of all US equity volume, capturing profits in milliseconds.[9]

As one trader proudly put it to me, "We have built the most efficient market in history—for trading fifty-share lots."

And from his perspective, he's right. The market has been optimized for those who trade fastest in the smallest increments, not for the companies building long-term value or the investors trying to own them. The companies that create the value being traded are called "issuers"—as if they were mere dispensers.

What does all this have to do with you? Most of the leaders I admire did not start out thinking about civic infrastructure or any such lofty term. They simply noticed something wrong in the world around them. As they pulled on that thread, they developed deep conviction in their particular ethos and mission. They wanted to change the way things are—for the better. They wanted to tackle a truly hard problem: reduce carbon emissions, revolutionize healthcare, improve education, democratize financial systems, or build open alternatives to the platforms that dominate our lives.

But as they go down the road of a harder-is-easier mission, something unexpected happens. Quite often, they realize they need to build more than a company. Even industry-wide change is not enough. It starts to feel daunting. They wonder who they are to decide the rules that govern our whole society. Sadly, many shy away from embracing this responsibility. As a result, our shared infrastructure is left to decay or, worse, become captured by people with no ethos at all.

But you don't have to shy away. In the last chapter, we explored the power of standards thinking to drive industry-wide change; this chapter explores *infrastructure thinking* as a way of looking not just at one industry's landscape but at the foundational rules and parameters that determine what industries can exist at all. Perhaps these are the very rules you need to change. Perhaps changing them is the only way to truly see your mission actualized in the world.

Civic infrastructure organizations share three common attributes:

1. **They possess rule-setting or coordinating power.** Their decisions become everyone else's constraints; their standards enable others to cooperate. When the Financial Accounting Standards Board (FASB) changes an accounting rule, every public company in America must comply. The local public library may seem like a humble example, but it too radiates enormous power. (These effects may seem soft or intangible, but this is mistaken. For example, libraries have been shown repeatedly to generate economic value far beyond their costs.[10])
2. **They're tiny relative to what they govern.** The Financial Accounting Standards Board has just seven board members, yet they dictate how trillions in assets get calculated.[11] You probably didn't even know there was an International Earth Rotation Service (IERS) in charge of "leap seconds," which can make changes to billions of phones without their owners' knowledge.[12]
3. **Trust is their essential currency.** Without widespread belief in their legitimacy, they can collapse without warning. So many casualties of modern "disruption"—from newspapers to unions to political parties—still exist but are no longer able to serve the same civic function. Contrary to many advocates of creative destruction, there is no guarantee that a vital function will be replaced. We must choose.[13]

When I was just starting LTSE, my new colleagues at the NYSE gave me a lovely tour of the marble building, which, if you ever get the chance, is really quite special. The old trading floor. The ornate boardrooms where titans of industry once gathered. And there, behind glass, the original Buttonwood Tree Agreement that kicked off the whole enterprise. The NYSE started as twenty-four brokers meeting under a buttonwood tree in 1792. This founding document of American capitalism is barely a page long. Twenty-four brokers agreed to two things: trade only with each other and charge a fixed commission of a minimum of 0.25%.[14]

That's it. No marble building. No impressive facade. Just a price-fixing cartel, written on a scrap of paper.

This should remind you of UL, Sea-Land, and the internet itself from the previous chapter. Each started with a coordination problem, then found an entrepreneurial solution that later became essential infrastructure.

FICO started the same modest way: Bill Fair and Earl Isaac invested $400 each to convince skeptical bankers that algorithms could assess credit risk.[15] By the time Fannie Mae and Freddie Mac began requiring FICO scores for the mortgages they would purchase, every lender in America had to get on board. Today, FICO scores are used by 90% of major lenders.

Unicode started as three engineers' side project in 1987—today it governs every piece of text on every device on Earth.[16]

Anything can be different if we want it to be. In other places, it is. German workers sit on corporate boards.[17] Swiss citizens can overturn laws by referendum.[18] In Singapore, the government owns 90% of the land, and 80% of the population lives in public housing built on this land.[19] Japan has nursing rooms in public locations that can be easily located via an app.[20] Different societies build different civic infrastructure, encoding different values.

The challenges of our era are civilization scale: AI governance, climate stability, pandemic preparedness, biodiversity collapse, epistemic crisis. Yet we lack the civic infrastructure to address them. New technologies and changing values mean we are about to get a whole lot of institutional turnover whether we choose it or not. The opportunities are massive. Yet most entrepreneurs are blind to them.

The cost of inaction is steep. When we don't build infrastructure intentionally, it gets built accidentally. And, almost always, badly.

For example, US transit construction costs run eight to twelve times higher than in peer nations. People attempt to justify this with all manner of just-so stories ranging from the uniqueness of American culture to various technical challenges. But rigorous research has shown that this cost bloat stems from governance structures that separate decision-makers from consequences.[21]

Things are even worse in healthcare. Medical errors kill hundreds of thousands of Americans annually; they are the third leading cause of death in this country.[22] They persist because hospitals—even nonprofit ones—face perverse incentives: Admitting errors invites lawsuits, while treating complications generates revenue. Malpractice settlements buy silence through nondisclosure agreements (NDAs) rather than surfacing cases to learn from. This is not the fault of doctors and nurses; it reflects the same structural forces we've seen throughout this book.[23]

What is especially frustrating is that frontline practitioners have worked out how to fix the problem of medical errors. Hospitals that implement transparent error reporting, blameless investigation systems, and systematic learning see dramatic reductions in preventable harm.[24] And yet the errors persist, year after year.

The situation may seem hopeless, but despair is a choice. Consider what happened in aviation. After a series of fatal crashes in the 1960s, this country formed the National Transportation Safety Board (NTSB), with real power to investigate every crash and name names.[25] The industry adopted what's called *just culture*, where errors lead to learning, not punishment. Aviation deaths dropped 95%.[26] Although individual airlines sometimes suffer from this transparency, the whole industry gains far more.

So why don't we have a National Patient Safety Board? Well, check the dates. The NTSB was first proposed in the years before the rise of shareholder primacy. The foundational report on systemic medical errors—the Institute of Medicine's *To Err Is Human*—was published in 1999. There is simply too much gravity pulling hospitals—yes, hospitals!—to lobby against it. This is what passes for good governance today.[27] The infrastructure we refuse to build is worth more to some than the lives it would save.

Every day, another independent pharmacy closes its doors—not because they're bad at business but because pharmacy benefit managers (PBMs) have rigged the game. They own their own pharmacies and steer patients there, using the data from independent pharmacy claims to poach their customers. Three PBMs—CVS Caremark, Express Scripts, and OptumRx—control sales of 80% of all prescriptions through what regulators describe as "confusing, unfair, opaque" practices—and outrageously high prices.[28] Meanwhile, 27% of Americans skip medications they need because they can't afford them.[29] One pharmacist put it bluntly: "People are being harmed, and it is because of PBM greed."[30]

When pharmacists describe their own circumstances, they say, "We cannot negotiate any aspect of our contracts with PBMs in any meaningful way. It is truly take-it-or-leave-it."[31] One Kentucky pharmacist reported that in a single day, 150 prescriptions were reimbursed below their purchase cost.[32]

PBMs operate through a complex rebate system. Drug manufacturers pay PBMs to get their products on formularies, and the rebate is based on the medication's list price.[33] The higher the price, the larger the rebate they receive. A $3,000 branded drug might generate $900 in rebates for the PBM; a $160 generic, perhaps $5. This creates a perverse incentive to keep cheaper drugs off formularies, steering patients toward expensive medications even when affordable alternatives exist.

This rebate pattern shows up all over civic infrastructure. "Payment for order flow" in stock trading, payola in music radio, slot fees in grocery stores—call them rebates or kickbacks, the mechanism is the same: Middlemen get paid to steer decisions away from the best choice toward the most profitable one for them. (Do I even need to add that Costco does not accept slot fees or rebates?)

This is civic infrastructure gone bad. Organizations meant to coordinate drug benefits have become rent-seeking monopolies, extracting value at every turn while providing the thinnest veneer of service.

Dr. Alex Oshmyansky looked at this system and saw an opportunity not to reform PBMs but to replace them entirely.[34] A radiologist outraged by the Martin Shkreli price-gouging scandal, Oshmyansky founded a non-profit pharmacy in 2015 to sell drugs at cost. But he couldn't make it work as a non-profit because he was unable to raise funding beyond his own investment. Undeterred, he took his mission to Y Combinator in 2018, where mentors urged him to switch to a for-profit model. Eventually, he found the combination that should sound familiar by now.

Oshmyansky reincorporated as a public benefit corporation (PBC) and then took a shot in the dark. He cold-emailed Mark Cuban with his plan to bypass the PBM middlemen entirely. Cuban was stunned by what he discovered about the industry's markups. "Prior to us, there was no transparency whatsoever and so nobody knew what the price of any medication was," Cuban explained. He became not just an investor but the company's loudest champion and eventually cofounder, lending his name to what became the Mark Cuban Cost Plus Drug Company. "These pharmacy benefit managers are dictating prices . . . basically stealing money from employers and employees."[35]

Cost Plus Drugs tells customers the actual manufacturer cost of each drug and adds exactly 15% markup plus a $5 pharmacy fee.[36] Since Cost Plus Drugs is a public benefit corporation, it is legally committed to transparency. It's required to "publish all contracts" online. Every price, every deal: completely public.

Next, Cost Plus Drugs constructed a 22,000-square-foot manufacturing facility in Dallas to become a licensed drug wholesaler, bypassing the rebate system entirely.[37] Generic Tecfidera, the multiple sclerosis drug, costs $6,617 at traditional pharmacies where PBMs control the transaction; at Cost Plus Drugs, it's $39.50, just above the manufacturer's cost.[38] A leukemia drug that costs $2,000 at retail sells for $30 at Cost Plus Drugs.[39] A study in the Annals of Internal Medicine found that Medicare alone could save $3.6 billion annually on just eighty-nine generic drugs if it used Cost Plus Drugs pricing.[40]

Cost Plus Drugs reached 1.5 million customers within a year. But the real shockwave came when Blue Shield of California dropped CVS Caremark.[41] Blue Shield's CEO identified the breaking point. They'd found a cancer drug for $160 per month (versus $3,000 retail), but CVS Caremark refused for months to add it to their formulary. "They initially refused and they kept refusing," he said. "It's like pulling teeth to get that to happen."[42] Blue Shield now uses Cost Plus Drugs for generics, expecting to save $500 million annually. CVS stock dropped 8.5% on the announcement.[43] Cuban has long argued that "the dominant three PBMs put stock price over health."[44]

Cost Plus Drugs is rewiring the relationships between doctors, pharmacists, pharmaceutical companies, and the employers who provide insurance. They are becoming a new part of the infrastructure that determines how the entire healthcare system works. And every employer who switches, every patient who saves thousands, and every news story about the price differences weaken the old infrastructure's gravitational pull.

The implications reach beyond drug pricing. Cuban believes Cost Plus Drugs could become a path to universal coverage through radically transparent, market-based providers. He may or may not be right about the future. But either way, his proposal demonstrates how civic infrastructure can change the landscape of what can be debated.

Social media algorithms amplify outrage, reward trolling, and turn neighbors into enemies. The institutions our grandparents relied on to forge consensus have been hollowed out. We can all tell that our sense of shared reality has fractured, but nobody quite knows how to put Humpty Dumpty back together again. Colin Megill thought he might. A Seattle programmer, he watched the Arab Spring's promise dissolve into chaos on social media, then watched Occupy Wall Street tear itself apart in flame wars. He decided the root cause was that online forums amplify conflict because conflict drives engagement. So in 2012, Megill and two cofounders built Pol.is to encode the opposite values.[45] They engineered a platform that was good at finding consensus, not controversy.

Its algorithm is deceptively simple: Everyone in a community is invited to submit one-line statements to Pol.is, which then offers everyone else in the community the chance to vote on whether they agree or disagree with each one. There's no commenting and therefore no provocations, baiting, or arguing. The algorithm acts as a neutral tallying system, clustering participants by their actual opinion patterns, not their declared tribes. Its goal is to find the statements that bridge otherwise opposing groups. Instead of optimizing for engagement, it boosts the statements that achieve consensus across different clusters and lets divisive statements sink into obscurity.

The platform has a track record of defusing real-world crises. In Taiwan, when Uber-versus-taxi protests paralyzed Taipei in 2015, the government deployed Pol.is instead of calling traditional town halls.[46] Within weeks, twenty thousand participants found that, beneath the street protests and angry rhetoric, both sides actually agreed on most points. There turned out to be wide support for measures such as equal regulations, proper insurance, and taxing both kinds of ride services. The government implemented these consensus findings, and both sides accepted the outcome. Taiwan went on to use Pol.is for twenty-six national issues in the years that followed, with 80% of the cases leading to concrete government action.[47]

Austria's eighty-four-member climate assembly used it to test recommendations with five thousand citizens.[48] New Zealand newspapers deployed it to build consensus on everything from sugar policy to tax reform.[49] Trust emerges from transparency because everyone can see the same data, the same clusters, and the same consensus points emerging. Instead of manipulating public opinion, Pol.is helps communities discover the truth about themselves.

The ultimate proof is that Pol.is works even in hell. In 2021, Twitter's management grew concerned about toxic discourse. They built their Community Notes feature on the Pol.is architecture. Even surrounded by Twitter's engagement-maximizing algorithms, the system successfully identifies truthful notes that people across tribal divides can accept. It's like building a pocket of breathable air inside a toxic waste dump.[50]

Megill and his tiny team have kept Pol.is open source and nonprofit.[51] They have encoded their values into the architecture itself, building civic infrastructure that others can adopt. The next time you see a community paralyzed by division, realize that this is a choice.

The consensus is there, buried under the noise. Thanks to Pol.is, we have the ability to find it—if we have the will.

Both Cost Plus and Pol.is are still relatively early in their journey to becoming civic infrastructure. I include them to counteract the feeling that such large, imposing institutions feel out of reach. I often have leaders bemoan to me "Why don't you include examples of startups?" when I teach this concept. But that's precisely the point. Every single example we've seen—from Novo Nordisk's single insulin lab to NYSE's simple price-fixing agreement—was once just a startup. Their indomitable scale is no reason to be intimidated. Rather, it is a reason to think bigger. These opportunities are all around us, often requiring nothing more than the conceptual clarity to see them.

Consider credit unions. In 1908, immigrant mill workers in Manchester, New Hampshire, faced a problem: They needed credit, but banks wouldn't serve them. Too poor, too foreign, too risky. So they pooled their money to create St. Mary's Cooperative Credit Association, America's first credit union.[52] Members own the institution, one member gets one vote regardless of wealth, and all profits return to members as better rates. The idea spread to communities across America, who realized they could build their own financial infrastructure rather than beg for better treatment from commercial banks. During the Great Depression, while nine thousand banks failed and millions lost their savings, credit unions expanded.[53] Today, 143 million Americans have accounts at credit unions.[54]

And yet their massive success hasn't been replicated in other domains. We all know Wikipedia for knowledge,[55] Signal for privacy,[56] Khan Academy for education;[57] our most important digital systems are overseen by non-profits like the Apache Software Foundation[58] and the Linux Foundation.[59] They don't write code; they provide constitutional governance for the open-source communities that power most of the world's websites and smartphones. We have singletons, not movements. We marvel at them, but we do not emulate them.

Once again, the false binary of for-profit versus non-profit blinds us. Entrepreneurs cannot see opportunities in the interstitial spaces where they have been conditioned not to look.

Building civic infrastructure is a bit like the final exam for the principles of this book. Miss even one answer, and the whole thing collapses. It's also a bit like carving the Grand Canyon with water and gravity. If you are willing to persist and persevere, you can make something impossible seem inevitable. It's also likely to feel like a long march through the desert. At LTSE, we had to develop our own indicators of flow: each regulatory clarification, each ally gained, each precedent established. These were drops of water finding the path downhill, slowly but inevitably carving the channel for others to follow.

Building LTSE was unquestionably the most arduous startup I've ever undertaken. I honestly don't think I could have done it without applying everything in this book:

"Harder is easier." LTSE is an ordinary, everyday, ho-hum five-sided marketplace. Its value proposition has to work for founders and managers, public market investors and investment bankers, venture capitalists, stock traders and market makers, and regulators too—all at the same time. Only by serving all of them at once could we unlock the transformative value we hoped to achieve. But how do you satisfy regulators who want predictability while building something genuinely new? How do you serve venture capitalists who need liquidity and returns while promoting long-term holding? The contradictions almost drove me crazy. One of our investors quipped, "Well, at least nobody will be crazy enough to try to compete with you."

Mission drive. LTSE employees are among the most dedicated I have ever met. Almost every person who works there could have made far more money finding a cozy spot inside the *status quo*. They choose LTSE because they truly believe fundamental change is possible. We owed it to them to build a management system worthy of that commitment.

"Fiduciary to who?" Just like Sol Price, we take our fiduciary duties seriously. Not just to shareholders but to the companies and members we oversee. We've gone to extraordinary lengths to insulate decision-making from outside pressure. Every policy, every decision, and every trade-off gets evaluated against our mission.

Financial gravity. In civic infrastructure, funding structures encode power relationships. If the organizations you're supposed to regulate pay your bills, and you're desperate for revenue, you've already lost. In fact, one savvy trader once warned me, years before we began trading stocks, that if we ever finally got the exchange running, we would see a surge of volume in the early days, and then one day, once that revenue was baked into the business plan and future forecasts, the call would come: "We're giving you a lot of volume. Sure would be a shame if something happened to it. Perhaps we could discuss some rule changes." I thought he was paranoid. But then it happened. We were prepared to say no and built to survive the immediate loss of volume that came as a result.

"Intelligent loss of sales." Yes, we make money from trading, but we've deliberately structured our business to minimize dependence on high-frequency traders and speculators. Our listing standards deter short-term companies by design. Instead, we cater only to the very best companies, the ones organized around a philosophy of long-term value creation and the aspiration to be mission-controlled in everything they do.

Structural integrity. LTSE is a three-entity constellation that makes it possible to make promises people can believe. Each entity reinforces the others while maintaining appropriate independence. We have aligned cap tables and intercompany agreements, just like we discussed in Chapter 10. Many people called it complicated, but to me, it is actually the simplest solution to a complex problem. When a large potential customer wanted to list but didn't meet our standards, they were turned away automatically, even though the revenue would have transformed our trajectory. The standards are the standards.

Standards and mission transmission. Here's where we had our biggest breakthrough—and our biggest failure. Initially, we had rigid, rules-based listing requirements, including a few I had proposed back in the final pages of *The Lean Startup*. We got pretty close to getting this approved before we were ambushed by financial firms that objected to one of the specific rules. But changing that rule would have required betraying other firms that were committed to it. One size fits none.

It almost killed the company. But as it turned out, necessity provided the mothering we needed. Forced to pivot, we birthed a breakthrough: principles-based standards. Each company proposes how they'll implement our five core principles. Then, once they commit, it's legally binding. Since our standards require public disclosure, they are subject to true enforcement. No greenwashing allowed.

An ethos of human flourishing. At the end of the day, LTSE's original mission—to become a sanctuary for company builders—reflects this ethos in the most fundamental way. Every decision we make is evaluated through this lens. Not "Does this maximize revenue?" but "Does this create an environment where builders can focus on long-term value creation?"

I'm enormously proud of the progress we have made to date and especially of the remarkable customers, partners, and team that have come together to support this mission. For all that it has achieved, LTSE is by far the hardest—and least likely to succeed—project I have ever worked on. It's only in its first innings.

I stepped aside as CEO in 2022, in part to write this book. The company today is led by an extraordinary leadership team helmed by Maliz Beams. The work of civic infrastructure necessarily unfolds across decades. By the time you read this, LTSE will have written new chapters I can only imagine today, authored by the leaders who will advance this mission in the years to come.

LTSE CASE STUDY: If you're interested in learning more about LTSE, its history and present, scan the QR code or go to incorruptible.co/ltse-case-study.

But that uncertainty is itself instructive. Building civic infrastructure requires accepting that you might only succeed in laying the groundwork for others to build upon. When I was a younger entrepreneur, I would have found this impossible to accept. I was impatient for success, fame, riches, all manner of worldly rewards. These longings were sometimes helpful motivators but far more often distractions. They would have been fatal to LTSE.

The scale of civic infrastructure requires a distinctive personal ethos. What would I feel satisfied having built regardless of whether it succeeds or fails?

Whatever the future brings, my hope is that this work will help others birth new civic institutions that extend this mission far beyond what any single company could achieve alone. Either way, our goal should be that someday, when our children ask us, "At that moment in history, what were you doing?" we will be able to answer them.

Over the broad sweep of this book, we have been steadily zooming outward: from the spark of an idea, to the organization it becomes, to its management system, its culture, its structure, and finally everything caught in its orbit. Here in Part III, we've zoomed out even further and seen how organizations can project their own gravity, create standards, and ultimately participate in building the very architecture of our civilization. We've been climbing these hierarchies looking for the source of legitimate authority, the person in charge, the wizard behind the curtain. *Who is the bank?* We have seen CEOs and tenant farmers—and everyone in between—be brought low by this question.

But here's where it gets trippy. Pull back far enough, and you discover that the ultimate source of all this gravitational force, the thing that gives civic infrastructure its power, standards their pull, and organizations their mass, isn't institutional at all. Turn the ladder upside down, and you may experience a moment of vertigo.

You're not stuck in traffic. You are traffic.

Chapter Fifteen

YOU ARE TRAFFIC

> He who fights monsters should be careful lest he thereby become a monster. And if you gaze long into an abyss, the abyss also gazes into you.
>
> —**Friedrich Nietzsche**
> *Beyond Good and Evil*
> 1886

You're not stuck in traffic. You are traffic.

We ended the last chapter with this observation, and it's worth sitting with for a moment. Throughout this book, we've been climbing a hierarchy, looking for the highest authority that governs CEOs and tenant farmers alike. An organization may begin as an idea in the mind of an individual person or a small team. As it is built, layer by layer, more and more people add their voice, their hands, their will. But also their influence. By the time we zoom out to a whole organization, what has happened to that original intention? Has it been amplified and protected or damaged by internal or external corruption? Who sets its rules? Who controls its money? Who is in charge of making sure its ethos is upheld? We've zoomed out while looking up, always searching for the ultimate authority. *Who is the bank?*

The answer has been lurking between the lines of this entire book. Way back in Chapter 5, I noted that every organization gets to choose for itself how it will contribute to "human flourishing" and endure the resulting competitive consequences. Did that sound a bit like relativism to you? And did that bother you?

Good. Hold on to that feeling.

Let's talk about those competitive consequences for a moment. Throughout, we've seen organizations aligned with human flourishing generate seemingly impossible advantages. They attract better talent, inspire deeper loyalty, create unshakable trust. But why does it happen?

Because we all carry an instinct—sometimes buried, sometimes dampened, but always present—to move toward our own flourishing and to support what helps others flourish too. Some of us are drawn to products that make life easier. Others to beauty that elevates the everyday. Still others to innovations that promote health or belonging or justice. The particular expression varies, but underneath them all runs the same current. When organizations genuinely align with human flourishing, they tap into this universal instinct. That's the source of the magnetic powers from *harder is easier*. That's why all the alignment techniques in Part II actually work.

Notice one more thing. When we studied financial gravity, we saw how it works: driven primarily by people's perception of what values they must embrace in order to further their goals. This nonstop pull can be tremendously destructive, as when organizations are held down by a critical mass of shortsighted profiteering. But it can also be a source of great strength, as in *mission transmission*. Either way, it is a major source of tension in modern life—between the still, small voice that knows better and the unconscious pressure to conform.

But where does this gravitational pull actually come from?

You are generating it right now.

I know how that sounds. Here you are, maybe reading this during your commute or in a stolen moment between meetings, and I'm telling you that you're the secret architect of the entire economic system. It seems absurd. After so many chapters of emphasizing structural causes, this may sound to some like a retreat—as if we could solve climate change by recycling. But I have something different in mind.

Think back to what we discovered when we first defined gravity. Every transaction transmits force. Every moment of attention creates pull. Every choice adds mass to the order it supports.

Indeed, in this era of surveillance capitalism and attention economy, organizations are obsessed with . . . you. I've sat in countless meetings where executives debate what to do with their product. Add features or remove them? Raise prices or lower them? Use a healthier ingredient even though it adds three cents to the cost? The room fills with spreadsheets, market research, competitive analysis. The analysis almost always comes down to one thing, which goes by the innocuous-sounding phrase "willingness to pay." Companies spend untold millions trying to decode it. Will customers pay the extra three cents? Will you?

"Willingness to pay" is only one name for this obsession. The same idea appears in so many other places: employment brand, customer retention, switching costs, capital inflows, customer lifetime value, and more. Every click, every swipe, every like, every purchase fuels their algorithms. They all boil down to the same thing: *What will you do?* You—the customer, the subscriber, the potential investor, the employee. Even when you think nobody is looking, every choice you make reverberates in gravitational waves.

Of course, there is one way to avoid having to measure willingness to pay: sell addictive products. The same ill logic applies to tobacco and social media as well as many varieties of the benign-sounding business strategy of "vendor lock-in." As we saw in Chapter 1, this corruption breaks the logic of capitalism itself. Why? Because only voluntary, uncoerced, fully informed exchanges are sure to create surplus value. An addict cannot consent. Their "choice" has been hijacked.

I once talked to an early Instagram employee who shared their anguish at watching the ratio of organic posts to advertised posts slowly shift under years of Facebook's ownership. They were falling behind competitors because the product was loaded with too much advertising. Yet they couldn't give up the extra advertising revenue, not even for a quarter.

By now, we have a clear understanding of why this happens. Jim Sinegal likened it to heroin—once started, it is almost impossible to stop. In Chapter 7, we saw how the "surrogation" of false proxies leads companies astray, sometimes with deadly consequences, as at Johnson & Johnson. These companies themselves are addicts, desperate for advertising revenue, for clicks, for outrage—whatever feeds their insatiable hunger. This addiction breaks capitalism's core logic just the same. They are addicts making more addicts. It is, in the end, pathetic.

Only you can help them break this cycle. If you are not yet addicted, do not begin. And if you still have the strength, walk away. As a customer, as an employee, as an investor, you have the power to refuse. Typically this is framed as a "collective action problem," as if there is no point in doing the right thing unless you've already agreed with others to do the same. But seeing it in this way causes us to miss a surprising source of power. Remember how gravity works: It emerges from perception. Every transaction sends a signal. In the age of surveillance capitalism, those signals are tracked, aggregated, and analyzed with obsessive precision. When you walk away, that action becomes their data—and someone's OKR. When enough people make similar choices, even without coordinating, leaders see the pattern. That's how individual gravity becomes a collective force. Naturally, when organizers or civic infrastructure help accelerate this aggregation, they magnify this force. (Perhaps there are entrepreneurial opportunities in these murky depths.)

And we give this power away so cheaply, so thoughtlessly. We are busy, we are overtaxed, we have a full plate with the people right in front of us who we need to take care of. Plus, systems can be opaque, and the impact of our consumer, investment, and employment choices is hard to fully understand. And so we end up investing our retirement savings in the very systems we complain about. We buy from whoever has the slickest marketing or the most convenient platform. We work for companies we don't believe in—sometimes because we genuinely cannot find any other viable option but often because we've been wounded into a cynical belief that it doesn't matter or "that's just how things are." And with each choice, we add our small bit of gravity to the system, making it feel more permanent, more inevitable.

Ursula K. Le Guin described our "inevitable" financial and economic systems thus: "Its power seems inescapable. So did the divine right of kings."[1] As we've seen, many of the structures that govern modern life are younger than the trees in your local park. Their inevitability is an illusion. The future we build depends not on some distant "them" making better decisions but on us recognizing the power we already have. Our individual choices can solidify and strengthen what is or draw energy away from the *status quo* and toward far better alternatives. But knowing that systems can change is one thing. Believing you personally have the power to change them is another.

There is a second book hidden inside this one that I did not write but could have.

I'm a company builder at heart, so I naturally see the world through organizational eyes. Every story, every bit of advice is told from the point of view of the organization itself. Founders, builders, leaders are the protagonists of these stories. But I could easily have given the same advice and told the same stories from the point of view of the individuals affected. Just like Newton's gravity, the financial kind pulls both ways. In sociology, this is called structuration: Organizations may be emergent intelligences, but the people who make them up also have independent agency.[2] Your choices are constrained by organizations, yes. But your participation or refusal shapes them right back. Every tool in this book can be used to amplify your vision of human flourishing, or it can be used to reinforce the idea that the *status quo* is "how things just have to be."

In case you missed it, let me repeat. Every story in this book—every single one—can be read in reverse, centering a different protagonist.

Let me show you what I mean. Mission-driven companies attract better talent—is this recruiting advice or guidance about where to work? Customers show fierce loyalty to values-aligned companies. This is also a shopping guide. Investors routinely kill the golden goose. Is this a parable—or the playbook for a new kind of investment firm?

Selective pressure, carefully applied, can redirect whole organizations toward human flourishing. Even if you never start a company, you are a builder nonetheless. Choose accordingly.

When you choose to work for a company that values human flourishing, you're not just making a career decision; you're participating in *mission transmission*. Your labor becomes a vote for that organization's approach to the world. When you refuse to work for extractive companies, you're contributing to a talent scarcity that forces them to change or die. When you buy a product, you're supporting or even shaping standards that entire industries will eventually adopt. We credit Volvo with setting in motion the events that led to the universal use of three-point safety belts in cars. But the prosperity cascade only started because early adopters bought those cars and wore the belts. That's what created the data that clued in the insurance industry. Those anonymous early drivers have their fingerprints on the millions of lives saved since.

Each gravitational choice ripples outward. A company sees demand, competitors take notice, suppliers adapt, regulations follow. Standards don't fall from the sky; they emerge from the gravitational pull of millions of individual choices. When you move your retirement savings to funds that invest in human flourishing, you're not just managing your portfolio; you're architecting civic infrastructure. Capital flows where you direct it, and capital creates the institutional landscape that shapes everyone's choices.

So why do we feel so powerless? Why does the current system feel so inevitable, so permanent, so impossible to change?

I have spent many years of my life being told that my work was pointless, that the way things are is inevitable, and that I was doomed to fail. That the thing I wanted to build or change or scale was impossible. People said this even about the humble A/B split test in *The Lean Startup*, not to mention the many other ideas I've championed since then.

Now, I am not asking for your sympathy. I have thick skin and have learned to love feedback, even the hostile kind. But doomerism is something different. When confronted with the mere idea that there is a better way, quite a lot of people get genuinely angry. They invest incredible amounts of time arguing—not that the new idea is bad but that it is *doomed to fail.* I used to let it get me down every time it happened. But over time, the very monotony of it clued me in to an insight. If a reform will inevitably fail, why spend so much time and money trying to convince me not to make the attempt? Why not just let me inevitably fail and enjoy the spectacle?

There's a vast pundit-industrial complex dedicated to amplifying the just-so stories: Shareholder primacy is natural law. Markets are perfectly efficient. Lethargy (or even malignancy) is a by-product of scale. I eventually came to see that the people getting angry are just repeating this inherited orthodoxy. When they argue for the inevitability of the *status quo*, they're trying to shape the gravitational field. If everyone believes reform is impossible, then this becomes true. And all too often, sadly, this prophecy is self-fulfilled.

Your optimism is the fuel that must be burned to make this engine turn.

Look around. The very people telling you that individual choices don't matter are the same ones spending billions to influence those choices. So make your choice to pull toward the world you want to live in, not the one they want to keep you in. What does that look like in practice? Let me share some examples—not prescriptions but possibilities that might spark your own thinking.

As a customer, you're engaged in mission transmission every bit as much as the mission-locked companies we studied in Chapter 12. The same rules apply. If you want to see your values amass gravitational force, (1) choose the values-aligned vendor when you can and (2) see it as your obligation to give new vendors a chance. I can't tell you how many people complain about the *status quo* to me but also say they're "too busy" to take a risk on a new startup trying to fix the very problems they're complaining about—even as a customer.

Every dollar earned in extraction has a cost to the future we're longing for. But every dollar earned by creating genuine value is pure gravity pulling the whole world toward human flourishing.

As a source of talent, your labor is one of the most powerful gravitational forces you control. When you take a job, you're not just trading time for money; you're adding mass to an organization's gravitational field. Your skills, creativity, and reputation become part of what pulls others toward that company's vision of the world. This is why companies fight so hard for talent. They know that where the best people go, others follow.

I want to share a thought experiment with you. Imagine yourself as an organization of one. You can apply the same gravitational analysis we've used throughout this book to your own choices. Just as organizations must choose between maximizing human flourishing or extracting value, so must you. But this does not need to be a stressful choice.

If your work aligns with human flourishing, then you should feel free to prosper without limit. If you create more value than you capture, then by definition, anything you make helps others even more.

But what if your work isn't aligned? Or if you're just not sure?

In that case, you're lending your gravitational mass in ways that may undermine your own values. Gravity is treacherous because as you're strengthening it, it reshapes you. Your values align with what gets rewarded. Your definition of "normal" shifts. I can't tell you how many people I know feel trapped in lucrative jobs that they realize—or at least suspect—are extractive. They wind up adding years of gravitational force to systems they oppose. The future they wanted becomes that much harder to build because they helped strengthen its opposite.

If you find yourself in this situation, I totally understand. Sometimes that kind of work choice is unavoidable. Or sometimes we have other, more urgent priorities. It happens. In our world today, there are far too many people who struggle to meet their basic needs or take care of their families. This battle is not for them. If you're struggling, I honor your struggle, and everyone else should too. Do what you have to do.

But if you're fortunate enough to have choices, this thought experiment is for you. There is a third path, distinct from the two that feel most obvious. You don't have to compromise, slowly becoming what you once opposed. But you also don't have to drop out entirely, retreating into cynicism or purely private satisfactions. Instead, you can seek opportunities to shape the world to *your* ethos. We all know people who earn more money than they need from an employer they despise. Research shows that above a certain income threshold, additional earnings don't increase happiness (studies vary, but most agree that happiness plateaus above an annual salary of $100,000 in developed economies).[3] Again, if you earn more than that and your earnings are aligned with human flourishing, there is no ethical conflict. Earn as much as you can. But if not, be as rigorous as Costco with its margin cap. Calculate exactly how much money you need and why.

Are you supporting yourself, your family, a loved one in need? Building genuine security? Put a number to it.

I call this threshold the *maximum ethical salary*—your personal margin cap. If you find yourself with the option to earn more than that from an employer misaligned with the "builder's intuition" of value creation, do one of these things instead:

- Whenever you get a raise, before that gets reflected in your spending, see if you can use that surplus to work fewer hours, fewer days, or less intensively. Use the extra time and energy to network or find values-aligned work.
- If you need a cushion to exit, get to work. Accumulate the cushion and then execute an exit plan.
- Contribute your surplus labor and energy to a worthwhile cause. This is not just about volunteering. Find someplace you can contribute to by building, like an open-source project. Who knows, maybe you'll find a new job that way.
- Better yet, start a company aligned with human flourishing. This is, in the end, one of the most satisfying ways to profit.

Whatever you do, do it consciously. Write it down. Don't let gravity slowly shape you.

I've had many people come to see me worried about their path, and in every case, we've been able to get them into a new and better situation. They often wind up making far more money, in addition to sleeping better at night. Some became founders who are now independently wealthy, all by choosing to align their work with human flourishing.

While you're at it, invest those profits in companies that prioritize human flourishing too. After all, you've seen the evidence across these pages that they outperform for their investors too. That's you.

Throughout this book, we've seen how much more effective it is to find breakthrough solutions rather than asking people to settle for less. Jim Sinegal didn't ask customers to pay more for a hot dog; he insisted his COO "f'ing figure it out." Tony's Chocolonely doesn't serve inferior chocolate. Their bars are 28% larger, cost less, and taste great. Devoted Health doesn't compromise on health outcomes. Costco makes excellent returns even with capped margins. The organizations that truly serve human flourishing don't need sacrifice. They win by being better.

In 2020, Brian Chesky told me something that helped me suddenly make sense of the forces and dynamics in this book: "Businesses are built on love and trust."[4] Not just the good ones. All of them. Even mercenary companies depend on employees who love someone enough to perform work for money and who trust that they'll be paid if they do what the organization demands.

This is why your choices matter so much. You can lend your gravity to organizations that commit to maximizing human flourishing, that embrace love and trust. Whether as an employee, investor, or customer, you'll be better off. After all, when given the chance to compete fairly, these companies just make more money. It's that simple.

Our task now is to imagine a world where this reality is generally recognized. Just take a moment to contemplate that future, one where gravity pulls inexorably toward human flourishing. That gravity would pull the next generation into a future we can scarcely imagine.

To see this dream to fruition, nobody has to attend meetings or learn secret handshakes. But we do have to use the gravity we've been given, however much or little it may be, to maximize our mission transmission.

One more thing.

Fifteen chapters ago, I told you about The Professor, a biotech founder whose breakthrough could be used to save lives or create bioweapons. Top scientists were refusing to join him because they feared investor corruption. That's why he sought my help. The story of our conversations launched this entire book.

Who was the protagonist of that story? Naturally, I told the story from The Professor's point of view. He was the one seeking solutions and trying to build something useful and important. And he was the one who embraced new ideas about governance, saw the need for long-term thinking, and courageously protected that builder's intuition about what profit really means.

But you can see more clearly now. Who came first? The scientists. Their challenging questions, their refusal to settle for fuzzy answers—that's what created the gravitational force that pushed The Professor to my door. They did not organize with one another formally. They didn't have a multistep plan or even any answers at all for the questions they were asking. They simply did something we can all do: They showed up for the conversation with their genuine values, their conscience, their real concerns and reservations, and they let those values guide what they said and did.

They were having the right conversation but fumbling with shadows: the scientists wielding power they didn't understand, sending The Professor to seek solutions he couldn't name.

Now you are armed to do better. Not just with words but with physics.

Every story in this book can be read this upside-down way, revealing a different protagonist altogether.

Turn back to the Introduction and read The Professor's story again. You'll see it differently now.

Epilogue

QUEEN OF THE DEAD

A book lives like Merlin, in reverse. These words died the moment I set them down on the page. They are only born when you read them. They live only as you metabolize them. You get the final say.

I know that few readers will walk this journey with me all the way to the end. So for those of you who have come this far, perhaps you will walk just a few steps further.

This book has been littered with open secrets and hidden truths. Which of these you choose to perceive is up to you. You are the arbiter of their meaning and their impact. Perhaps you will use these tools to build a new and vibrant future. Excellent. But perhaps you have realized that each one can also be used in reverse. Is financial gravity a force to be reckoned with—or a way to get ahead? If you wish, you may use these words in that way. You are the living and do not need my blessing. But I give it anyway. Do what you need to do.

I have taken it for granted that you will choose to resist gravity with the tools in your hands. But, of course, you have always known the opposite choice is available. You have felt it your whole life. Perhaps even now you have realized the wealth, the fame, the career acceleration that may be yours, gravity lifting you as easily as sailing. Perhaps you will publish a thorough takedown of these ideas and reap the incalculable rewards. I picture you now, taking notes as you read, pencils and knives sharpened. You easily find the seams in the argument. If you have understood my message so far, you have by now realized an uncomfortable truth. What you write does not need to be correct in order to advance your career. Your takedown need only elevate you into the perception of the proper few. I wish you luck.

But perhaps one day, even as you are writing your notes, preparing for your ascent, you will have a moment of confusion. You may wake suddenly as if out of a dream and have a moment of altered perception. You will look around, bewildered, at a barren wasteland, strip-mined already. And you will look up in terror at the megalithic beasts that roam there. Their shadowy, spidery skeletons protrude to the endless sky, joints gripped in dark sinews. The ground trembles as they stride, masters of all they see, as if in sympathy with your own fears.

But they are not alone. And this will be your first glimpse of her, even more terrible than they. Armed with her mother's golden scythe, she strikes one blow after another. You hear the dull crunch of metal on bone. The violence of this forlorn battlefield may frighten you even more.

But follow her gaze, and you may have an abrupt reversal of perception. You are suddenly struck by the lumbering, zombie quality of these old beasts. Their very sinews entrap people, half asleep, doing their bidding. Long and twisting hierarchies of bondage. Stochastic action, hardly awake. Yet forward, always forward, in its motion.

Suddenly you realize that her scythe is an instrument not of violence but of mercy. She directs your gaze higher. You see that the spidery sinews stretch not just upward in space but backward in time. These joints are gripped by thousands upon thousands of grotesque puppet strings, stretching back to cruel fathers and brutal conquistadors. They are the not even past, still pulling the strings. For those trapped inside, even as they strive not to stumble, they long for her embrace. Your terror gives way to pity.

She turns her iron gaze toward you, and you tremble again. Fear not. She is looking past you. Follow her eyes once more.

Scurrying along the cracked ground of this bleak wilderness, you catch a glimpse of a small, furtive, brilliant light. Too bright and too fast to perceive directly as it weaves and dodges. Only then do you realize it is not one but many, popping in and out of the interstitial spaces. Like mammals among dinosaurs, they are poised, waiting for their moment.

Your eyes turn upward, and now finally, she meets your gaze. And in the moment, her expression strikes you like a question. An invitation. You look down at your own hands. You grasp the choice she has asked you to make. Hands turned upward, toward the sky. Or turned away, to the dusty ground.

And just like that—the waking dream is over. Turn back awake to reality, the vision naturally forgotten. Resume your work. Take notes. Thrive.

And yet some time later—Weeks? Months? Years?—you may have a moment of sharp, sudden recall. The look on her face. Gripped with sudden curiosity, you will wonder what happened next. Did you turn your hands upward, to lend your work to hers?

Well—did you?

APPENDIX

IMPLEMENTATION GUIDES

Ready to take the next step? I've put together a series of implementation guides for all stages of company development. Each one includes templates, examples, more case studies, and other resources. I also maintain a list of vendors who are aligned with the principles in *Incorruptible*.

To access these resources, visit incorruptible.co/guides-for-builders.

Or scan the QR code:

THE *INCORRUPTIBLE* COMMUNITY

The blueprint and ideas in this book are tools for putting into practice. The *Incorruptible* Community is a place to pool experience while doing it. Members can get support when they need it and offer their own learning and wisdom to others.

It's a network of people committed to building organizations that last, including founders, executives, investors, employees, customers, and citizens of all kinds.

To join the community, visit community.incorruptible.co.
Or scan the QR code:

READERS' GUIDES

Regardless of formal role or title, the ideas and mechanisms in *Incorruptible* are for everyone. We all have agency and influence over the organizations in our lives, even if we don't always feel that way. We all have opportunities to help build a more prosperous future.

Each guide is designed to help its readers apply *Incorruptible*'s principles from a particular perspective. They include reflection questions, practical tips, and techniques specific to each position:

- For consumers
- For employees
- For investors
- For board members
- For founders

To access the readers' guides, visit incorruptible.co/all-reader-guides.

Or scan the QR code:

GLOSSARY

Career equity: The professional reputation and future job opportunities that directors, lawyers, and executives prioritize, often at the expense of a specific company's long-term mission.

Fiduciary duty: A legal obligation to act in the best interest of another party. In modern business, this is often narrowly interpreted as a duty to maximize shareholder value.

Financial gravity: The psychological and systemic pressure that pulls organizations and individuals toward financial values, fueled by the desire to succeed in future transactions.

***Harder-is-easier* mission:** A strategy where an organization chooses a difficult, principled path (like refusing to raise prices during inflation) to unlock "magnetic powers" of trust and loyalty that eventually make execution easier.

Mission drive: The management discipline and rigorous use of *holistic metrics* to ensure that an organization only profits via the attainment of its mission.

Public benefit corporation (PBC): A legal corporate form that requires directors to balance the stockholders' financial interests with a specific "public benefit" stated in the charter.

Shareholder primacy: The dominant theory of corporate governance, which holds that the sole purpose of a corporation is to maximize the wealth of its shareholders.

Spiritual holding company (SHC): A separate legal entity (like a trust or foundation) that holds governance authority over a company specifically to safeguard its animating "spirit" or purpose in perpetuity.

Steward ownership: An ownership structure that "unbundles" power and money, ensuring that control of a company remains with people dedicated to its mission rather than with outside investors.

Surrogation: A psychological phenomenon where people stop seeing a metric as a *measure* of a goal and start treating the metric as the *goal itself.*

For a full glossary of terms used in *Incorruptible,*
scan the QR code or go to incorruptible.co/glossary-of-terms.

Acknowledgments

A book like this would be nothing without the stories that bring its concepts to life. I want to thank first and foremost the courageous leaders, employees, customers, and investors of the organizations who have allowed me to tell their story in these pages. You are the true pioneers who have paved the way for the millions who will follow. Thank you.

This book introduced the term *torchbearers* to describe the unsung heroes who steadfastly push a mission forward. This book has been lucky to have a true *torchbearer* for the entirety of its many years of gestation: Melanie Rehak. As you can imagine, many of the events described herein required my total focus and left little time for research or writing. Melanie kept the project alive through many such episodes. She has been my longtime collaborator, editor, and researcher. I am immensely grateful for her indefatigable spirit and her facility with the pen.

This book involved extensive research, case study development, and an immense amount of fact-checking. In this I was aided by my research team, helmed by Melanie Rehak. Fact-checking and research were provided by Robin Lorsch Wildfang. Thanks also to Tom White and Alistair Kitchen. Needless to say, any errors that remain are my own.

Many of the interviews cited in this book were conducted as part of the production of *The Eric Ries Show*. Thanks to Jordan Bornstein and the whole team at Pen Name for their help bringing it to life. To see the results, check out https://ericriesshow.com/.

We owe a tremendous debt to the many academics and researchers who have established the empirical basis for so many of the claims in this book. There are far too many to thank by name, but please check the notes. Their dedication to rigor, to experimentation, and to the idea that knowledge should be broadly accessible is admirable.

The book was supported by an incredible early-reader community. More than six hundred test readers generated more than ten thousand comments. I read every single one, and hundreds of them had a direct impact on the final manuscript. I am indebted to every reader who took the time to give such thoughtful feedback. Thanks also to the team behind helpthisbook.com, Rob Fitzpatrick and Devin Hunt, who made collecting and organizing this feedback a breeze.

Thanks also to the students of the Solveit course, as well as the fast.ai and Answer.AI communities, many of whom became early readers through the Solveit platform, using AI-powered close reading to analyze, respond to, and customize the ideas in the book. Your feedback was immensely helpful.

For especially valuable feedback through the writing process, I want to especially thank for their contributions Mark Selleck, Tim O'Reilly, Kieran Snyder, Sarah K. Cowan, Scott Stern and his students at MIT, Alex Komoroske and the entire In the Woods community, David Berger, Olga Svitelska and the EO SF chapter, Jordan Myska Allen, Steve Newman, Manisha Snoyer, Joseph Oorebeek, Ian Paul Graham, Bridget Harris, Markos Moulitsas, Roy Bahat, Judy Samuelson, Cate Hall, Kim Scott, Leah Solivan, and Nicole Itano.

Thanks to the work of Answer.AI, I benefited through the late stages of editing and researching from a completely custom large language model-enabled canvas that helped immensely, powered by the Solveit platform. Solveit also helped make sense of those ten thousand test reader comments. I am indebted especially to the Answer.AI philosophy of "human-in-the-loop" use of large language models, which seeks not to replace human creativity but to enhance it. To try this amazing invention for yourself, go to solve.it.com.

At LTSE: Maliz Beams, Steve Goldstein, John Bautista, Michelle Greene. Foundational legal work was done by Annette Nazareth. Special thanks to all of the investors who have supported our work through its many hills and valleys. Over the years this book has been in development, I was also ably supported by chiefs of staff Holly Grant and Benjamin Ehrlich. Although they have since gone on to more impressive things, I am grateful for their support and friendship.

At the Lean Startup Co.: Jonathan Bertfield and Loriann Watson.

At Answer.AI: my cofounder, Jeremy Howard, for his tireless work to ensure the benefits of artificial intelligence are democratically and broadly shared, as well as the entire team who is bringing this vision to life. Thanks also to Erik Gaasedelen, Curtis Allan, Johno Whitaker, and Rens Dimmendaal.

At Virgil: special thanks to Luke Versweyveld and team, who have helped many startups incorporate these provisions from their earliest stages.

At Unshackled: Shaherose Charania and Manan Mehta.

The Purpose Foundation has introduced and advocated for many "steward ownership" ideas. I am grateful to Annika Rosalie Schneider and Achim Hensen for their pioneering work in this area.

The indomitable Marny Sumrall has been my launch partner for this book, coordinating countless details behind the scenes as well as the mastermind behind the *Incorruptible* Community: community.incorruptible.co.

My career has been blessed with many longtime collaborators who have been my stalwart allies through thick and thin. Special thanks to my executive assistant, Brittany Hart. At CAA, thanks to my speaking agent, Peter Jacobs.

Marcus Gosling has been a partner of mine stretching all the way back to my earliest startups. His design sense is unparalleled. I am extremely grateful he has chosen to reprise his work on the cover of this book, as he did for *The Lean Startup* and *The Startup Way*. He also designed the illustrations that accompany each chapter.

At Authors Equity: Madeline McIntosh, Carly Gorga, Rose Edwards, Deb Lewis, Andrea Bachofen, Craig Young, Nina von Moltke, Sarah Christiensen-Fu, Erin Vandeveer, James Clear, and the entire team have been a pleasure to work with. Thank you for pioneering a new approach to publishing and for the love and care you have poured into this book. Thanks also to Anna Knighton for the book's interior design. Thanks to Nina Nocciolino for publicity support.

I have benefited from exceptional editorial support from Laureen Mutuski and David Georgi. Thank you for all that you have given to this manuscript.

At Crown, thanks to Paul Whitlatch for his early support for this project and to David Drake for his longtime belief in my work.

To my UK partners: thanks to Gordon Wise and Elliot Prior at Curtis Brown, as well as Matt James, Pippa Wright, Sahina Bibi, and Elise Harvey at Penguin Life.

My longtime advisor, sounding board, and comrade-in-arms is the incredible Christy Fletcher, now at UTA. We have been partners now through so many different ventures that extend far beyond publishing, and I am filled with gratitude for your wisdom, prescience, and integrity. Thank you for making this entire enterprise possible. Thanks to the whole team at UTA, especially Melissa Chinchillo, Yona Levin, and Claire Yoo.

My life as a writer began long before I even knew the word *entrepreneurship*. I want to thank my family for helping me build an incorruptible foundation. Their values have left an imprint that infuses every page. To my parents, Andrew and Vivian, and my sisters, Nicole and Amanda—and their incredible spouses and children—thanks for supporting me through all these long years.

To my own children, I hope one day you will be proud of the work for which you have sacrificed so much time with your father. I love you more than words can say. Everything I do is inspired by a dream of the future you will one day inherit. May you bask in its sunshine always.

For my beloved Tara, my inspiration, my partner, and my most important editor: I feel so blessed we have been able to build this adventure of a life together. Thank you.

Notes

Introduction

1 https://www.startuplessonslearned.com/2020/06/out-of-crisis-8-brian-chesky-part-2.html, retrieved January 27, 2026.

Chapter One: The Mystery of the Golden Goose

1 For this and what follows on Sol Price, see, for example, https://www.washingtonpost.com/wp-dyn/content/article/2009/12/14/AR2009121403336.html, retrieved September 7, 2025.
2 Robert E. Price, "Sol Price: Retail Revolutionary: The FedMart Years—1954 to 1975," *Journal of San Diego History* 56, no. 4 (2010): 197, https://sandiegohistory.org/journal/v56-4/v56-4price.pdf, retrieved July 1, 2025.
3 Robert E. Price, *Sol Price: Retail Revolutionary and Social Innovator* (San Diego History Center, 2012), 61.
4 Price, *Sol Price*, 77.
5 Price, *Sol Price*, 62.
6 Price, "Sol Price," 197.
7 Price, *Sol Price*, 84.
8 https://www.supermarketnews.com/grocery-operations/2012-hall-of-fame-sol-price, retrieved February 5, 2026.
9 Price, *Sol Price*, 57.
10 See https://www.sandiegoreader.com/news/1982/apr/01/cover-mean-business-sol-price-and-the-fedmart-sto/, retrieved September 7, 2025, for this and what follows.
11 Price, *Sol Price*, 110.
12 "Fedmart Retail Chain," *New York Times*, April 29, 1982. See also "FedMart Liquidating Retail Operations," *UPI Archives*, April 28, 1982; and "Mean Business: Sol Price and the FedMart Story," *San Diego Reader*, April 1, 1982.
13 Price, *Sol Price*, 79.
14 See, for example, https://www.sandiegoreader.com/news/1982/apr/01/cover-mean-business-sol-price-and-the-fedmart-sto/ and https://mastersinvest.com/newblog/2019/6/29/learning-from-sol-price, both retrieved September 7, 2025.
15 https://www.danielscrivner.com/who-is-sol-price-lessons-from-the-discount-store-pioneer-who-built-fedmart-and-inspired-walmart-and-costco/, retrieved December 26, 2025.
16 Price, *Sol Price*, 113.
17 Robert Owen, "Third Essay," in *A New View of Society and Other Writings*, ed. Gregory Claeys (Penguin, 1991), 44, retrieved July 1, 2025, https://ia803202.us.archive.org/13/items/772200_202307/A%20New%20View%20of%20Society%20and%20Other%20Writings.pdf: "Indeed, after experience of the beneficial effects from due care and attention to the mechanical implements, it

became easy to a reflecting mind to conclude at once, that at least equal advantages would arise from the application of similar care and attention to the living instruments . . ."

18 https://newlanark.org/introducing-robert-owen/, retrieved July 9, 2025.

19 Robert Owen, *The New Existence of Man upon the Earth* (Effingham, Wilson, Royal Exchange, 1815 and 1817), vol. 2, lvii.

20 James O'Toole, *The Enlightened Capitalists: Cautionary Tales of Business Pioneers Who Tried to Do Well by Doing Good* (Harper Business, 2019), Kindle, location 917 of 1354.

21 https://newlanark.org/introducing-robert-owen/, retrieved July 1, 2024.

22 https://www.scottishmaritimemuseum.org/3d_collections/silent-monitor/, retrieved September 8, 2025.

23 Owen, *New View of Society*, 66.

24 Owen, *New View of Society*, 9.

25 Owen, *New View of Society*, 62.

26 Alexander Cullen, *Adventures in Socialism: New Lanark Establishment and Orbiston Community* (John Smith and Son, 1910), 41.

27 "Robert Owen Timeline," Robert Owen Museum, 2008, https://www.robertowenmuseum.co.uk/wp-content/uploads/2019/11/Robert-Owen-Timeline-with-literature-references.pdf, retrieved January 17, 2026.

28 https://newlanark.org/about-new-lanark/timeline/48-timeline/247-walkers/ and more generally https://newlanark.org/about-new-lanark/timeline/, both retrieved September 8, 2025.

29 https://www.theatlantic.com/magazine/archive/1883/10/historic-notes-of-life-and-letters-in-massachusetts/539484/, retrieved July 1, 2025.

30 O'Toole, *Enlightened Capitalists.*

31 Sears was originally incorporated as A. C. Roebuck Inc. in 1892, then changed its name to Sears, Roebuck and Company in 1893. https://tile.loc.gov/storage-services/master/pnp/habshaer/il/il0700/il0736/data/il0736data.pdf, retrieved January 20, 2026.

32 This number varies a bit depending on the source: https://inequality.org/article/sears/ says employees owned one-third of the company under Wood, while https://americanbusinesshistory.org/general-robert-wood-the-forgotten-man-who-changed-sears-and-the-world/ gives this 25% for the 1970s, fifteen years after Wood's retirement. Both articles retrieved November 4, 2025.

33 https://prospect.org/economy/sears-gutted-ceo/ and https://www.cnn.com/2018/10/18/business/eddie-lampert-sears, both retrieved December 26, 2025.

34 https://www.cbsnews.com/news/bleeding-sears-vows-to-fight-like-hell-to-stay-alive/, retrieved December 26, 2025.

35 https://www.cbsnews.com/news/eddie-lampert-why-buy-faded-sears/, retrieved December 26, 2025.

36 https://www.cnn.com/2018/10/15/business/sears-bankruptcy, retrieved December 26, 2025.

37 https://www.library.hbs.edu/hc/polaroid/a-research-and-manufacturing-company/commercialization-of-the-polarizer/, retrieved September 8, 2025.

38 Steve Jobs, quoted in https://www.nytimes.com/2011/10/07/opinion/the-man-who-inspired-jobs.html, retrieved July 1, 2025.

39 https://www.boston.com/uncategorized/noprimarytagmatch/2012/10/03/history-of-polaroid-and-edwin-land/, retrieved January 17, 2026.

40 https://www.smithsonianmag.com/arts-culture/why-polaroid-inspired-both-steve-jobs-and-andy-warhol-61708948/, retrieved July 1, 2025.

41 https://www.nytimes.com/2001/10/13/business/deep-in-debt-since-1988-polaroid-files-for-bankruptcy.html, retrieved December 26, 2025.

42 Cadbury's started as a grocery shop in 1824, and Bournville Village and the factory mentioned here were built in 1878 by the sons of the original founder; https://www.cadbury.co.uk/about/history/our-story/, retrieved July 1, 2025.

43 https://www.thegrocer.co.uk/analysis-and-features/cadburys-200-years-of-takeovers-triumphs-and-transformations/688914.article, retrieved September 8, 2025, for this and what follows.

44 https://www.tastingtable.com/1794073/cadbury-creme-eggs-recipe-change/, retrieved September 8, 2025.

45 https://www.businessinsider.com/cadbury-creme-egg-sales-plummet-2016-1, retrieved September 8, 2025.

46 https://www.bbc.com/news/articles/c0lg9y791kyo, retrieved September 8, 2025.

47 *Mergers, Acquisitions and Takeovers: The Takeover of Cadbury by Kraft*, House of Commons Business, Innovation and Skills Committee, Ninth Report of Session 2009–10. Warren Buffett, a major Kraft shareholder, called Kraft's strategy "dumb" and cut his stake from 9% to 6%; see Raffaella Sadun, David J. Collis, Amram Migdal, and Kerry Herman, "Irene Rosenfeld at Mondelēz International: Crafting a Corporate Strategy," Harvard Business School Case 718-403, November 2017 (revised November 2021).

48 https://www.fundinguniverse.com/company-histories/toys-r-us-inc-history/, retrieved January 7, 2026.

49 https://www.reuters.com/article/business/how-5-billion-of-debt-caught-up-with-toys-r-us-idUSKCN1BV0FQ/, retrieved September 8, 2025.

50 https://apgianninifoundation.org/history/, https://www.occ.treas.gov/about/who-we-are/history/history-of-the-occ/1866-1913/1866-1913-bank-of-america.html, and https://www.reuters.com/article/business/bank-of-america-gets-big-government-bailout-idUSTRE50F1Q7/, all retrieved January 20, 2026.

51 https://www.richmondfed.org/publications/research/econ_focus/2013/q3/-/media/4EDF64C581574974B9AAE6B3D7C88A9A.ashx, retrieved January 20, 2026.

52 Andrew Tangel and John Sindreu, "What Went So Wrong with Boeing?," *Wall Street Journal*, October 25, 2024, retrieved February 13, 2026.

53 https://www.sciencedirect.com/science/article/abs/pii/S1044028324001169, retrieved December 26, 2025.

54 https://www.youtube.com/watch?v=YDwDMF_f5rM, retrieved December 26, 2025.

55 https://www.forbes.com/sites/steveschaefer/2015/04/10/ges-50-billion-buyback-continues-corporate-americas-binge-on-its-own-stock/ and https://www.cgaa.org/article/ge-stock-buyback, both retrieved November 12, 2025.

56 Daniel Nelson, "Taylorism and the Workers at Bethlehem Steel, 1898–1901," *Pennsylvania Magazine of History and Biography* 101, no. 4 (October 1977): 487–505.

57 https://www.tandfonline.com/doi/abs/10.1080/09672567.2012.683877.

58 Though this may sound bracing to modern ears, this idea has ancient provenance. Aristotle contrasted *chrematistics* (unlimited money-making for its own sake) with *oikonomia* (household management aimed at living well), calling the former "unnatural" (*Politics*, Book I, ca. 350 BCE). Centuries later, Karl Polanyi called this distinction "probably the most prophetic pointer ever made in the realm of the social sciences" (*The Great Transformation*, 1944). Thomas Aquinas condemned avarice but argued wealth could be virtuous "when obtained justly" (*Summa Theologica*, II-II, Q78). Modern thinkers continue this tradition: Mariana Mazzucato argues that "much of what is passing for value creation is just value extraction in disguise" (*The Value of Everything*, 2018); see also Marjorie Kelly, *Wealth Supremacy* (2023), and Judy Samuelson, *The Six New Rules of Business* (2021).

59 Adam Smith: "Give me that which I want, and you shall have this which you want, is the meaning of every such offer" (*The Wealth of Nations*, 1776). Frédéric Bastiat: "By virtue of exchange, one man's prosperity is beneficial to all others" (*Economic Harmonies*, 1850). Carl Menger: both sides gain because each values what they receive more than what they give (*Principles of Economics*, 1871). Milton Friedman: "If an exchange between two parties is voluntary, it will not take place unless both believe they will benefit from it" (*Free to Choose*, 1980).

60 *Oxford Latin Dictionary* (Oxford University Press, 1968), 540.

61 Brian Broughman and Jesse M. Fried, "Do Founders Control Start-Up Firms That Go Public?," *Harvard Business Law Review* (2020), https://journals.law.harvard.edu/hblr/wp-content/uploads/sites/87/2020/03/HLB104_crop.pdf, retrieved September 9, 2025: "Among firms that reach IPO, 60% of founders are no longer CEO. With little voting power, only half of the others survive three years as CEO."

62 For more on Costco, see https://www.acquired.fm/episodes/costco, retrieved September 10, 2025.

63 For more on Mondragon, see https://www.newyorker.com/business/currency/how-mondragon-became-the-worlds-largest-co-op, retrieved September 10, 2025.

64 https://www.johnlewispartnership.co.uk, retrieved September 10, 2025.

65 For the history of Zeiss, see https://www.zeiss.com/corporate/en/about-zeiss/past/history/ernst-abbe.html; for longevity, see https://www.opticaljournal.com/zeiss-celebrates-175-years-of-innovation-passion-and-the-courage-to-develop/; for the foundation statutes, see https://www.carl-zeiss-stiftung.de/fileadmin/mediamanager/downloads/carl-zeiss-stiftung-statut_engl-english-25022021.pdf, all retrieved January 18, 2026; for their employment ethos, see Martin Abraham and Bernhard Prosch, "Long-Term Employment Relationships by Credible Commitments: The Carl Zeiss Foundation," *Rationality and Society* 12, no. 3 (2000).

66 https://www.ch.vanguard/content/dam/intl/europe/documents/en/vanguard-in-a-nutshell-eu-en.pdf, retrieved September 10, 2025.

67 https://investors.thehersheycompany.com/en_us/home/corporate-governance-board-and-management/corporate-governance.html, retrieved September 10, 2025.

68 https://therobinreport.com/rei-a-radical-co-op/, retrieved November 4, 2025.

69 https://www.novonordisk.com/about/our-heritage.html, retrieved November 4, 2025.

70 For obvious reasons, Marie Krogh is not officially considered a cofounder of Novo Nordisk. However, in 2009, the August Krogh Prize, created by the Organization of Danish Medical Societies in 1969 and awarded annually to an outstanding health researcher in Denmark, was renamed the Marie and August Krogh Prize at the request of the Novo Nordisk Foundation, which "proposed the name change as a result of increasing awareness of Marie Krogh's role in the years leading up to the establishment of the Foundation and her role as a pioneering woman researcher"; https://novonordiskfonden.dk/en/prizes/marie-og-august-krogh-prisen/, retrieved December 25, 2025.

71 https://novoholdings.dk/novo-group, retrieved January 18, 2026.

Chapter Two: Who Is the Bank?

1 Aristotle, *Rhet.* I.2, 1356a6–8.

2 Airbnb founder Brian Chesky described this vividly: "I felt like I lost control of my company not from the investors but from the employees. We were all going in a thousand different directions and I didn't know what to do. . . . I want to help founders keep control of their company. And keep control of their company is not vis-à-vis investors. It's vis-à-vis your own team." See https://www.youtube.com/watch?v=ViqxJY_AG_w, retrieved January 28, 2026.

3 https://phys.org/news/2024-12-ants-superior-humans-group-problem.html, retrieved September 10, 2025.

4 https://www.youtube.com/watch?v=ZHpu7ngQxwE.

5 The term "emergent" was introduced by philosopher G. H. Lewes in *Problems of Life and Mind* (1875) to describe effects that cannot be reduced to the sum of their components. The term "superorganism" was coined by entomologist William Morton Wheeler in "The Ant-Colony as an Organism" (*Journal of Morphology* 22 [1911]), arguing that ant colonies behave as unified wholes with their own identity and processes. E. O. Wilson's *The Insect Societies* (Harvard University Press, 1971) provided a landmark modern synthesis, building on Wheeler's earlier work.

For an integrative treatment of intelligence as an emergent phenomenon in neural systems, see K. L. Downing, *Intelligence Emerging* (MIT Press, 2015).

6 See A. W. Woolley, C. F. Chabris, A. Pentland, N. Hashmi, and T. W. Malone, "Evidence for a Collective Intelligence Factor in the Performance of Human Groups," *Science*, October 29, 2010. The researchers found converging evidence of a general "c factor"—analogous to individual IQ—that predicts a group's performance across a wide variety of tasks. See also T. W Malone and A. W. Woolley, "Collective Intelligence," in *The Cambridge Handbook of Intelligence*, 2nd ed., ed. R. J. Sternberg (Cambridge University Press, 2010), 780–801, https://doi.org/10.1017/9781108770422.033, retrieved January 28, 2026.

7 See, for example, J. Aubouin-Bonnaventure, S. Chevalier, N. Morel, et al., "Collective Intelligence in Work Teams: A New Multilevel Construct and Scale," *Current Psychology* 44 (2025): 10375–91, https://doi.org/10.1007/s12144-025-07818-8, retrieved January 28, 2026.

8 John Steinbeck, *The Grapes of Wrath* (Penguin, 1984), 37.

9 Dan Davies, *The Unaccountability Machine: Why Big Systems Make Terrible Decisions—and How the World Lost Its Mind* (University of Chicago Press, 2024).

10 https://www.3m.com, retrieved December 26, 2025.

11 https://effectuation.org/hubfs/Journal%20Articles/2016/06/3m-struggle-between-efficiency-and-creativity.pdf, retrieved July 2, 2025. Also for what follows.

12 3M's "15% time" (or "15% culture") is a policy introduced around 1948 that allows employees to spend up to 15% of their work time pursuing projects of their own choosing. The Post-it note was famously invented during an employee's 15% time. See https://www.3m.com/3M/en_US/careers-us/working-at-3m/life-with-3m/, retrieved January 28, 2026.

13 Brian Hindo, "3M's Innovation Crisis: How Six Sigma Almost Smothered Its Idea Culture," *BusinessWeek*, June 11, 2007.

14 https://www.designnews.com/industry/3m-shelves-six-sigma-in-r-d, retrieved September 10, 2025.

15 A 2023 peer-reviewed study in the *Annals of Global Health*, based on internal company documents, found that 3M and DuPont "knew broadly about the dangers the chemicals pose by 1970" but withheld the information from regulators and the public. See Nadia Gaber, Lisa Bero, and Tracey J. Woodruff, "The Devil They Knew: Chemical Documents Analysis of Industry Influence on PFAS Science," *Annals of Global Health* 89, no. 1 (January 1, 2023): 37, https://doi.org/10.5334/aogh.4013. See also https://www.ag.state.mn.us/Office/Communications/2018/02/20_3M.asp and https://abcnews.go.com/Health/3m-agrees-103b-settlement-claims-polluted-drinking-water/story?id=100333076, retrieved December 26, 2025.

16 https://www.latimes.com/archives/la-xpm-2005-jul-01-fi-boeing1-story.html, retrieved September 10, 2025.

17 https://www.theguardian.com/commentisfree/2019/sep/11/boeing-capitalism-deregulation, retrieved July 2, 2025.

18 https://www.chicagotribune.com/2004/02/29/so-why-does-harry-stonecipher-think-he-can-turn-around-boeing/, retrieved December 26, 2025.

19 https://www.seattletimes.com/business/boeing-aerospace/boeings-long-fall-and-how-it-might-recover/, retrieved September 10, 2025.

20 https://fortune.com/article/fortune-archives-the-ultimate-manager/, retrieved November 4, 2025.

21 The $68 billion was distributed between 2010 and 2019; https://www.cnbc.com/2024/07/18/boeing-path-forward.html, retrieved September 10, 2025.

22 https://www.npr.org/2020/01/09/795123158/boeing-employees-mocked-faa-in-internal-messages-before-737-max-disasters, retrieved July 2, 2025.

23 https://www.npr.org/2020/01/09/795123158/boeing-employees-mocked-faa-in-internal-messages-before-737-max-disasters, retrieved July 2, 2025.

24 https://www.bbc.com/news/business-51058929, retrieved September 10, 2025.

25 https://www.theguardian.com/world/2019/mar/10/ethiopian-flight-302-second-new-boeing-737-max-8-to-crash-in-four-months, retrieved January 8, 2026.

26 https://chiefexecutive.net/jim-mcnerney-named-chief-executives-2015-ceo-of-the-year/, retrieved September 10, 2025.

27 McNerney was no longer CEO at the time of the crashes. Responsibility for the 737 MAX program (and subsequent crashes) has been tied to multiple leaders, the board, and the general cultural changes in the years prior. See, for example, https://www.library.hbs.edu/working-knowledge/why-boeings-problems-with-737-max-began-more-than-25-years-ago, https://www.wsj.com/business/boeing-max-starliner-dreamliner-ortberg-468f3000, and https://www.managerism.org/topics/companies-industries/thinkpiece-no-38-2, all retrieved July 18, 2025.

28 https://www.imd.org/research-knowledge/disruption/articles/why-you-will-probably-live-longer-than-most-big-companies/, retrieved November 4, 2025.

29 https://investing-aid.com/how-long-is-the-average-stock-holding-period-and-why-it-has-declined/, retrieved November 4, 2025.

30 https://www.equilar.com/blogs/558-ceo-tenure-rates.html, retrieved November 4, 2025.

31 https://www.pewresearch.org/politics/2024/06/24/public-trust-in-government-1958-2024/, retrieved September 10, 2025.

32 https://www.businesstimes.com.sg/opinion-features/how-americans-trust-big-business-went-bad-worse, retrieved September 10, 2025.

33 https://jamanetwork.com/journals/jama/article-abstract/2738392, retrieved September 10, 2025.

34 https://digitalcontentnext.org/blog/2023/10/31/americans-are-losing-trust-in-the-media-what-can-we-do-about-it/, retrieved November 4, 2025.

35 https://research.lifeway.com/2023/07/13/americans-trust-in-the-church-remains-near-historic-low/, retrieved November 4, 2025.

36 https://paulgraham.com/foundermode.html, retrieved September 10, 2025.

37 https://www.nbcnews.com/tech/tech-news/it-s-not-just-marissa-yahoo-has-history-troubled-ceos-n696966, retrieved July 2, 2025.

38 https://www.nytimes.com/2021/03/30/podcasts/ezra-klein-podcast-ted-chiang-transcript.html, retrieved July 2, 2025.

Chapter Three: Gravity

1 Even at the dawn of the twentieth century, the impossibility of flight was considered a settled fact. Papers from that time are loaded with quotes like "aerial flight is one of that great class of problems with which men can never cope" (https://todayinsci.com/N/Newcomb_Simon/NewcombSimon-Quotations.htm, retrieved January 19, 2026). A 1903 *New York Times* editorial predicted that a working flying machine "might be evolved by the combined and continuous efforts of mathematicians and mechanicians in from one million to ten million years" (https://www.nytimes.com/1903/10/09/archives/flying-machines-which-do-not-fly.html, retrieved January 19, 2026). Sixty-nine days later, the Wright brothers flew at Kitty Hawk. Astronaut Dave Williams, in his book *Why Am I Taller?*, called this "perhaps the most infamous bad prediction of all time."

2 These psychological mechanisms are well established. Key frameworks include Joseph Henrich and Francisco Gil-White's dominance-prestige theory (https://doi.org/10.1016/S1090-5138(00)00071-4, retrieved January 17, 2026), Patricia Hawley's resource control theory (https://doi.org/10.1006/drev.1998.0470, retrieved January 17, 2026), and Mark Van Vugt's work on status hierarchy (https://doi.org/10.1002/9781119125563.evpsych232, retrieved January 17, 2026). For empirical validation, see Joey Cheng et al. (https://doi.org/10.1037/a0030398, retrieved January 17, 2026).

3 Seventy-eight percent of surveyed CFOs would sacrifice long-term value to smooth earnings, with 55% willing to avoid positive net present value projects—investments where the projected

cash generated exceeds the cost—if it meant missing quarterly consensus earnings. See J. R. Graham, C. R. Harvey, and S. Rajgopal, "The Economic Implications of Corporate Financial Reporting," *Journal of Accounting and Economics* 40, nos. 1–3 (2005): 3–73, https://doi.org/10.1016/j.jacceco.2005.01.002, retrieved January 19, 2026. This is a classic study, much cited. Similar conclusions have been reached in more recent studies, including J. R. Graham, "Presidential Address: Corporate Finance and Reality," *Journal of Finance* 77, no. 4 (2022): 1975–2049, https://doi.org/10.1111/jofi.13161, retrieved January 19, 2026; "DNA of the CFO," EY, 2023, https://www.ey.com/en_gl/cfo-agenda/dna-of-the-cfo-survey, retrieved January 19, 2026; and "The Case Against Corporate Short Termism," McKinsey Global Institute, August 4, 2017, https://www.mckinsey.com/mgi/overview/in-the-news/the-case-against-corporate-short-termism, retrieved January 19, 2026.

4 See, for example, J. Pfeffer, "Organization Theory and Structural Perspectives on Management," *Journal of Management* 17, no. 4 (1991): 789–803.

5 https://news.stanford.edu/stories/2022/12/explains-recent-tech-layoffs-worried, retrieved September 10, 2025.

6 John Mackey, *The Whole Story: Adventures in Love, Life and Capitalism* (Matt Holt Books; BenBella Books, 2024), 376.

7 Mackey, *Whole Story*, 110.

8 Mackey, *Whole Story*, 74.

9 https://www.cnbc.com/2018/09/20/how-john-mackey-started-whole-foods-which-amazon-bought-for-billions.html, retrieved September 10, 2025.

10 Mackey, *Whole Story*, 156.

11 Mackey, *Whole Story*, 156.

12 https://www.barrons.com/articles/SB50001424052748704101304577038310951868528, retrieved November 5, 2025.

13 https://www.washingtonpost.com/business/on-small-business/when-we-were-small-whole-foods/2014/07/29/5203bd98-1680-11e4-9349-84d4a85be981_story.html, retrieved November 5, 2025.

14 https://www.washingtonpost.com/business/on-small-business/when-we-were-small-whole-foods/2014/07/29/5203bd98-1680-11e4-9349-84d4a85be981_story.html, retrieved September 10, 2025.

15 J. Mackey, "I No Longer Want to Work for Money," *Fast Company*, February 2007.

16 https://www.strategy-business.com/article/From-Whole-Foods-to-holistic-health-A-founders-story, retrieved September 10, 2025.

17 https://1stock1.com/1stock1_201.htm, retrieved January 26, 2026.

18 https://www.strategy-business.com/article/From-Whole-Foods-to-holistic-health-A-founders-story, retrieved September 10, 2025.

19 Mackey, *Whole Story*, 383.

20 https://www.forbes.com/sites/stevedenning/2013/01/05/the-new-management-paradigm-john-mackeys-whole-foods/, retrieved September 10, 2025.

21 See, for example, https://time.com/91192/whole-foods-stock-plummets-as-natural-and-organic-food-competition-grows/ or https://finance.yahoo.com/news/whole-foods-wfm-stock-down-21 1603035.html, both retrieved September 10, 2025.

22 Mackey, *Whole Story*, 384.

23 https://www.corpgov.net/2017/02/whole-foods-proxy-access-proxy-score-82/, retrieved January 28, 2026.

24 https://www.foxbusiness.com/markets/whole-foods-shares-leap-after-jana-takes-8-3-stake, retrieved September 10, 2025.

25 Mackey, *Whole Story*, 361.

26 https://www.cnbc.com/2017/04/10/jana-partners-takes-whole-foods-stake-to-mull-sale-speed-turnaround.html, retrieved September 10, 2025.

27 https://www.cnbc.com/2017/07/19/jana-sheds-entire-stake-in-whole-foods.html, retrieved September 18, 2025.
28 https://www.denverpost.com/2017/06/14/whole-foods-ceo-calls-investor-greedy/, retrieved September 18, 2025.
29 Mackey, *Whole Story*, 368.
30 Mackey, *Whole Story*, 367.
31 Mackey, *Whole Story*, 369.
32 https://www.bloomberg.com/news/articles/2017-08-28/amazon-cuts-prices-at-whole-foods-as-much-as-50-on-first-day, retrieved September 10, 2025.
33 https://fortune.com/2017/09/12/amazons-price-cuts-whole-foods/, retrieved September 10, 2025.
34 https://www.cnbc.com/2017/07/19/jana-sheds-entire-stake-in-whole-foods.html, retrieved September 10, 2025.
35 https://www.janapartners.com/, retrieved September 10, 2025.
36 https://www.cannaeholdings.com/news-releases/news-release-details/cannae-holdings-inc-announces-strategic-partnership-jana, retrieved September 10, 2025.
37 Whole Foods had appeared on the list every year since its inception in 1998—one of only twelve companies to do so; see https://media.wholefoodsmarket.com/whole-foods-market-celebrates-20-years-as-one-of-fortunes-100-best-companie/. For 2018, see https://fortune.com/ranking/best-companies/2018/, retrieved November 12, 2025.
38 See https://www.businessinsider.com/whole-foods-employees-reveal-why-stores-are-facing-a-crisis-of-food-shortages-2018-1 and https://www.bostonglobe.com/business/2018/01/19/people-are-mad-about-empty-shelves-whole-foods/EXWLpibflCXCJQNnf9O73K/story.html, both retrieved January 7, 2026.
39 Mackey, *Whole Story*, 386.
40 https://www.businessinsider.com/amazon-big-grocery-reorg-leaders-integrate-whole-foods-2025-6, retrieved December 30, 2025.
41 https://corpgov.law.harvard.edu/2020/07/08/the-role-of-long-term-institutional-investors-in-activism/, retrieved September 10, 2025.
42 Mackey, *Whole Story*, 386.
43 Owen Davis, "The Greedy Bastards Won," Dealbreaker, June 16, 2017, https://dealbreaker.com/2017/06/the-greedy-bastards-won, retrieved September 10, 2025. This article was published online after the Amazon acquisition of Whole Foods.
44 Davis, "Greedy Bastards Won."

Chapter Four: The New Governance

1 The mechanics of why this is the case are explained later in this chapter.
2 According to Rand Fishkin, "The Twitter board had severe misgivings about what this transaction would mean for the company's mission" (private correspondence, November 11, 2025). Additionally, while the board could have resisted according to the business judgment rule, doing so would have opened them to being sued under the Revlon Doctrine. See https://www.nbcnews.com/business/business-news/elon-musk-buying-twitter-what-it-means-and-is-it-possible-explainer-rcna24389, retrieved January 17, 2026.
3 According to the *LA Times*, outgoing GM CEO Rick Wagoner "said the biggest mistake he ever made as chief executive was killing the EV1." See https://www.latimes.com/archives/la-xpm-2009-mar-31-fi-gm-cars31-story.html, retrieved January 17, 2026. For a detailed account, see Michael Shnayerson, *The Car That Could: The Inside Story of GM's Revolutionary Electric Vehicle* (Random House, 1996). For an accessible overview, see the documentary film *Who Killed the Electric Car?*, directed by Chris Paine (Sony Pictures Classics, 2006). Also see Colleen Cunningham, Florian Ederer, and Song Ma, "Killer Acquisitions," *Journal of Political Economy* 129, no. 3 (March 2021):

649–702, available at https://ssrn.com/abstract=3241707 or http://dx.doi.org/10.2139/ssrn.3241707, retrieved January 27, 2026. There is more on killer acquisitions in Chapter 11.

4 Pop Quiz answer: Greater. A "classified" (or "staggered") board elects only a fraction of directors each year, making it harder for activists to gain control quickly. Anything that makes it harder to take over a company is said to cause "entrenchment" by governance experts because it insulates management from shareholder pressure. Whether that's good or bad depends entirely on your perspective. We'll revisit this issue in Chapter 9. For more, see https://corporatefinanceinstitute.com/resources/management/staggered-board-of-drectors/, retrieved January 17, 2026.

5 *Silicon Valley*, season 3, episode 8, "Bachman's Earnings Over-Ride," directed by Jamie Babbit, on HBO.

6 For what follows, see https://www.theguardian.com/business/nils-pratley-on-finance/2021/aug/12/the-vectura-board-has-stretched-fiduciary-duty-beyond-breaking-point and https://www.theguardian.com/business/2021/aug/12/pressure-grows-on-vectura-board-to-reject-philip-morris-takeover-bid, both retrieved July 18, 2025.

7 https://www.pmi.com/media-center/press-releases/press-details/?newsId=24151, retrieved December 30, 2025.

8 See https://www.pmi.com/media-center/press-releases/press-details?newsId=24151 and https://www.bloomberg.com/news/articles/2024-09-17/philip-morris-to-sell-uk-inhaler-maker-vectura-at-a-loss, retrieved January 7, 2026.

9 https://www.bbc.com/news/business-58582382, retrieved December 30, 2025.

10 https://www.cdc.gov/nccdphp/priorities/tobacco-use.html, retrieved December 30, 2025.

11 https://thorax.bmj.com/content/77/6/537, retrieved July 18, 2025.

12 https://www.pmi.com/media-center/press-releases/press-details, retrieved September 10, 2025.

13 https://www.theguardian.com/business/nils-pratley-on-finance/2022/jan/11/time-for-unilevers-boss-to-deliver-more-than-mayonnaise, retrieved July 18, 2025.

14 See, for example, "Corporation, Business," in C. Geisst, *The Encyclopedia of American Business History*, Almanacs of American Life, 2 vols. (Facts on File, 2005); R. E. Seavoy, *Origins of the American Business Corporation, 1784–1855: Broadening the Concept of Public Service During Industrialization* (Greenwood Press, 1982).

15 https://1752.com/about-us/history/, retrieved September 10, 2025.

16 https://news.law.fordham.edu/jcfl/2018/11/18/a-brief-history-of-the-corporate-form-and-why-it-matters/, retrieved September 10, 2025.

17 Joseph Kinnicut Angell and Samuel Ames, *On the Law of Private Corporations Aggregate* (Hilliard, Gray, Little and Wilkens, 1832), 273.

18 Limited liability emerged as a distinct corporate attribute over the course of the nineteenth century. New York enacted the first general incorporation statute with liability protections in 1811, initially a form of "double liability" where shareholders could be required to contribute up to the par value of their shares, but no more. (See http://clsbluesky.law.columbia.edu/2026/01/21/how-the-business-of-privateering-contributed-to-the-evolution-of-corporate-law/.) England followed with the Limited Liability Act of 1855, which allowed companies to limit shareholder liability by registration. (See https://www.legislation.gov.uk/ukpga/Vict/18-19/133/enacted.) By 1860, similar regimes were in place in France and most US states. As legal historian Ron Harris has argued, limited liability in the "modern sense" only became a uniform attribute of all corporations in the twentieth century; before that, multiple liability regimes coexisted. (See https://www.cambridge.org/core/journals/journal-of-institutional-economics/article/new-understanding-of-the-history-of-limited-liability-an-invitation-for-theoretical-reframing/B12B69696AC81304A2738ADE4FFF4556.) The protection was revolutionary: Without it, investors risked their entire personal fortune if a company's debts exceeded its assets. Limited liability made broad share ownership possible for ordinary people who could not afford catastrophic risk. All retrieved January 27, 2026.

19 For a contemporary account of the "Erie War," see https://www.theatlantic.com/magazine/archive/1868/07/the-great-erie-imbroglio/628100/. Note that this episode involved dubious conduct on both sides. For example, one New York state senator accepted a $75,000 bribe from Vanderbilt and $100,000 from Gould, kept both sums, and voted in Gould's favor. (See https://historycollection.com/blood-money-and-railroads-how-americas-most-powerful-titans-waged-the-shocking-erie-war/.) The point is not to endorse such conduct but to emphasize how differently such matters are viewed today. The directors' aggressive defense was not seen as a breach of their duty to the corporation. Today, by contrast, once a sale is viewed as inevitable, the board's role transforms from "defenders of the corporate bastion to auctioneers charged with getting the best price for the stockholders at a sale of the company." Revlon, Inc. v. MacAndrews & Forbes Holdings, Inc., 506 A.2d 173 (Del. 1986). (See https://casetext.com/case/revlon-inc-v-macandrews-forbes-holdings.) All retrieved January 17, 2026.

20 Delaware General Corporation Law, Chapter 273, approved March 10, 1899. Section 1 permitted "any number of persons, not less than three" to "establish a corporation for the transaction of any lawful business." However, note that Section 7 still required the certificate of incorporation to state "the nature of the business or objects or purposes proposed to be transacted, promoted or carried on." See https://www.scribd.com/document/31223483/Delaware-General-Corporation-Law-of-1899-21-Del-Laws-273, retrieved January 17, 2026.

21 For more on this, see, for example, Robert C. Clark, *Corporate Law* (Little, Brown, 1986), chaps. 1–2.

22 This principle, known as *respondeat superior* ("let the master answer"), dates to seventeenth-century English common law. The Latin maxim *qui facit per alium facit per se* means "he who does an act through another is deemed in law to do it himself." The foundational case taught in American law schools is A. Gay Jenson Farms Co. v. Cargill, Inc., 309 N.W.2d 285 (Minn. 1981), which established the standard test for when a creditor's control over a debtor creates an agency relationship, and thus liability. See https://casetext.com/case/a-gay-jenson-farms-co-v-cargill-inc, retrieved January 27, 2026. The astute reader can already see how this is going to cause tension—when brought into a fiduciary context—with the essential notion of corporate limited liability.

23 For the history of the legislative charter system, see https://www.amacad.org/publication/daedalus/american-corporation, retrieved January 17, 2026. For the origins of trust law and fiduciary duties in English common law, see https://ora.ox.ac.uk/objects/uuid:3aeaa887-e57d-41ab-ae9d-e9f1fb14e1f0, retrieved January 17, 2026. For the development of agency law from Roman *mandatum*, see https://oxfordre.com/classics/view/10.1093/acrefore/9780199381135.001.0001/acrefore-9780199381135-e-3909, retrieved January 17, 2026. Believe it or not, there is no term in the literature for the kind of incorporation that existed between the advent of general incorporation and the development of shareholder primacy. I suggest "purposeful incorporation."

24 Guth v. Loft, Inc., 5 A.2d 503, 510 (1939), https://case.law/caselaw/?reporter=del-ch&volume=23&case=0255-01, retrieved September 10, 2025.

25 Legal scholar Lynn Stout has argued that this turn to the agency framing is simply wrong as a matter of law: directors are not agents and shareholders are not principals. The corporation itself is the principal, and directors are its fiduciaries. As Stout wrote, "At law, a fundamental characteristic of any principal/agent relationship is the principal's right to control the agent's behavior. But shareholders lack the legal authority to control directors or executives." See https://scholarship.law.cornell.edu/cgi/viewcontent.cgi?article=2311&context=facpub, retrieved January 27, 2026.

26 https://corpgov.law.harvard.edu/2023/04/04/the-erb-principles-for-corporate-political-responsibility/, retrieved December 30, 2025. See also Milton Friedman, "The Social Responsibility of Business Is to Increase Its Profits," *New York Times Magazine*, September 13, 1970, 32–33, 122–24.

27 See, for example, https://businesslawreview.uchicago.edu/online-archive/rethinking-limits-revlons-general-prohibition-exploring-interference-corporate, retrieved December 30, 2025, for more on this case.

28 It is an open question whether Milton Friedman himself was the cause or a mere symptom of

this shift. See, for example, *Stop Blaming Milton Friedman!*, https://openscholarship.wustl.edu/cgi/viewcontent.cgi?article=6540&context=law_lawreview, retrieved January 28, 2026. I want to especially emphasize that there is no democratically endorsed law enacting shareholder primacy. As a result, some scholars have treated it almost like a mass delusion. For a rigorous analysis, see Lynn A. Stout, "The Shareholder Value Myth," Cornell Law Faculty Publications, Paper 771 (2013): "Shareholder primacy is an abstract economic theory that lacks support from history, law, or the empirical evidence. In fact, the idea of a single shareholder value is intellectually incoherent." For more, see https://scholarship.law.cornell.edu/cgi/viewcontent.cgi?article=2311&context=facpub.

29 For a detailed history of how shareholder primacy became judge-made law, see Robert J. Rhee, "A Legal Theory of Shareholder Primacy," *Minnesota Law Review* 102 (2018): 1951–2002, https://scholarship.law.umn.edu/cgi/viewcontent.cgi?article=1121&context=mlr, retrieved January 17, 2026.

30 https://www.levernews.com/svb-chief-pressed-lawmakers-to-weaken-bank-risk-regs/, retrieved September 19, 2025.

31 Before the collapse, SVB frequently used this as their official public-facing mission statement. See, for example, https://www.williamfry.com/knowledge/sponsorship-of-the-silicon-valley-bank-reception/, retrieved January 17, 2026. However, SVB was a Delaware C corp, and their actual charter read, "The purpose of the Corporation is to engage in any lawful act or activity for which corporations may now or hereafter be organized under the General Corporation Law of Delaware" (see https://www.sec.gov/Archives/edgar/data/719739/000071973919000034/exhibit31amendedandrestate.htm, retrieved January 17, 2026). This "neutral" charter meant they fell under the sway of shareholder primacy.

32 See, for example, Dominic Barton and Mark Wiseman, "The Error at the Heart of Corporate Leadership," *Harvard Business Review* 96, no. 3 (2018): 70–79; McKinsey and FCLTGlobal, *Measuring the Economic Impact of Short-Termism* (McKinsey, 2017), https://www.mckinsey.com/~/media/mckinsey/featured%20insights/long%20term%20capitalism/where%20companies%20with%20a%20long%20term%20view%20outperform%20their%20peers/mgi-measuring-the-economic-impact-of-short-termism.ashx, retrieved January 17, 2026; https://www.wlrk.com/docs/IsShortTermBehaviorJeopardizingTheFutureProsperityOfBusiness_CEOStrategicImplications.pdf, retrieved January 17, 2026.

33 Here is the logic. Recall that traditional fiduciary duty drew from two common law traditions. Under trust law, trustees protect and preserve for beneficiaries; beneficiaries don't control the trustee and don't bear liability. Under agency law, agents maximize for principals; principals control the agent and bear liability for the agent's actions (respondeat superior).

Shareholder primacy insists that corporations be treated as agents of investors, maximizing their returns above all. This is incompatible with limited liability. If shareholders truly are "principals" who control corporate "agents," they should logically bear liability for corporate actions. Thus, advocates for shareholder primacy are undermining the legal and philosophical foundation for limited liability itself.

And the public has noticed. As corporations behave in ways the public finds harmful—while shareholders collect profits and disclaim responsibility—support for the corporate form erodes. There have been numerous calls for a "corporate death penalty"—judicial dissolution of corporate charters for egregious wrongdoing. (See Mary Kreiner Ramirez and Steven A. Ramirez, *The Case for the Corporate Death Penalty* [NYU Press, 2017].) If shareholders want to preserve limited liability, they should stop allowing their allies to insist they are principals deserving of agency duties.

34 Personal interview with David Berger, April 25, 2025.

35 https://hummedia.manchester.ac.uk/schools/soss/economics/discussionpapers/EDP-1002.pdf, retrieved November 5, 2025.

36 https://news.yale.edu/2020/11/17/polarization-us-politics-starts-weak-political-parties, retrieved November 5, 2025.

37 https://hms.harvard.edu/news/deaths-rose-emergency-rooms-after-hospitals-were-acquired-private-equity-firms, retrieved November 5, 2025.

38 For three additional key ideas, we return to Lynn Stout. First, the idea that shareholders own corporations is a fallacy: "Although laymen sometimes have difficulty understanding the point, corporations are *legal entities that own themselves*, just as human entities own themselves. What shareholders own are shares." Second, shareholder primacy doesn't even benefit shareholders: "The dynamic is much the same as that presented by fishing with dynamite. In the short term, the fisherman who switches from using baited lines to using dynamite sees an increase in the size of his catch. But when many fishermen in the village begin using dynamite, after an initial increase, the collective catch may diminish steadily. Shareholders may experience the same regrettable result when they push managers to 'maximize shareholder value.'" Let's give her the final word: "Shareholder-value ideology is based on wishful thinking, not reality. As a theory of corporate purpose, it is poised for intellectual collapse." *The Shareholder Value Myth* (Berrett-Koehler Publishers, 2012), 8.

Chapter Five: The Blueprint

1 You can hear Dwuane tell her story in her own words at https://www.youtube.com/watch?v=m_yv86sCQNY, retrieved September 16, 2025.

2 This and any other quotations from Todd Park that are not otherwise attributed in an endnote come from *The Eric Ries Show*, podcast, "How the Former U.S. CTO Built a $3B Healthcare Company Powered by Love | Todd Park," November 6, 2025, https://www.youtube.com/watch?v=cFll3HNXR1E, retrieved January 28, 2026.

3 https://www.athenahealth.com/about/who-we-are, retrieved January 8, 2026.

4 https://www.castlighthealth.com, retrieved September 16, 2025.

5 https://www.emersoncollective.com/articles/right-care-right-place-right-time, retrieved July 7, 2025.

6 For this and more on Devoted, see https://www.healthcarefinancenews.com/news/himsscast-devoted-healths-5-star-rating-success-due-its-prime-directive-backed-tech, retrieved November 12, 2025, and its accompanying list of podcasts. See also https://medicareabc.com/devoted-medicare-advantage-plans/, retrieved November 12, 2025.

7 https://tracxn.com/d/companies/devoted-health/__nmiBadft21nnUP-nWEEAloTvR_grXaYBipctTJsUys4/funding-and-investors#funding-rounds, retrieved September 16, 2025.

8 https://obvious.com/portfolio/devoted-health, retrieved July 7, 2025.

9 https://www.emersoncollective.com/articles/right-care-right-place-right-time, retrieved July 7, 2025.

10 https://www.letlifehappen.com/why-devoted-health-has-put-family-at-the-center-of-its-mission/, retrieved September 16, 2025.

11 https://www.smithsonianmag.com/history/in-ponzi-we-trust-64016168/, retrieved September 7, 2025.

12 https://www.in2013dollars.com/us/inflation/1920?amount=15000000&, retrieved September 7, 2025.

13 https://www.accountingtools.com/articles/deferred-liability, retrieved November 12, 2025.

14 https://www.investopedia.com/terms/e/externality.asp, retrieved November 12, 2025.

15 I'm simplifying here, but this principle has a long pedigree. The idea that profit only represents real value creation when it exceeds the opportunity cost of capital dates back to Robert Hamilton in *An Introduction to Merchandise* (Murray and Cochrane, 1802). Alfred Marshall formalized this as "economic profit" in *Principles of Economics* (1890). The broader implication—that society benefits when individuals pursue legitimate profit—goes back further still. As Adam Smith wrote in *An Inquiry into the Nature of and Causes of the Wealth of Nations* (University of Chicago, 1977, reprint of the 1776 edition), "The natural effort of every individual to better his own condition . . . is so powerful, that it is alone, and without any assistance, not only capable of carrying on the society to wealth and prosperity."

16 One 2012 estimate found that for every tobacco-related death, the industry earned approximately $6,000 in profit. See Michael Eriksen, Judith Mackay, and Hana Ross, eds., *The Tobacco Atlas*, 4th ed. (American Cancer Society, 2012).

17 https://oig.hhs.gov/oei/reports/oei-09-16-00410.asp and https://www.propublica.org/article/cigna-pxdx-medical-health-insurance-rejection-claims, both retrieved January 3, 2026.

18 See Atul Gupta et al., "Does Private Equity Investment in Healthcare Benefit Patients? Evidence from Nursing Homes," NBER Working Paper 28474, 2021, https://www.nber.org/papers/w28474, retrieved January 3, 2026.

19 On monopoly rents as a private tax on productive activity, see Henry George, *Progress and Poverty* (D. Appleton and Company, 1879). On rent seeking more broadly, see Gordon Tullock, "The Welfare Costs of Tariffs, Monopolies, and Theft," *Western Economic Journal* (1967), https://doi.org/10.1111/j.1465-7295.1967.tb01923.x; and Anne Krueger, "The Political Economy of the Rent-Seeking Society," *American Economic Review* (1974), https://assets.aeaweb.org/asset-server/files/9452.pdf, both retrieved January 17, 2026.

20 See Mark DesJardine and Rodolphe Durand, "Disentangling the Effects of Hedge Fund Activism on Firm Financial and Social Performance," *Strategic Management Journal* (2020), https://www.hec.edu/en/news-room/activist-hedge-funds-short-term-gains-offset-drop-companies-value-long-term-new-research-finds, retrieved January 17, 2026.

21 Lest you think this view is only held by noneconomists, consider Simon Kuznets, who invented the concept of GDP in 1934. He warned from the start that "the welfare of a nation can scarcely be inferred from a measure of national income." By 1962, he had become an outspoken critic of the narrow view of profit. He won the Nobel Prize in 1971, and in his Nobel lecture, he called conventional measures a "measure of our ignorance" because they "do not reflect many costs"; https://www.weforum.org/stories/2021/12/stakeholder-capitalism-episode-1-a-brief-history-of-gdp/, retrieved January 3, 2026.

22 As Steen Thomsen writes, "Colin Mayer (2023, 2024) . . . explain[s] that profits generated by creating problems for society are not true profits since they do not take into consideration the social costs (negative externalities) of the problems they create. These costs are not paid by companies (and do not appear in profit and loss statements) but by their stakeholders, and they are precisely emphasized in current discussions of ESG and CSR. A sustainable purpose (which aims to be truly profitable also in a social sense) therefore internalizes externalities and aims to create value for society net of social costs." Thomsen, "Corporate Purpose"; see also Colin Mayer, "Reflections on Corporate Purpose and Performance," *European Management Review* 20, no. 4 (2023): 719–24; and Colin Mayer, *Capitalism and Crises: How to Fix Them* (Oxford University Press, 2024), 181–96, https://doi.org/10.1093/oso/9780198887942.001.0001, accessed September 25, 2025.

23 Park, "How the Former U.S. CTO Built."

24 https://www.youtube.com/watch?v=cFll3HNXR1E, retrieved January 17, 2026.

25 https://www.devoted.com/providers-ready/, retrieved December 31, 2025.

26 https://www.letlifehappen.com/why-devoted-health-has-put-family-at-the-center-of-its-mission/, retrieved September 16, 2025.

27 https://endpoints.news/devoted-health-2024-financials-reveal-revenue-growth/, retrieved October 1, 2025.

28 https://www.devoted.com/resources/2021-company-update/, retrieved July 7, 2025.

29 https://www.devoted.com/resources/delivering-better-care/, retrieved July 7, 2025.

30 https://www.youtube.com/watch?v=ss-SI2Szjxk, retrieved July 9, 2025.

31 Note that Costco's payment method for suppliers is a little more complicated than just net-thirty-day payments. Suppliers can opt to be paid earlier than thirty days by accepting/offering a discount using a system called C2FO. See https://costco.c2fo.com/costco, https://www.sec.gov/Archives/edgar/data/1940372/000149315222028154/ex10-6.htm, and https://www.acquired.fm/episodes/costco, retrieved July 9, 2025.

32 https://companiesmarketcap.com/gitlab/marketcap/, retrieved September 7, 2025.

33 https://www.washingtonpost.com/archive/opinions/1993/12/23/japans-secret-w-edwards-deming/b69b8c00-4c5d-483a-b95e-4aeb1d94d2c6/, retrieved September 7, 2025.

34 The "double bottom line" measures both financial and social returns; the "triple bottom line" adds environmental impact (often summarized as "people, planet, profit"). These frameworks attempt to balance multiple objectives rather than integrating them into a single measure. See, for example, https://www.forbes.com/sites/lorikozlowski/2012/10/02/impact-investing-the-power-of-two-bottom-lines/ and https://sustainlab.co/blog/the-triple-bottom-line-making-your-company-more-sustainable, both retrieved November 13, 2025. Stout, "Shareholder Value Myth."

35 Fred Reichheld, *The Ultimate Question: Driving Good Profits and True Growth* (Harvard Business School Press, 2006). Reichheld defines bad profits as "earnings at the expense of customer relationships—whenever a customer feels misled, mistreated, coerced or abused."

36 https://www.si.edu/newsdesk/about/stats, retrieved July 8, 2025.

37 https://projects.propublica.org/nonprofits/organizations/530206027, retrieved July 8, 2025.

38 https://www.forbes.com/companies/goodwill-industries-international/, retrieved July 8, 2025.

39 https://www.goodwill.org/about/, retrieved July 9, 2025.

40 https://www.macrotrends.net/stocks/charts/PM/philip-morris/net-income, retrieved September 7, 2025.

41 "Economic Trends in Tobacco," Centers for Disease Control and Prevention, September 17, 2024, https://www.cdc.gov/tobacco/php/data-statistics/economic-trends/index.html, retrieved January 2025. This includes more than $240 billion in healthcare spending and nearly $372 billion in lost productivity.

42 https://www.uschamber.com/co/start/strategy/nonprofit-vs-not-for-profit-vs-for-profit, December 31, 2025.

43 From "Ulysses," by Alfred, Lord Tennyson. The full poem can be read here: https://www.poetryfoundation.org/poems/45392/ulysses, retrieved January 17, 2026.

Chapter Six: Harder Is Easier

1 https://www.snopes.com/fact-check/costco-founder-kill-hotdogs/, retrieved July 7, 2025.

2 https://www.investing.com/analysis/costco-balances-premium-valuation-with-consistent-doubledigit-growth-200666556, retrieved November 13, 2025.

3 https://www.foodbible.com/news/us-food/costco-hot-dogs-same-price-after-40-years-676312-20250502, retrieved November 13, 2025.

4 https://www.directorsandboards.com/uncategorised/singlebusiness-about-more-making-money/, retrieved July 7, 2025. Sol Price frequently joked about his influence. I'll let the *Acquired Podcast* guys tell the story: "There's a really funny Sol quote from later in his life. He's asked about how he feels about essentially being the father of modern American retailing. He thinks about it, he laughs, and says, you know, maybe I should have worn a condom." From their great episode about Costco: https://www.acquired.fm/episodes/costco, retrieved January 17, 2026.

5 https://www.directorsandboards.com/uncategorised/singlebusiness-about-more-making-money/, retrieved July 7, 2025.

6 https://www.directorsandboards.com/uncategorised/singlebusiness-about-more-making-money/, retrieved July 7, 2025.

7 https://www.sandiegouniontribune.com/2021/08/01/first-price-club-opens-in-san-diego-45-years-ago/, retrieved January 5, 2026.

8 https://www.historylink.org/File/3609, retrieved January 5, 2026.

9 https://thehill.com/homenews/4696314-costcos-new-cfo-makes-announcement-about-1-50-hot-dog-combo/, retrieved January 19, 2026.

10 https://www.eatthis.com/big-mac-cost/ and https://www.foodandwine.com/mcdonalds-big-mac-prices-per-state-cashnetusa-report-2025-11727992, both retrieved November 13, 2025.

11 https://knowyourmeme.com/memes/subcultures/costco-hot-dog, retrieved September 15, 2025.

12 https://www.nbcdfw.com/news/business/money-report/costcos-iconic-1-50-hot-dog-combo-has-a-viral-t-shirt-design-celebrating-its-cult-status/3283856/, retrieved July 7, 2025.

13 Confirmed in conversation between the author and Jim Sinegal, April 15, 2025.

14 https://finance.yahoo.com/news/whopping-number-hot-dogs-costco-173000068.html, retrieved July 7, 2025.

15 https://fortune.com/2024/06/01/costco-ceo-hot-dog-price-story/, retrieved July 7, 2025.

16 https://www.foxbusiness.com/lifestyle/costcos-pepsi-to-coke-switch-goes-viral-members-sound-off, retrieved September 15, 2025.

17 https://www.seattletimes.com/business/complete-qa-with-costco-founder-ceo-jim-sinegal/, retrieved July 7, 2025.

18 https://www.usatoday.com/story/money/food/2022/09/26/costco-hot-dog-soda-combo-price/8118306001/, retrieved July 7, 2025.

19 https://financhill.com/blog/investing/costco-stock-vs-sp-500, retrieved September 15, 2025.

20 https://www.financecharts.com/stocks/COST/performance, retrieved September 15, 2025.

21 https://finance.yahoo.com/news/prediction-costco-stock-underperform-p-221500955.html, retrieved September 15, 2025.

22 https://www.cnbc.com/2025/04/04/grocery-may-soon-go-up-is-costcos-130-membership-worth-the-money.html, retrieved July 7, 2025.

23 https://www.wsj.com/business/retail/how-costcos-kirkland-signature-brand-became-a-powerhouse-29a8132d, retrieved July 7, 2025.

24 Fourteen percent on brand names and 15% on Kirkland products, according to https://managementconsulted.com/podcast/costco-business-model-breakdown and https://thepricingconundrum.substack.com/p/the-dark-side-of-costcos-pricing, both retrieved July 7, 2025.

25 https://www.bloomberg.com/news/articles/2013-06-06/costco-ceo-craig-jelinek-leads-the-cheapest-happiest-company-in-the-world, retrieved October 1, 2025.

26 https://www.costco.com/wcsstore/CostcoUSBCCatalogAssetStore/feature-pages/16w0604-sustainability-ethics.pdf, retrieved September 16, 2025.

27 https://fs.blog/sol-price-customer-best-friend/, retrieved October 1, 2025.

28 https://www.caseiq.com/resources/employee-relations-best-practices-costco/, retrieved September 16, 2025.

29 https://retailwire.com/discussion/is-elevated-pay-core-driver-costcos-success/, retrieved September 15, 2025.

30 https://retailwire.com/discussion/is-elevated-pay-core-driver-costcos-success/, retrieved September 15, 2025. See also Zeynep Ton's research and work at the Good Jobs Institute, a summary of which can be found at https://www.hbs.edu/bigs/costco-and-other-retailers-prove-a-good-jobs-strategy-works, retrieved December 9, 2025.

31 https://mastersinvest.com/newblog/2019/7/5/learning-from-costcos-jim-sinegal, retrieved July 7, 2025.

32 https://www.alumni.hbs.edu/stories/Pages/story-bulletin.aspx?num=7060, retrieved January 19, 2026.

33 *The Eric Ries Show*, podcast, "AI Will Break the Internet—Cloudflare CEO's Big Prediction | Matthew Prince," August 28, 2025, https://www.ericriesshow.com/matthew-prince-ai/, retrieved January 28, 2026.

34 Matthew Prince, personal correspondence with the author, November 6, 2025.

35 https://blog.cloudflare.com/introducing-universal-ssl/, retrieved November 14, 2025.

36 https://www.cloudflare.com/press/press-releases/2014/cloudflare-offers-the-industrys-first-universal-ssl-for-free/, retrieved November 14, 2025.

37 https://w3techs.com/technologies/details/cn-cloudflare, retrieved November 14, 2025.

38 https://www.macrotrends.net/stocks/charts/NET/cloudflare/market-cap, retrieved February 27, 2026.

39 For more on the sources and consequences of this organizational "friction," see Stanford professors Robert Sutton and Huggy Rao's *The Friction Project* (St. Martin's Press, 2024).

40 Jeremy Howard, personal correspondence with the author, May 2025.

41 It's important to understand that intentionally "milking" a "cash cow" has been considered a strategy best practice for decades. The Boston Consulting Group began promoting it as part of their "growth-share matrix" in the late 1960s. The term "cash cow" was introduced by Bruce D. Henderson in "The Product Portfolio," *BCG Perspectives*, no. 66 (Boston: Boston Consulting Group, 1970). "Products with high market share and slow growth are 'cash cows.' Characteristically, they generate large amounts of cash, in excess of the reinvestment required to maintain share. This excess need not, and should not, be reinvested in those products." See https://web-assets.bcg.com/img-src/BCG_The_Product_Portfolio_tcm9-139921.pdf, retrieved January 17, 2026.

42 Howard, personal correspondence.

43 Howard, personal correspondence. See also https://www.globenewswire.com/news-release/2025/02/14/3026595/0/en/Enlitic-Inc-to-Showcase-AI-Enabled-Workflows-at-ViVE-2025.html, retrieved January 19, 2026.

44 Prince, "AI Will Break the Internet."

45 Donald Sull, Charles Sull, and Ben Zweig, "Toxic Culture Is Driving the Great Resignation," *MIT Sloan Management Review*, January 11, 2022, https://sloanreview.mit.edu/article/toxic-culture-is-driving-the-great-resignation/, retrieved September 16, 2025.

46 https://www.kornferry.com/insights/this-week-in-leadership/purpose-a-year-in-review, retrieved September 28, 2025.

47 https://www.fiercehealthcare.com/payer/devoted-health-closes-1-15b-series-d-funding-round, retrieved July 7, 2025.

48 https://www.gurufocus.com/news/2135765/charlie-munger-daily-journal-2018-shareholder-meeting-part-2, retrieved July 7, 2025.

49 Park, "How the Former U.S. CTO Built."

50 https://www.youtube.com/watch?v=Te5QF9rRJCI&list=PLWhCgHlnjGmGekUM1nB9hjG-qa8gfsGYB&index=7, retrieved July 8, 2025.

51 https://www.deloitte.com/us/en/pages/advisory/solutions/the-importance-of-trust-in-your-organization.html/, retrieved July 8, 2025.

52 https://fs.blog/sol-price-customer-best-friend/, retrieved September 16, 2025.

53 https://www.newyorker.com/culture/infinite-scroll/the-age-of-enshittification, retrieved November 14, 2025. See also Seth Godin, "Trading Trust," *Seth's Blog*, February 16, 2024, https://seths.blog/2024/02/trading-trust/, retrieved January 17, 2026.

54 https://www.harvardbusiness.org/insight/good-leadership-it-all-starts-with-trust/, retrieved July 8, 2025.

55 https://deloitte.wsj.com/riskandcompliance/trust-increasingly-hard-to-win-easier-than-ever-to-lose-951e641e and https://www.deloitte.com/us/en/about/four-factors-of-trust.html, both retrieved August 27, 2025.

56 https://www.weforum.org/stories/2022/08/why-trust-is-key-to-leading-companies-unlocking-value/, retrieved January 5, 2026.

57 Lin Lin, Ngou Teng Pun, and Ping-Wen Sun, "Impact of Investor Trust on Public Firms' Stock Price Efficiency and Cost of Capital: Insights from a Firm-Level Measure for Investor Trust," *Economic Modelling* 138 (2024): 106786. https://doi.org/10.1016/j.econmod.2024.106786, retrieved September 16, 2025.

58 https://corporate-adviser.com/nearly-73pc-of-young-people-demand-sustainability-in-investment-portfolios-research/, retrieved September 17, 2025.

59 https://www.bcg.com/publications/2024/driving-company-value-with-stakeholders-perceptions, retrieved July 8, 2025.

60 https://www.edelman.com/news-awards/only-one-third-of-consumers-trust-most-of-the-brands-they-buy. See also https://www.brandwatch.com/blog/brand-loyalty/ (Bain research on loyal customer lifetime value) and https://www.braze.com/resources/articles/building-long-term-customer-loyalty (Braze study on repeat purchase motivations), all retrieved January 5, 2026.

61 https://2719723.fs1.hubspotusercontent-na1.net/hubfs/2719723/NPS%203.0%20memo

/Net%20Promoter%203.0%20-%20Inspiration%20from%20Fred%20Reichheld.pdf, retrieved July 8, 2025. See also Fred Reichheld's book, *Winning on Purpose: The Unbeatable Strategy of Loving Customers* (Harvard Business Review Press, 2021).

62 Mari Sako, "Does Trust Improve Business Performance?," in *Organizational Trust: A Reader*, ed. Roderick M. Kramer (Oxford University Press, 2006; online ed., Oxford Academic, October 31, 2023), https://doi.org/10.1093/oso/9780199288496.003.0010, retrieved January 17, 2025.

63 https://hbr.org/2020/01/are-you-undervaluing-your-customers, retrieved July 8, 2025.

Chapter Seven: Mission Drive

1 Park, "How the Former U.S. CTO Built."

2 https://smhc.co.uk/collection/chouinard-salewa-karabiners-1972/, retrieved September 18, 2025.

3 *The Eric Ries Show*, podcast, "From Blacksmith to Billionaire: The Making of Patagonia's Ethos | David Gelles," September 11, 2025, https://www.ericriesshow.com/from-blacksmith-to-billionaire-the-making-of-patagonias-ethos/, retrieved January 28, 2026.

4 David Gelles, *Dirtbag Billionaire: How Yvon Chouinard Built Patagonia, Made a Fortune, and Gave It All Away* (Simon & Schuster, 2025), Kindle edition, 128.

5 Gelles, *Dirtbag Billionaire*, 128–29.

6 Gelles, *Dirtbag Billionaire*, 111–12.

7 Gelles, *Dirtbag Billionaire*, 80.

8 Gelles, "From Blacksmith to Billionaire."

9 Gelles, *Dirtbag Billionaire*, 136–37. I have simplified this story somewhat, as these negotiations were quite complicated. For example, at one point, Doug Tompkins gave Patagonia a onetime $5 million line of credit, to be tapped only in case of emergency. Gelles tells the story this way: "'I'll never use a penny of it,' McDivitt told him. She never did."

10 Gelles, *Dirtbag Billionaire*, 140–41.

11 Gelles, *Dirtbag Billionaire*, 128–29.

12 https://sustainable.org.nz/learn/news-insights/let-my-people-go-surfing-8-philosophies-from-patagonia-for-your-business/, retrieved September 18, 2025.

13 https://www.outsideonline.com/culture/active-families/why-site-childcare-essential, retrieved September 18, 2025.

14 https://paulgraham.com/foundermode.html, retrieved September 29, 2025.

15 https://www.patagonia.com.au/pages/supply-chain-environmental-responsibility-program, retrieved November 14, 2025.

16 Gelles, *Dirtbag Billionaire*, 203.

17 See, for example, https://www.forbes.com/sites/davidrock/2020/01/09/the-nli-interview-patagonias-dean-carter-on-how-to-treat-employees-like-people/ and https://initiatives.weforum.org/industry-net-zero-accelerator/case-study-details/patagonia-sparking-the-sustainability-cultural-shift-at-every-level/aJYTG00000001H34AI, both retrieved September 18, 2025.

18 https://brandingstrategyinsider.com/patagonia-in-the-making-my-founders-story/, retrieved January 17, 2026.

19 I know some readers will feel I am exaggerating here. I assure you, this is considered a well-established point among governance experts. For example, see Leo E. Strine Jr., "Our Continuing Struggle with the Idea That For-Profit Corporations Seek Profit," *Wake Forest Law Review* 47, no. 135 (2012): "Stockholders' best interest must always, within legal limits, be the end. Other constituencies may be considered only instrumentally to advance that end."

20 Hansmann and Kraakman call this "a widespread normative consensus that corporate managers should act exclusively in the economic interests of shareholders." Note the use of "should" here. Are you part of this consensus? Henry Hansmann and Reinier Kraakman, "The End of History for Corporate Law," *Georgetown Law Journal* 89 (2001): 439, 441, https://doi.org/10.2139/ssrn.204528, retrieved January 17, 2026.

21 *Caveat emptor* is a Latin phrase meaning "let the buyer beware." Interestingly, this is not an ancient Roman idea; it originated in Tudor England (see https://people.howstuffworks.com/caveat-emptor.htm, retrieved January 17, 2026). For centuries it governed commerce: Buyers bore all risk. In the twentieth century, "there was a paradigm shift from 'let the buyer beware' to 'let the seller beware'"—through consumer protection laws, product liability, and the principle that sellers should be responsible for defects buyers cannot reasonably detect. For an accessible roundup of this history, see https://blog.ipleaders.in/doctrine-of-caveat-emptor/, retrieved January 17, 2026.

Most readers have only ever known the soft world of *caveat venditor*. But shareholder primacy has been quietly eroding this reversal: If a company's sole obligation is to shareholders and regulators fail to impose sufficient penalties (or companies lobby to weaken them), the buyer is once again on their own. For more on why shareholder primacy requires companies to ignore externalities (i.e., you), see Michael Jensen, "Value Maximization, Stakeholder Theory, and the Corporate Objective Function" (2001).

22 See Lawrence G. Foster, *Robert Wood Johnson: The Gentleman Rebel* (1999) and https://www.jnj.com/our-heritage/from-company-president-to-national-business-leader-the-story-of-robert-wood-johnson-ii, retrieved September 28, 2025.

23 See https://www.jnj.com/our-heritage/8-fun-facts-about-the-johnson-johnson-credo, retrieved November 14, 2025. It's important for mission-driven companies to explicitly name these commitments and give them teeth. For example, Airbnb publicly commits to support five stakeholders: "Guests, Hosts, Communities, Shareholders, and Employees," with explicit principles and metrics for each; see https://news.airbnb.com/serving-all-stakeholders/. Note that neither Johnson nor Sol Price used the trendy modern word "stakeholder." I follow them in using the more old-fashioned term "fiduciary" instead.

In 2019, 181 CEOs signed the Business Roundtable's statement declaring that companies should serve "customers, employees, suppliers, communities, and shareholders"—but carefully avoided ranking them, insisting "each of our stakeholders is essential." See https://opportunity.businessroundtable.org/ourcommitment. A Harvard Law School study later found this was mostly for show. See https://papers.ssrn.com/sol3/papers.cfm?abstract_id=3899421. The pandemic provided an immediate natural experiment to see if these "stakeholder" commitments were real. A Wharton study found that when the pandemic hit, BRT signatories were more likely to lay off workers than nonsignatories. See https://www.marketplace.org/2020/08/19/how-are-ceos-doing-on-their-stakeholdlers-pledge/, all retrieved January 5, 2026.

24 https://www.washingtonpost.com/local/obituaries/seward-johnson-johnson-and-johnson-heir-who-sculpted-real-life-images-in-bronze-dies-at-89/2020/03/14/05b242ee-653e-11ea-845d-e35b0234b136_story.html, retrieved September 28, 2025.

25 James O'Toole, "Connecting the Dots Between Leadership, Ethics and Corporate Culture," *Ivey Business Journal* (September/October 2009), https://iveybusinessjournal.com/publication/connecting-the-dots-between-leadership-ethics-and-corporate-culture/, retrieved September 29, 2025. See also https://www.mgmtstories.com/all-the-balls-are-red/, retrieved January 5, 2026.

26 O'Toole, *Enlightened Capitalists*, 167.

27 https://www.jnj.com/our-heritage/8-fun-facts-about-the-johnson-johnson-credo, retrieved January 2, 2026.

28 O'Toole, "Connecting the Dots."

29 https://www.annualreports.com/HostedData/AnnualReportArchive/j/NYSE_JNJ_2002.pdf, retrieved January 5, 2026.

30 https://knowledge.wharton.upenn.edu/article/patients-versus-profits-at-johnson-johnson-has-the-company-lost-its-way/, retrieved September 29, 2025. See also https://www.radicalcandor.com/podcast/cult-of-the-credo-7-36, retrieved January 17, 2026.

31 https://www.cbsnews.com/news/how-jj-misled-the-fda-over-its-phantom-recall-of-motrin/, retrieved September 29, 2025.

32 See https://www.corpgov.net/2015/04/johnson-johnson-jnj-proxy-score-44/ and https://www.justice.gov/archives/opa/pr/mcneil-ppc-inc-pleads-guilty-connection-adulterated-infants-and-childrens-over-counter-liquid, respectively, both retrieved November 14, 2025.

33 https://knowledge.wharton.upenn.edu/article/patients-versus-profits-at-johnson-johnson-has-the-company-lost-its-way/, retrieved November 14, 2025. See also https://www.radicalcandor.com/podcast/cult-of-the-credo-7-36, retrieved January 17, 2026.

34 https://www.marketwatch.com/story/jj-ceos-retirement-benefits-valued-at-1435-mln-2012-03-14 and https://www.reuters.com/article/business/jj-ceo-weldon-retirement-pay-seen-at-1435-mln-idUSL2E8EEFAG/, retrieved September 29, 2025.

35 Reuters's investigation revealed that from at least 1971 to the early 2000s, J&J's raw talc and finished powders sometimes tested positive for small amounts of asbestos. See "Johnson & Johnson Knew for Decades That Asbestos Lurked in Its Baby Powder," Reuters, December 14, 2018, https://www.reuters.com/investigates/special-report/johnsonandjohnson-cancer/, retrieved November 14, 2025. See also Gardiner Harris, *No More Tears: The Truth Behind Johnson & Johnson's Baby Powder* (Random House, 2024).

36 Henderson et al.'s 1971 case study described talc particles "deeply embedded" in ten of thirteen ovarian tumors examined; W. J. Henderson et al., "Talc and Carcinoma of the Ovary and Cervix," *Journal of Obstetrics and Gynaecology of the British Commonwealth* 78 (March 1971): 266–27, https://cdn.cnn.com/cnn/2017/images/11/15/talc.and.carcinoma.of.the.ovary.and.cervix.1971.pdf, retrieved January 19, 2026.

37 "Johnson & Johnson Knew"; Internal J&J documents show positive asbestos tests from multiple labs between 1971 and the early 2000s.

38 In 1976, J&J assured the FDA that no asbestos was "detected in any sample" from a specific period while withholding results from three labs that had found asbestos, including one reporting "rather high" levels. "Johnson & Johnson Knew."

39 New York attorney general consent judgment, June 11, 2024. J&J's research director warned they should "protect our powder franchise" by eliminating respirable fibers while acknowledging "no final product will ever be made which will be totally free from respirable particles"; see https://ag.ny.gov/sites/default/files/settlements-agreements/2024.06.11.jnj-talc-consent-judgment-new-york.pdf, retrieved November 14, 2025.

40 As of 2024, J&J faced more than 62,000 talc-related lawsuits; Diana Novak Jones, "Lawyers Increase Talc Ad Spending After J&J's $9 Billion Settlement Offer," Reuters, November 5, 2024, https://www.reuters.com/legal/litigation/lawyers-increase-talc-ad-spending-after-jjs-9-billion-settlement-offer-2024-11-05/, retrieved November 14, 2025.

41 J&J's April 2023 bankruptcy filing for LTL Management proposed $8.9 billion to resolve talc claims. Jef Feeley and Steven Church, "J&J to Pay $8.9 Billion to Settle Talc-Cancer Lawsuits," Bloomberg, April 4, 2023, https://www.bloomberg.com/news/articles/2023-04-04/j-j-to-pay-8-9-billion-to-settle-talc-litigation-cancer-claims, retrieved November 14, 2025.

42 Seth Godin, "Avoid False Proxies," *Seth's Blog*, June 5, 2023, https://seths.blog/2023/06/avoid-false-proxies/, retrieved July 8, 2025.

43 https://www.prnewswire.com/news-releases/historic-national-customer-rage-survey-record-level-of-product-and-service-problems-incite-surly-customers-to-yell-more-and-seek-revenge-for-their-hassles-301765053.html, retrieved September 18, 2025.

44 https://customercaremc.com/2023-national-customer-rage-study/, retrieved September 18, 2025.

45 The concept of surrogation was developed by Jongwoon Choi, Gary Hecht, and William B. Tayler, "Strategy Selection, Surrogation, and Strategic Performance Measurement Systems," *Journal of Accounting Research* (forthcoming), available at SSRN, https://ssrn.com/abstract=1910383 or http://dx.doi.org/10.2139/ssrn.1910383, retrieved January 17, 2026. Roger Martin expanded on this with the Southwest Airlines example in *When More Is Not Better* (Harvard Business Review Press, 2020).

46 https://finance.yahoo.com/news/number-go-up-is-alive-and-well--and-not-just-in-crypto-morning-brief-110129908.html, retrieved January 28, 2026.

47 See https://trellis.net/article/patagonias-comprehensive-plan-counter-rising-emissions/. Creating new accounting frameworks that enable companies to more easily internalize externalities is an emerging area of research. For examples, see Harvard Business School's Impact-Weighted Accounts project, https://www.hbs.edu/impact-weighted-accounts/; and the True Cost Accounting movement, https://clf.jhsph.edu/projects/true-cost-food, all retrieved January 5, 2026.

48 https://www.southwest.com/swa-resources/pdfs/communications/one-reports/2023-One-Report_Online_Final.pdf, retrieved September 18, 2025.

49 https://www.patagonia.com/stories/planet/our-footprint/patagonia-clothing-made-where-how-why/story-18467.html, retrieved February 13, 2026.

50 https://eu.patagonia.com/gb/en/our-footprint/working-with-factories.html, retrieved November 13, 2026.

51 See https://www.patagonia.com/our-footprint/migrant-workers.html, retrieved November 15, 2025, for this and what follows.

52 https://www.patagonia.com/stories/planet/our-footprint/the-unacceptably-high-cost-of-labor-a-new-migrant-worker-standard-from-patagonia/story-17743.html, retrieved February 13, 2026.

53 https://www.fairlabor.org/wp-content/uploads/2021/10/patagonia_reaccreditation_assessment_october_2017_0.pdf, retrieved September 28, 2025.

54 Ian Hickson, "Reflecting on 18 Years at Google," *Hixie's Natural Log*, November 22, 2023, https://ln.hixie.ch/?start=1700627373&count=1, retrieved February 13, 2026.

55 See https://arxiv.org/abs/1706.03762 and https://analyticsindiamag.com/ai-features/attention-is-all-you-need-gets-no-attention-at-all/, both retrieved January 5, 2026.

56 See https://digiday.com/marketing/alphabet-google-ditches-dont-evil-motto-right-thing/ and https://www.cnbc.com/2018/05/21/google-seems-to-have-removed-most-mentions-of-dont-be-evil-from-its-code-of-conduct.html. This loss of ethos is a recurring theme among ex-Googlers; for examples, see Ross LaJeunesse (eleven years), "nothing more than just another corporate marketing tool," https://medium.com/@rossformaine/i-was-googles-head-of-international-relations-here-s-why-i-left-49313d23065; Ian Hickson (eighteen years), "that Google is no more," https://ln.hixie.ch/?start=1700627373&count=1; Steve Yegge (thirteen years), "they can no longer innovate," https://steve-yegge.medium.com/why-i-left-google-to-join-grab-86dfffc0be84; Raph Levien (eleven years) and Claire Stapleton (twelve years), https://www.cnbc.com/2019/12/31/google-veterans-the-company-has-become-unrecognizable.html; Meredith Whittaker (thirteen years), https://guykawasaki.com/meredith-whittaker-revolutionizing-tech-privacy-and-power/. As one employee put it, "There is an abiding devotion to revenue and seemingly endless growth"; https://edition.cnn.com/2023/03/20/tech/google-layoffs-employee-culture/index.html, all retrieved January 5, 2026.

57 Google fines: $170M (2019), https://www.ftc.gov/news-events/news/press-releases/2019/09/google-youtube-will-pay-record-170-million-alleged-violations-childrens-privacy-law; EU advertising: €1.49B (2019), https://ec.europa.eu/commission/presscorner/detail/en/IP_19_1770. "Don't be evil" lawsuits: shareholders (2016), https://arstechnica.com/gadgets/2025/06/google-settles-shareholder-lawsuit-will-spend-500m-on-being-less-evil/; employees (2021), https://www.npr.org/2021/11/29/1059821677/google-dont-be-evil-lawsuit; both settled. All sources retrieved November 15, 2025.

58 Hickson, "Reflecting on 18 Years at Google."

59 This advice, that companies should "institutionalize their intentions," originates from the mentorship President Obama provided to Brian Chesky: https://fortune.com/article/airbnb-ceo-brian-chesky-went-to-night-school-with-barack-obama/, retrieved January 5, 2026.

Chapter Eight: The Invisible Leader

1 https://www.eosworldwide.com/blog/103242-eos-netflix-culture-deck, retrieved November 15, 2025. The original version of the deck can be found here: https://www.slideshare.net/slideshow/culture-2009/8469957, retrieved January 5, 2026.

2 For an introduction to Follett and her impact, see Michele Zanini, "Mary Parker Follett: The First Prophet of Management," https://www.michelezanini.com/mary-parker-follett-the-first-prophet-of-management/. For more scholarly views, see Jess Gregory, "Mary Parker Follett, a Modern Conceptualization of Power Nearly a Century in the Making," NERA Conference Proceedings 2023, https://digitalcommons.lib.uconn.edu/cgi/viewcontent.cgi?article=1006&context=nera-2023; and Melissa A. Schilling, "Decades Ahead of Her Time: Advancing Stakeholder Theory Through the Ideas of Mary Parker Follett," *Journal of Management History* 6, no. 5 (2000): 224–42.

3 Pauline Graham, ed., *Mary Parker Follett: Prophet of Management* (Beard Books, 2003), 108.

4 https://infed.org/mobi/mary-parker-follett-community-creative-experience-and-education/, retrieved November 15, 2025.

5 See Mary P. Follett, *The New State* (Longmans, Green, 1918), for a discussion of this principle.

6 See Mary Parker Follett, *Dynamic Administration: The Collected Papers of Mary Parker Follett*, ed. Henry C. Metcalf and L. Urwick (Harper & Brothers, 1941), 166–67.

7 See https://timkastelle.org/blog/2017/12/before-tom-peters-before-peter-drucker-we-had-mary-parker-follett/, retrieved November 15, 2025. Drucker's praise is from the foreword he wrote to the best modern collection of Follett's writing: Pauline Graham, ed., *Mary Parker Follett: Prophet of Management* (Boston: Harvard Business School Press, 1995).

8 "The history of management needs to be rewritten. Management science does not, as it is usually depicted, begin with Taylor and Fayol. . . . Instead, the history of management is, and has been the story of two distinct, opposing schools of thought that emerged side-by-side, at the dawn of the 20th century. Pioneered by two practical philosophers: Mary Parker Follett and Frederick Winslow Taylor"; Niels Pflaeging and Silke Hermann, "The Invention of Managements: From Follett & Taylor Onwards," *BetaCodex Network White Paper* 17 (2021), https://www.researchgate.net/publication/350888714, retrieved January 28, 2026.

9 https://www.expressnews.com/business/article/heb-top-5-forbes-list-private-companies-spacex-19999828.php, retrieved January 5, 2026.

10 https://abc7news.com/post/free-groceries-texas-grocery-store-heb-power-outage-weather/10359388/, retrieved September 28, 2025.

11 https://www.washingtonpost.com/lifestyle/2021/02/19/texas-heb-lost-power/, retrieved July 8, 2025.

12 https://www.texasmonthly.com/news-politics/how-heb-became-emergency-preparedness-model/, retrieved September 18, 2025.

13 https://www.marketingsociety.com/the-library/inside-story-what-it-took-keep-texas-grocery-chain-running-chaos-hurricane-harvey, retrieved September 18, 2025.

14 https://www.dallasfed.org/research/swe/2022/swe2204/swe2204d, retrieved July 8, 2025.

15 https://careers.heb.com/about-us, retrieved November 15, 2025.

16 https://www.expressnews.com/news/texas/article/H-E-B-frequent-Google-questions-17656827.php, retrieved January 28, 2026.

17 Todd Park first turned me onto the idea of a "reservoir of trust," a phrase coined by Starbucks founder Howard Schultz. In a 2010 HBR interview, Schultz said he aimed to "preserve and enhance the integrity of the only assets we have as a company, our values, our culture and guiding principles, and a reservoir of trust with our people" (see https://hbr.org/podcast/2010/06/howard-schultz-on-starbucks-tu.html). Under his leadership, Starbucks repeatedly made *Fortune*'s 100 Best Companies to Work For list. But like many companies in earlier chapters, Starbucks has struggled with succession without institutional safeguards: "For more than two

decades, the coffee empire has tried and failed to find a lasting successor" (see https://insights.som.yale.edu/insights/has-starbucks-finally-found-the-right-leader). Schultz has recognized this as a loss of cultural cohesion (see https://www.cnbc.com/2025/06/11/starbucks-howard-schultz-backs-ceo-brian-niccol.html), all retrieved January 5, 2026.

18 See Godin, "Trading Trust"; and *The Eric Ries Show*, podcast, "How to Build Trust and Win Your Customer's Attention with Seth Godin," August 1, 2024, https://www.ericriesshow.com/seth-godin/, retrieved February 11, 2026.

19 Clayton Christensen made the same observation in his 2012 book *How Will You Measure Your Life?*: "It's easier to hold to your principles 100% of the time than it is to hold to them 98% of the time."

20 For more on the Trust Battery, see *The Eric Ries Show*, podcast, "Lessons on Creating a $17 Billion Dollar Learning Company, Going Viral with an Owl, and Ditching Short-Term Thinking with Luis von Ahn (Duolingo)," February 10, 2025, https://www.ericriesshow.com/luis-von-ahn/, retrieved January 28, 2026. Shopify CEO Tobi Luttke has also spoken about the importance of the trust battery as a concept: "It's a mental model for how to think about the relationship between people." See https://www.youtube.com/watch?v=Y9eXTlKMRBc, retrieved January 7, 2026.

21 https://blog.duolingo.com/handbook/, retrieved November 15, 2025.

22 https://ovayozabalogun.medium.com/i-visited-duolingos-office-1d732381919a, retrieved September 18, 2025.

23 *The Duolingo Handbook* (Duolingo, 2025), 36.

24 See Walter J. Ong, *Orality and Literacy: The Technologizing of the Word* (Methuen, 1982); Lynne Kelly, *Knowledge and Power in Prehistoric Societies: Orality, Memory, and the Transmission of Culture* (Cambridge University Press, 2015).

25 Park, "How the Former U.S. CTO Built."

26 Howard Schultz, personal correspondence with the author, April 27, 2025.

27 https://ir.gitlab.com/overview/default.aspx, retrieved July 9, 2025.

28 https://downtimeproject.com/podcast/gitlabs-2017-postgres-outage/, retrieved November 15, 2025.

29 https://handbook.gitlab.com/handbook/, retrieved September 18, 2025.

30 *The Eric Ries Show*, podcast, "How GitLab Scaled to 30M Users with Transparency, Remote Work, and the Ultimate Employee Handbook | Sid Sijbrandij," July 10, 2025, https://www.ericriesshow.com/Sid-Sijbrandij/, retrieved January 28, 2025.

31 https://about.gitlab.com/company/, retrieved November 17, 2025.

32 https://increment.com/on-call/the-benefits-of-transparency/, retrieved July 9, 2025.

33 https://increment.com/on-call/the-benefits-of-transparency/, retrieved July 9, 2025.

34 https://www.brmbl.io/handbook/handbook-usage/, retrieved July 9, 2025.

35 https://slab.com/blog/short-toes-how-gitlabs-values-shape-company-documentation/, retrieved July 9, 2025.

36 Sijbrandij, "How Gitlab Scaled to 30M Users."

37 https://handbook.gitlab.com/handbook/about/#count-handbook-pages.

38 Sijbrandij, "How Gitlab Scaled to 30M Users."

39 https://handbook.gitlab.com/handbook/values/, retrieved September 18, 2025.

40 https://about.gitlab.com/company/, retrieved November 17, 2025.

41 https://www.forbes.com/sites/alexkonrad/2021/10/14/gitlab-reaches-15-bil-market-cap-as-shares-jump-in-ipo/, retrieved September 18, 2025; https://about.gitlab.com/company/, retrieved November 17, 2025.

42 https://stockanalysis.com/stocks/gtlb/statistics/, retrieved July 9, 2025.

43 https://www.nasdaq.com/articles/google-buys-more-gitlab-stock-what-investors-need-to-know, retrieved September 18, 2025.

44 https://news.microsoft.com/source/2018/06/04/microsoft-to-acquire-github-for-7-5-billion/, retrieved September 18, 2025.

45 https://www.linkedin.com/posts/sijbrandij_today-i-shared-on-our-earnings-call-that-activity-7041159814810390528-fJQC/, retrieved September 18, 2025.

46 https://ir.gitlab.com/news/news-details/2024/GitLab-Names-Bill-Staples-as-New-CEO/default.aspx, retrieved January 5, 2026.

Chapter Nine: Constitutional Governance

1 https://www.lightreading.com/business-transformation/twilio-ipo-stock-soars-92-, retrieved September 18, 2025.

2 https://softwarestackinvesting.com/checking-in-on-twilio-twlo/, retrieved September 18, 2025.

3 https://www.twilio.com/en-us/blog/company/leadership-updates/twilio-leadership-update, retrieved July 9, 2025.

4 https://klse.i3investor.com/web/blog/detail/future_tech/2024-01-09-story-h-210613311-CEO_of_chat_tech_plumber_Twilio_is_leaving_the_building, retrieved September 18, 2025.

5 https://www.twilio.com/en-us/press/releases/twilio-announces-pricing-of-initial-public-offering?utm and https://www.twilio.com/en-us/press/releases/twilio-announces-fourth-quarter-and-full-year-2016-results0, both retrieved November 16, 2025.

6 https://www.sec.gov/Archives/edgar/data/1447669/000144766924000034/twlo-20231231.htm, retrieved November 16, 2025.

7 https://www.macrotrends.net/stocks/charts/TWLO/twilio/revenue, retrieved September 29, 2025.

8 The main institutional-investor proponent of the dual-class sunset is CII, the Council of Institutional Investors. For their perspective on why the sunset is justified, see https://www.cii.org/dualclass_stock, retrieved January 18, 2026. Notably, the word "mission" does not appear on the page. Only a minority of IPOs feature dual-class "supervoting" structures. Among companies that do adopt them, roughly half include time-based sunsets. See Jay R. Ritter, "Dual Class IPOs, by Tech and Non-Tech, 1980–2024," https://site.warrington.ufl.edu/ritter/files/IPOs-Dual-Class.pdf; and Cooley, "Considerations for Implementing a Multi-Class Share Structure," February 5, 2025, https://capx.cooley.com/2025/02/05/considerations-for-implementing-a-multi-class-share-structure/, both retrieved January 5, 2026.

9 See, for example, https://law.justia.com/codes/delaware/2022/title-8/chapter-1/subchapter-i/section-102/, retrieved January 18, 2026, which describes the use of this language.

10 See, for example, https://www.law.cornell.edu/wex/public_benefit_corporation, retrieved September 18, 2025.

11 https://www.anthropic.com/company, retrieved September 18, 2025.

12 https://www.patagoniaworks.com, retrieved September 18, 2025.

13 https://delcode.delaware.gov/title8/c001/sc15/, retrieved September 18, 2025.

14 For a more complete list, see https://en.wikipedia.org/wiki/List_of_benefit_corporations, retrieved November 16, 2025.

15 It's only this simple if you do it before you have shareholders though. After that, conversion requires shareholder approval. https://corpgov.law.harvard.edu/2022/02/18/converting-to-a-delaware-public-benefit-corporation-lessons-from-experience/, retrieved July 9, 2025.

16 https://www.latent.space/p/answerai, retrieved January 5, 2026.

17 This teaching appears across wisdom traditions spanning millennia. Laozi, Tao Te Ching, ch. 76 (6th–4th c. BCE): "The hard and stiff will be broken. The soft and supple will prevail." The Babylonian Talmud, Taanit 20b (3rd–5th c. CE), records, "A person should always be soft like a reed, and he should not be stiff like a cedar." Aesop's fable "The Oak and the Reed" (Perry Index 70) circulated orally from the 6th c. BCE, with the earliest written versions by Babrius (2nd c. CE, Fable 36) and Avianus (ca. 400 CE, Fable 16). Jean de La Fontaine rendered it as "Je plie, et ne romps pas" ("I bend and do not break") in *Fables* I.22, verse 21 (Paris, 1668). Geoffrey Chaucer gave us the earliest English version—"And reed that boweth down for every blast, / Ful lightly, cesse wynd, it wol aryse"—in *Troilus and Criseyde* II.1387–89 (ca. 1385).

18 The Second Annual Rome Conference on Artificial Intelligence, Ethics, and Corporate Governance, June 19–20, 2025. Special thanks to David Berger for his work on this event.

19 "2004 Founders' Letter," Alphabet Investor Relations, https://abc.xyz/investor/founders-letters/2004/, retrieved July 9, 2025.

20 https://www.nytimes.com/2022/08/11/business/media/new-york-times-valueact-stock.html, retrieved July 20, 2025.

21 https://www.alibabagroup.com/en-US/ir-corporate-governance-partnership, retrieved September 19, 2025.

22 https://www.inc.com/allison-fass/peter-thiel-mark-zuckerberg-luck-day-facebook-turned-down-billion-dollars.html, retrieved July 9, 2025.

23 Park, "How the Former U.S. CTO Built."

24 https://corpgov.law.harvard.edu/2024/10/16/re-thinking-the-hostility-towards-dual-class-share-structures-when-dual-class-shares-work-better/, retrieved January 28, 2026.

25 See https://www.nytimes.com/2017/06/21/technology/uber-ceo-travis-kalanick.html, https://www.wsj.com/articles/zynga-moves-to-single-class-share-structure-1525293576, https://edition.cnn.com/2019/09/24/tech/wework-ceo-adam-neumann-stepping-down,andhttps://www.nytimes.com/2022/02/08/business/dealbook/peloton-ceo-sale.html, all retrieved November 17, 2025.

26 https://www.nytimes.com/2004/02/28/business/international-business-2-year-fight-pays-off-for-hollinger-shareholders.html, retrieved November 16, 2025.

27 https://www.ncbi.nlm.nih.gov/pmc/articles/PMC5971364/, retrieved November 16, 2025.

28 https://academic.oup.com/brain/article/132/5/1396/354862, retrieved November 16, 2025.

29 https://www.leidos.com/company/history/our-founder, retrieved September 19, 2025.

30 J. Robert Beyster, *The SAIC Solution: How We Built an $8 Billion Employee-Owned Technology Company* (Wiley, 2007), 11.

31 Beyster, *SAIC Solution*, 3.

32 https://cleo.rutgers.edu/wp-content/uploads/2007/02/None-of-Us-Is-As-Smart-As-All-of-Us.pdf, retrieved September 19, 2025.

33 https://www.washingtontechnology.com/2014/07/beyster-outlines-what-went-wrong-with-saics-employee-ownership-model/355756/, retrieved September 19, 2025.

34 https://www.washingtontechnology.com/2014/07/beyster-outlines-what-went-wrong-with-saics-employee-ownership-model/355756/, retrieved July 13, 2025.

35 https://www.sec.gov/Archives/edgar/data/353394/000119312505228499/d425.htm (see page 13), retrieved November 16, 2025.

36 https://beyster.com/saics-employee-ownership-continues-to-shift-blasi-speaks/, retrieved November 16, 2025.

37 https://www.annualreports.com/HostedData/AnnualReportArchive/s/NYSE_SAI_2003.pdf, retrieved September 19, 2025.

38 https://www.sandiegouniontribune.com/2009/06/19/saic-vote-could-end-control-by-employees/, retrieved October 1, 2025.

39 https://investors.leidos.com/static-files/d65e3bf9-0857-4bc4-b17e-e52d5cf70fd5, retrieved September 19, 2025.

40 https://beyster.com/shareholder-decisions-and-annual-yacht-competition/, retrieved September 19, 2025.

41 https://www.govtech.com/archive/new-york-citytime-scandal-nets-500-million-settlement.html, retrieved September 19, 2025.

42 https://www.crainsnewyork.com/article/20100613/REG/306139981/clocking-citytime-the-craziest-contract-ever, retrieved September 19, 2025.

43 https://www.nyc.gov/assets/doi/downloads/pdf/june11/pr_citytime_s2%20indictment_62011.pdf, retrieved September 19, 2025.

44 https://www.justice.gov/archive/usao/nys/pressreleases/March12/saicdpa.html, retrieved September 19, 2025.

45 For Leidos, see https://pcg.law.harvard.edu/wp-content/uploads/brtpurposearchive/A.Corporate-Governance-Guidelines/Leidos.pdf; for SAIC, see https://www.dailycsr.com/SAIC-Corporate-Governance-Integrity-Innovation-Inclusion-Board-Diversity_a4195.html, both retrieved January 5, 2026.

46 https://www.washingtontechnology.com/2014/07/beyster-outlines-what-went-wrong-with-saics-employee-ownership-model/355756/, retrieved July 20, 2025.

47 See SAIC, Definitive Proxy Statement (DEF 14A), filed April 26, 2013, US Securities and Exchange Commission, listing director independence status, https://www.sec.gov/Archives/edgar/data/1336920/000119312513174327/d516258ddef14a.htm, retrieved November 16, 2025.

48 https://www.govinfo.gov/content/pkg/CPRT-107SPRT80393/html/CPRT-107SPRT80393.htm, retrieved January 2, 2026.

49 See Peter J. Wallison, *All the Rage: Will Independent Directors Produce Good Corporate Governance?* (American Enterprise Institute, 2006); and Kathleen Day, "After Enron, a New Focus on Boards," *Washington Post*, March 8, 2002, https://www.washingtonpost.com/archive/business/2002/03/08/after-enron-a-new-focus-on-boards/ba063772-1f0a-44ec-99d4-3ec58731ea6d/, retrieved January 5, 2026.

50 Most companies have a nominations and governance committee whose charter spells out admission criteria for directors. The pledge can be added here as a prerequisite for all board members.

51 Research consistently demonstrates that professional codes create powerful counter-gravitational fields. The Hippocratic oath reduces medical errors and increases patient advocacy even when it conflicts with institutional pressure. Engineering codes prevent structural failures by making professional licenses contingent on safety standards. Legal ethics rules protect client confidentiality even against prosecutorial pressure. Accounting standards maintain audit independence through career consequences for violations. These systems work because they create stronger gravitational fields than any individual employer—violating professional standards destroys long-term career prospects across an entire profession, making ethical behavior the rational choice even under intense short-term pressure. See, for example, https://www.researchgate.net/profile/Anca-Yallop/publication/281207466_The_Use_and_Effectiveness_of_Codes_of_Ethics_-_A_Literature_Review/links/55db3fea08aeb38e8a8b81ea/The-Use-and-Effectiveness-of-Codes-of-Ethics-A-Literature-Review.pdf and https://www.sciencedirect.com/science/article/abs/pii/S0167268116301093?via%3Dihub, both retrieved September 10, 2025.

52 J. Heese, G. Pérez-Cavazos, and C. D. Peter, "When Executives Pledge Integrity: Evidence on CFO Integrity Oaths and Financial Reporting Quality," *Accounting Review* 98, no. 7 (2023): 261–88, https://doi.org/10.2308/TAR-2021-0600, retrieved January 20, 2026. Difference-in-difference analysis of 120 firms with oath-taking CFOs vs. 717 without, showing 20% reduction in earnings manipulation and 15% reduction in operational manipulations.

53 J. H. Zickfeld et al., "Effectiveness of Ex Ante Honesty Oaths in Reducing Dishonesty Depends on Content," *Nature Human Behaviour* 9, no. 1 (2024): 169–87, https://doi.org/10.1038/s41562-024-02009-0, retrieved January 18, 2026. This study of 21,506 participants found specific pledges reduced dishonest reporting from 31.3% to 18.5%.

54 On voluntary commitment, see Charles A. Kiesler, *The Psychology of Commitment* (Academic Press, 1971); Darwyn E. Linder et al., "Decision Freedom as a Determinant of the Role of Incentive Magnitude in Attitude Change," *Journal of Personality and Social Psychology* 6, no. 3 (1967). On ex-ante honesty pledges and design details, see Janis H. Zickfeld et al., "Effectiveness of Ex Ante Honesty Oaths in Reducing Dishonesty Depends on Content," *Nature Human Behaviour* (2024); Eyal Peer et al., "How Pledges Reduce Dishonesty: The Role of Involvement and Identification," *Journal of Experimental Social Psychology* 113 (2024). On oath-taking and timing, see Nicolas Jacquemet et al., "Truth Telling Under Oath," *Management Science* 65, no. 1 (2019). On social observability, see Ann-Kathrin Koessler, "Pledges and How Social Influence Shapes Their Effectiveness," *Journal of Behavioral and Experimental Economics* 98 (2022). On tying commitments to decision points, see Peter M. Gollwitzer, "Implementation Intentions," *American Psychologist* 54, no. 7 (1999).

55 David J. Berger, Steven Davidoff Solomon, and Aaron J. Benjamin, "Tenure Voting and the U.S. Public Company," *Business Lawyer* 72, no. 2 (2017): 295–336. For additional research on quality shareholders and long-term performance, see Lawrence A. Cunningham, "The Case for Empowering Quality Shareholders," *BYU Law Review* 46, no. 1 (2021), https://digitalcommons.law.byu.edu/lawreview/vol46/iss1/5, retrieved January 20, 2026.

56 https://www.ecgi.global/sites/default/files/working_papers/documents/finalbechtkamisarenkapajuste_2.pdf, retrieved September 20, 2025.

57 https://www.sec.gov/files/rules/sro/iex/2018/34-82948-ex3.pdf, retrieved January 5, 2026.

58 Alphabet's Class C shares carry no votes at all. Berkshire Hathaway's Class B shares have 1/10,000th the voting power of Class A shares, making them effectively economic-only for most purposes. This structure is also common in family businesses; see https://www.dwt.com/blogs/family-business-resource-center/2018/06/stocks-in-family-business-voting-or-nonvoting. For more on separating voting and economic rights, see the Purpose Foundation's guidebook for lawyers at https://purpose-economy.org/content/uploads/purpose-guidebook-for-lawyers10022021.pdf. Germany is currently considering legislation to make this structure even simpler to implement: In April 2025, Germany's new coalition government announced plans to introduce a dedicated "steward-owned company" legal form (the VE-GmbH) that would allow companies to lock in mission protection without requiring separate foundation structures. See Anne Sanders and Noah Neitzel, "Steward Ownership: Concept, Potential and Implementation in Germany and the Netherlands," SSRN, 2025, https://papers.ssrn.com/sol3/papers.cfm?abstract_id=5178366, all retrieved January 28, 2026.

59 https://www.nber.org/papers/w26519, retrieved September 20, 2025.

60 https://s26.q4cdn.com/656283129/files/doc_downloads/governance_doc_updated/Airbnb-ESG-Factsheet-(Final).pdf, retrieved January 18, 2026.

61 https://www.rei.com/newsroom/article/rei-co-op-board-of-directors-announces-2025-election-results, retrieved September 20, 2025.

62 https://corporate.vanguard.com/content/corporatesite/us/en/corp/articles/announcing-largest-fee-cut-vanguard-history.html, retrieved September 20, 2025.

63 See https://www.johnlewispartnership.co.uk/about/who-we-are.html, retrieved September 20, 2025, for this and what follows on John Lewis.

64 https://www.johnlewispartnership.co.uk/content/dam/cws/pdfs/Juniper/FYR/John-Lewis-Partnership-plc-2024-25-Full-Year-Results-Announcement.pdf, retrieved September 20, 2025.

65 https://www.bbc.com/news/business-65520696, retrieved September 20, 2025 and https://www.independent.co.uk/news/business/john-lewis-reported-to-be-exploring-plan-to-sell-shares-to-raise-investment-b2303755.html, retrieved October 10, 2025.

66 https://www.retailgazette.co.uk/blog/2023/05/john-lewis-crunch-vote/ and https://www.youtube.com/watch?v=1kZinylNii8, retrieved October 10, 2025.

67 See, for example, https://insights.som.yale.edu/insights/in-defense-of-dual-class-shares and https://www.hbs.edu/faculty/Pages/item.aspx?num=54523&, retrieved September 20, 2025.

68 Rajendra S. Sisodia, David B. Wolfe, and Jagdish N. Sheth, *Firms of Endearment: How World-Class Companies Profit from Passion and Purpose*, 2nd ed. (Pearson Prentice Hall, 2014).

69 https://www.deloitte.com/us/en/programs/monitor-institute/articles/driving-business-value-with-corporate-purpose.html, retrieved September 20, 2025.

70 Jump Associates, *The Payback on Purpose: How Purpose-Driven Companies Outperform the Competition* (Jump Associates, October 24, 2023).

71 James Madison, "The Structure of the Government Must Furnish the Proper Checks and Balances Between the Different Departments," *Federalist*, no. 51, in *The Federalist Papers*, from the *New York Packet*, February 8, 1788, Library of Congress, https://guides.loc.gov/federalist-papers/text-51-60, retrieved January 20, 2026.

72 https://www.nytimes.com/2005/07/17/business/yourmoney/how-costco-became-the-antiwalmart.html, retrieved September 20, 2025.

73 https://www.corpgov.net/2014/01/costco-cost-how-i-voted-why-i-proposed-simple-majority-standard-proxy-score-25/, retrieved September 20, 2025.

74 https://investor.costco.com/governance/governance-documents/default.aspx, retrieved September 20, 2025.

75 https://boardmember.com/the-costco-way-a-conversation-with-tony-james/, retrieved September 20, 2025.

76 https://www.dailykos.com/storyonly/2007/8/30/131038/492, retrieved September 20, 2025.

77 https://www.dailykos.com/storyonly/2007/8/30/131038/492, retrieved September 20, 2025.

78 https://www.seattleweekly.com/news/company-for-the-people/, retrieved November 16, 2025.

79 https://www.issgovernance.com, retrieved November 16, 2025.

80 https://www.corpgov.net/2016/01/costco-wholesale-proxy-score-57/, retrieved September 20, 2025.

81 https://www.corpgov.net/2014/01/costco-cost-how-i-voted-why-i-proposed-simple-majority-standard-proxy-score-25/, retrieved September 20, 2025.

82 http://www.srp.law.harvard.edu/2014-declassification-proposals.shtml, retrieved September 20, 2025.

83 https://www.fool.com/investing/2021/03/09/if-you-invested-1000-in-costcos-ipo-this-is-how-mu/ and https://dqydj.com/sp-500-return-calculator/, both retrieved September 20, 2025.

84 https://www.corpgov.net/2014/01/costco-cost-how-i-voted-why-i-proposed-simple-majority-standard-proxy-score-25/, retrieved September 20, 2025.

85 https://progressivegrocer.com/kroger-adopts-corporate-governance-best-practices-board-backs-annual-elections, retrieved January 3, 2026.

86 https://progressivegrocer.com/kroger-adopts-corporate-governance-best-practices-board-backs-annual-elections, retrieved September 20, 2025.

87 See https://local12.com/news/local/kroger-market-share-drop-threatens-grocery-national-ranking-cincinnati-chain-high-prices, https://www.supermarketnews.com/consumer-trends/in-2024-kroger-albertsons-is-not-even-close-to-being-a-grocery-monopoly-, and https://www.supermarketperimeter.com/articles/12868-kroger-to-shutter-60-underperforming-stores, all retrieved January 5, 2026.

88 You can compare Costco and Kroger's stock performance here: https://www.financecharts.com/compare/KR%2CCOST (Costco +2,011% vs. Kroger +606% vs. S&P 500 +624% from 2006 to 2025). For market share comparisons, one analyst called Kroger's performance "like Costco in reverse." See https://www.grocerydive.com/news/grocery-market-share-united-states-biggest-winners-losers/758672/, retrieved January 5, 2026.

89 https://s201.q4cdn.com/287523651/files/doc_downloads/govdocs/Corporate-Governance-Guidelines.pdf, retrieved September 20, 2025.

90 Peter Kajüter, Florian Klassmann, and Martin Nienhaus, "The Effect of Mandatory Quarterly Reporting on Firm Value," *Accounting Review* 94, no. 3 (2019): 251–77.

91 Peggy Hsieh, Timothy Koller, and S. R. Rajan, *The Misguided Practice of Earnings Guidance* (McKinsey, 2006).

92 Hui Liang James, Nilakshi Borah, and Roger Lirely, "The Effectiveness of Board Independence in High-Discretion Firms," *Quarterly Review of Economics and Finance* 85 (2022): 103–17, https://doi.org/10.1016/j.qref.2020.10.021, retrieved January 18, 2026.

93 M. Cremers and S. M. Sepe, "Board Declassification Activism: The Financial Value of the Shareholder Rights Project," SSRN Working Paper, 2017.

94 Jeffrey Sonnenfeld and Steven Tian, "Re-Thinking the Hostility Towards Dual-Class Share Structures: When Dual-Class Shares Work Better," *Harvard Law School Forum on Corporate Governance*, October 16, 2024.

95 https://www.msci.com/research-and-insights/blog-post/how-ownership-can-shape-outcomes, retrieved January 3, 2025.

96 A. Dumitrescu and M. Zakriya, "Governance, Information Flow, and Stock Returns: Evidence from a Natural Experiment," *Journal of Corporate Finance* 72 (2022): 102168.

97 J. R. Copland, D. F. Larcker, and B. Tayan, *The Big Thumb on the Scale: An Overview of the Proxy Advisory Industry*, Stanford Graduate School of Business Closer Look Series, Working Paper no. 3679 (Stanford, CA: Stanford University, 2018).

98 US House Financial Services Subcommittee, "Testimony in House Hearing: 'Exposing the Proxy Advisory Cartel: How ISS & Glass Lewis Influence Markets,'" *Harvard Law School Forum on Corporate Governance*, May 5, 2025, retrieved January 3, 2025, https://corpgov.law.harvard.edu/2025/05/05/testimony-in-house-hearing-exposing-the-proxy-advisory-cartel-how-iss-glass-lewis-influence-markets-2/, retrieved January 3, 2025.

99 ISS recommends votes against any "company [that] employs a common stock multi-class capital structure with unequal voting rights," with an exception for "newly-public companies with a sunset provision of no more than seven years from the date of going public." See https://www.issgovernance.com/file/policy/2025/Benchmark-Policy-Changes-For-Comment-2026.pdf, retrieved January 18, 2026. Note, once again, that the word "mission" does not appear in this policy document.

100 https://www.johnlewispartnership.co.uk/content/dam/cws/pdfs/Juniper/jlp-constitution.pdf, retrieved September 20, 2025.

101 https://tracxn.com/d/companies/airbnb/__7LQipbu68GsySiuAjesyrgEJvq6FIc-aAcJ5SCz-p7Mk/funding-and-investors, https://tracxn.com/d/companies/spacex/__UIpPfXSDe2O53VUbJNlNoPlcSwZr-1f_r0ie4BjsSaw/funding-and-investors, and https://tracxn.com/d/companies/anthropic/__SzoxXDMin-NK5tKB7ks8yHr6S9Mz68pjVCzFEcGFZ08/funding-and-investors, all retrieved November 17, 2025.

Chapter Ten: The Constellation View

1 https://www.newyorker.com/business/currency/how-mondragon-became-the-worlds-largest-co-op, retrieved September 20, 2025, for the storyline of what follows on Mondragon.

2 https://www.imd.org/research-knowledge/case-studies/can-social-enterprises-scale-while-remaining-sustainable-the-mondragon-cooperatives/, retrieved January 6, 2026.

3 https://www.mondragon-corporation.com/en/anual-report/in-numbers/, retrieved July 11, 2025.

4 William Foote Whyte and Kathleen King Whyte, *Making Mondragon: The Growth and Dynamics of the Worker Cooperative Complex* (Cornell University Press, IRL Press, 1991), 58, https://www.jstor.org/stable/10.7591/j.ctt1287dbf.9.

5 https://www.diariovasco.com/20090314/alto-deba/caja-laboral-cumple-anos-20090314.html, retrieved July 13, 2025.

6 https://corporate.mcdonalds.com/corpmcd/franchising-overview.html, retrieved January 18, 2026.

7 https://www.coca-cola.com/gb/en/about-us/faq/how-many-bottling-partners-and-employees-are-part-of-coca-cola-s and https://investors.coca-colacompany.com/about, both retrieved September 20, 2025.

8 https://www.marketing-now.co.uk/article/168479/freedom-within-a-framework-how-virgin-groups-brand-boss-navigates-40-businesses, retrieved September 20, 2025.

9 https://breznikar.com/articles/what-percent-of-hotels-does-marriott-own/1781, retrieved September 20, 2025.

10 https://www.inter.ikea.com/en/this-is-inter-ikea-group/the-ikea-franchise-system, retrieved September 20, 2025.

11 https://ccg.cbs.dk/wp-content/uploads/sites/32/2023/06/Foundation-Ownership-at-IKEA.pdf, 3, retrieved January 18, 2026.

12 https://www.sec.gov/Archives/edgar/data/320193/000032019320000096/a10-kexhibit2119262020.htm, retrieved September 20, 2025.

13 https://www.sec.gov/Archives/edgar/data/1067983/000095017024019719/brka-ex21.htm, retrieved September 20, 2025.

14 https://factsanddetails.com/korea/South Korea/Chaebols and Samsung/entry-7403.html, retrieved September 20, 2025.

15 https://arizmendiarrietafundazioa.org/img/2020/01/the-key-factors-of-success-of-mondragon-experience.pdf, retrieved September 20, 2025.

16 https://hcn.eu/partner/caja-laboral-kutxa/, retrieved September 20, 2025.

17 https://kittykroger.wordpress.com/2012/10/11/the-origins-of-the-mondragon-cooperative-in-1943-father-arizmendi/, retrieved September 20, 2025.

18 https://www.nceo.org/employee-ownership-blog/two-coops-leave-mondragon-corporation, retrieved September 20, 2025.

19 Wolfgang Streeck, "Beneficial Constraints: On the Economic Limits of Rational Voluntarism," in *Contemporary Capitalism: The Embeddedness of Institutions*, ed. J. Rogers Hollingsworth and Robert Boyer (Cambridge University Press, 1997).

20 https://drpop.org/mondragon-what-is-solidarity/, retrieved September 20, 2025.

21 Anjel Errasti, Ignacio Bretos, and Aitziber Nunez, "The Viability of Cooperatives: The Fall of the Mondragon Cooperative Fagor Electrodomésticos," *Review of Radical Political Economics* 49, no. 2 (2017): 181–97, https://doi.org/10.1177/0486613416666533, retrieved January 20, 2026.

22 Bruce Schneier, *Liars and Outliers: Enabling the Trust That Society Needs to Thrive* (John Wiley & Sons, 2012).

23 https://www.theverge.com/2021/9/15/22675130/facebook-instagram-teens-mental-health-damage-internal-research, retrieved September 20, 2025.

24 https://novonordiskfonden.dk/app/uploads/Novo-Nordisk-Foundation-2023-Annual-Report.pdf, retrieved September 20, 2025.

25 https://wellcome.org/about-us/investments, retrieved September 20, 2025.

26 https://www.carlsbergfondet.dk/en/about-the-foundation/the-carlsberg-family/carlsberg-research-laboratory/, retrieved September 20, 2025.

27 *The Causes and Effects of the Lehman Brothers Bankruptcy*, hearing before the Committee on Oversight and Government Reform, US House of Representatives, October 6, 2008, https://www.govinfo.gov/content/pkg/CHRG-110hhrg55766/pdf/CHRG-110hhrg55766.pdf, retrieved January 20, 2026; and http://news.bbc.co.uk/2/hi/business/8235141.stm, retrieved September 25, 2025.

28 R. Coase, "The Nature of the Firm," *Economica* 4, no. 16 (1937): 386–405.

29 Park, "How the Former U.S. CTO Built."

30 https://awealthofcommonsense.com/2016/07/the-strategy-tax/, retrieved January 4, 2026.

31 https://www.carlsberggroup.com/newsroom/carlsberg-research-laboratory-celebrates-150-years-of-breakthroughs-that-are-bigger-than-beer/, retrieved November 17, 2025.

32 https://www.westcommunitycu.org/resources/shared-branch.htm, retrieved January 20, 2026.

33 https://science.nasa.gov/mission/voyager/voyager-1/, retrieved January 4, 2026.

34 Kate Vitasek, Karl Manrodt, and Jim Kling, *Vested Outsourcing: Five Rules That Will Transform Outsourcing* (Palgrave Macmillan, 2011).

35 https://www.marketscreener.com/quote/stock/JONES-LANG-LASALLE-INCORP-13180/news/JONES-LANG-LASALLE-Procter-Gamble-Names-Jones-Lang-LaSalle-Supplier-of-the-Year-597855/, retrieved December 3, 2025.

36 https://files01.core.ac.uk/download/pdf/29400991.pdf, retrieved September 20, 2025.

37 https://exploremondragon.com/wp-content/uploads/07.-THE-STRUCTURE-OF-MONDRAGON-CORPORATE-GOVERNING-BODIES.pdf, retrieved December 3, 2025.

38 https://www.inc.com/magazine/20101101/how-i-did-it-eileen-fisher.html, retrieved January 6, 2026.

39 https://www.grantsforwomen.org/2012/11/women-entrepreneurs-receive-eileen.html, retrieved January 6, 2026.

40 https://medium.com/fifty-by-fifty/eileen-fisher-designing-for-change-f6877b4130f1, retrieved January 4, 2026.

41 https://thestoryexchange.org/eileen-fisher-passing-ceo-reins-lisa-williams-patagonia/, retrieved November 17, 2025.
42 https://medium.com/fifty-by-fifty/eileen-fisher-designing-for-change-f6877b4130f1, retrieved November 17, 2025.
43 https://actecfoundation.org/podcasts/purpose-trusts-patagonia/, retrieved September 20, 2025.
44 See https://data.worldbank.org/indicator/CM.MKT.LDOM.NO?locations=US and https://www.ecgi.global/system/files/2024-06/paper_half-the-firms-double-the-profits-public-firms-transformation-1996-2022_2.pdf, both retrieved December 10, 2025.
45 https://www.biteassetmanagement.com/wp-content/uploads/2024/08/Bite-Asset-Management-Research-Insights-Staying-private-for-longer.pdf, retrieved November 17, 2025.
46 https://www.mckinsey.com/industries/private-capital/our-insights/global-private-markets-report, retrieved November 17, 2025.
47 https://blog.exit-planning-institute.org/emotional-considerations-transitions, retrieved September 20, 2025.
48 https://www.businessinsider.com/bob-moore-bobs-red-mill-founder-employee-owned-company-2024-2, retrieved September 21, 2025.
49 https://www.nytimes.com/2010/07/18/jobs/18boss.html, retrieved September 21, 2025.
50 https://www.nytimes.com/2024/02/13/business/bob-moore-dead.html, retrieved September 21, 2025.
51 https://www.nceo.org/employee-ownership-blog/bob-moore-iconic-founder-bobs-red-mill-passes-away-age-94, retrieved September 21, 2025.
52 https://www.snackandbakery.com/articles/112256-bobs-red-mill-ceo-on-achieving-employee-ownership, retrieved September 21, 2025.
53 https://www.fiftybyfifty.org/2018/08/king-arthur-flours-recipe-for-success/, retrieved September 21, 2025.
54 https://www.common-trust.com/blog/clegg-autos-employee-ownership-trust-benefits-for-employees, retrieved September 21, 2025.
55 See https://www.prnewswire.com/news-releases/common-trust-raises-2-6m-in-seed-funding-to-support-small-businesses-to-exit-through-employee-ownership-buyouts-301922920.html and https://techcrunch.com/2023/09/11/common-trust-2-6m-business-succession-plan/, both retrieved September 21, 2025.
56 https://www.patagonia.com/ownership/, retrieved December 3, 2025.
57 https://employeeownership.co.uk/Site/Site/content/News-and-Insights/EO-Knowledge-Programme/EO-Knowledge-Programme-findings.aspx, retrieved September 21, 2025.
58 See https://www.nceo.org/articles/research-employee-ownership-corporate-performance, retrieved September 21, 2025, for this and the rest of the information in this paragraph.
59 Douglas Kruse, "Does Employee Ownership Improve Performance?," *IZA World of Labor* (2022): 311, https://doi.org/10.15185/izawol.311.v2, retrieved January 3, 2026.
60 See, for example, Joseph Blasi, Douglas Kruse, and Dan Weltmann, "Firm Survival and Performance in Privately Held ESOP Companies," in *Sharing Ownership, Profits, and Decision-Making in the 21st Century* (2013); see also https://cleo.rutgers.edu/articles/largest-study-yet-shows-esops-improve-performance-and-employee-benefits/, retrieved December 10, 2025.
61 For more on the variety and forms of mission lock vehicles, see the Purpose Foundation's overview of steward ownership: https://purpose-economy.org/content/uploads/purposebooklet_en.pdf.
62 https://www.zeiss.com/corporate/en/about-zeiss/past/history.html, retrieved September 21, 2025.

Chapter Eleven: The Spiritual Holding Company

1 I am grateful to Annika Schneider for introducing me to this concept of "unbundling" power and money. For more, see https://www.steward-ownership.com/.

2 For an accessible introduction to "steward ownership" and the data that supports this approach, see the *Purpose Foundation* book here: https://steward-ownership.com/steward-ownership-101.

3 https://ccg.cbs.dk/wp-content/uploads/sites/32/2023/06/Industrial-Foundations-and-Danish-Society1.pdf, retrieved September 21, 2025.

4 https://pellervo.fi/wp-content/uploads/2024/03/A_Survey_on_Finnish_Co_operatives__Business_Performance__Challenges__and_the_Sustainable_Mindset-2.pdf, retrieved January 18, 2026.

5 https://www.statista.com/topics/7633/credit-unions-in-the-us/, retrieved September 21, 2025.

6 https://www.cuinsight.com/banks-tax-hypocrisy-will-hurt-main-street-not-credit-unions/, retrieved January 18, 2026.

7 https://www.cicopa.coop/publications/second-global-report-on-cooperatives-and-employment/, retrieved September 21, 2025.

8 https://project-equity.org/news/employee-ownership-insider/proof-for-employee-ownership/, retrieved January 18, 2026.

9 See, for example, Steen Thomsen, *The Danish Industrial Foundations* (Djøf Publishing, 2017); Christian Børsting and Steen Thomsen, "Foundation Ownership, Reputation, and Labour," *Oxford Review of Economic Policy* 33, no. 2 (2017): 317–38.

10 We owe a debt to Steen Thomsen's pioneering research in this area. For example, see Steen Thomsen, Thomas Poulsen, Christa Børsting, and Johan Kuhn, "Industrial Foundations as Long-Term Owners," *Corporate Governance: An International Review* 26 (2018): "The probability of surviving beyond age 40 is 30 percent for foundation-owned firms and 10 percent for other firms. The survival probability is always higher for foundation-owned firms." Foundation-owned companies also showed more stable ownership, lower management turnover, more conservative capital structures (higher equity ratios), and higher scores on a long-termism index covering finance, investment, and employment. PDF available at https://ccg.cbs.dk/wp-content/uploads/sites/32/2023/06/Corporate-Governance-2018-Thomsen-Industrial-foundations-as-long%E2%80%90term-owners.pdf; more research available at https://ccg.cbs.dk/research-papers-enterprise/.

11 It has been a long time since Western philosophers spent time rigorously debating the nature of a soul. But when they did, they worked out clear arguments for why it would be incorruptible. Scholastic thought, for example, argued that a soul is incorruptible when it has (1) self-subsistence: it exists in its own right, not merely as a property of something else; (2) immateriality: its form is not tied to physical matter that can decay; (3) absence of internal contraries: it contains no opposing forces that would destroy it from within; and (4) natural appetite for perpetual being: it inherently seeks to continue existing. A spiritual holding company satisfies all four: Its mission and governance structure persist independent of any particular personnel or assets (self-subsistence); its essential form exists in information and relationships rather than physical substrates (immateriality); constitutional governance channels conflict into resolution rather than destruction (no internal contraries); and its very design prioritizes mission continuity (appetite for perpetual being). See Thomas Aquinas, *Summa Theologica*, part I, question 75, articles 2 and 6; for a non-Christian framework, see Maimonides, *Guide for the Perplexed*, part III, chapters 51 and 54.

For modern readers, this will all sound very metaphysical. Not to worry. Modern thinkers have given us tools to make similar claims on a purely material basis. Christian List and Philip Pettit argue that organizations with proper decision structures can constitute genuine agents with beliefs and responsibilities distinct from their members (*Group Agency* [Oxford University Press, 2011]). Peter French argues corporations can be moral persons, not mere legal fictions ("The Corporation as a Moral Person," *American Philosophical Quarterly* 16, no. 3 [1979]); see also Tom Donaldson, *Corporations and Morality* (Prentice Hall, 1982). Andy Clark and David Chalmers's extended mind thesis shows that cognitive processes can span people, tools, and institutional structures ("The Extended Mind," *Analysis* 58, no. 1 [1998]), while Edwin Hutchins's work on distributed cognition demonstrates how organizational systems possess emergent cognitive properties (*Cognition in the Wild* [MIT Press, 1995]). A major open question is whether organizations satisfy the criteria for what Maturana and Varela call an autopoietic system: one that continuously produces and maintains its own identity (*Autopoiesis and Cognition* [D. Reidel, 1980]).

12 For more on Dario Amodei, see https://www.forbes.com/profile/dario-amodei/ or https://www.businessinsider.com/dario-amodei, both retrieved September 21, 2025.

13 Paul Christiano, Jan Leike, Tom B. Brown, Miljan Martic, Shane Legg, Dario Amodei, "Deep Reinforcement Learning from Human Preferences," arXiv, 2017, https://arxiv.org/abs/1706.03741, retrieved January 18, 2026.

14 https://arxiv.org/abs/1606.06565, retrieved September 21, 2025.

15 See, for example, Daniel C. Dennett, *From Bacteria to Bach and Back: The Evolution of Minds* (W. W. Norton, 2017); Nick Bostrom, *Superintelligence: Paths, Dangers, Strategies* (Oxford: Oxford University Press, 2014); Eliezer Yudkowsky, "Artificial Intelligence as a Positive and Negative Factor in Global Risk," in *Global Catastrophic Risks*, ed. Nick Bostrom and Milan M. Ćirković (Oxford: Oxford University Press, 2008), 308–45.

16 https://openai.com/charter/, retrieved July 11, 2025.

17 https://www.theverge.com/2019/7/22/20703578/microsoft-openai-investment-partnership-1-billion-azure-artificial-general-intelligence-agi, retrieved September 21, 2025, and https://www.techrepublic.com/article/news-openai-structure-explained/ and https://www.datastudios.org/post/how-openai-was-funded-from-nonprofit-donations-to-billions-in-investments-and-global-partnerships, both retrieved November 17, 2025. In October 2025, OpenAI converted its structure to a public benefit corporation; the OpenAI Foundation (the renamed non-profit) holds a 26% stake, while Microsoft holds 27%.

On safety concerns, see https://law.stanford.edu/2025/03/21/ai-partnerships-beyond-control-lessons-from-the-openai-microsoft-saga/. Roughly half of OpenAI's AI safety researchers departed in 2024; former researcher Tom Cunningham wrote in his farewell message that the team faced "a growing tension between rigorous analysis and functioning as a de facto advocacy arm for OpenAI." See https://www.wired.com/story/openai-economic-research-team-ai-jobs/, all retrieved February 19, 2026.

18 See https://corpgov.law.harvard.edu/2023/10/28/anthropic-long-term-benefit-trust/ and https://www.anthropic.com/news/the-long-term-benefit-trust, both retrieved September 21, 2025.

19 https://www.lesswrong.com/posts/6tjHf5ykvFqaNCErH/anthropic-s-responsible-scaling-policy-and-long-term-benefit, retrieved November 17, 2025.

20 https://www.reuters.com/technology/crypto-exchange-ftx-sell-shares-ai-startup-anthropic-2024-02-22/, retrieved September 21, 2025.

21 https://techcrunch.com/2025/07/30/meta-to-spend-up-to-72b-on-ai-infrastructure-in-2025-as-compute-arms-race-escalates/, retrieved November 17, 2025.

22 Private conversation, January 9, 2026.

23 https://techcrunch.com/2026/01/07/anthropic-reportedly-raising-10b-at-350b-valuation/, retrieved January 23, 2026.

24 https://tracxn.com/d/companies/anthropic/__SzoxXDMin-NK5tKB7ks8yHr6S9Mz68pjVCzFEcGFZ08/funding-and-investors, retrieved September 21, 2025.

25 For these figures, see https://aitechtrend.com/anthropics-rapid-rise-generative-ai-revenue-surges-to-3-billion/ and https://www.anthropic.com/news/anthropic-raises-series-f-at-usd183b-post-money-valuation, both retrieved November 17, 2025.

26 https://www.axios.com/2025/05/27/ai-harris-100-poll-move-slow, retrieved July 13, 2025.

27 https://www.tekedia.com/anthropic-revenue-soars-to-3bn-as-enterprise-demand-for-generative-ai-surges/, retrieved November 17, 2025.

28 https://time.com/6980000/anthropic/, retrieved July 13, 2025.

29 https://www.grundfos.com/hello, retrieved July 13, 2025.

30 https://www.pdjf.dk/en/, retrieved September 21, 2025.

31 https://www.pdjf.dk/en/purpose-and-charter/, retrieved July 13, 2025.

32 https://www.pdjf.dk/en/about-us/, retrieved September 21, 2025.
33 https://www.globaldata.com/company-profile/grundfos-holding-as/analysis/, retrieved September 21, 2025; and https://www.grundfos.com/media/reports-and-publications/grundfos-annual-report-2024, retrieved November 17, 2025.
34 Grundfos, *Annual Report 2024* (Bjerringbro, Denmark: Grundfos, 2024), 31, https://www.grundfos.com/content/dam/global/page-assets/about-us/annual-reports/Grundfos-Annual-Report-2024.pdf, retrieved January 18, 2026.
35 https://www.pdjf.dk/en/board-of-directors/, retrieved September 21, 2025. The foundation's charter specifies that these four external members are elected for four-year terms by simple majority vote of the board of directors. Candidates must possess "a highly qualified technical and/or financial and/or sales and/or general management background" and "must not be employed in the day-to-day management of the Grundfos Group."
36 This is described in detail at https://www.pdjf.dk/en/about-us/, retrieved November 17, 2025.
37 https://www.grundfos.com/about-us/who-we-are/leadership-structure-and-ownership, retrieved September 21, 2025.
38 https://www.pdjf.dk/en/list-of-donations/, retrieved September 21, 2025.
39 https://www.forbes.com/sites/danielasirtori/2017/03/20/from-climber-to-billionaire-how-yvon-chouinard-built-patagonia-into-a-powerhouse-his-own-way/, retrieved January 4, 2026.
40 Gelles, "From Blacksmith to Billionaire."
41 https://www.patagoniaworks.com/press/2022/9/14/patagonias-next-chapter-earth-is-now-our-only-shareholder; see also Harvard Business School case study at https://www.hbs.edu/faculty/Pages/item.aspx?num=63834 and CNBC coverage at https://www.cnbc.com/2022/09/15/yvon-chouinard-donates-patagonia-to-fight-climate-change-protect-land.html, retrieved January 4, 2026.
42 https://www.patagoniaworks.com/press/2022/9/14/patagonias-next-chapter-earth-is-now-our-only-shareholder, retrieved January 4, 2026, and https://www.nytimes.com/2024/01/30/climate/patagonia-holdfast-philanthropy.html, retrieved September 21, 2025.
43 https://www.ktllp.cpa/purpose-trusts-a-quick-guide/, retrieved January 20, 2026.
44 Gelles, *Dirtbag Billionaire*, 255.
45 https://www.patagoniaworks.com/press/2022/9/14/patagonias-next-chapter-earth-is-now-our-only-shareholder, retrieved January 4, 2026.
46 https://www.patagoniaworks.com/faq, retrieved September 21, 2025.
47 https://www.patagoniaworks.com/press/2022/9/14/patagonias-next-chapter-earth-is-now-our-only-shareholder, retrieved January 4, 2026.
48 Gelles, "From Blacksmith to Billionaire."
49 "Billionaire No More: Patagonia Founder Gives Away the Company," *New York Times*, September 14, 2022, https://www.nytimes.com/2022/09/14/climate/patagonia-climate-philanthropy-chouinard.html, retrieved January 4, 2026.
50 See, for example, https://ccg.cbs.dk/wp-content/uploads/sites/32/2023/06/156267789.pdf, retrieved July 13, 2025.
51 On ROA, ROE, and Tobin's Q, see David Schroeder and Steen Thomsen, "Foundation Ownership and Financial Performance: International Evidence," 2025, https://papers.ssrn.com/sol3/papers.cfm?abstract_id=5357750. On earnings volatility, see https://www.cbs.dk/en/research/departments-and-centres/department-of-international-economics-and-management/center-corporate-governance/news/industrial-foundations-live-forever. On ESOP layoff resilience, see https://project-equity.org/news/employee-ownership-insider/proof-for-employee-ownership/, all retrieved on January 18, 2026. For foundational research establishing this pattern, see Steen Thomsen, "Foundation Ownership and Economic Performance," *Corporate Governance* 4, no. 4 (1996): 212–21.
52 https://link.springer.com/chapter/10.1057/9780230346499_12, retrieved September 21, 2025.
53 See, for example, a list of related articles at http://www.tifp.dk/en/research-materials, retrieved July 13, 2025.
54 Børsting and Thomsen, "Foundation Ownership, Reputation, and Labour."

55 The *Acquired Podcast* has a very entertaining version of this story here: https://www.acquired.fm/episodes/novo-nordisk-ozempic, retrieved January 18, 2026. For a more scholarly treatment, see Kurt Jacobsen, *Novo Nordisk* (Copenhagen: Gads Forlag, 2023).

56 https://www.acquired.fm/episodes/novo-nordisk-ozempic, retrieved January 4, 2026.

57 https://www.novonordisk.com/about/our-heritage.html, retrieved January 4, 2026.

58 See https://www.sec.gov/Archives/edgar/data/353278/000162828018001266/novo-b20xf12x31x17.htm for the estimated number of shareholders and https://www.investing.com/equities/novo-nordis-historical-data for Novo's average daily trading volume, both retrieved January 6, 2026.

59 https://www.novonordisk.com/investors/stock-information/share-and-ownership-structure.html, retrieved September 21, 2025.

60 https://www.spiegel.de/international/business/interview-with-weight-loss-drugs-inventor-lotte-bjerre-knudsen-a-f2815950-ff24-4e87-b7e9-b6d6c1982d57, retrieved September 21, 2025.

61 See https://www.sec.gov/Archives/edgar/data/1117399/000110465906062320/a06-20059_16k.htm. In 2012, Merck shut down Serono's Geneva R&D headquarters, ending programs "from basic research to clinical trials"; see https://www.nature.com/articles/nbt0712-569, both retrieved January 6, 2026.

62 Lest you think I am exaggerating, you should know that the practice of acquiring rivals specifically to shut down their R&D is well documented—and studied. Colleen Cunningham, Florian Ederer, and Song Ma found that a whopping 5.3%–7.4% of pharmaceutical acquisitions are "killer acquisitions" designed to cancel programs; see https://www.journals.uchicago.edu/doi/10.1086/712506. A 2024 European Commission study confirmed the pattern, finding approximately eighteen transactions per year in the pharmaceutical sector followed by unexplained discontinuation of overlapping R&D projects; see https://www.learlab.com/news/study-on-killer-acquisitions-in-the-pharma-sector/, both retrieved January 6, 2026.

63 https://all-things-nordic.com/2023/09/29/novo-nordisks-market-capitalisation-is-larger-than-denmarks-annual-gdp/, retrieved September 21, 2025. Although Novo's stock peaked above $600 billion, it has recently come down due to difficulties related to the US obesity drug market. See https://www.bloomberg.com/news/articles/2025-11-07/why-novo-nordisk-is-struggling-and-what-trump-s-ozempic-wegovy-price-deal-means, retrieved January 28, 2026.

Chapter Twelve: Mission Transmission

1 For Costco's official supplier requirements, including X-ray inspection, pathogen testing, and unannounced audits, see https://azzule.com/wp-content/uploads/2022/11/Food-Safety-Quality-Audit-Expectations-V2.0-Costco.pdf. For an example of Costco's testing exceeding industry norms, see https://www.yahoo.com/lifestyle/articles/rigorous-testing-costcos-kirkland-milk-170000743.html. For research on how large retailers' private standards elevate safety throughout supply chains, see https://link.springer.com/chapter/10.1007/978-3-319-15227-1_4, all retrieved January 18, 2026.

2 These figures come from the best available data, which spans different years. For Costco's 6,925 food safety audits in FY 2010 and their requirement that all food vendors have an annual audit, see https://www.food-safety.com/articles/3710-case-study-costco-wholesale-food-safety-from-the-top-down. For the FDA's 17,609 domestic facility inspections in 2010, see https://www.oversight.gov/sites/default/files/documents/reports/2017-09/oei-02-14-00420.pdf, 27. Based on these 2010 figures, Costco performed about 28% of the combined audit/inspection workload. Since then, FDA inspections have declined to an average of 8,353 per year from FY 2018–23 (see https://www.gao.gov/products/gao-25-107571), making the disparity likely even larger today. For the finding that 56% of FDA-regulated facilities went five or more years without inspection (2004–8), see https://www.qualityassurancemag.com/news/hhs-releases-results-of-study-on-fda-inspections-of-domestic-facilities/.. For Costco's 9% grocery market share (Q2 2025), see https://csimarket.com/stocks/competitionSEG2.php?code=COST, all retrieved January 18, 2026.

3 https://oig.hhs.gov/reports/all/2025/fda-food-safety-inspections-of-domestic-food-facilities/ retrieved July 14, 2025.
4 https://www.impactphl.org/news-archive/perspectives/vol19, retrieved July 14, 2025.
5 https://www.latimes.com/news/la-na-gatesx07jan07-story.html, retrieved July 14, 2025.
6 https://deming.org/demings-14-points-for-management/, point 4, retrieved July 14, 2025.
7 See https://www.patagonia.com/stories/planet/our-footprint/how-we-got-here-organic-cotton/story-97024.html and https://ga-institute.com/Sustainability-Update/looking-at-sustainable-cotton-patagonia-is-a-well-known-pioneer/, both retrieved November 24, 2025.
8 https://www.scribd.com/document/292942335/Toyota-Supplier-Case-Study, retrieved January 4, 2026, and https://toyotatimes.jp/en/toyota_news/together_with_our_suppliers/002.html, retrieved November 24, 2025.
9 https://news.airbnb.com/airbnb-provides-update-on-its-unprecedented-250-million-support-program-for-hosts/ and https://news.airbnb.com/airbnb-announces-1-billion-host-endowment-fund/, both retrieved January 4, 2026.
10 https://www.costco.com/confidential-ethics-hotline-for-suppliers.html, retrieved November 24, 2025.
11 https://ciw-online.org/blog/2019/10/ffp-sotp-season-7/, retrieved November 24, 2025.
12 This act followed years of relentless activism highlighting abuses in Nike's supply chain. In a May 1998 speech, Nike CEO Phil Knight acknowledged, "The Nike product has become synonymous with slave wages, forced overtime, and arbitrary abuse." Nike subsequently became the first major apparel company to publish its complete supplier list in 2005. See https://theworld.org/stories/2016/07/30/how-nike-solved-its-sweatshop-problem, retrieved January 18, 2026.
13 https://www.fairtradecertified.org/blog/leading-with-fair-trade-how-patagonia-became-a-leader-in-ethical-sourcing/, retrieved January 4, 2026.
14 https://www.hbs.edu/faculty/Pages/item.aspx?num=41251, retrieved July 14, 2025.
15 For this and what follows, see https://www.sama.com/our-story, retrieved November 24, 2025.
16 RLHF stands for "reinforcement learning from human feedback." This technology made generative AI chatbots like ChatGPT possible. And without the HF provided by humans (often in low-wage countries like those served by Sama), RLHF would not work at all. See Christiano et al., "Deep Reinforcement Learning."
17 https://www.sama.com/leila-janah-founder, retrieved November 24, 2025.
18 *The Eric Ries Show*, podcast, "AI's Human Backbone: The Hidden Hands That Shape The Technology | Wendy Gonzalez (Sama)," October 24, 2024, https://www.ericriesshow.com/wendy-gonzalez-sama/, retrieved July 29, 2025.
19 See https://www.sama.com/blog/ethical-and-sustainable-sourcing and https://time.com/6246018/facebook-sama-quits-content-moderation/, both retrieved July 29, 2025.
20 https://www.sama.com/blog/building-an-ethical-supply-chain, retrieved July 29, 2025.
21 https://www.sama.com/report/2023-impact-report, retrieved July 29, 2025.
22 On local job multipliers, see Enrico Moretti, "Local Multipliers," *American Economic Review* 100, no. 2 (2010): 373–77, https://doi.org/10.1257/aer.100.2.373. On employment and community well-being, see Timothy J. Bartik, "Bringing Jobs to People: Improving Local Economic Development Policies" (W. E. Upjohn Institute for Employment Research, 2020), https://doi.org/10.17848/pol2020-023; Sarah A. Burgard and Katherine Y. Lin, "Bad Jobs, Bad Health? How Work and Working Conditions Contribute to Health Disparities," *American Behavioral Scientist* 57, no. 8 (2013): 1105–27, https://doi.org/10.1177/0002764213487347. On workplace participation and civic engagement, see Carole Pateman, *Participation and Democratic Theory* (Cambridge University Press, 1970); for empirical support, see Wolfgang G. Weber, Christine Unterrainer, and Barbara Höge, "Psychological Research on Organisational Democracy: A Meta-Analysis," *Applied Psychology* 69, no. 3 (2020), https://doi.org/10.1111/apps.12205, all retrieved January 18, 2026.
23 See UC Berkeley Labor Center, "A Downward Push: The Impact of Wal-Mart Stores on Retail Wages and Benefits" (2007), https://laborcenter.berkeley.edu/a-downward-push-the-impact

-of-wal-mart-stores-on-retail-wages-and-benefits/; Good Jobs First, "Harms of Big Box Retail," https://goodjobsfirst.org/harms-big-box-retail/; Lukas Lehner, Zachary Parolin, Clemente Pignatti, and Rafael Schmitt, "Monopsony Power and Poverty: The Consequences of Walmart Supercenter Openings" (2024), https://papers.ssrn.com/sol3/papers.cfm?abstract_id=4975258. For an accessible overview, see Rogé Karma, "The Walmart Effect," *The Atlantic*, December 2024, https://www.theatlantic.com/economy/archive/2024/12/walmart-prices-poverty-economy/681122/, all retrieved January 18, 2026.

24 On Costco's wage spillovers, see Reuters, "Costco's Japan wages provide pathway to firing up nation's low pay economy," https://www.reuters.com/business/retail-consumer/costcos-japan-wages-provide-pathway-firing-up-nations-low-pay-economy-2024-06-06/ and https://www.marketdash.io/stock-market-news/54748/when-costco-comes-to-town-something-surprising-happens-to-local-wages-and-businesses. On Costco as a supplier to small businesses, see https://www.heraldnet.com/business/costco-growing-as-a-supplier-for-small-businesses/. On the "good jobs strategy," see Zeynep Ton, *The Good Jobs Strategy* (Houghton Mifflin Harcourt, 2014); and "Costco and Other Retailers Prove a 'Good Jobs' Strategy Works," Harvard Business School, https://www.hbs.edu/bigs/costco-and-other-retailers-prove-a-good-jobs-strategy-works. For an accessible overview, see https://youtu.be/ldQAZNXecBY, all retrieved January 18, 2026.

25 Park, "How the Former U.S. CTO Built."

26 https://www.wbrc.com/2025/06/21/it-makes-them-feel-empowered-fairfield-housing-community-opens-onsite-garden/, retrieved November 24, 2025.

27 See https://www.youtube.com/watch?v=5QD8N6JPqa0 and https://2024conference.bioneersarchive.org/speaker/odessa-flores-vasquez/, both retrieved January 18, 2026.

28 Park, "How the Former U.S. CTO Built."

29 Listen to https://shorefast.org/news-stories/zitas-story/ or read https://carleton.ca/news/story/zita-cobb-fogo-island/ for this and what follows, retrieved November 24, 2025.

30 https://www.nytimes.com/2024/11/08/travel/fogo-island-inn-zita-cobb-interview.html, retrieved November 24, 2025.

31 https://entreedestinations.com/blog/economic-nutrition-canadas-eastern-shores/, retrieved November 24, 2025.

32 On Fogo Island Fish and hand-line cod fishing, see https://fogoislandfish.ca/pages/fogo-island-fish. On "Economic Nutrition" labels, see https://shorefast.org/economic-nutrition/ and https://shorefast.org/news-stories/economic-nutrition-for-the-places-we-live/. On fair wages and pricing, see https://sustainableheritagecasestudies.ca/2022/01/14/community-led-tourism-at-fogo-island/. On GDP, see https://www.canada.ca/en/atlantic-canada-opportunities/campaigns/impacts/shorefast-foundation.html, all retrieved January 18, 2026.

33 Bill Trelstad, Wendy Smith, and Natalie Slawinski, *Shorefast: A Strange and Familiar Way to Reimagine Capitalism*, Harvard Business School Case 320-098 (Boston: Harvard Business School Publishing, 2020).

34 https://www.tamarackcommunity.ca/latest/leading-the-way-to-creating-sustainable-connected-communities, retrieved November 24, 2025.

35 https://www.norc.org/research/projects/assessing-child-labor-in-west-africa-cocoa-farming.html, retrieved September 27, 2025.

36 https://fortune.com/2021/04/11/ethical-chocolate-business-tonys-chocolonely-child-labor/, retrieved July 14, 2025.

37 https://tonyschocolonely.com/pages/tonys-timeline, retrieved November 24, 2025.

38 https://thebusinessdownload.com/tonys-chocolonely-paving-the-way-to-exploitation-free-chocolate/, retrieved November 24, 2025.

39 Tony's Chocolonely Nederland B.V., *Annual FAIR Report 2017–2018* (2018), PDF, https://thechocolatelife.com/Content/files/2022/05/Tonys_Annual_Report_2018-2019_en.pdf, retrieved November 24, 2025: "The Dutch market is all grown up. . . . We're still the Number 1 national chocolate brand."

40 https://online.flippingbook.com/view/189607595/92/, retrieved February 17, 2026.
41 https://tonyschocolonely.com/pages/living-income-model, retrieved July 29, 2025.
42 Translated from the original Dutch, "En we zouden nooit, nooit, het commerciële belang van de Tony's reep laten prevaleren boven het belang van de cacaoboer." https://teunvandekeuken.nl/10-jaar-tonys-y-teun-speecht/, retrieved July 29, 2025.
43 https://www.tonysopenchain.com/whos-in/mission-allies/feastables, retrieved January 20, 2026.
44 https://thechocolatelife.com/tonys-open-chain-interactive-report/, https://www.tonysopenchain.com/whos-in/mission-allies, and https://thechocolatelife.com/exploring-tonys-open-chain-podsavechocolate-ep-124/, retrieved July 14, 2025.
45 https://www.specialtyfood.com/news-media/news-features/specialty-food-news/chocolate-prices-sales-jump-following-u-k-grocer-commitment/, retrieved January 20, 2026.
46 https://tonyschocolonely.com/pages/tonys-5-sourcing-principles, retrieved November 24, 2025.
47 https://respect.international/wp-content/uploads/2022/05/Tonys-Chocolony-annual-report.pdf, 69, retrieved January 20, 2026.
48 https://tonyschocolonely.com/pages/clmrs, retrieved July 14, 2025.
49 https://respect.international/wp-content/uploads/2022/05/Tonys-Chocolony-annual-report.pdf, retrieved July 14, 2025.
50 https://www.cocoainitiative.org/news/stories-ici/johns-apprenticeship-journey, retrieved July 14, 2025.
51 https://www.cocoainitiative.org/news/stories-ici/joseph-child-protection-champion, retrieved January 20, 2026.
52 https://www.linkedin.com/posts/tony%27s-chocolonely_worlddayagainstchildlabor-letthemplay-activity-7338899718636273664-RTxp/, retrieved July 14, 2025.
53 https://tonyschocolonely.com/blogs/news/cocoa-farmers-cost-of-living-crisis-cocoa-price, retrieved July 14, 2025.
54 https://tonyschocolonely.com/pages/mission-lock, retrieved November 24, 2025.

Chapter Thirteen: The Power of Standards

1 https://www.volvogroup.com/en/about-us/heritage/three-point-safety-belt.html, retrieved September 25, 2025.
2 https://www.media.volvocars.com/us/en-us/media/pressreleases/15458?preview=true&t=f3839743-951f-4a34-bacf-f1773eca5e15, retrieved July 14, 2025.
3 https://www.media.volvocars.com/global/en-gb/media/pressreleases/10705/1970-1979-a-historical-review, retrieved July 14, 2025; and https://statisticsanddata.org/data/top-countries-by-motor-vehicle-production-1950-2020/, retrieved January 20, 2026.
4 https://www.curbsideclassic.com/automotive-histories/automotive-history-french-deadly-sins-m-c-escher-edition-part-1-fiat-ford-chrysler-rootes-simca-the-impossible-equation/, retrieved January 20, 2026.
5 Volvo has become a case study for how brands create value by simplifying otherwise complex decisions for customers; see https://www.researchgate.net/publication/340506516_Transforming_brand_core_values_into_perceived_quality_a_Volvo_case_study. One recent estimate pegged the value of the Volvo brand at €10.3 billion; see https://brandfinance.com/press-releases/from-icons-to-innovators-nordic-brands-balance-tradition-and-innovation-in-2025, both retrieved January 20, 2026.
6 Donald W. Reinfurt, Claudio Z. Silva, and Andrew F. Seiva, *A Statistical Analysis of Seat Belt Effectiveness in 1913–1915 Model Cars Involved in Towaway Crashes*, vol. 1 (US Department of Transportation, National Highway Traffic Safety Administration, 1975), https://rosap.ntl.bts.gov/view/dot/1108, retrieved January 20, 2026. The study of fifteen thousand tow-away crashes found that three-point belts reduced moderate or worse injuries by 56.5% compared to unbelted occupants.
7 Highway Loss Data Institute, *Automobile Insurance Losses, Injury Coverages by Highway Loss Data*

Institute: Comparisons of Claim Frequencies of Volkswagen Rabbits with Automatic and Manual Seat Belts, 1975, 1976, and 1977 Models (Highway Loss Data Institute, 1977), https://openlibrary.org/books/OL4458094M/Automobile_insurance_losses_injury_coverages, retrieved January 20, 2026.

8 https://web.archive.org/web/20140529033515/http://www.nhtsa.gov/cars/rules/import/fmvss/, retrieved September 27. 2025.

9 https://www.ul.com/about/history, retrieved September 25, 2025.

10 https://ulse.org/insight/129-years-past-present-and-future-safety-science/, retrieved July 14, 2025.

11 https://www.ul.com/about/history, retrieved September 25, 2025.

12 https://1752.com/about-us/history/, retrieved September 25, 2025.

13 In *The Box: How the Shipping World Made the Economy Bigger* (Princeton University Press, 2006), xi, Marc Levinson notes that this story is probably apocryphal, as there is no contemporary evidence for it.

14 https://www.library.hbs.edu/working-knowledge/the-truck-driver-who-reinvented-shipping, retrieved July 14, 2025.

15 https://heavyhaultexas.com/freightwaves-classics-pioneers-malcom-mclean-changed-the-freight-world-with-intermodal-containers/, retrieved September 25, 2025.

16 https://transportgeography.org/contents/chapter1/the-setting-of-global-transportation-systems/idealx-first-containeriship-1956/, retrieved October 2, 2025.

17 Levinson, *Box*, 107.

18 https://www.library.hbs.edu/working-knowledge/the-truck-driver-who-reinvented-shipping, retrieved July 14, 2025.

19 For this and what follows, see Levinson, *Box*, 18–21.

20 https://worksthatwork.com/2/intermodal-container, retrieved July 29, 2025.

21 Levinson, *Box*, 171.

22 https://www.imo.org/en/ourwork/safety/pages/containers-default.aspx, retrieved September 25, 2025.

23 https://www.library.hbs.edu/working-knowledge/the-truck-driver-who-reinvented-shipping, retrieved July 15, 2025.

24 https://knowledge.wharton.upenn.edu/article/seth-bergers-full-court-press-building-a-company-from-the-ground-up/ and https://www.aspeninstitute.org/people/bart-houlahan/, both retrieved November 25, 2025.

25 See https://shoremount.zendesk.com/hc/en-gb/articles/4410704961041-How-did-the-B-Corp-movement-begin. As the founders later recalled, "all the good they'd put into the business was seen as worthless to the money people." See https://growgood.co/a-shoe-that-changed-the-world-how-the-b-corp-movement-started/, both retrieved January 27, 2026.

26 https://www.awakin.org/v2/calls/408/jay-coen-gilbert/, retrieved January 4, 2026.

27 https://blog.mycorporation.com/2013/09/b-corp-experts-weigh-in-jay-coen-gilbert/, retrieved January 20, 2026.

28 https://bailard.com/beyond-profits-the-rise-of-b-corps-and-benefit-corporations/, retrieved January 4, 2026.

29 https://www.bcorporation.net/en-us/news/press/b-lab-publishes-new-b-corp-standards-raising-the-bar-for-businesses-worldwide/, retrieved January 4, 2026.

30 https://www.newhope.com/brands/industry-companies-launches-purpose-pledge-for-ethical-business-accountability, retrieved January 18, 2026.

31 https://www.purposepledge.org/, retrieved January 20, 2026.

32 https://sustainablebrands.com/read/14-brands-new-standard-purpose-driven-business, retrieved January 20, 2026.

33 For more on the Evergreen certification, see https://www.tugboatinstitute.com/what-is-evergreen/, retrieved February 20, 2026; for more on the philosophy of Evergreen companies, see Dave Whorton and Bo Burlingham, *Another Way: Building Companies That Last . . . and Last . . . and Last* (Portfolio, 2025).

34 From an interview with Rune Kvist, February 20, 2025.

35 Kvist interview.

36 https://www.prnewswire.com/news-releases/the-artificial-intelligence-underwriting-company-launches-with-15m-to-help-enterprises-deploy-ai-with-confidence-302512447.html, retrieved November 26, 2025.

37 See A. L. Russell, "'Rough Consensus and Running Code' and the Internet-OSI Standards War," *IEEE Annals of the History of Computing* 28, no. 3 (July–September 2006): 48–61, https://doi.org/10.1109/MAHC.2006.42, retrieved January 20, 2026.

38 https://www.cloudflare.com/en-gb/learning/ddos/glossary/open-systems-interconnection-model-osi/, retrieved January 8, 2026.

39 https://www.lenovo.com/us/en/glossary/arpanet/, retrieved January 20, 2026.

40 https://groups.google.com/g/comp.os.minix/c/dlNtH7RRrGA/m/SwRavCzVE7gJ, retrieved September 26, 2025.

41 https://news.ycombinator.com/item?id=9263336m, retrieved September 26, 2025.

42 See https://www.themarginalian.org/2011/12/02/steve-jobs-1995-life-failure/ and https://www.youtube.com/watch?v=kYfNvmF0Bqw, both retrieved January 4, 2026.

Chapter Fourteen: A New Civic Infrastructure

1 https://www.sec.gov/files/form1.pdf.

2 He wasn't exaggerating. Here is LTSE's original Form 1 application, filed years later: https://www.sec.gov/rules/other/2018/long-term-stock-exchange/long-term-stock-exchange-1.htm.

3 Eric Klinenberg defines social infrastructure as "the physical places and organizations that shape the way people interact." See Eric Klinenberg, *Palaces for the People: How Social Infrastructure Can Help Fight Inequality, Polarization, and the Decline of Civic Life* (Crown, 2018). Mario Small's work shows how organizations like childcare centers and churches shape people's social networks in ways they don't control. See Mario Small, *Unanticipated Gains: Origins of Network Inequality in Everyday Life* (Oxford University Press, 2009).

4 See, for example, North's Nobel Prize lecture, https://www.nobelprize.org/prizes/economic-sciences/1993/north/lecture/, retrieved July 15, 2025, or his book, *Institutions, Institutional Change and Economic Performance* (Cambridge University Press, 1990).

5 Hernando de Soto, *The Mystery of Capital: Why Capitalism Triumphs in the West and Fails Everywhere Else* (Basic Books, 2003).

6 Self-regulatory organizations (SROs) like stock exchanges and FINRA are private entities granted regulatory authority by the SEC under the Securities Exchange Act of 1934. Courts have extended a form of immunity to SROs based on their quasi-governmental status. See Rohit A. Nafday, "From Sense to Nonsense and Back Again: SRO Immunity, Doctrinal Bait-and-Switch, and a Call for Coherence," *University of Chicago Law Review* 77, no. 2 (2010): 847–85.

7 See, for example, the forty-hour work week (https://blogs.loc.gov/inside_adams/2024/01/40-hours-5-days/), the HACCP food safety system (https://spinoff.nasa.gov/moon-landing-food-safety), organic certification (https://nationalaglawcenter.org/overview/organic/), and GAAP accounting standards (https://www.sechistorical.org/museum/galleries/rca/rca02b-status-gaap.php). For more on the counterintuitive way that such regulations accelerate rather than hinder progress, see Jason Crawford (https://www.technologyreview.com/2021/07/13/1028295/proud-solutionist-history-technology-industry/). For an accessible history, see JoAnne Yates and Craig N. Murphy, *Engineering Rules: Global Standard Setting Since 1880* (Johns Hopkins, 2019), all retrieved January 18, 2026.

8 https://www.politifact.com/factchecks/2016/jul/06/mark-warner/mark-warner-says-average-holding-time-stocks-has-f/, retrieved September 27, 2025.

9 https://www.sec.gov/marketstructure/research/hft_lit_review_march_2014.pdf, retrieved September 27, 2025.

10 Texas public libraries were found to return $4.64 for every dollar invested (https://www.tsl.texas

.gov/roi, retrieved January 20, 2026). Similar studies across the US consistently find returns of four to five dollars per dollar spent. For more on libraries as civic infrastructure, see Klinenberg, *Palaces for the People*.

11 https://www.fasb.org/about-us, retrieved July 15, 2025.

12 https://www.iers.org/IERS/EN/Home/home_node.html, retrieved September 27, 2025.

13 Schumpeter himself warned that "the capitalist process in much the same way in which it destroyed the institutional framework of feudal society also undermines its own." Capitalism "broke not only barriers that impeded its progress but also flying buttresses that prevented its collapse . . . removing partners of the capitalist stratum, symbiosis with whom was an essential element of the capitalist schema." The result: "Dematerialized, defunctionalized and absentee ownership does not impress and call forth moral allegiance as the vital form of property did. Eventually there will be nobody left who really cares to stand for it." Joseph Schumpeter, *Capitalism, Socialism and Democracy* (Harper & Brothers, 1942), 139–42.

14 See https://www.thewallstreetexperience.com/blog/meet-the-famous-buttonwood-tree-of-wall-street/, retrieved August 29, 2025, and https://digitalcommons.fairfield.edu/cgi/viewcontent.cgi?article=1102&context=business-facultypubs, retrieved July 11, 2025.

15 https://www.fico.com/en/history, retrieved September 27, 2025.

16 Joe Becker of Xerox and Lee Collins and Mark Davis of Apple began investigating a universal character set in 1987. Becker coined the name "Unicode" and published the first proposal in 1988. The Unicode Consortium was incorporated in 1991; see https://www.historyofinformation.com/detail.php?id=2487, retrieved January 20, 2026.

17 MitbestG 1976, Sections 7–9.

18 https://www.servat.unibe.ch/icl/sz00000_.html, retrieved November 26, 2025. See article 141.

19 https://marketurbanism.com/2020/08/05/the-limits-of-the-singapore-housing-model/, retrieved October 2, 2025.

20 https://www.timeout.com/tokyo/news/find-nursing-rooms-and-diaper-stations-across-japan-with-mama-papa-map-070224, retrieved January 20, 2026.

21 See https://www.hsrail.org/blog/why-transit-projects-cost-more-in-the-u-s-than-almost-anywhere-else-and-what-we-can-do-about-it/. The Transit Costs Project at New York University found that procurement governance problems alone create a 1.85× cost multiplier. When agencies lack internal capacity, they rely on consultants who consume 21% of project costs (versus 5%–10% in France), creating a governance trap where those overseeing contracts depend on those they're supposed to monitor. See https://transitcosts.com/executive_summary/ and https://transitcosts.com/transit-costs-study-final-report/, all retrieved November 26, 2025.

22 Martin A. Makary and Michael Daniel, "Medical Error—the Third Leading Cause of Death in the US," *BMJ* 353 (2016): i2139, https://www.bmj.com/content/353/bmj.i2139, retrieved November 26, 2025: Medical errors are the third leading cause of death, 251,454 annually.

23 As hospital administrators have professionalized, they too have come under the sway of governance-class "best practices." The AHA's 2022 governance survey found that 58% of boards devote less than 20% of their time to quality (https://www.jointcommission.org/en-us/knowledge-library/blogs/dateline-tjc-2023-09-refocus-your-boards-attention-on-quality-and-patient-safety); a 2025 HHS Office of Inspector General report found that hospitals did not even capture half of patient harm events—in many cases because "it was not standard practice to capture them" (https://oig.hhs.gov/reports/all/2025/hospitals-did-not-capture-half-of-patient-harm-events-limiting-information-needed-to-make-care-safer/, retrieved February 20, 2026). And boards don't pay for what they don't prioritize: A national study of non-profit hospital CEO compensation found no association between CEO pay and quality outcomes (https://jamanetwork.com/journals/jamainternalmedicine/fullarticle/1748832). All retrieved January 20, 2026.

24 Michigan's Keystone ICU project cut central line infections by 66% using simple checklists; Peter J. Pronovost, J. Bryan Sexton, and Michael Holzmann, "An Intervention to Decrease Catheter-Related Bloodstream Infections in the ICU," *New England Journal of Medicine* 355,

no. 26 (2006): 2725–32. See also https://psnet.ahrq.gov/issue/hospital-survey-patient-safety-culture-2014-user-comparative-database-report, retrieved November 26, 2025.

25 "History of the National Transportation Safety Board," NTSB, August 20, 2024. https://www.ntsb.gov/about/history/Pages/default.aspx, retrieved November 26, 2025.

26 https://skybrary.aero/articles/just-culture and https://www.faa.gov/newsroom/out-front-airline-safety-two-decades-continuous-evolution, both retrieved November 26, 2025: US aviation fatalities declined 95% from 1970 to 2019 despite massive growth in air travel.

27 For the report, see https://nap.nationalacademies.org/resource/9728/To-Err-is-Human-1999--report-brief.pdf. The latest "compromise" proposes a board that would need permission to investigate and couldn't name facilities (see https://www.congress.gov/bill/118th-congress/house-bill/7591/text). For more, see https://kffhealthnews.org/news/article/will-a-national-patient-safety-board-modeled-after-the-ntsb-actually-fly/, all retrieved January 18, 2026.

28 https://www.pioneerrx.com/blog/the-state-of-pharmacy-benefit-managers-2022-report, retrieved July 15, 2025.

29 https://www.goodrx.com/healthcare-access/research/third-of-americans-dont-fill-prescriptions-due-to-cost, retrieved July 30, 2025.

30 https://www.wpxi.com/news/washington-news-bureau/congress-trying-tackle-rising-prescription-drug-costs-by-cracking-down-pbms/6SVEPP36E5EADGGCJ4J5VYQEUI/, retrieved July 15, 2025.

31 Kevin J. Duane, PharmD, written testimony before the United States House Committee on Oversight and Accountability, "The Role of Pharmacy Benefit Managers in Prescription Drug Markets, Part I: Self-Interest or Health Care?," May 23, 2023, 3, https://oversight.house.gov/wp-content/uploads/2023/05/Kevin-Duane-written-testimony-5.23.23.pdf, retrieved July 30, 2025.

32 https://www.foxbusiness.com/lifestyle/independent-pharmacies-fear-closures-amid-financial-strain, retrieved July 30, 2025.

33 https://www.rightwayhealthcare.com/blog/the-generic-drug-pricing-game, retrieved January 5, 2026.

34 https://time.com/6962877/alex-oshmyansky/, retrieved September 27, 2025, for what follows.

35 https://www.fiercehealthcare.com/health-tech/mark-cuban-wants-keep-shaking-healthcare-heres-cost-plus-drugs-next-move, retrieved July 15, 2025.

36 https://www.markcubancostplusdrugcompany.com, retrieved September 27, 2025.

37 https://dallasinnovates.com/mark-cubans-cost-plus-drugs-to-begin-manufacturing-drugs-in-dallas-deep-ellum-this-week/, retrieved September 27, 2025.

38 https://omrf.org/wp-content/uploads/2024/04/MARK-CUBAN-COST-PLUS-DRUG-INFO.pdf and https://smithrx.com/blog/affordable-multiple-sclerosis-treatment-unlocking-savings-with-mark-cuban-cost-plus-drugs, both retrieved September 27, 2025.

39 https://jrreport.wordandbrown.com/2024/08/20/mark-cubans-cost-plus-drug-co-vows-total-transparency-to-shatter-drug-prices/, retrieved September 27, 2025.

40 Hussein Lalani, Aaron S. Kesselheim, and Benjamin N. Rome, "Potential Medicare Part D Savings on Generic Drugs from the Mark Cuban Cost Plus Drug Company," *Annals of Internal Medicine* (2022), https://doi.org/10.7326/M22-0756, retrieved September 27, 2025.

41 See https://www.cnn.com/2023/08/17/business/blue-shield-california-new-pharmacy-care and https://www.reuters.com/business/healthcare-pharmaceuticals/blue-shield-california-drop-cvs-caremark-pharmacy-benefit-manager-wsj-2023-08-17/, both retrieved January 2026.

42 https://fortune.com/2023/08/17/mark-cuban-online-pharmacy-cost-plus-drugs-amazon-blue-shield-cvs/, retrieved July 15, 2025.

43 https://www.cnbc.com/2023/08/17/blue-shield-of-california-taps-amazon-cost-plus-for-pharmacy, retrieved July 15, 2025.

44 https://www.drugchannels.net/2024/03/mark-cuban-five-ways-that-big-pbms-hurt.html, retrieved January 4, 2026.

45 https://pol.is/home2, retrieved January 5, 2026.

46 https://blog.pol.is/uber-responds-to-vtaiwans-coherent-blended-volition-3e9b75102b9b, retrieved January 5, 2026.
47 https://democracy-technologies.org/participation/consensus-building-in-taiwan/, retrieved January 5, 2026.
48 Federal Chancellery of Austria, *The Austrian Climate Council: Final Report* (Vienna, 2022), https://www.bundeskanzleramt.gv.at, retrieved January 5, 2026.
49 C. Megill, "Pol.is: Scaling Deliberation for Mass Participation," *Pol.is Case Studies* (2019), https://compdemocracy.org/Case-studies/, retrieved January 5, 2026.
50 https://arxiv.org/pdf/2210.15723, retrieved December 19, 2025.
51 https://colinmegill.com/, retrieved November 26, 2025.
52 https://www.stmarysbank.com/about-us/who-we-are/our-history, retrieved September 27, 2025.
53 For the history of credit unions in the US, see https://www.cutoday.info/THE-feature/A-Piece-of-History-That-Almost-Wasn-t, retrieved September 27, 2025.
54 https://ncua.gov/files/publications/analysis/quarterly-data-summary-2025-Q1.pdf, retrieved September 27, 2025.
55 https://en.wikipedia.org/wiki/Wikipedia, retrieved September 27, 2025.
56 https://www.cnn.com/2025/02/09/tech/secure-chat-apps-signal-tor-browser/index.html, retrieved January 28, 2026.
57 https://annualreport.khanacademy.org, retrieved September 27, 2025.
58 https://www.apache.org, retrieved September 27, 2025.
59 https://www.linuxfoundation.org, retrieved September 27, 2025.

Chapter Fifteen: You Are Traffic

1 https://www.americanrhetoric.com/speeches/ursulakleguinnationalbookawardspeech.htm, retrieved September 27, 2025.
2 https://www.ebsco.com/research-starters/sociology/structuration-theory, retrieved January 20, 2026.
3 The original finding that happiness plateaus around $75,000 (in 2009 dollars) comes from Kahneman and Deaton (see https://www.pnas.org/doi/10.1073/pnas.1011492107). The idea of a fixed threshold has been contested (see https://www.pnas.org/doi/10.1073/pnas.2208661120), but even such research shows the happiness impact of increased salary reaches significant diminishing returns. Beyond this narrow question, substantial research (not to mention ancient wisdom) has repeatedly shown that income does not drive life satisfaction. For example, see the Harvard Study of Adult Development, which tracked participants for eighty-five years (see https://news.harvard.edu/gazette/story/2017/04/over-nearly-80-years-harvard-study-has-been-showing-how-to-live-a-healthy-and-happy-life/). All retrieved January 18, 2026.
4 https://www.startuplessonslearned.com/2020/06/out-of-crisis-8-brian-chesky-part-2.html, retrieved September 27, 2025.

Index

About the Author

Over the last two decades, ERIC RIES's ideas about continuous innovation, long-term thinking, governance, and market reform have reshaped company building and management practices. He is the creator of the Lean Startup method and the author of the *New York Times* bestseller *The Lean Startup*, *The Leader's Guide*, and *The Startup Way*. As a founder, Eric has put his own ideas into practice with the Long-Term Stock Exchange (LTSE); Answer.AI, an AI R&D lab; Virgil, a legal services startup; and IMVU. On *The Eric Ries Show*, he talks with world-class technologists, thought leaders, and executives building for the long term. He lives in the San Francisco Bay Area with his wife and three children.